POWER MOVES

POWER MOVES

Transportation, Politics, and Development in Houston

KYLE SHELTON

UNIVERSITY OF TEXAS PRESS AUSTIN

This book was supported in part by
Lowell Lebermann Jr.

Printed in the United States of America
First edition, 2017
First paperback reprint, 2018

Requests for permission to reproduce material from this work should be sent to:
Permissions
University of Texas Press
P.O. Box 7819
Austin, TX 78713-7819
utpress.utexas.edu/rp-form

♾ The paper used in this book meets the minimum requirements of ANSI/NISO Z39.48-1992 (R1997) (Permanence of Paper).

Library of Congress Cataloging-in-Publication Data

Names: Shelton, Kyle, 1985– author.
Title: Power moves : transportation, politics, and development in Houston / Kyle Shelton.
Description: First edition. | Austin : University of Texas Press, 2017. | Includes bibliographical references and index.
Identifiers: LCCN 2017009406| ISBN 978-1-4773-1429-6 (cloth : alk. paper) | ISBN 978-1-4773-1465-4 (pbk. : alk. paper) | ISBN 978-1-4773-1466-1 (library e-book) | ISBN 978-1-4773-1467-8 (non-library e-book)
Subjects: LCSH: Transportation—Texas—Houston—History. | Transportation and state—Texas—Houston. | City planning—Texas—Houston—Citizen participation.
Classification: LCC HE310.H8 S53 2017 | DDC 388.409764/1411—dc23
LC record available at https://lccn.loc.gov/2017009406

doi:10.7560/314296

TO MY FAMILY

CONTENTS

POWER MOVES

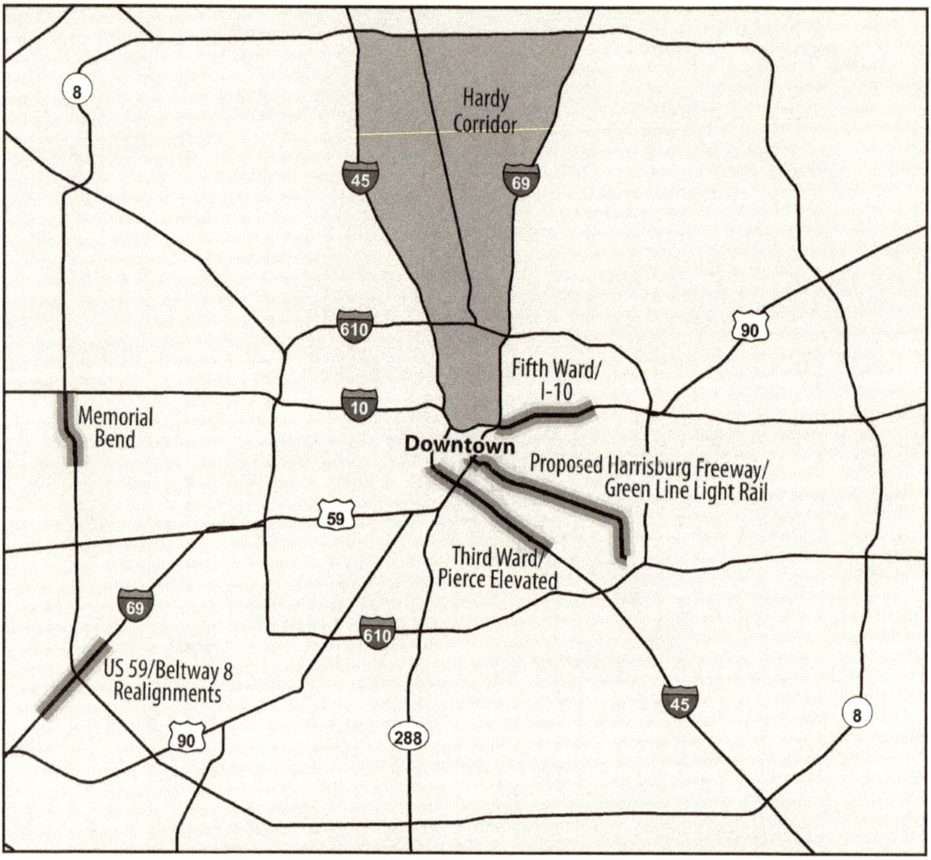

Fig. 0.1. Houston Highway and Rail Map with Case Studies Highlighted
This map shows the current extent of Houston's highway network. Overlaid on top of the map are those areas that serve as case studies within the following chapters. Map by Jean Aroom and Hannah Krusleski, Rice University GIS/Data Center.

INTRODUCTION

I.

About a mile to the northeast of downtown Houston, Texas, roads seem to occupy every plane. One runs below, recessed into the earth. Another soars above on concrete piles. A third is a bridge, level with the ground a few paces back. Moving south down Jensen Drive, the bridge is suspended between the rushing traffic on Interstates 10 and 69 (formerly US Highway 59). At the halfway point of the bridge, a look to the east affords a view of the massive interchange of these two freeways. Originally built in the 1960s, the flyover ramps, main lanes, and frontage roads tore a neighborhood apart to make way for improved metropolitan mobility. Today the road seems like a given. It fits the landscape. Its curves hug the contours of the reengineered land, and its decks have stood for years. It's hard to picture what stood there before. Homes, businesses, places of worship, and schools have faded for all but the few who remember their presence before the upheaval of construction.

When they were built, the roadways disrupted the Fifth Ward, a historically African-American section of the city. The ward—anchored by its main commercial drag, Lyons Avenue—was a vibrant and cohesive part of black life in Houston during the nineteenth and twentieth centuries. The road erased much of this history. The interchange alone claimed nearly nine hundred structures; as the freeways ran north and east, they claimed several thousand more in the ward and other communities. Beyond simply removing structures, the road's construction disrupted established patterns of life in the Fifth Ward. Its lanes bisected routes students took to school and those adults followed to run daily errands or get to work. Along with existing rail lines, the road put a concrete barrier between the neighborhood and the city, boxing the ward in with massive infrastructure. To the south, I-10; to the west, the then US 59; to the north and east, rail yards. Entry and exit meant crossing markers that signaled a neighborhood apart.

Like decisions made in countless other American cities, the choice by the Texas Highway Department to run the road through the predominantly minority ward was not accidental. During the 1950s and 1960s, as a part of wider urban renewal efforts, officials from many states and cities worked jointly to place highways through urban minority and working-class neighborhoods. At a time of immense demographic change in American cities, white officials hoped removing "blighted" communities would help revitalize central cities and that new roads and efficient traffic planning would help draw white suburbanites back into town for work and play. This official perspective, of course, did not sit well with residents of the communities affected by the interventions. But African-American Fifth Warders, like other ethnic and racial minorities across the nation, faced entrenched racism and classism that prevented effective contestation. At the time the road was built in the 1960s, residents lacked the political and economic influence needed to stop, redirect, or even lessen the impacts of the project. Fifth Warders had almost no warning that the road was being planned. Many learned of its routing only after the first steps of construction began. The lack of public information limited residents' opportunities to object. Thousands were moved before any form of resistance could be organized. But even as the road rose above and below the landscape, other Houstonians drew lessons from the experience of the Fifth Warders.

II.

Speaker after speaker rose to address the elected officials presiding over an April 1983 public forum at St. Patrick's Catholic Church on Houston's north side. The diverse collection of Houstonians in attendance came to weigh in on two pending transportation plans for Houston and Harris County. The first called for the construction of a countywide toll road system. The second would build a heavy rail mass transit network. Both systems planned to use an old rail corridor just blocks from the church for a route. Residents from this corridor, a mixture of white-collar and blue-collar African-American, white, and Latino Houstonians, feared that the building of the projects would threaten their homes and daily rhythms. Cognizant of the destruction caused by earlier road construction in neighborhoods throughout Houston, corridor residents preferred the rail option, believing it would be less disruptive and better serve their communities. One homeowner exclaimed, "We don't want the toll road to come in and uproot our homes for the benefit of just a few people. We don't want it to come in and devastate our community."[1]

Houstonians whose homes sat removed from proposed routes, including many white-collar, white suburbanites with long daily commutes in personal vehicles, felt differently. These residents worried about their taxes going to support a system that would provide them with little service. Lee Swanson, one such suburbanite, campaigned for the toll roads, arguing that they were the "best solution" for Houston's traffic problems. Far from disrupting lives, Swanson maintained, the road would instead "tie the [metropolitan] community together." As the hour grew later, patience grew thin. Citizens on both sides of the debate interrupted speakers with cheers and boos.[2] Houstonians came to the forum with competing understandings of their communities and city, and through arguments about the proposals they articulated those visions. The meeting changed few minds. The projects, framed by residents as either catastrophes or solutions, represented another step in a decades-long debate over the shape of the city and its infrastructure—a debate that did not stop when the votes over the transit system and the toll road were tallied.

III.

In May 2015, when the light rail line, known locally as the Green Line, opened, a rider's journey ended abruptly at the Altic/Howard Hughes Station, despite route maps showing two additional stops. The tracks ran a few hundred yards past the last stop, disappeared for about a half mile, and reappeared to run past the final two, where the stations were completed, but not yet in use. The gap in the tracks existed because of a delay caused by a roiling debate within Houston's East End community about whether to build an overpass or an underpass where the light rail crossed a set of freight rail tracks. During the initial stages of line construction, the Metropolitan Transit Authority of Houston and Harris County (METRO), the region's largest public transit agency, proposed the building of an overpass. After substantial public feedback and a concerted local push against the idea, however, METRO agreed to instead build an underpass. But initial engineering work found an unstable pollution plume left by the petroleum tanks of derelict service stations, and the agency said the pollution made construction of the underpass unviable. METRO moved forward with the overpass plans. This shift caused uproar among community members who supported the underpass and thought they had that choice secured.

The underpass/overpass debate was just the latest conflict in decades of tension between East End residents and officials attempting to plan and construct transportation infrastructure for and through the neighborhood. The East End, a set of predominantly Mexican-American communities, has a long history of being shaped by industrial infrastructure. Because of its location along the Houston Ship Channel, the East End has housed freight traffic, heavy trucks, and industrial uses since the early twentieth century. At the same time that it has been dominated by industrial traffic, the personal transportation system for community members has almost always been lacking. Electric streetcars served the area until the late 1930s, and once they were removed the area received only minimal private bus service well into the 1970s. Mobility for most meant walking, using a private car, or waiting on slow and unreliable buses. Then, in the late 1960s, officials announced that they intended to run a highway, the Harrisburg Freeway, through the center of the East End. Residents protested vociferously. The East Enders' awareness of the consequences of road building in the Fifth Ward and long-held frustrations about infrastructural intrusions spurred the protest. Their fight against the road contributed to the eventual abandonment of the plan.

The light rail line and the rejected roadway are linked together, physically and politically, by the communities' contentious history with transportation infrastructure. In concrete terms, the rail runs down the same street that highway planners intended to use as the route for the highway that was rejected in the 1970s. This overlap exemplifies the ways in which previous decisions can either lead to or preclude future choices. In the decades since they helped defeat the road plan, East End residents have demanded better transit service and improved infrastructure for their neighborhoods. The road fight showed that if they applied constant political pressure to METRO or other officials, they might achieve some of their goals. Decades of such lobbying pushed METRO to build the light rail line in the community. Even as the rail was laid, some East Enders remained skeptical of the agency's role in the area. Many viewed the rail not as a provider of mobility, but instead as a spur for redevelopment—a push that many East Enders still fear will displace them. METRO sees the light rail as a sign of the agency's efforts to serve residents and to create a working system for the area. The line was paid for entirely by METRO at a cost of almost $600 million, certainly a signal of commitment to the community. And despite periods of tension, the agency worked closely with residents and community representatives during its planning. Thanks to the long-running participation of East End residents in mobility debates, the Green Line process—from plan, to construction, to overpass debate—was far different from that which occurred during previous transportation debates.

The decisions made in each of these moments shaped more than just a city's transportation network. They remade the landscapes of Houston's Fifth Ward, Hardy corridor, and East End. They continue to influence the form and function of those communities today. The infrastructural debates of previous eras, and the physical legacies they left behind, shaped subsequent choices across the city, which in turn birthed the current built environment of the Houston metropolitan area. The passionate participation of a cross-section of Houstonians in these three transportation debates also reflected a larger political sea change that occurred in Houston's politics and urban development between 1950 and today. When Houstonians fought for or against highways, considered the merits of mass transit, or advocated for other infrastructural outcomes, they not only altered the urban landscape but also seized a larger role in metropolitan growth decisions.

By transforming elements of the built environment from inert materials into arenas in which they could claim and assert political power, residents crafted a set of rhetorical and political actions that constituted what I term infrastructural citizenship. In this case, citizenship is not defined by nationality or legal standing, but instead by the quotidian acts residents used to construct themselves as political participants. Most expressions of infrastructural citizenship in Houston emerged in the form of transportation activism. During efforts to protect or shape their communities, Houstonians staged protests, wrote letters, and attended countless public meetings. They organized historical preservation campaigns, lobbied city officials, and paid for independent planning efforts. They argued that their homes and local streets should be held in the same esteem as regional highways and downtown redevelopments. With each action, residents used the particular infrastructural debates around transportation decisions to assert their rights as citizens.[3] The tactics pursued by residents reflected an inability to shift the early stages of decision-making and instead were moves that attempted to impact final results. Residents worked to delay projects, draw attention to concerns, and protest decisions of which they did not approve.[4] Even if those efforts failed to achieve their desired outcomes, as many did, the simple act of projecting their hopes onto the structures allowed citizens to reshape their meaning.[5]

Houstonians engaged in transportation battles were far from alone in their use of infrastructural citizenship. Since World War II, citizens across America, not connected by any specific racial, economic, or political categorization, have embraced elements of the actions and ideas that constitute infrastructural citizenship in hopes of garnering control over their cities, streets, and homes. The examples from Houston highlighted in this book resonate with countless others from around the nation. Houstonians turned to fights about transportation infrastructure to cope with the immense physical, economic, and political tumult occurring in both urban and suburban America after World War II. Residents in other cities and regions fought over changes in development practices, the location of hazardous wastes, and even the impacts of energy infrastructure.[6] The transportation fights in Houston quickly expanded to inform other metropolitan debates. Houstonians cared deeply about how mobility systems would serve them and connect the city, but they also channeled frustrations about a wide variety of issues into campaigns around transportation infrastructure. Beyond pushing for specific modes or routes, Houstonians used infrastructural conflicts to advocate for the protection of their communities, as an entry point into broader political debates, and as a way to forward their own visions for the city.[7] Through these actions, citizens challenged the status quo of urban development and reconfigured the balance of metropolitan political power by inserting themselves into its fabric.

Struggles over how to best shape a city—where to build homes, businesses, parks, or schools; how to provide access to those spaces; how to power and operate them; and how to pay for them—are universal. Over the course of the twentieth century, debates about highways and mass transit systems became increasingly influential, if understudied, elements of the effort to define American metropolitan growth. Much of the literature on metropolitan growth that does exist is focused on the earlier part of the twentieth century.[8] The history of these debates, and of the nation's changing urban built environment more generally, is traditionally framed through the actions of the government officials, engineers and architects, private companies, and real estate developers who planned and built the systems that served American cities. This official perspective took shape in both the black-and-white ink of engineering renderings and in the final positioning of steel girders. Their viewpoints are the most visible—both on the landscape and in scholarship—because they were the most concrete. They were the ones that usually got built. However, using the frame of infrastructural citizenship allows competing definitions of the built environment to come to the fore. It acknowledges the possibility that a single highway could bring promise or dread depending upon the location of an off-ramp. One community of residents may have supported a road because it brought them into town more quickly. Another may have rejected it because it cut them off from a school or grocery store. The fact that a single infrastructural debate could oscillate from the metropolitan scale to the level of a single home, and from public debate to private domain, demonstrates the universality of the subject and the significance of its study.

Although infrastructural citizenship can and should be located by historians in events that occurred prior to 1940, the combination of increasingly empowered citizens and the roiling redevelopment that occurred in American cities after 1945 resulted in uniquely contentious metropolitan infrastructure debates. This fertile political moment allowed for the scaffolding of infrastructural citizenship—and its many iterations—to emerge. Increasing citizen activism, on both the left and the right of the political spectrum, was essential to shifting the nature of infrastructural debate and project construction.[9] Nationally, citizen protest against official-driven infrastructural planning, particularly urban highways, began to crop up in the late 1950s at a time when hundreds of millions of dollars were flowing into projects to build downtown roadways and remake urban cores. This undercurrent turned into a flood by the late 1960s as a wide variety of Americans fought for influence over the infrastructural future of their cities.[10] As federal officials devolved a variety of decision-making powers to the local level during the second half of the twentieth century, citizens seized on opportunities to influence policy.[11] By the mid-1970s, much of this debate had shifted toward arguments about investing in public mass transit.[12] Fights over what transportation mode to prioritize intensified through the late twentieth century and continued into the twenty-first century in Houston and across the nation.[13]

The citizen-led push to shape postwar infrastructure put pressure on government officials and helped shift the planning of major projects from a process that excluded citizens altogether toward one that required significantly more citizen participation. That level of involvement continues today, and transportation decisions are among the most publicly scrutinized and fractious decisions that a city, region, or state can make. Increased involvement in decisions did not directly equate with increased decision-making power, though. Although individuals have gained a louder voice in transportation decisions, theirs is not always the one that carries the day. Parsing through Houston's historical and contemporary transportation fights sheds light onto where citizens have made gains, what the durability of those victories are, and where citizens continue to face limits on their ability to effect change. Lessons drawn from Houstonians' transportation activism can help situate the broader efficacy of infrastructural citizenship as a tool that allowed citizens to participate in the decision-making process and to help shape their cities.

As a form of political activism, infrastructural citizenship connects with several national political trends of the later twentieth century. The fights over highway infrastructure link to broader mass mobilization campaigns for democratic decision-making and civil rights that reverberated through American cities in the postwar period, from the War on Poverty to labor movements. Organizers and activists from these movements were not siloed; nor were the everyday citizens who participated in them. There was a free flow of leadership among these movements, with each drawing lessons and strengths from others. Fights around infrastructure were no different. Leaders in Houston's debates were often active in the city's civil rights movement and other community campaigns. While many parallel citizen-led efforts lost momentum in the face of political opposition from the Nixon and Reagan administrations, or as a result of a lack of financial resources, transportation debates remained an active and contested realm in most major cities. This longevity may be partially due to the amorphous nature of infrastructural and transportation fights. They are ever-present and affect a wide range of citizens. Unlike the War on Poverty and the civil rights movement, though, transportation activism created less durable allegiances and less effective long-term activism. Individuals fought projects on a one-off basis, making sustained activity much more difficult and limiting the long-term influence of groups that formed in response to discrete projects.

As transportation fights stretched into the 1970s and 1980s, they became imbricated with a second, seemingly contradictory stream of political activism—the conservative fiscal and political turn rooted in predominantly white suburbs.[14] Suburban infrastructural activism was a part of a much larger push for local control by white suburbanites that aimed to stem racial integration and keep suburban taxes from supporting majority-minority cities. The rise of suburban conservative politics also created a metropolitan crisis of political contestation between cities and suburbs. This metropolitan fragmentation made regional governance an antagonistic rather than a cooperative endeavor. Furthermore, it still clouds how we conceptualize urban and suburban mobility and the connections between these metropolitan places. This book calls for infrastructural contests to be elevated within discussions of the mass political activism in the 1960s, 1970s, and 1980s.[15]

Because examples of infrastructural citizenship are not confined to particular geographic, political, racial, or socioeconomic boundaries, scholars must compare how citizens from different contexts embodied the concept. Houston's example, again, will prove instructive. Given the city's rapid physical expansion after World War II, no part of the city or group of residents completely escaped the consequences of transportation infrastructure development.[16] Although African-American and Mexican-American residents absorbed many of the consequences of highway construction, they were not alone in facing the negative impacts; nor were they the only groups who resisted official plans.[17] Roads ran through the suburbs as well.[18] Because of the ubiquity of transportation infrastructure, all metropolitan citizens confronted its elements in their daily lives. And several times during Houston's history, seemingly disconnected groups aligned to fight for or against transportation systems. Despite such brief alignments, Houstonians faced divergent scales of destruction and possessed significantly different amounts of political power depending upon their race, class, and geographic location. These differences directly influenced the outcomes of transportation debates and cannot be ignored.

The Americans who participated in infrastructural struggles did not explicitly articulate their actions as expressions of infrastructural citizenship. However, most activists recognized that infrastructure debates afforded them a public, long-term, and potentially transformative topic around which they could advocate for their interests. I turn to the concept of infrastructural citizenship, then, not because it was deployed by historical or even present-day actors, but instead because it offers an organizing idea by which we can conceptualize how thousands of Americans have participated in the shaping of urban built environments since World War II. During discrete infrastructural fights that have occurred over the past seventy years, at a variety of scales and in a variety of places, a diverse set of citizens embraced a common set of rhetorical and political arguments about the placement, construction, and use of infrastructure.

Citizen responses to large-scale infrastructure projects, particularly highways and mass transit systems, must be privileged as formative and dynamic elements of urban development and politics in postwar American cities.[19] Histories of the construction and impact of infrastructure have multiplied in recent years, but, despite this upsurge, work remains to be done on how metropolitan residents conceived of and reacted to infrastructure construction and its aftereffects.[20] Earlier works concerned with infrastructure development, such as those in urban politics, have either privileged the organizational efforts of white elites like Jane Jacobs or focused much-needed attention on the damaging consequences of construction for lower-income and nonwhite communities. Rarely have scholars joined these histories or situated these fights as key political battles within metropolitan urban politics.[21] Even more rarely have scholars engaged with how residents responded to infrastructure after its construction. In this book I have attempted to address each of these gaps and to build upon our understanding of how major urban infrastructures affect the lives of urban residents before, during, and after their construction.

HOUSTON, AN UNKNOWN METROPOLIS

Houston has been an aspirational city since its founding in 1836. From the first, boosterism was a central ingredient in the city's growth. The Allen brothers, the city's founders, sold their humid, mosquito-infested land to potential settlers as the healthiest place in Texas, with "an abundance of excellent spring water, and enjoying the sea breeze in all its freshness." And although few sea breezes could be felt fifty miles inland from the Gulf of Mexico, the Allens' claims of economic prosperity proved prescient. "Trade will flow to [Houston]," they asserted, "making it, beyond all doubt, the great interior commercial emporium in Texas," one served both by rail and by water.[22] By the 1920s, their visions had come to pass. Houston had beaten out regional rivals thanks to the construction of a navigable ship channel, a hurricane that crippled Galveston, and the discovery of oil northeast of the city.[23] The city captured much of the oil trade, and by the 1920s boosters were comparing the city to New Orleans. Houston expanded after World War II, and residents, bullish on its future, celebrated its millionth resident in 1954, touted its reputation as "Space City," and objected to those who depicted it as a tier below New York, Chicago, or Los Angeles. Today, as Houston continues to expand, boosters and the national press are selling it as "America's Next Great Global City," on par with any international metropolis.

In reality, though, the city has been defined less by outsized examples of Texas boosterism than by dependence on a natural resource–based economy, speculative and expansive residential and commercial real estate development organized by an elite-driven growth regime, continued in-migration from all over the globe, and an unequal socioeconomic and political hierarchy overtly shaped by racism and discrimination. The expansion these forces fomented—in population growth, economic production, and the sheer size of Houston's geographic footprint—vaulted the city from a regional trade center into the upper echelon of American metropolitan areas. The region's deep ties to the energy sector made it a global hub and brought national and international pressures to bear on local policies and practices.[24] For all its success, Houston's racist history and the entrenched socioeconomic inequalities present in the city's education, employment, and housing practices prevented all Houstonians from sharing in the city's success equally. Despite Houston's incredible historical transformations and the current-day challenges those shifts have created, the city is vastly understudied. No more than a two dozen or so histories are devoted to it, and none of these draw the connection between the city's historical civic activism and the shaping of its sprawling built environment. Other disciplines have not done much better with documenting the city's past or present.[25] Compared to other cities of its size and import, Houston has been somewhat neglected, and much of how it came to be and what it is becoming remains unrecorded.

Given Houston's present circumstances, understanding its past is critical. In 1940, Houston was the nation's twenty-first largest city, with 384,000 residents. By 2014 it had jumped to fourth place, with a population of 2.2 million. An incredible diversification accompanied this increase. Between 1960 and today, the proportion of people of color in the region went from 35 percent to more than 60 percent.[26] Twenty-five percent of today's Houstonians were born outside of the United States.[27] Compared to other major cities, Houston's current demographic breakdown is the closest to that which is projected for the nation as a whole by 2050. The metropolitan region is 38 percent white, 36 percent Hispanic, 17 percent black, and 7 percent Asian.[28] To Stephen Klineberg, a sociologist and the founding director of the Kinder Institute for Urban Research at Rice University, who has studied the city for more than three decades, Houston's demographic reality makes it "the place where America's future will be worked out."[29] And it is not just Houston that reflects the nation's changing makeup. Fort Bend County, to Houston's southwest, is one of the most diverse counties in the nation, and it is predominantly suburban.[30] Studying why such a mixture of residents settled in the region and how they coexist politically, socially, and culturally is vital because it can inform similar processes in cities across the nation as they continue to diversify in the coming decades.

If the Houston metropolitan area today is a microcosm for what the nation is becoming, the city's past models many of the undulations that remade American cities after World War II. These shifts turned the south into the

Sunbelt and redirected the economic and demographic growth of the nation. Between 1950 and 1980, Houston transitioned from a medium-sized, biracial, southern city into a sprawling multiracial metropolis. This transition began in the 1920s and 1930s through in-migration from the rural South and Mexico. Houston's Cold War–centric economy and energy-sector expansion brought white migrants in from the Northeast and the Midwest. The city began to diversify further in the 1960s and 1970s as small streams of Middle Eastern and Asian immigrants came to the region. Then, in 1982, the dual forces of a deep economic recession and violence in Central America propelled a major change in migration patterns to Houston. A huge influx of migrants from El Salvador and Guatemala came to the city in the early 1980s.[31] Since then, the growth rate of Latino Houstonians has far outstripped that of other groups. With more and more nonnative Houstonians, non-southerners, and international migrants, the identity of the city has likewise changed considerably from parochial and inward-looking to global and expanding.[32]

Despite this overall diversification and the steady growth of individuals' political power during the late twentieth century in Houston, the pool of elite Houstonians maintaining control over the city's decision-making has grown only slightly larger and slightly more diverse since its founding. Houston, like many other US cities, has been driven by a consortium of business leaders and elected officials working together in dogged pursuit of economic success, often at the expense of other considerations, such as equity and environmental protection.[33] The absence of political machines or significant labor unions that could swing political contests meant that elites could ignore residents on most decisions. Houston's de facto public-private growth machine has consisted of business leaders from a variety of sectors—real estate, shipping, agriculture, and energy—working in concert with elected allies over the course of nearly two centuries to cement the city's position as a primary economic hub for the American South and Southwest.[34] Until the 1970s, this leadership group was almost solely composed of wealthy white men whose decisions rippled outward to shape the city.[35]

Although the city's "old boys' club" began to recede as Houstonians of color and women began to break into positions of power beginning in the 1970s and 1980s, most notably with the election of Kathy Whitmire as mayor in 1981, the majority of the city's and region's top decision-makers remained mostly white and mostly male up to today. The entrance of women and nonwhite leaders into positions of formal power was a significant shift that offered access to power for many communities and formerly disenfranchised groups. The rise of these leaders to power, in fact, succeeded thanks to the political organization of groups concerned with their lack of voice in the city's status quo approach to governance. However, the ascent of a small pool of leaders did not topple the elite-driven functioning of the city or result in equally distributed political power. It simply broadened the pool of elite decision-makers. The longevity of Houston's elite leadership is a legacy of the city's racist, discriminatory past and still confronts the city in the form of limited political participation and often opaque, elite-driven governance. Racial and economic inequity is interconnected with the city's persistent elite-driven control and remains a major issue.[36] Although racism is no longer codified, there is no denying that in the second half of the twentieth century and the first decades of the twenty-first the legacy of entrenched racism, along with the persistent realities of economic inequality, have remained. The limiting effects both forces have had on the political power of nonwhite groups have continued to affect how black, Latino, and especially lower-income Houstonians have participated in these important debates.[37]

Many of Houston's constitutive elements, from its economic prosperity to its ethnic diversity, were shaped by and helped shape the city's infrastructural debates. As in other realms of city governance, for most of the twentieth century members of Houston's power elite, especially the city's largest real estate developers, influenced the placement of roadways. This type of influence was a possibility closed to other residents well into the 1970s. Too often, though, discussions of metropolitan politics, especially Sunbelt politics, get locked onto the actions of these elites, eliding how nonelites responded to or challenged elite decision-making power.[38] City and state officials, joined by elite allies, certainly won many battles over growth and have rightfully been highlighted as central to urban power structures, but in no city did these groups come out winners in every conflict; nor did they operate in a vacuum. Neighborhood-level pushback by citizens in transportation debates led to compromise and to some outright victories against the perceived power brokers in the city. But such victories remain exceptions in other areas, from education to electoral politics.

The city's transportation infrastructure fights seem to fit an established and historically resonate narrative: wealthier, mostly white Americans win; black, Latino, and poorer Americans lose. Yet, behind that narrative, the fact remains that a diverse collection of Houstonians have used the common set of actions and language of transportation activism and infrastructural citizenship to stake claims to democratic rights and civic decision-making power. That shared experience and common action is important. Even while outcomes of the strategy often diverged, breaking along lines of race, class, and privilege, the fact that many Americans employed and continue to employ the tactic makes it worth exploring. Isolating the appeal and implementation of infrastructural activism, while not ignoring the disproportionate consequences communities faced or the political inequalities that allowed those unequal outcomes to take place, can highlight the evolving role infrastructure decisions have played in the development of urban America. The transportation debates laid out in the this book highlight the profound mix of anxiety and hope that Houstonians have attached to structures of mobility over the past seventy years. The weight of these debates in one city hint at the broader significance that transportation systems and infrastructure more broadly have assumed in American metropolises since 1950.

HIGHWAYS, TRANSIT, AND THE AMERICAN URBAN FORM

Highways underpinned every aspect of Houston's postwar development and have been key pieces to the city's functioning since the 1950s. Roads reflected and enabled the desire of Houston's developers and political elites to grow the region's economy, footprint, and national profile. Like their peers in other major cities during the postwar period, middle-class white Houstonians pined for suburban homes and sought to escape both real and perceived problems in central cities. Local and regional officials, with immense support from the state and federal government, responded to this pressure by implementing policies that enabled and encouraged outward growth.[39] As real estate developers and speculators built the suburban homes for which many clamored, governments at every level built the roads. Highways quickly became a self-fulfilling infrastructure, physical diviners of the region's built form. New roads enabled expansion and justified calls for further highway construction.

Houston's position on a flat coastal plain allowed for snowballing patterns of suburban development during the postwar period and encouraged the construction of highways. While at its founding the surrounding area was swampy and fecund, by draining, channelizing, damming, and reclaiming land for development Houstonians carved out a gigantic space in which to grow. This reformation created new problems, such as subsidence and flooding, but the claiming of once waterlogged land also drove the city's expansion by spurring real estate development and, more importantly, the speculative buying and selling of land on the city's edges. Hindered by neither natural boundaries nor neighboring cities, Houston grew in almost every direction.[40]

Houston's physical boundaries expanded in step with the region's population growth. In 1940, the city encompassed 73 square miles. By 1960, after three huge annexations, the city controlled nearly 350 square miles.[41] Today, of American cities with more than 100,000 people, Houston is the third largest by square mileage at 628 square miles, behind only Anchorage, Alaska, and Jacksonville, Florida. Annexation offered city officials the chance to control and benefit from the massive immigration to the region by capturing the tax base of growing areas. Despite the city's expansions, however, officials could not keep pace with suburban development; nor could they compete with every area municipality in the annexing of desirable areas. Moreover, the competitive nature of annexation compelled overreaches on territory and created a slew of service problems for Houston.[42] Despite the strains put on city and county governments by the rapid pace of expansion, regional municipalities continued to develop, and highways stitched this growth together.

The constitution of postwar Houston around the car and the highway system was not unique, but Houston's version of the automobile metropolis should be seen as a model of America's car-centric growth after World War II. Similar to other southern and southwestern cities that were built up after the rise of the automobile, Houston lacked a dense core or a legacy transit system. Alongside its regime of massive highway construction, these conditions led to the creation of a car-dependent city marked by low-density development and possessing few mass transit options.[43] The creation of this landscape happened remarkably fast. In 1950, the city possessed one highway, the Gulf Freeway, which ran between Houston and Galveston and put just over twenty-six miles of highway-standard roadways in Harris County. Today, the county is home to more than 1,200 miles of highways, and construction is underway on the region's third major ring road, which runs nearly thirty miles from the historical core of the city.[44] The building of this highway-centric transportation system paid huge dividends to powerful suburban real estate developers and the politicians they supported. In the decades after World War II, these city and regional decision-makers viewed transportation choices as a tool of economic development, and they rarely considered how their choices would limit future decisions about mobility.

The interconnected processes of increased individual car usage and the construction of physical and policy landscapes that required and catered to cars contributed to the "essentialization" of automobiles both in Houston and in the larger American society by the 1950s.[45] Nowhere was this prioritization made more obvious than in the decline of transit. In contests over use of the public street and access to public funds, automobile advocates framed highways as a public good that should be supported by tax dollars at the same time that they painted mass transit as a private endeavor.[46] The success of this tactic, combined with layers of onerous local regulations on transit companies, resulted in the bankruptcy of most private companies at the same time that millions in public money poured into the construction of auto infrastructure. Across the country transit options dwindled in the face of a quickly metastasizing car culture. Mass transit systems all but disappeared outside of eastern cities with legacy systems. Trains and buses could not provide the escape, speed, flexibility, or convenience that citizens craved and cars provided.

Despite the popularity and ubiquity of car ownership, the loss of transit options took a large toll on those who could not or did not own cars. Although Americans romanticized the open road, access to auto-derived freedom and even basic mobility was far from a given. Rather, the ability to move was determined, to a great extent, by one's race, age, class, and gender.[47] Car ownership rates among African Americans, for example, while on the rise in the 1950s, remained about half that of white Americans, making this group more dependent upon public transportation.[48] Even today, while car ownership has risen across all racial groups, minority Americans are still far less likely to own a vehicle than white Americans.[49] As cities became increasingly auto-centric, this meant circumscribed mobility and second-class citizenship for those who could not afford cars.

Beyond becoming irreplaceable elements of the urban landscape, highways, and some transit systems, also installed simultaneous proximity and distance between city and suburbs. The routes shrunk the temporal distance between central city office buildings and suburban homes, but they also lengthened the social, economic, and racial space between metropolitan residents. Many white urbanites responded to the metropolitan changes of the 1950s and the falling away of race-based boundaries in the 1960s by reinscribing separation through physical distance and economic exclusivity.[50] Car-based metro areas appealed to suburbanites' growing anti-urban sentiments by offering quasi-rural landscapes that remained within driving distance of major cities.[51] By using their personal automobiles to escape groups, lifestyles, or spaces they found undesirable, suburbanites practiced "secessionist automobility."[52] Such attitudes, whether conscious or not, helped establish major divides between American central cities and their suburbs.

Houston's transportation history again provides an important example of the legacies of car-centric growth. While the building of freeways was integral to Houston's success and has defined the shape of the city and region, the choice to build roads has become a path-dependent reality that has limited other mobility options and restricted Houstonians' visions for what the city could become.[53] Time and again when the city faced a mobility crisis, Houstonians and their leaders chose to double down on cars and larger roadways, neglecting meaningful transit investment until almost 1980 and cementing the region's outward growth. Only in recent years have alternative mobility futures entered the discussion of the city's transportation future, and, despite this uptick, economic, social, and political investments into highway development far outstrip those given to other modes. Houston's mobility choices over the past several decades have been informed by a mix of the individual preferences of Houstonians, the actions of real estate developers, and a matrix of government transportation policies and subsidies. As metropolitan Houston diversified, suburbanized, and underwent huge political shifts after World War II, its decision-making process became increasingly fraught. The area's transportation debates occurred within this context, and the resolutions of the fights shed light on how the metropolitan area took shape.

Understanding how such car-based urban and metropolitan planning has altered the physical form, transportation options, and decision-making processes of American cities is a secondary aim of this book. This analysis can in turn be used to inform future decision-making about the growth of cities. Houston will provide the backdrop for this investigation. This is a crucial topic given that cities across the United States are currently grappling with the historical legacies of their auto-centric transportation systems. While cities continue to suburbanize, new outlying communities increasingly resemble the urban areas they are purposefully built apart from. At the same time, many central cores are densifying and attracting new residents. Transporting metropolitan residents across massive urbanized areas has become a major obstacle for the regional governments involved. In many metro areas, residents and officials are incorporating new approaches to mobility, and some are seeking to bring investments in transit, pedestrian, and biking infrastructure into the same stratosphere as that given to roadways. At the same time, cities are facing immense questions about equity, affordability, and access to employment that are intimately tied up in the form and function of a region's transit system. Although no city will be moving completely away from highway-based mobility in the near future, finding new paths forward is essential to thinking about how our cities will grow in the face of new demographic pressures and attitudes, changing economic realities, and shifting forms of energy production.

The tendency for American cities over the past seventy years to grow outward is not implicitly wrong, but it is undeniably a choice. Suburban and exurban American development arose and grew as a result of a set of government policies, the efforts of speculative real estate developers, and the choices of individual Americans. These are choices that cities and citizens have made and will most likely continue to make in some form for years to come. But they are choices that also must be more concretely and transparently linked to their outcomes, to their effect on the built form of the metropolitan region and its everyday functioning. The combination of a seemingly endless expansion of our nation's infrastructure and funding streams that have not been able to keep up with maintenance demands on roads, bridges, or transit has contributed to a major infrastructural crisis, one without a clear way out.[54] Likewise, the (re)urbanization of American cities cannot be approached without a critical, historical eye. Like American suburbs, the shapes of cities today reflect decades of racism, inequity, and undemocratic decision-making processes. Indeed, many of the areas of the urban core that are redeveloping and are the target of quality-of-life improvements are historically minority, often low-income communities. Just as residents in these areas faced unjust treatment at the hands of highway planners in the 1960s, so today are many confronted with escalating rents, little government support, and the accumulated effects of decades of inequality.

The growth of metropolitan areas was and is a messy affair. It is tied up with individual lives and desires, political alliances, and economic bottom lines. Transportation and infrastructure debates hold an integral spot in this messiness. Similar to other formative yet unrecognized forces of urban reshaping, such as demolition, infrastructural conflicts are often assumed to be secondary political arguments.[55] They are centered on the background structures of everyday life—on the routes, traffic, and trip times. Most Americans focus on these systems and the debates behind them only when struck by their convenience or inconvenience. Americans see the highway more immediately when they are stuck in traffic. They object to a change in a bus route when it leaves the street in front of their house, but rarely notice a shift in another person's route. They organize for or against major infrastructure, but ignore many smaller design shifts or public subsidies. By exploring the conflicts around Houston's transportation and mobility changes, this book insists that these debates come to the fore.

INFRASTRUCTURAL CITIZENSHIP AND ITS ELEMENTS

The concept of infrastructural citizenship builds from recent scholarship in anthropology, geography, history, and mobility studies that defines infrastructure as more than the concrete, metal, or fiber-optic networks that shuffle humans and the resources we use across the globe.[56] Hard infrastructure—the pathways and technologies that permit commerce, travel, and exchange—cannot be ignored, but recent work has moved away from concentrating solely on these networks. Instead, scholars have used soft infrastructure—the constitutive social, economic, and political structures that formulate the foundation of any infrastructure—to study its place in society. The best studies of infrastructure interweave hard and soft, echoing anthropologist Brian Larkin's definition of infrastructure as "technology entangled in political domains."[57] Just as a study of urban politics presents a messy tangle of interests, alliances, and power struggles, so, too, can an interrogation of particular infrastructural systems lay bare countervailing definitions and uses from a number of actors.

Transportation structures are among the most tangible and common infrastructural elements in American cities.[58] Their centrality suggests that they be privileged in studies of the shifting nature of the relationship between officials, residents, and the built environment. Highways and streets have strict regulations prescribed by officials, and scholars have shown how leaders have used infrastructure and its rules to impose larger political or social goals onto landscapes and citizens.[59] In Houston, and other postwar American cities, officials used highways to facilitate suburbanization and to attempt to prop up the central business district. Despite the nearly total power of these decision makers, citizens forwarded their own perspectives on large projects and redefined spaces through uses that often stood in opposition to the expectations of officials.[60] Challenging the official version of construction and redevelopment through infrastructural debates and transportation activism, citizens complicated the place and legacy of these structures.[61]

Unlike other elements of the built, political, and social environment, transportation networks cannot be avoided. One may not be served by a phone or sewage line, may not participate in elections or hold a job, but every urban resident moves, in one form or another, across the city's mobility network. The network that facilitates this movement evolves over time as officials attempt to structure, order, and facilitate the types of movement they deem best. However, that view often brooks against citizens' own mobility choices and use of infrastructure. The ensuing conflicts between these sets of actors transform the urban and suburban built environment, change urban planning practices, and alter societal notions of technology, speed, and time.[62]

Transportation structures, and the mobility they allow, are simultaneously ephemeral and permanent parts of urban life. A pedestrian's route may change on a daily basis, or a commuter may take the same drive each morning for decades. Mobility practices can shift with the turn of the wheel or the acceleration of a gait. Yet all these uses are carried out on a system of semipermanent pieces of the cityscape. Infrastructural decisions made in the past reverberate for decades because of the durability of the structures. Overpasses and sidewalks are built to last. Steel, concrete, and asphalt persist for years. But these systems are also in a constant state of deterioration, maintenance, and remaking. In many ways the transient, yet solid nature of transportation structures imitates the city itself. The meanings of spaces can change in a moment. So, too, can seemingly permanent structures be demolished. Buildings, roads, and cities continue to be made and remade, if only to be imagined and forgotten anew by those who look upon them.

Several secondary concepts—mobility, place, and participation—are couched within the definition of infrastructural citizenship and exemplified through Houstonians' application of the concept via transportation activism. These components help deepen the discussion of how infrastructural choices shape cities and the lives of their inhabitants.

POLITICS OF MOBILITY

Transportation infrastructure is, of course, connected to movement. But these structures do far more than direct the physical motions of urban dwellers. Highways, train tracks, and the vehicles that carry people through a city's built environment shape the lives of those who use or encounter them on a daily basis. More than simply determining where and how one can travel, these systems impose a tangible order onto the cityscape that stretches far beyond the corridors through which they run and helps residents cognitively organize the city.[63]

The inherent connection between transportation structures and the movements of urban residents links the contestations of infrastructural citizenship to an underlying politics of mobility. Mobility, here, means much more than the simple act of movement. It also describes how people perceive movement and the spaces and systems that allow it, and the role it plays in their daily lives.[64] Making mobility a part of infrastructural citizenship lends the idea dynamism. By framing transportation structures and the mobility they have permitted as political, contestable categories, we can investigate how transportation decisions were made, and by whom, and recognize which populations gained the benefits or suffered the consequences of these efforts.[65] A great deal of work has already been done on how urban residents actively attempted to shape early twentieth-century cities through mobility fights, but few works document the same process in the second half of the century.[66] Because of this absence, we underestimate the role that transportation fights play in the creation of American cities today.

Tying a politics of mobility framework to infrastructural citizenship also permits me to consider in this book how access to or denial of mobility has affected the lives of citizens in ways that have gone beyond just getting to jobs, schools, or stores. In totality, the term acknowledges that mobility could possess deeper, more contradictory meanings for residents: freedom or oppression, modernity or backwardness, privilege or poverty. Through these meanings, mobility illuminates the intersection of politics, culture, and urban development in Houston. Adding social and cultural elements to what remains too often a solely political and economic discussion around highway and transportation decision-making illustrates how interwoven mobility infrastructure is with other facets of our urban worlds.

PLACE

Each of the Houstonians discussed in this book possesses a set notion of place, one inextricably tied to his or her interactions with the landscape. The planning and building of roadways and mass transit systems altered Houstonians' relationship to place by installing physical boundaries across the city and, at the same time, providing a means for movement that transgressed those borders. More intimately, the connection or severance created by a highway or transit system disrupted people's notions of their homes and neighborhoods. Major infrastructure projects forcibly remade the spaces Houstonians passed through each day. Often, construction rendered previous landscapes unrecognizable. Such changes disrupted what urban theorist Kevin Lynch calls the "legibility" of an area, by disconnecting it from other parts of the city or changing established pathways.[67] For those who experienced firsthand the destruction of a neighborhood, the landscape transformation turned a place that once connoted home to one instead signifying anxiety, unwelcomeness, or even fear.[68]

Over time, though, once-alien landscapes become accepted and known. Definitions of place are fluid. They are linked both to the elements of past landscapes that persist and to the new meanings installed by redevelopment. Roads become a part of a neighborhood, traffic a daily occurrence. Speeding cars, the ding of a bus stopping, and the voices of pedestrians become background noise. To understand how residents conceive of their neighborhoods and homes, their places, we must pay attention to how the past and present meanings of a landscape converge.[69] Moreover, individuals are never simply acted upon by the construction of new infrastructure; they also respond to its presence. While physical structures have regimented space in particular ways, Houstonians' use and contestation of those structures have endlessly redefined their sense of place and connection to the city.[70]

Notions of place are foundational to the rhetoric of infrastructural citizenship. Many Houstonians who participated in major mobility debates did so largely in order to protect or improve their homes and neighborhoods. Roadways and transit networks, therefore, cannot be viewed solely at the metropolitan scale. Scholars must zoom in on particular spaces and work to understand how different groups of residents might come to view the same place in completely different terms. To a suburban Houstonian, a new highway section through downtown reads simply as a more useful commuter space. But to the Houstonian displaced by the roadway, the new landscape is foreign and destructive. Both groups turned to expressions of infrastructural citizenship and advocated for their desired outcomes through its words and actions. To square competing views of place, to diagnose whose idea of the city was valued most by formal decisions, we must bring as many perspectives as possible to bear on our definition of landscape and the city.

PARTICIPATION

For many scholars of the civil rights movement and the citizen democracy movements of the 1970s and 1980s, the promise of creating a truly democratized, citizen-driven, local decision-making apparatus broke against the conservative turn of national politics in the early 1980s.[71] Grassroots efforts to pull lower-class and minority Americans more centrally into metropolitan politics took hold in some cities, but none could sustain power for long. As many of the longest-running citizen-participation groups fizzled out or shifted in their missions, few grew in their place. Yet efforts to carve out space for democratic participation did not completely disappear. Rather, they moved to discrete topics, such as infrastructural debates, where neighborhood-level coalitions or special-interest groups attempted to influence the outcome of an election or a planning choice by applying pressure to elected officials.[72] In these debates, ephemeral alliances sometimes arose among strange bedfellows—white suburbanites voting alongside black urban residents on a particular project, for example. But such alliances rose and fell alongside project timelines, rarely extending beyond a particular debate and with limited significance for overall regional politics.

The limitations of such efforts, though, should not prevent a deep dive into the influence of transportation debates on the shape and functioning of American cities. Since the 1970s, transportation debates have provided a venue for Americans to influence the shape of their cities. The highway revolt provided a template for citizens who wanted to stop or alter major projects. New federal regulations in the 1970s forced officials to include citizens more directly in the finalizing of plans, and these regulations also gave citizens a tool through which they could slow or stop projects they disliked. Countless transit referenda and highway bond issues also gave Americans the ability to directly weigh in on the choices their cities made. Citizens seized on these opportunities as other avenues for engagement fell by the wayside. They did not always succeed in these fights. In fact, citizens have failed to alter infrastructure choices far more often than they have won. Not all Americans chose—or were able—to participate in transportation decision-making. Indeed, many of the fights were incredibly localized and limited to those with direct interest in the outcome. Often, successes failed to roll forward because political organizing focused on a single project was less durable than that around a more multifaceted, continuous topic, such as voting rights or economic justice. But these realities do not lessen the importance of the fights. This argument does not insist that transportation fights represent the most important venue for democratic participation. Rather, it asserts that these debates are among the most accessible and prevalent. Transportation choices have become an important civic battlefield in many American cities, and their anatomy must be better analyzed.

Skeptics of the democratized transportation decision-making angle might argue that rather than reflecting a productive trend, citizen participation in transportation debates stems from the not-in-my-backyard (NIMBY) tendencies of participants. Most people do not want projects that will hurt their own interests, but are less inclined to fight those that only affect others.

Some have argued that such a protectionist stance cripples cities' ability to effectively plan and build out major projects.[73] To a certain extent, this is a valid critique. There are examples of many projects that would benefit the whole that have been derailed by localized efforts to stop or change a route. Moreover, many successful NIMBY fights are led by elite white residents with economic and political power other citizens do not possess. This disparity must be acknowledged. However, just as importantly, we must be careful not to simply label all examples of citizen organization NIMBYism; nor should we dismiss all NIMBY fights as selfish. Either approach dismisses the validity of citizens' attempts to protect their neighborhoods and rejects the validity of an individual's sense of place.

For all the successes that citizens have had participating in transportation debates, the process is far from fully democratic. Elected officials, economically powerful developers and businesspeople, and engineers still possess far more power over transportation choices than everyday citizens. Turnout in transit and road referenda, similar to other local elections, is low in most American cities. But despite these limitations, citizen participation in mobility fights should not be ignored. These conflicts have allowed a wide variety of Americans to gain a larger say in civic decisions over the past seventy years. Citizen participation in transportation decisions makes them messier. It makes the public debate more vigorous. And, in the end, often leads to a different system than that originally laid out by officials.

CHAPTER OUTLINE

Power Moves explores its arguments about infrastructural citizenship, Houston's iteration of the concept through transportation activism, and the impacts of car-based planning in six chapters. The first three deal solely with decisions about roadways between 1950 and 1975. The final three consider decisions made about automobiles and transit between 1973 and today. The first three chapters consider Houston's embrace of highway construction, the effects of that building program, and the first instance of successful citizen pushback against a roadway. These chapters demonstrate how the political process that shaped the city's transportation network slowly became more open between 1950 and 1975 as citizens became more engaged. The next two chapters consider mobility debates and referenda held in 1973, 1978, and 1983 that considered the idea of building a mass transit system in Houston. The final chapter moves to the present day to consider the legacies of the choices made in those earlier votes and Houston's current transportation system. The debates around these votes demonstrated how politics and decision-making about transportation in the city had changed since 1950. The choices those citizens of the region who voted in the three referenda made structured the area's transportation system—and the city itself—into the present day.

Chapter 1 provides the historical context of Houston's postwar rise to national prominence and highlights the central position that transportation structures played in enabling its ascent. In particular, it explains how the city made highways its primary purveyor of mobility by the early 1950s. It draws a picture of Houston's political climate and establishes the state of Houstonians' engagement with infrastructure and mobility in the immediate postwar period. Highlighting the positions of corporate leaders, suburban real estate developers, and elected officials, this chapter demonstrates the top-down nature of decision-making in 1950s Houston. It also examines the political priorities championed by this leadership group. From resistance to zoning to an embrace of annexation, the common thread between these practices was the encouragement of economic growth and the maintenance of tight control over city politics in order to maintain elite influence. The chapter concludes by describing the region's postwar highway development and the changes it brought to Houston's physical shape.

Chapter 2 picks up on the opening chapter's discussion of the construction and planning of the city's transportation system by focusing on three major road projects built during the 1950s and early 1960s. The process of developing these highways displayed how elite Houstonians and officials drove the planning process, and, for the most part, ignored the concerns of everyday Houstonians. By looking closely at projects that cut through central city neighborhoods populated by African Americans and at the planning of a road through an all-white suburb, this chapter will demonstrate citizens' relative lack of power in transportation planning during the postwar period and the broad effects of highways on residents' lives. Although roads shaped all parts of the city, the projects that ran through African-American and Mexican-American areas undeniably took a larger physical toll, displacing far more residents and claiming many more homes through eminent domain. Citizens throughout the region could do little to change this initial round of construction, but as this chapter concludes, the actions residents took began to establish the foundation for later exertions of infrastructural citizenship via transportation activism. Residents attempted to resist these seemingly inevitable projects and in the process shifted the way Houstonians engaged in debates about mobility and the networks that allowed it.

Chapter 3 documents a shift in whose vision of infrastructure and mobility influenced the city's transportation choices. It captures one of the earliest examples of successful citizen pushback against top-down decision-making in Houston. Focusing on a proposal to construct a highway through the predominantly Mexican-American East End, this chapter examines how citizens conceptualized and organized against the roadway, what arguments they advanced, and why they succeeded in blocking the roadway. East Enders resisted highway plans by employing the rhetoric of infrastructural citizenship and practicing transportation activism. They called for decisions about the neighborhood and its infrastructure to be built around democratic self-determinism, environmental justice, and civil rights. Combined with changes to federal laws about public works oversight and a nationwide funding crisis, the resistance of citizens helped derail the highway project.[74] This signaled one of the first times that Houstonians successfully implemented their own visions for mobility and served as a rebuttal to the previously unimpeachable planning power of city elites and officials.

Chapter 4 documents how during the 1970s, at the same time that East Enders debated the construction of the highway, all Houstonians considered the merits of creating the city's first publicly owned mass transit agency. In 1973 they rejected the creation of the Houston Area Rapid Transit Authority (HARTA). And then, in 1978, the Metropolitan Transit Authority of Houston and Harris County (METRO) was successfully created. Emerging at a time when cities across the United States were considering rail-based mass transit systems as a way to ease traffic congestion and address environmental problems, the HARTA and METRO votes represented the region's first postwar opportunities to alter its approach to mobility. The city's changing political atmosphere manifested itself in the debates. In the HARTA vote, a unique coalition of African-American, Mexican-American, and working-class white suburbanites opposed the plan and helped to reject the proposal. This organic alliance demonstrated the peculiarities of the metropolitan power structure and challenges historical narratives about the relationship between cities and suburbs in the 1970s. In the METRO campaign, a similar alliance of African-American, Mexican-American, and, this time, wealthier suburban whites who lived in areas that the transit authority would serve determined the outcome of a metropolitan-wide vote. These groups used their political power to gain concessions before helping to approve METRO.

The Authority's inauguration not only signaled the continued importance of citizen input to transportation planning, but also offered African-American and Mexican-American Houstonians another opportunity to assert their own political desires into regional discussions.

Chapter 5 documents how the debate around two additional transportation referenda led to the dissolution of the fragile alliance that had been formed during the HARTA and METRO votes between the city's citizens of color and white suburbanites. The referenda consisted of a second attempt to create a rail system and a vote to commission a Harris County toll road authority. A powerful civic group, The Metropolitan Organization (TMO), came out on the side of the rail plan. An interracial network of church groups from within the city's inner loop, the group believed rail held greater promise for central city residents than the toll road proposal. Supporters of the tollway plan, mostly white suburbanites from both affluent and working-class municipalities, decided that they no longer wanted to support Houston-based transit systems. They supported toll roads that could move them throughout the metropolitan area with ease. Transportation activists on both sides articulated arguments built around the precepts of infrastructural citizenship. The debate laid bare the tensions between city and suburban citizens that had remained dormant in Houston longer than in other cities and showed the staying power of auto-centric planning. In the end, the toll road plan won out, and for the next two decades transportation development in the region remained road-based and suburb-oriented. Despite Houston's history of balanced metropolitan politics, the 1983 outcomes made it clear that white suburbanites possessed the ability to implement their visions of infrastructural citizenship in a way that mostly nonwhite urban residents could not.

Chapter 6, the final chapter, moves forward to the present day. Through a case study of one arm of the newly implemented light rail system, this chapter will examine the legacies of Houstonians' transit decisions and show just how deeply assertions of infrastructural citizenship and the limits of transportation activism have become ingrained into the political and social structures of the city. The Green Line light rail runs along almost the exact same route as the proposed Harrisburg Freeway of the 1970s. However, unlike the residents who waged the fight of the 1970s, the residents of Houston's East End in the 2000s were engaged in the process of planning, and indeed, in bringing the light rail to their community. The example shows that Houstonians today have more say over the infrastructural and mobility choices being made in the region than ever before. The public feedback processes and increasingly more equal political arena means that citizens from across the region have the ability to voice their own ideas about the future of the city in ways that were nearly impossible in the 1950s. This does not mean, however, that citizens have the final say over major decisions. As the Green Line example shows, citizen participation does not mean a guaranteed outcome. The process undertaken to create and build the line, though, reflects a very different system than that which operated in Houston for most of the postwar period.

This book traces how a wide variety of Houstonians engaged in debates about mobility and the nature of transportation structures in order to shape the city in ways that served their interests. Over sixty-five years, Houston transitioned from a city dominated, but not controlled, by a small cohort of white elites into a metropolitan area whose multiethnic electorate weighed in on the choices of both the city and the wider region. The decisions Houstonians made and continue to make about their transportation networks and the visions those choices projected held increasingly important roles in shaping the physical city. Houstonians may never agree on what mobility means and what systems should be put in place to accommodate it, but by striving to define and secure it for themselves, they formulated Houston's unique system and built the structures along which Houstonians still move today.

CHAPTER 1

BUILDING A HIGHWAY METROPOLIS

The Origins and Advent of Houston's Postwar Growth

> *This is Houston. It is a city that refuses to stand still for anybody. It is a city where the old—except in its sturdiest forms—quickly disappears, in which the new quickly becomes the old, in which change is relentless and rushing. It is a city on the move, with few to observe its movement, for most of its citizens are moving with it, moving too swiftly to stand aside and watch. . . . Pause, if you safely can, somewhere beside the Gulf Freeway. The movement will dazzle you. But do not stand still too long . . . you might get run over. Or—what is worse in Houston—you surely will get left behind.*
>
> W. D. BEDELL, *HOUSTON POST*, 1957

Despite Houston's growing pains it was clear to many national observers between 1945 and 1960 that the city represented the future of urban America. Houston and its inhabitants seemed to never stop moving. From home to work, from city center to suburb, along local streets and smooth new highways, Houstonians' movement, both their economic and physical mobility, provided the city with the essential elements of its postwar reputation. Its pulsating activity orbited around symbols of the city's growth: the headquarters of the national petroleum companies that dominated downtown; the massive oil refineries and petrochemical companies along the ship channel; the nascent but bustling medical center; lot after lot and subdivision after subdivision of suburban tract housing; and the expanding road network that connected all these places. Behind this movement stood an economic boom that began during World War II and persisted in the decades after the war. This growth brought hundreds of thousands of migrants to the city—whites and African Americans from East Texas and Louisiana, Mexican Americans from the Rio Grande Valley and northern Mexico, and, increasingly, white Americans from beyond the South and the Southwest.

These people brought their own life experiences, politics, and visions for the future with them and added them to Houston's already complicated mixture. Housing needs for newcomers led to a massive residential build-up that transformed the ranches and fields around the city into homes and subdivisions and made vast amounts of wealth for real estate speculators. Lucrative wartime industries—especially petrochemicals and petroleum refining—transitioned into postwar operation and drove the expansion of Houston's economy.[1]

As national media profiles of the city hinted, though, Houston's rapid transformation from city to metropolis did not come without problems. Writing for the *Saturday Evening Post* in 1947, George Sessions Perry described the city as groping its way toward greatness: "It is an incipient heavyweight champion in its pimply-faced adolescence, virile, disordered, in selected spots beautiful, but primarily awesome and unstoppable."[2] Houston's population increase and outward physical expansion gave the city a reputation of strength, yet those very forces also precipitated some of Houston's most pressing infrastructural and political challenges. Suburban residential development placed immense service demands on local governments. City departments worked diligently to build and expand sewage and water networks, local streets, and drainage systems, but the construction of these systems and other infrastructure lagged throughout the city. Suburban municipalities absorbed thousands of the area's migrants and with their newfound numbers challenged Houston's dominance of metropolitan politics. The combination of the city's longtime resistance to zoning and the Houston metropolitan region's rapid growth resulted in a volatile mixture of land uses and complicated local planning efforts. An accumulation of automobiles led to congested highways and demands for new transportation structures. Changing demographics forced city politicians and their elite allies to scramble to maintain the status quo and to protect their power. As Houstonians attempted to address these issues, they disagreed over what their city needed and how it should grow.

Houstonians did not experience the benefits of the city's growth or the pains of its problems in equal measure. White-collar and blue-collar white residents, on the one hand, found gainful employment in a number of industries and benefited from access to cheap homes throughout the region. African-American and Mexican-American residents, on the other hand, faced differing forms of discrimination that prevented them from accessing the spoils of Houston's postwar growth—higher-paying jobs and better housing—at the same rates as white Houstonians. The majority of African

Americans and Mexican Americans continued to work in low-level oil industry jobs, as laborers at places such as the Port of Houston, or as service workers. Blacks remained disenfranchised until the 1960s. Race-based segregation limited their access to public resources and kept them confined to particular areas of the city. Houstonians of Mexican origin, while enfranchised and defined as white throughout most of the twentieth century, nonetheless faced discrimination based upon their nationality and confronted similar economic and social boundaries as blacks that prevented them from securing public resources.

Compounding the effects of such discrimination, African-American and Mexican-American Houstonians dealt with the negative consequences of Houston's growth on a daily basis. The poor physical condition of neighborhoods populated by these Houstonians demonstrated that Houston officials were neglecting communities of color in order to focus resources on white, wealthier parts of the city. The Houston government invested little public money in improving these areas prior to the 1960s. Streets were often unpaved or lacked proper drainage; health-care, educational, and recreational facilities were woefully inadequate. However, continued in-migration of African-American and Mexican-American immigrants changed the political dynamics of the city beginning in the late 1950s. Backed by the electoral power of a growing constituency and empowered by civil rights victories at the state and national levels, these Houstonians clamored ever more insistently for a seat at the city's table.[3]

This chapter argues that the construction of the region's highway network and the contemporaneous, interconnected expansion of suburban development between 1945 and 1960 triggered and reflected changes taking place within the region because of its demographic and territorial growth. These shifts set the stage for future conflicts about how the city and its region would grow and move. The geographic spread of residents, and the subsequent shift in mobility priorities, resulted in a diffusion of political power throughout the region, weakening Houston officials' once nearly complete control of metropolitan decision-making and necessitating a greater degree of metropolitan-wide planning than ever before. To both the elected officials contending with growth and the residents creating it, highways seemed to provide a solution to many of the problems the region faced. The construction of highways not only transformed the way Houstonians moved, but also rearticulated how residents interacted with one another and understood their city by reshaping its built environment. Citizens projected a variety of meanings onto the planning and construction of the city's highways, articulating their own understandings of infrastructural citizenship in the process. With near unanimity, they recognized transportation structures as vital to the future of the city. Yet, what Houstonians could not agree upon, and what became increasingly contested over the course of the remainder of the twentieth century, was who would hold the power to determine the shape these structures took, and whose interests they would serve. These disagreements would form the root of a number of political debates over the ensuing several decades.

The diverse set of Houstonians who participated in postwar growth and transportation discussions offered competing expectations for mobility. Elected officials and wealthy elites, an overwhelmingly white and male group, viewed mobility as central to ensuring that the region continued to grow economically and physically. For this reason they worked diligently to remove constraints caused by traffic congestion or limited infrastructure. For suburbanites, again predominantly white and middle to upper class, but also consisting of working-class whites in municipalities along the ship channel, mobility meant easy access to sites of employment, recreation, and consumption. They expected politicians and planners to provide them with roads that could take them from their driveway to points throughout the region in their private automobiles and at low cost. For city residents, people from a number of racial groups and economic classes, mobility was more complicated. After the war, Houstonians in the central city could access the city's limited private bus companies, but by that point all who could afford them, mostly white Houstonians and a smaller percentage of wealthier African-American and Mexican-American Houstonians, owned private cars. Like their suburban counterparts, car-owning Houstonians pressured officials to provide the infrastructure they required. Regional car owners supported investment in roads and did not raise a fuss as the city's private mass transit system deteriorated. Other city residents, mainly from lower economic stations and predominantly African American or Mexican American, relied on walking or buses for their daily movements. Even if they experienced segregation on the buses, as blacks did until the 1960s, or if the systems failed to adequately meet the service demand in their neighborhoods, as was the case for most Houstonians, the systems were essential to their daily movements. The decline of the city's bus system and the splintering of neighborhoods by roadways, then, meant a great deal of disruption to riders and pedestrians alike. Unfortunately for members of these groups, in the immediate postwar period they possessed very little political power, or at least not enough to cancel out the demands of their more influential counterparts.

Between 1945 and 1960, elected officials, their professional staffs, and a small but influential coterie of elites—leaders from the Houston Chamber of Commerce, executives of major corporations, land and real estate developers, and oilmen—dominated, but never completely controlled, local decision-making.[4] Martin Melosi argues that one of the main distinctions between prewar and postwar Houston was that the infrastructure decisions of city officials rippled outward to affect the development of the region in the postwar years in ways they had not prior to the war.[5] Highways captured the metropolitan influence these leaders possessed exceedingly well. Houston's leaders hoped that road construction would stimulate the regional economy by driving suburban development and increasing land values. Moreover, they intended for the building of the highway system to secure their control over the entire region by linking outlying citizens and communities ever more closely to the central city.[6] The immense influence of the city's leaders during the postwar period made their choices about roadways, and mobility in general, the de facto choices of the entire metropolitan area.

While officials may have touted highways as beneficial for all Houstonians, few nonprofessional, nonelite residents played a role in their planning during the 1950s and 1960s. This dearth of citizen oversight mirrored national patterns in highway decision-making and reflected the realities of Houston politics.[7] Not only did officials, usually planners and engineers, decide what systems would be built and where they would run, they also determined which parts of Houston and which Houstonians would receive the benefits or suffer the consequences of their construction. However, nonelite Houstonians were not entirely absent from the process of creating the region's transportation network or its meaning during this period. Citizens influenced the city's embrace of highways by buying cars, demanding autocentric infrastructure, and moving to the suburbs. Each of these actions was an assertion of infrastructural citizenship—first the purchase of an infrastructurally specific tool, then political lobbying for more roads, and finally the selection of a home that required such infrastructure to be in place. Houstonians were far from complacent in the building up of the highway metropolis. As the consequences of road development—displacement, traffic noise, and altered neighborhoods—became clear after the first round of major construction ended in the early 1960s, affected citizens complained and expressed hesitancy about further implementation. As later chapters will show, this hesitancy would grow into outright resistance by the late 1960s and 1970s.

ANTECEDENTS TO HOUSTON'S POSTWAR GROWTH

As the quotation that opened this chapter makes clear, Houston's postwar expansion and seemingly ever-changing urban landscape fascinated the American public during the 1950s. Postwar portraits of Houston, however, too often depicted the city as an overnight sensation and ignored the decisions and policies that had jump-started its ascent from regional capital to international metropolis during the preceding half century. Stepping away from the glossy magazine versions of Houston allows one to see the roots of the city's economic and physical development. Many of the same processes and actors that shaped Houston's growth between 1900 and 1945 remained influential as the city entered the postwar period. Understanding the place of different demographic groups in Houston during the prewar era, however, is essential to understanding the decisions Houstonians made about mobility later on.

Between 1900 and 1960, Houston's economic elite—a group of white, male bankers, real estate developers, lumber and cotton magnates, and oilmen—dominated decision-making in Houston. The members of this group generally did not hold elected office, but their close political allies, such as Mayor Oscar Holcombe, who served off and on as the city's leader for a total of twenty-two years between 1921 and 1956, often acted on their behalf.[8] Jesse Jones, one of the city's leading businessmen and its most influential citizen from the 1920s to the 1950s, never sought elected office but nonetheless parlayed his business success and influence into an important role in the national Democratic Party. His financial acumen was so highly respected that Republican president Herbert Hoover appointed him to the Reconstruction Finance Corporation in 1932. President Franklin Roosevelt made him chairman of the organization in 1933 and US secretary of commerce in 1940. These positions put a Houstonian in charge of millions of dollars in federal funds during the Great Depression.[9] In addition to Jones, other leaders, such as M. D. Anderson and Will Clayton, owners of one of the world's largest cotton-trading companies; the brothers George and Herman Brown, owners of the construction company Brown and Root; and Gus Wortham, owner of American General, an insurance company, each supported important local, state, and federal politicians, including Lyndon B. Johnson and Albert Thomas during the 1930s and 1940s. They maintained close relationships with these politicians as they moved into positions from which they would help develop Houston after World War II.[10] As the city grew in the postwar period, suburban developers joined this group of elites.

The close relationship that elites maintained with government officials from the local, state, and national levels permitted them to implement their visions for the future of the city during the postwar period. They justified their influence by maintaining that their actions were selfless, aimed not at enriching themselves, but instead at improving the city as a whole.[11] While these elites financially benefited from many of the reforms and policies they supported, initiatives to modernize the city's banking system and update its infrastructure systems also stoked Houston's general advancement and growth.[12] Such results allowed elites to paint themselves as Houston-first boosters and to gain even more decision-making power.[13] From their position of influence, elites could also criticize practices or policies such as zoning, higher taxation, or the enshrinement of civil and labor rights that they believed threatened either their own economic and political interests or the economic growth of the city. By resisting such policies and spurning progressive social practices, elites helped foster an undemocratic atmosphere in Houston where the votes and concerns of working-class and poor Houstonians of all races were routinely ignored by elected officials and their elite supporters.[14] With limited organizing outlets—neither labor unions nor political machines held much sway—working-class Houstonians had few opportunities to voice displeasure about elite choices.

Neither the city's rapid growth nor the wealth of many of its elites would have been possible without Houston's access to an abundance of natural resources and the links created between the city and global economies from the early 1900s onward.[15] Prior to 1900, agricultural products such as lumber and cotton, packaged in the city before being sent to either Galveston or New Orleans for sale, buoyed Houston's economy. Then, in the early 1900s, three key developments placed the city at the center of the Texas oil boom and changed its economy drastically.[16] The destruction of Galveston by a hurricane in 1900, the discovery of oil outside of Houston at Spindletop in 1901, and the construction of a deep-sea port and ship channel in the 1910s propelled Houston's transformation into an "energy-intensive metropolis," in which the oil industry inextricably shaped the economy and the physical environment.[17] By the 1930s, oil was the largest producer of wealth in the region. Natural gas was also a major export. The nation's petrochemical industry came to Houston during World War II. Seemingly overnight, dozens of refineries and factories populated the shorelines of the ship channel all the way to Galveston Bay.[18] The concentration of the oil industry and its derivatives drew secondary, supply-chain businesses to the city, increasing oil's economic footprint.[19] Oil also dramatically affected the region's built and natural environment, with new infrastructures cropping up to allow for its growth. Although the oil industry brought wealth and prestige to the city, it also created costs, in the form of health problems and industrial pollution. Houston officials and many residents made a calculated choice to embrace the oil industry and absorb its impacts.[20]

The construction and improvement of transportation networks aided the development of Houston's resource-based economy and influenced the built environment of the city. Prior to 1900, Houston was mainly a railway hub and collection point for inland resources.[21] Rail continued to be a major freight system for the city well into the twentieth century. After a hurricane destroyed Galveston in 1900, though, Houston had an opportunity to take water-borne commerce away from its regional rival. Local business leaders and elected officials at the municipal and national levels leapt at the chance. Using a mix of funds from the city and federal governments, they created a deep-sea port and the Houston Ship Channel in the 1910s.[22]

While the ship channel and freight railways influenced the industrial and economic development of the city, commuter transportation shaped the city's residential and commercial patterns. Houston's first mass transit firm, the Houston City Railway Company, began to operate a horse-drawn streetcar in 1868. By 1891, electrified streetcars were the norm, and by 1927 track mileage had reached a peak of ninety miles. These lines spurred the development of residential neighborhoods farther from downtown, with streetcar suburbs popping up in River Oaks, Houston Heights, and Magnolia Park. By the mid-1920s, private automobiles began to eat into ridership, and private bus companies, with more flexible routes, competed with the streetcars for patrons. By 1940, all of Houston's streetcars were gone, driven out by the combination of low ridership and financial problems.[23] By World War II, auto transit—both car and bus—dominated the city, but Houston lacked a formal highway plan until the 1940s. State and city officials recognized that roads, like rail before them, offered an opportunity to connect the city to the hinterlands, and they hoped that highways would afford the region access to the nation's flowering trucking industry.[24] Leaders began to seriously formulate plans for a metropolitan road system during the war. The construction of the first highways and the growing number of private automobiles, combined with the poor management of the private bus companies, caused a free fall in bus ridership during the 1950s. By the end of the decade, bus companies were struggling to maintain service levels, following the same pattern the streetcars had taken.

Regulations, and their absence, also influenced the city's built environment. Houston's lack of a zoning ordinance led to several physical outcomes for the city. Residents considered enacting zoning regulations four times between 1927 and 1965, but voters rejected each proposal.[25] Many elite businessmen, particularly real estate developers, argued against zoning because they believed it compromised the city's adherence to free-market principles. But behind this ideological rhetoric lay an economic truth, the absence of rigid zoning rules allowed developers to determine the direction of the city's growth by placing commercial and residential projects in any area they wished.[26] The fact that development was unencumbered by zoning also encouraged a state of constant transition in Houston's built environment, with structures going up or coming down on a nearly daily basis. The construction of highways through Houston neighborhoods in the 1950s and 1960s, and the displacement they caused, were not anomalies, then, but rather another iteration of the city's changing landscape. Houstonians were not of one mind about such patterns, as demonstrated by resistance to highways, historical preservation drives, and campaigns for zoning. The city's lax land-use regulations also complicated attempts to plan future infrastructure systems and, in some cases, qualify for federal funding.[27]

The absence of zoning and other such regulations did not affect the lives of Houstonians in the same way. Several residential neighborhoods, particularly those populated by wealthier white Houstonians, relied on segregation, distance, high property values, and deed restrictions or restrictive covenants to protect the character of their neighborhoods.[28] For the first half of the twentieth century, segregation kept African Americans hemmed into historically black neighborhoods in the city center. Discrimination and economic limitations likewise kept Houstonians of Mexican origin concentrated in particular parts of the city. After the US Supreme Court, in *Shelley v. Kraemer*, outlawed explicitly racial restrictions in 1948, previously white communities near African-American and Mexican-American neighborhoods began to integrate. Without legal justification for keeping these groups out, white residents attempted to organize their neighbors to prevent home sales to members of these groups and resorted to violence to keep black families from moving into their neighborhoods. In 1953, for example, the home of the first black family to move into the previously all-white Riverside subdivision was bombed.[29] As it became clear that even such drastic measures would not keep African-American and Mexican-American Houstonians out of formerly white neighborhoods, whites moved to subdivisions away from traditionally black and Latino neighborhoods, hoping that distance and high home prices would keep their neighborhoods exclusive. By rewriting restrictions to prevent residents from renting rooms, creating businesses, or using properties for any practices deemed detrimental to the property values and peace of mind of their neighbors, communities hoped to keep home values high enough to make it difficult for lower-income residents to purchase a home. This approach was particularly effective in the city's most economically exclusive and politically powerful neighborhoods, such as River Oaks. Residents here put a great deal of resources toward maintaining deed restrictions. Less prosperous neighborhoods could not defend deed restrictions to the same extent, and this contributed to white flight and slow integration in the areas nearest African-American and Mexican-American neighborhoods.[30]

Since Houston's founding in 1836, the city has been framed, by Houstonians and non-Houstonians alike, as a model of free-market capitalism.[31] This reputation persisted into the decades between 1950 and 1985, and Houston's postwar elected officials and elites continued to promote the city as a bastion of laissez-faire capitalism. They argued that the hard work and business acumen of residents, combined with a commitment to limited government and low taxation, could foster economic success. Despite building a reputation for both themselves and the city as a champion of the free market, though, after World War II much of Houston's infrastructure growth depended upon the financial support of the federal and Texas state governments. Houston officials and elites coveted investment in roads, oil pipelines, and the port, because they believed it would encourage economic growth. At the same time, officials and elites resisted public subsidies for social programs such as public housing because they worried that the federal oversight attached to such programs could threaten their political hold on the city.[32] They also thought that investing in lower-income areas might lead to further questioning of the political status quo. To justify these concerns, they argued that these practices would result in higher taxes and make Houston beholden to federal dollars.[33]

Despite their public dislike of federal money, this funding was essential to the rise of some of Houston's most important postwar elites. The Brown brothers would not have been the major players they were after World War II without the wartime contracts their company, Brown and Root, received to build oil pipelines and construct ships for the US Navy. Similar contracts continued after the war, when they rebuilt war-damaged areas and constructed North Atlantic Treaty Organization (NATO) air bases throughout

Europe. The corporation used this momentum to become one of the largest construction companies in the nation. By the 1960s, Brown and Root was one of only two construction firms in the United States to have revenues of more than $1 billion.[34] The Browns were not alone in receiving federal support during World War II. Like other southern and southwestern cities, Houston as a whole received significant federal investment. Between contracts let to businesses like Brown and Root, the building of two oil pipelines, and support for the petrochemical industry, the federal government sent nearly $265 million to Houston during the war.[35] This was a huge investment for a city supposedly allergic to federal money, and it helped to vault Houston into the postwar period with a strong economy. Infrastructure continued to be a major source of federal and state investment into Houston during the 1950s and 1960s as the interstate system was planned and constructed. Even as city officials accepted millions of dollars to support Houston's roads, they continued to resist funds for social programs until the mid-1960s, when civil rights agitation and federal policy changes forced leaders to accept more funding.

POSTWAR GROWTH

The people of the region celebrated the arrival of the millionth Houstonian on July 3, 1954. The same day, developer Frank Sharp announced plans to open a huge suburban development, Sharpstown, in Southwest Houston.[36] The timing of the two events demonstrated the link between Houston's decades of population growth and the explosion of suburban developments oriented around new highways. Articles celebrating Houston's population achievement framed the success both as a result of wise past decisions and as an indication of the city's promising future. The *Houston Post* drew a straight line from Houston's four decades of "industrial and business growth" since the building of the ship channel to its huge postwar population influx. Further down that line stood the hundreds of new residential subdivisions, such as the ones Sharp announced on "Millionth Day." These communities succeeded because they met the needs and expectations of the professional Americans who were flocking to Houston and of those Houstonians looking to move out of the city to its environs.[37] *Newsweek* viewed the city's millionth person and the announcement of Sharpstown as evidence of the effectiveness of Houston's approach to development. According to the magazine, over the past fifty years Houston had advanced from a "piece of muddy nothing in the middle of nowhere" to a towering metropolis that looked every day more and more like "the shape and shadow of America's future."[38]

Oil, and the wealth it created, remained a key cog in Houston's economy and culture after the war, often influencing the development of new parts of the city. Oil-rich businessmen and major petroleum companies invested in the burgeoning medical center and bet heavily on suburban real estate development. As companies poured their resources into the city, they also injected the interests of their firms into Houston's future. When Humble Oil—which later became ExxonMobil—created a real estate subsidiary, Friendswood Development Corporation, in the late 1950s, the company directly connected its corporate interests to city and metropolitan growth. Humble executives pushed for highway access to their real estate holdings, supported laws that made development easier, and actively campaigned to bring the new National Aeronautics and Space Administration (NASA) Space Center to Houston in the early 1960s. The siting of the center next to Friendswood's first major subdivision development created a financial windfall for the company.[39]

Oil companies were not alone in attempting to influence and gain from Houston's growth. Corporations such as Prudential Insurance chose to build in the growing medical center area in hopes of gaining from early entry into what many believed would become a second downtown. Prudential's choice proved prescient; by 1960, the medical center area housed over $94 million of taxable value, and another $30 million was in development.[40]

Transportation, and the commerce it allowed, continued to hold a central place in the city's economic expansion after the war. By the late 1940s, Houston's port was handling the second-greatest amount of cargo by weight in the United States, trailing only New York City, which made it the center of trade in the American South. The US Army Corps of Engineers had invested nearly $50 million in widening and dredging the channel.[41] In the late 1950s, port officials predicted that the transportation hub would only continue to grow. Looking forward, port manager J. B. Turner declared that Houston would continue to be a "Doorway to the World." Indeed, as it had for decades before, the city and its port benefited from their position at the tip of a funnel that collected the raw materials and trade products "from its own surrounding territories and the great hinterlands available to it," refining and repackaging them and then sending them on to global markets.[42] In 1963, nearly 11 percent of the city's workforce was employed at the port or in an ancillary business.[43]

Booming commerce and an expanding oil-based economy brought migrants to the city in droves. For decades prior to 1945, rural African-American Texans and Louisianans, Mexican-American immigrants from the Rio Grande Valley and northern Mexico, and white Americans from throughout Texas and the South came to the city for a variety of reasons.[44] After the war, though, Harris County experienced greater raw population increases than it had in the 1920s and 1930s, when the city had grown at its fastest rate because of the oil boom. Once again, oil was central to this movement. Jobs in refining, petrochemicals, engineering, and secondary industries drew hundreds of thousands to the city.[45] In addition to oil, the mass implementation of air conditioning, the expansion of manufacturing, and the suburban real estate boom contributed to the growth of Houston and other southern and southwestern cities.[46] The population of Houstonians of Mexican origin rose from 20,000 people in 1940 to more than 75,000 in 1960, an increase of 275 percent. The population of African Americans leapt from 86,000 to more than 215,000 by 1960, an increase of 150 percent. The white population of Harris County rose from 405,000 in 1940 to well over 918,000 by 1960, growing by more than 127 percent.[47] These three groups remained the most significant populations in the city until the late 1970s, when large numbers of Asian, Middle Eastern, and Central American immigrants began to come to the city.[48]

As a result of chain migration and Houston's patterns of segregated housing, the majority of these migrants found homes in established racially homogeneous neighborhoods.[49] A small percentage of African-American and Mexican-American migrants took advantage of suburban developments or settled in working-class municipalities like Pasadena, but white migration to those areas dwarfed that of both groups. The vast majority of African-American and Mexican-American migrants settled in or near the central city, where they encountered vibrant yet underserved neighborhoods.

The central city neighborhoods that accommodated African-American and Mexican-American migrants most readily displayed the strain of the city's expanding population, but migration taxed Houston's entire infrastructure.[50] Throughout the 1940s and 1950s, officials scrambled to construct systems that could keep the city operating smoothly. The concentrated settlement patterns of these communities also ensured that when highways cut through them, many residents would feel the consequences. Suburban areas, in contrast, generally avoided significant disruption, allowing suburbanites to dodge most of the negative experiences with highways early on in their construction. While economic growth and higher rates of employment contributed to a larger tax base and brought Houston national acclaim, the mass movement of people to its suburbs also threatened the city's position as the most dominant city within the region. Houston officials worried that a failure to provide services to new subdivisions would result in these areas joining competing municipalities through annexation. This could cause Houston to lose out on a chance to increase its tax base while helping a surrounding municipality grow. To avoid this outcome, officials worked closely with developers to create systems that could alleviate service problems. At the same time, city leaders expanded their annexation regimen to block the expansion of competing municipalities and turned to highway building to tie new developments to the city.[51]

By the mid-1950s, suburban residential development had become one of Houston's most important industries. Real estate had been a major wealth creator for the city's developers for decades, but prior to the 1930s the majority of that investment remained focused in and around the central business district. As the city grew, suburban speculation rose. David Bintliff, a prominent financier and developer, for example, began building subdivisions in the 1920s. During the 1930s and 1940s, he bought and sold several ranch properties in the southwestern part of the city, eventually owning and selling the land that later became Sharpstown. As it became clear that Houston would continue to thrive in the postwar period, Bintliff and other developers eagerly snapped up land surrounding the city. Bintliff saw that his "forte was to buy [land] around a booming metropolitan center and given time let these cities grow up and gobble me up."[52] By the late 1950s, real estate was a primary driver of the city's economy—and a huge wealth producer for developers like Bintliff who owned strategic parcels.

The rush to develop the thousands of acres of farmland around Houston caused a significant change to the landscape of Harris County. Over a twenty-year period, the county became progressively more urban as Houston expanded. The transition away from agricultural land use happened relatively quickly. Harris County reached the peak of its farm acreage in 1954, when 690,046 acres, about 60 percent of land in the county, made up its 3,869 farms. By 1974, after steady suburban development, the county housed 1,478 farms that covered 483,310 acres, less than 40 percent of the county's total area.[53] The expanding territory of Houston's corporate limits contributed to the shrinking of agriculture in Harris County. As Houston's population grew from 627,311 to 1,364,569 between 1940 and 1960, the city's jurisdictional boundaries expanded from 73 square miles to more than 340.[54] Within this increasingly large city, growth seemed to be occurring with little or no plan. Commenting on the nature of Houston's expansion in the 1950s, French journalist Pierre Voisin wrote that every developer "is doing just as he pleases, building here and there. . . . Houston is spreading like a spilled bucket of water."[55]

Behind the seemingly relentless expansion of the city, though, real estate speculators and elected officials worked closely to put a number of governance systems in place to accommodate and regulate suburban growth.[56] Municipal utility districts represented one such structure. These districts permitted developers to take on debt in order to provide service infrastructure to subdivisions not connected to the city's networks. The creation of a special district required a vote of subdivision residents and the approval of the state legislature. Once a district existed, developers could finance improvements and pass on debt to residents through taxation and fees. Developers often abused this system by installing a friend or family member as the sole resident of an undeveloped subdivision, holding the "election," which was guaranteed to pass, and then securing state approval. The Texas Legislature and local governments, far from stopping these abuses, encouraged them by approving districts whose elections occurred under dubious circumstances. Officials saw these entities as tools that could help stoke economic growth and operate as stopgaps for public service shortfalls. These districts blossomed around Houston after World War II, with sixty-two cropping up between 1949 and 1960, by far the most in any metropolitan area of the state.[57]

The advent of these districts led to the emergence of a common, yet problematic suburban growth pattern, what architect Lars Lerup has termed leapfrog development.[58] This pattern emerged as developers built subdivisions in unincorporated areas with low land values instead of purchasing more expensive acreage next to existing subdivisions or within the city. The strategy resulted in disconnected developments leapfrogging one another, a setup that made the provision of essential services nearly impossible and drove growth well beyond Houston's city limits. Texas annexation laws further contributed to the expansive nature of Houston's development by requiring annexing cities to take on the indebtedness of the areas they absorbed. For developers, this meant that they rarely had to pay off the debts they took on through municipal utility districts. These entities helped Houston provide services to underserved areas, but they also added millions in debt to municipal budgets and exacerbated metropolitan planning problems, because developers took little interest in integrating subdivisions into larger comprehensive plans. Once areas were annexed, such lack of foresight created a number of headaches for planners, officials, and residents.[59]

Houston and its satellite towns all recognized that annexation offered one of the easiest ways to capitalize on the area's growth. The desire to control valuable areas precipitated a massive annexation competition that dominated metropolitan politics for the next two decades. Prior to 1963, any Texas home-rule city had the power to annex land contiguous to its borders, a lax standard with the potential to inflame annexation battles. Before the war, no such competition existed, because Houston's satellite towns were small, and the development that occurred did so within areas clearly controlled by one municipality or another. This reality kept Houston in charge of metropolitan affairs and limited the use of annexation. However, Houston's satellite towns benefited from the same forces that propelled Houston's growth during the war. Between 1940 and 1950, several municipalities incorporated, and preexisting towns, including Pasadena and La Porte, grew significantly. The expansion desires of these small cities presented roadblocks to Houston's growth.[60]

Recognizing that as neighboring municipalities grew they would begin to hem in Houston's metropolitan influence, city leaders acted on their advantages while they could. Between 1945 and 1958, the Houston City Council used annexation to absorb a huge amount of land, including nearly all the subdivision development that had occurred beyond the city's boundaries during and immediately after the war. In 1948, approximately 85 percent of all subdivision platting occurred outside the city limits.[61] Motivated to bring this development into the city and add it to the city's tax rolls, the City Council enacted Houston's largest annexation ordinance to date in 1949, adding nearly 84 square miles of territory. The action brought 139,114 people into the city, and, just as importantly, prevented them from incorporating or joining another municipality. Even such a large action did not allow Houston to stay ahead of the area's growth, however. In 1956, Houston officials passed another annexation ordinance, and this time they expanded the city limits by another 184.8 square miles.[62] With these two major actions, Houston's jurisdictional territory more than quadrupled in less than a decade.[63]

In response to Houston's second large-scale annexation, several industrial cities along the ship channel—La Porte, Pasadena, and Deer Park—began employing annexation in order to stake their own claims to areas of valuable development. One typical move saw Deer Park and La Porte annex the land on which several chemical plants lay in an unincorporated part of Harris County, a move that added nearly $250 million in assessable property values to their tax rolls.[64] The most direct challenge to Houston's control of the metropolitan area occurred in 1960, when Pasadena, La Porte, Deer Park, and Lomax simultaneously passed ordinances that annexed 106 square miles of southeastern Harris County; Pasadena's ordinance allowed it to break out of the territorial box Houston officials had purposefully placed around the smaller city in earlier annexations to contain its growth. In the aftermath of this move, area municipalities passed dozens of annexation orders, prompting *Houston Post* journalist James Holley to note that "before the wave of annexation ceased," most of Harris County and the surrounding five other counties "had been blanketed by annexation ordinances."[65]

The actions of the smaller communities demonstrate the free-for-all nature of metropolitan growth in Houston during the 1950s and early 1960s. The competition complicated metropolitan planning efforts by turning neighboring municipalities into antagonists. Despite the fact that most disputes ended in Houston's favor, the use of annexation by the small municipalities demonstrated to Houston officials that they were no longer in complete control of the region. These conflicts presaged future negotiations and disagreements that would characterize the relationship between the city and its suburbs over the course of the 1960s and 1970s.

Worried that the disruptive annexation battles could stymie metropolitan and statewide growth, state officials decided to enact legislation designed to end the competition. Luckily for Houston officials, when the Texas Legislature passed the Municipal Annexation Act (MAA) of 1963, it gave the state's largest cities an advantage. The MAA quelled metropolitan annexation competition by assigning municipalities a defined extra-territorial jurisdiction (ETJ)—a territory outside of a city's corporate limits, which only that city could annex. The MAA determined ETJ sizes by population, which benefited large municipalities. The law established Houston's control over all unincorporated or unclaimed land within five miles of its city limits and gave the city the right to expand its territory by 10 percent each year.[66] Suburban communities had much smaller ETJs. With these expansive new powers, Houston officials placed large swaths of land into its ETJ to prevent suburban municipalities from encircling the city.

The MAA gave Houston the flexibility to avoid many of the problems other American cities confronted with their suburbs. Central cities across the nation competed with their bedroom communities for desirable territories, but few controlled as much territory or possessed the ability to claim more as freely as Houston. In other locations, suburban incorporation sometimes led to intense levels of metropolitan fragmentation. In both St. Louis and Oakland, for example, suburban municipalities annexed nearly all the land surrounding the central city, preventing the larger entity from expanding geographically or economically. The resultant stagnation of development contributed to economic declines in both cities.[67] Houston's ability to annex land during the postwar decades gave the city remarkable flexibility in its expansion. After passage of the MAA, new incorporations dropped decidedly within Harris County because Houston controlled most of the remaining unincorporated land.[68] The MAA also allowed Houston to continue dominating metropolitan politics and development. After securing territory, Houston officials pushed for the construction of an effective highway system in order to consolidate that power.

"TRAFFIC JAMS OR FREEWAYS": BUILDING HOUSTON'S HIGHWAY SYSTEM[69]

"Transportation in Houston is the story of the motor vehicle," declared *Houston Post* journalist Jim Mathis in 1958. "The city is built, some say, around four wheels and a gas tank instead of people."[70] While Mathis acknowledged the hyperbole in his statement, the underlying sentiment was not far from the truth. For all its roots in railroads and shipping, Houston after 1940 was an automobile city. By the late 1950s, observers seemed to have forgotten that streetcars, rail, and even horses had once used the streets of the now booming auto metropolis. No other aspect of Houston's built environment so shaped the physical character of the city after 1945 as highways. As Houston grew into an international metropolis, so grew its highways.

In Houston, as in cities across the world, highways and automobiles did not foist themselves onto residents; nor was the construction of roads what led to the embrace of auto-suburbs. Rather, it was the choices Americans made to turn to car travel and the auto-centric strategies, policies, and incentives implemented by governments at every level that made cars central to American lives and landscapes.[71] Although most Houstonians played little role in planning the initial elements of their road system, their embrace of automobiles necessitated its construction. In 1949, there were 290,000 registered vehicles in Harris County. By 1959, the number of registered vehicles had more than doubled, rising to 607,000, a number that forced officials to build a system that could serve them.[72] But even if officials built a system that responded to citizen demand, they also constructed it to meet their own desired outcomes, which were not necessarily aligned with those of all the city's residents. For Houston's elected officials, businessmen, and developers, accommodating cars meant building a system that could keep the city physically growing and commerce moving—and them in power. To meet those ends, city and state highway planners built roads that tied the growing suburbs and industrial areas to the central city, allowing suburban workers to access the central business district with ease. They also laid out roadways to serve the Port of Houston, the ship channel, and the NASA center. While these roads afforded commuters and suburbanites a great deal of mobility, there were drawbacks. Some highways cut central city neighborhoods in two, creating new boundaries and restricting access to various parts of town, as happened in the Fifth Ward. Coupled with the decline of public transit, the suburb-centric construction of roadways resulted in some Houstonians becoming less mobile even as more transportation structures were built.

Many Houston leaders viewed road construction and annexation as interlocking processes. Every mile of road constructed between the burgeoning suburban developments and the city allowed Houston to draw its outlying communities in and brought the officials' vision of an interconnected metropolitan area, with Houston at its helm, closer to reality. City leaders promoted metropolitan connectivity as key to development and argued that major projects, including "highways, freeways, major thoroughfares, major drainage channels, and flood control projects," could bind the region together.[73] Roads held a key position in bringing new business to the region as well. After World War II, relocating corporations—especially the all-important industrial concerns coming to the ship channel area—demanded road access.[74] Road development also presented businesses whose headquarters sat in the central business district with a new set of challenges. Executives from these companies recognized the necessity of expanding into suburban areas but also hoped to use roads to help stem the adverse effects of decentralization and inject energy back into downtown.[75] Local elected leaders and their professional staffs worked in concert with state and national highway officials to formulate Houston's highway system during the 1940s and 1950s. As they constructed the system, these leaders followed the contours put in place by Houston's economic growth, the interests of powerful developers and elites, and the mobility needs of its suburbanizing population.

The first major highway to open in Houston was the Gulf Freeway (now Interstate 45), which connected Houston and Galveston. Discussion of the roadway began in the 1930s, but action on the road's construction did not start until the end of World War II, after passage of the Federal-Aid Highway Act of 1944 earmarked adequate funding. Construction began in 1946, and the road opened in 1952.[76] The building of the Gulf Freeway set a number of precedents for the future development of Houston and its roadways. The highway was immensely popular; so many drivers used it that within three years the road had reached its capacity and was often congested.[77] Furthermore, the freeway gave Houstonians a sense of how highways could benefit the city and their individual mobility. Its construction signaled their embrace of roads and oriented their transportation choices toward road building for several decades. Traffic snarls on the freeway elicited calls for expansion from citizens and officials alike, refrains that would accompany every new road project. The freeway also demonstrated to developers how valuable road access could be, as property values rose considerably along the roadway and housing developments quickly sold out.[78] Finally, the road became a national trendsetter for engineering and planning standards with its six lanes of at-grade traffic and frontage roads.[79]

The construction and success of the Gulf Freeway spurred city, county, and state leaders to build a larger network of highways in and around Houston. The city's rampant growth brought a sense of urgency to this planning. In a 1954 editorial in the Houston Chamber of Commerce's monthly publication, *Houston*, Director of Transportation Eugene Maier called for a concerted effort to build new roads. Postwar growth, Maier maintained, had created service demands well above what "even the most imaginative public officials" could have forecast. Car registrations, population, and the size of the city all increased by huge margins during the early 1950s. Maier contended that a serious investment in highways might help alleviate the pressures created by these changes.[80] Scrambling to bring an effective system to the metropolitan area, state and local officials jointly approved the plans for a regional highway network in 1954 and announced it publicly in 1955 (fig. 1.1).[81]

Financing the system presented officials with their next hurdle. Unlike the Gulf Freeway, the metropolitan highway plan upon its inception lacked a consistent funding stream. The City of Houston attempted to pass several bond issues to raise money for right-of-way purchases and construction costs, but had mixed results as residents weighed the inconvenience of traffic against that of higher taxes.[82] The State of Texas had accrued a large nest egg for road maintenance during the war by not spending on new projects, but it could not foot the bill for the entire system.[83]

Passage of the Federal-Aid Highway Act in 1956 brought funding stability to the regional road network. Nationally, the act was itself an example of a politically contested infrastructural choice. The formulation of its component parts and the location of its routes throughout the nation emerged from

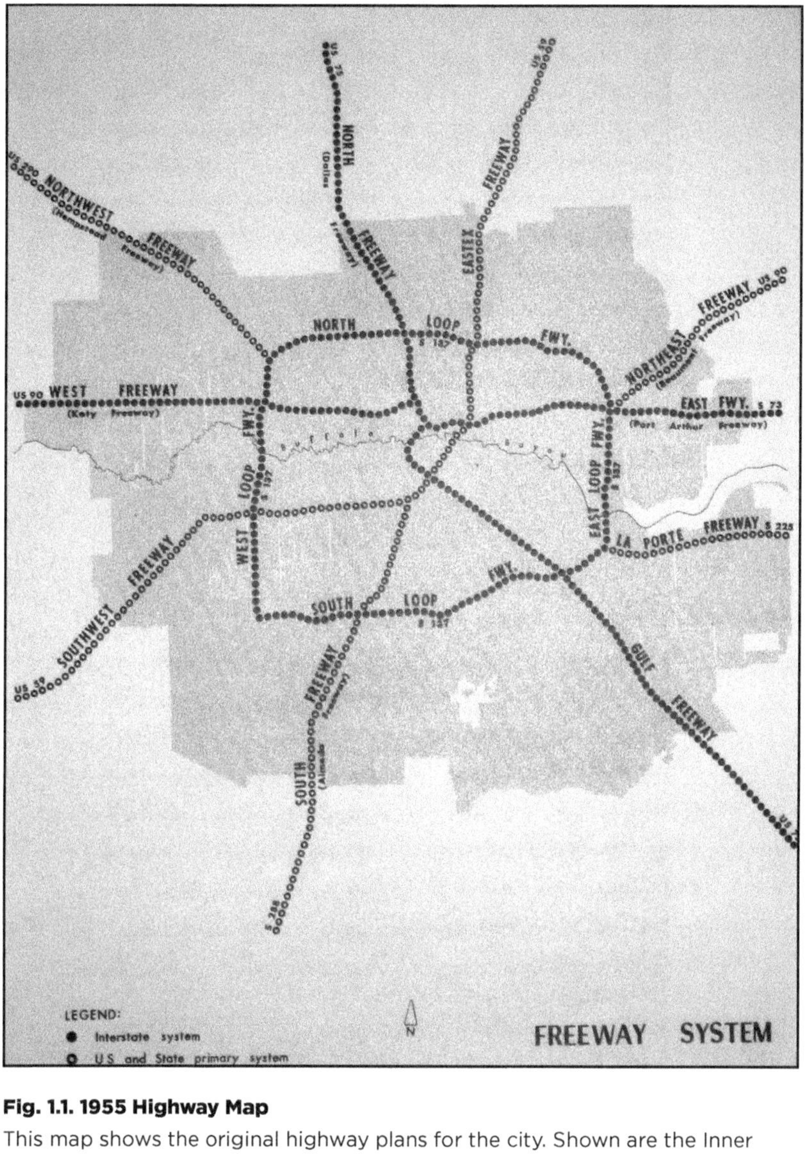

Fig. 1.1. 1955 Highway Map

This map shows the original highway plans for the city. Shown are the Inner Loop (now I-610) and several spoke highways, including the North Freeway to Dallas and the Gulf Freeway to Galveston (now I-45), the Southwest/Eastex Freeways (now US 59/I-69), and the West and East Freeways (now I-10), along with several state highways. City of Houston Planning Commission, *Annual Report 1955,* Texas Department of Transportation, Houston Branch Document Library.

a delicate negotiation between urban and rural legislators and different industry groups. The act's most important element, the federal government's agreement to pay for 90 percent of every route, ensured that states would be eager partners. Texas officials certainly were.[84] The financial incentives in the act allowed officials from Texas and Houston to purchase most of the required interstate right-of-way and begin construction on metropolitan roadways. Representing an even larger federal investment than the amount the federal government contributed for the ship channel, the original cost estimate for Houston's portion of the interstate system was $243 million, a number that indicated the breadth of Houston's road-building project. It was nearly half of the allotment the state was scheduled to receive.[85] Interstate funding also freed up local and state money for dedication to secondary highways and roads. The financial floodgates opened in the half-decade after the act's passage. Counting expenditures from all levels of government, more than $305,300,000 was spent on Houston area roadways from 1956 to 1961.[86]

As road planning and construction began, Houston business leaders recognized the importance of locating branches along or near the new roads. Executives from the city's largest companies contemplated decentralizing their operations and worked closely with the developers of suburban shopping centers and local officials to ensure that their secondary locations would benefit from proximity to highways. When Foley's Department Store decided to branch into the growing suburbs, the company leadership insisted that "close attention . . . be given to the State, County and City Freeway program" to ensure the success of the new stores.[87] Store officials opened direct lines of communication to the Texas Highway Department and monitored the construction status of the Southwest Freeway in order to make sure the road would adequately serve its branch store in the area.[88] Foley's leadership also joined with Sharpstown founder Frank Sharp to push for the extension of a bus route to the newly opened Sharpstown mall.[89] When they scouted for a new store in the southeastern part of the city, Foley's officials concentrated only on sites that abutted the Gulf Freeway.[90]

No part of the metropolitan area captured the economic and physical changes brought by the first stages of highway construction better than the Clear Lake area, southeast of the city. When the federal government and NASA announced the siting of the Manned Spacecraft Center (MSC) in Clear Lake in 1960, the area immediately became a hotbed for real estate development and jumped up the priority list for infrastructure expansion. The desirability of the area kicked off the annexation fight between Houston and Pasadena discussed earlier.[91] The MSC decision was a boon to the

Friendswood Development Corporation, which owned thousands of acres nearby and quickly announced plans to develop Clear Lake City, a residential community that would house and serve the predominantly white, professional MSC workers and their families. The growth potential of the MSC, Clear Lake City, and another Humble project, the Bayport Industrial Park, drove development around Clear Lake skyward in the early 1960s.

The MSC and Clear Lake City developments necessitated an overhaul of the area's highways and thoroughfares. The construction of these roads modeled the way officials used the structures to control the direction of metropolitan growth. In 1960, the Clear Lake area had a single two-lane market road, and only the Gulf Freeway provided highway access. As part of the MSC's construction, NASA teamed up with the Texas Highway Department to build NASA Road 1, which would connect the MSC directly to the Gulf Freeway (fig. 1.2). Even with this roadway complete, the highway department believed that the road network in the NASA area would need to be drastically

Fig. 1.2. NASA Road 1

Construction of the Manned Spacecraft Center and NASA Road 1 occurred simultaneously, as officials knew the MSC would need adequate road access. Texas Department of Transportation, Communications Division, Media Production, Photo Library, Jack Lewis, photographer, April 1, 1963.

expanded to serve workers and residents. Early in 1963, the department instituted a $100 million improvement plan to build "a network of good roads radiating in all directions" away from the MSC. Recognizing that many workers at the MSC and nearby industries would "prefer living away from the congestion of [the center's] immediate vicinity," highway officials offered a road plan that could easily bring commuting workers in from the surrounding suburban communities and even Houston itself.[92] Included in the plan were several other state highways that would crisscross the Clear Lake area and connect commuters to the Gulf Freeway.

The roads built to service the MSC area altered the landscape of southeastern Harris County. As the secondary highways and thoroughfares were developed around and near the MSC, real estate speculation escalated and land values rose just as they had upon completion of the Gulf Freeway.[93] Formerly small coastal towns, such as Kemah, Seabrook, and Taylor Lake, quickly became larger communities filled with MSC workers.[94] These communities promoted their road access to both the MSC and Houston as a primary reason to purchase a home in the community.[95] Road expansion in the Clear Lake area was typical of the entire region. The expanded road network linked the city's suburbs to Houston physically, economically, and cognitively. The roadways and the mobility they offered accelerated the dispersal of the metropolitan region by allowing Clear Lake and other suburbs to draw businesses and residents away from those parts of the metropolitan area that were less connected to the region's roadways.

At the same time that Houstonians were busily building up a road network, their once effective mass transit system was falling apart. As more Houstonians relied on cars for their daily mobility, fewer had reason to support mass transit. Like many other American cities throughout the 1940s and 1950s, Houston witnessed increasing numbers of citizens voting with their feet and pocketbook: forgoing mass transit and blocking measures to expand it.[96] These decisions, and the decline in transit service that accompanied them, created problems for Houstonians who still relied on the cheap mobility of the bus system to reach jobs, recreation, and other essential services. The city's streetcars ceased operation in 1940. Bus service peaked in 1947. Ridership fell throughout the 1950s, and the private bus companies found themselves struggling financially.[97] With service declining on private buses, some discussion of creating a public transit authority began. This conversation, though, faced two obstinate realities. First, many Houstonians and elected officials viewed public ownership of transit as an unwanted form of government intervention similar to zoning. Second, the majority of city, county, and state officials, as well as citizens, saw highways as the unquestioned future of the city's transportation system. While some discussion of the possibilities and merits of mass transit systems appeared in outlets such as the *Houston Chronicle*, with highway-centric attitudes dominating the conversation, gathering the necessary momentum for the creation of a publicly owned mass transit system seemed nearly impossible in the late 1950s and early 1960s.[98]

CONCLUSION

The combination of highway construction and outward urban growth in the 1950s and early 1960s drastically reshaped the Houston metropolitan area. Simultaneous suburban and highway development meant that noncentral homes would remain tied to roadways and the city. The declining distance between individual Houstonians and the nearest highway was one of the most important physical changes that highways brought to both suburban communities, such as Clear Lake City, and Central Houston. In 1960, 95 percent of Houstonians lived no more than 7.5 miles away from a freeway. Accounting for the roads that were under construction and looking forward to include future additions, projections concluded that by 1980, that distance would drop to 2.5 miles.[99] This number presaged the central place roads would come to inhabit in Houston's built environment within the next thirty years. As more and more roads were built and the highway network took shape, car rides and lane lines became a part of everyday life for most Houstonians.

Houston's growth both before and after World War II owed much to the city's geographic position on a flat, easily developable plain and to the ability among leading Houstonians to capitalize on that position through adroit business practices and economic expansion. In making choices that transformed the area's natural landscape to serve their purposes—whether that meant dredging Buffalo Bayou to turn it into a ship channel or linking subdivisions to the city with highways—Houston's elected leaders and elites also helped the city grow. The city's leaders were instrumental in directing Houston into and through the postwar period upon a wave of expansion. Whether elected or not, Houston's wealthiest and most powerful residents held tight to the reins of the city's growth and applied their vision of mobility to the city as a whole. The rest of Houston's citizens, though, were not powerless. Just as they pushed for roads by purchasing cars and demanding infrastructure for mobility around the metropolitan area, nonelite Houstonians influenced the city's path as it grew and prospered. Highway development and mass transit debates that took place over the ensuing three decades of the city's history offered citizens an avenue to assert their own ideas about the shape of the city, their rights to determine its future, and their conceptions of mobility. The remaining chapters weave these two strands—transportation structures and their place in struggles for political power—together. This will start with chapter 2, which shows that as the Texas Highway Department poured footings and planned overpasses, Houstonians became increasingly aware of how the roads they sought and celebrated would change their lives for better or worse.

CHAPTER 2

WHOSE HIGHWAYS?

Planning, Politics, and Consequences

In May 1962, flyers appeared under the front doors of homes in Memorial Bend, a white upper-middle-class Houston subdivision several miles northwest of downtown. A plat map of the neighborhood framed the top third of the page. A thick red line ran through the middle of ordered properties and over the top of several cul-de-sacs. "Attention Homeowners and Taxpayers," the headline read. "Are you aware that the City Planning Commission and Harris County are putting an eight-lane freeway, similar to the Gulf Freeway, through the Bend?"[1] Concerned neighbors dropped the flyers at every home in Memorial Bend. Others spread the word through neighboring subdivisions. By the time the residents came before the Houston Planning Commission a month later, they held a petition against the highway signed by more than 1,000 area residents.[2]

About that same time, across the city in the Fifth Ward, the predominantly African-American community that sat just a few miles from downtown Houston, a hammering noise rousted Ramona Toliver from her home. Standing on her front porch, a startled Toliver found the source of the noise when she observed a Texas Highway Department surveyor driving several orange-flagged staves into her front yard. The markers came up just short of her front door and sat on both sides of her garage, drawing a line right through its middle. Toliver confronted the surveyor, who reported that the staves marked the outer edge of the new interstate that would soon be coming through the ward. He informed her that her house and garage stood in the projected path, and that some, if not all, of her property would need to be taken to make way for the road. This was the first Toliver had heard of the interstate: "They didn't really announce it," she recalled. Frustrated, Toliver demanded that the worker get his supervisor. She wanted an explanation.[3]

As construction commenced on the ambitious highway system that city and state officials had laid out in their 1955 plan, variations of these two scenes played out across the region. For the first time, citizens came face to face with the roadways they had helped bring to fruition over the previous decade with their purchase of automobiles and their political support for roads, which were, in and of themselves, expressions of infrastructural citizenship. As officials announced the location of highways, however, many Houstonians learned that their homes and neighborhoods stood in the way. No longer dreaming of a potential system, but instead finding they would have to come to terms with an accumulation of alarming developments, citizens voiced growing concerns about highways starting in the late 1950s, deploying the rhetoric of infrastructural citizenship in an effort to protect their homes and neighborhoods.

While residents from every walk of life bore the costs of roadway construction, a small subset, those whose homes fell in or near the path of the roads, absorbed a preponderance of the negative effects. An accrual of consequences pushed these Houstonians to insist that plans be altered to save their homes and led others to call for an outright halt on road construction. However, the majority of Houstonians, powerful real estate developers, and city officials continued to push for new and wider roads. The tension among these viewpoints served to split Houstonians into two camps: those who generally supported road construction and those who opposed its unchecked expansion. These competing attitudes reflected different ideas about the purpose and shape of infrastructure. Although, as we shall see, those who supported the expansion of highways saw their vision come to fruition in most cases, this outcome did not prevent similar conflicts from roiling for several decades. The debate that began in the 1950s and 1960s cropped up with each new project proposal. And the contestation of projects became increasingly fraught as nonelite white, black, and Mexican-American Houstonians claimed more political power in the city's decision-making. The conflicts explored in this chapter show how a diverse set of Houstonians began to articulate competing visions for the future of the city's transportation network and attempted to put their ideas of home, neighborhood, and mobility to work in ways that matched those visions.

In the 1950s, Houstonians who attended Houston Planning Commission meetings to protest route plans or who demanded to speak to construction foremen to argue about property lines bumped against the reality that they possessed little control over the city's direction of growth. Because city officials and land developers carried out highway planning far removed from citizen oversight, Houstonians who questioned the city's approach to road building struggled to gain traction in early transportation debates. Officials possessed definitive ideas about how roads would benefit the city and what shape those roads should take.[4] Built around goals of traffic efficiency, their notions rarely matched those forwarded by the citizens who protested the routes.[5] At the same time that elected officials ignored the desires of citizens, they adhered closely to those of national groups—automobile manufacturers, the trucking industry, and drivers' advocacy organizations such as AAA—and local developers and business leaders whose interests were intimately tied to road construction.[6] In this regard Houston was not an anomaly. Across the nation during the 1950s, officials from the national, state, and local levels planned and implemented thousands of miles of highways and interstates with little citizen input.

The structure of the Federal-Aid Highway Act of 1956 encouraged officials to continue prioritizing urban expansion over the concerns of residents who stood in the way of roads.[7] The act codified the power that local and state leaders held in planning the nation's roadways by giving them complete control over routing decisions within urban areas.[8] It also provided a federal-local funding structure guaranteeing that the federal government would cover 90 percent of all interstate costs. This made interstates more palatable for localities that were wary of taking on debt. Because of the financial support attached to interstates, state officials concentrated on those projects and passed the costs for local highway and infrastructure development onto county and city governments. As chapter 1 demonstrated, the territorial and population growth of the postwar period had already stretched Houston's ability to meet the infrastructure demands of the city. The added burden of local road maintenance led city officials to devote the limited resources they did possess to building and maintaining routes that connected downtown to the suburbs or that served wealthier, more politically influential populations. These choices led to the continued neglect of transportation infrastructure in the poorest central city neighborhoods.[9]

This chapter will consider four road projects located in two distinct parts of Houston—the quickly expanding, almost exclusively white west side and the densely populated downtown Third and Fifth Wards, which in the 1950s and early 1960s contained the majority of the city's African-American population. The west side of the city had to contend with the construction of Houston's second ring road, the Outer Belt. Routes for Houston's two bisecting interstates ran through the Third and Fifth Wards. These projects not only demonstrated the physical impact roads brought to the areas through which they ran, but also reflected the range of reactions these structures elicited from Houstonians that lived there. As these examples will show, citizens had to struggle to be heard during the first stages of the construction process. Despite these difficulties, residents' initial responses anticipated later calls for participation in city planning and, eventually, outright resistance to road projects through escalating acts of transportation activism.

The routing and construction of highways through already settled parts of the city guaranteed that the roads would influence the lives of nearly all Houstonians. This conclusion counters the commonly held notion that the consequences of road construction fell solely onto the shoulders of disadvantaged groups. However, suburban and centrally located roads exacted very different costs on the parts of the city they crossed. It is undeniable that some residents suffered more severe consequences of road construction than others, and that those residents were overwhelmingly poorer and usually African American or Mexican American.[10] Likewise, it is clear that officials dealt with the complaints they received from Houstonians from different parts of the city in different ways. Different expressions of infrastructural citizenship received different hearings from public officials.

One major difference between the central city and suburban highway projects lay in the time frames for construction. The highways planned for predominantly white suburbs were more often than not projected routes that would not be built for decades, whereas city interstates were laid out and built in a relatively short amount of time. The vastly different periods of time between planning and construction resulted in vastly different experiences for Houstonians, with those whose lives were being uprooted by new roadways suffering a more immediate impact than those living in the suburbs who would have time to plan for a road's presence or contest its location. Because the suburban, mostly white residents possessed significant political and economic resources, their complaints, even if ultimately rejected, gained the attention of city and county officials in ways that poorer, nonwhite Houstonians' voices did not. The Texas Highway Department deemed Houston's downtown interstates priorities; as such, officials planned and constructed them quickly, often before citizen responses could coalesce.

The consequences of immediate construction were dramatic because new highways divided neighborhoods and displaced thousands of residents. Black Houstonians, the population overwhelmingly affected by Houston's interstate construction, possessed little political power when planning and construction began in the 1950s. They nonetheless railed against the negative consequences of the roadways. Although questions of electoral access and fights against segregation continued to dominate Houston's iteration of the civil rights movement, black Houstonians, like black citizens across the country, also contested problems with inadequate housing and transportation, increasingly articulating a rhetoric that can be seen as an expression of infrastructural citizenship.[11] By attempting to improve the physical conditions of their communities, Houstonians and others who fought what they saw as problematic transportation structures inaugurated another focus of the civil rights struggle, one rooted to the equal dispersal of infrastructural benefits and consequences. This demand persisted well into the 1980s, merging with concerns around environmental justice, and in many ways can still be found in community organizing to this day.[12]

Acknowledging the widespread, yet uneven impact of infrastructure projects is essential to understanding how Houstonians conceptualized and engaged with transportation infrastructure debates after World War II. Although the consequences of road building ranged in severity, the citizens affected by highways all felt wronged by the process. Road construction remade entire neighborhoods and landscapes, changing the way people understood their homes, streets, and place in the city.[13] With the effects of the first stage of highway construction providing a common motivation, a diverse array of Houstonians expressed frustration with the city's top-down development approach and agitated for a larger role in city planning. The expectations Houstonians brought to this push varied. White residents, particularly suburbanites, wanted to easily access the city in private automobiles and aimed to protect their homes from future road projects. African-American and Mexican-American residents of Central Houston shared those desires with white Houstonians, but also made transportation inequality—in terms of both planning and provision—a central focus of their ongoing civil rights agendas and of their assertions of infrastructural citizenship.[14]

THE ROAD PROJECTS

The first two projects this chapter discusses revolve around the western segment of Houston's second ring road, the Outer Loop (now Beltway 8). The original design for the road, which appeared on Houston-area highway plans in the early 1950s, called for it to encircle the city about twelve miles from downtown. Anticipating a road that would eventually be four lanes wide, city and county officials required that all developing subdivisions reserve a right-of-way of 150 feet for the road. The Memorial Bend Addition, platted in 1954, followed this requirement and commenced selling lots in 1955. By 1960, however, officials decided that projections of the city's growth required an expansion of previous road plans. They implemented new regulations that expanded the Outer Belt's right-of-way to three hundred feet and applied this width to already developed subdivisions. Plans that called for this width projected that it would allow for the eventual construction of a six-lane, at-grade highway. In Memorial Bend, this right-of-way would claim as many as thirty homes. Residents of the community, nearly all middle- and upper-class whites, objected to the plan. Citing their original plats and claiming that the road would lower their property values, many actively campaigned against the expansion. Though they were ultimately unsuccessful, their pressure led the Houston City Council and Houston Planning Commission to consider their complaints.

A second set of Outer Belt decisions in West Houston demonstrated the amount of influence developers held at this time. In the late 1950s and early 1960s, the developers R. E. Smith and Roy Hofheinz encouraged the Houston Planning Commission and the Harris County Commissioners Court to realign several parts of the Outer Belt. Smith and Hofheinz exemplified Houston's elite. Hofheinz served terms as both Houston mayor and Harris County commissioner prior to his move into development. Smith owned real estate throughout the metropolitan area, and in the mid-1950s he was one of Houston's richest residents. Like developers before and after them, Hofheinz and Smith brought their economic and political power to bear on the county court and other local decision-makers to seek alterations to the Outer Belt plans in ways that benefited their interests. The same local officials who dismissed the concerns of Memorial Bend residents and completely neglected African-American opinion in interstate planning gave quick and positive responses to the developers, which shows how much power the developers possessed.

The other two projects involved the construction of Interstates 10 and 45 through downtown Houston. The routes for these roads ran directly through the Third and Fifth Wards in the central city. Despite the fact that the two wards and their respective main streets—Dowling Street and Lyons Avenue—represented significant centers of black economic, political, and social life, officials made few attempts to prevent detrimental outcomes in these areas. The roads altered the physical landscape of both neighborhoods to a much greater degree than the Outer Belt altered Memorial Bend and other outlying areas. The changes forced the residents of the wards to redefine how they understood their communities and their connections to them. The roads also negatively affected the economic structures of both wards, disrupting businesses and displacing many of the residents who patronized them.[15]

Planning and construction for Interstate 10 East from Loop 610 to downtown occurred between 1956 and 1966. The two miles of the road between Lockwood Drive and US 59, which was a depressed, below-grade highway of six lanes, displaced more than 330 residences and businesses in the Fifth Ward. The interchange of 59 and I-10 claimed 890 more. Construction on the northern end of Interstate 45, entering into downtown, followed the route of the original Gulf Freeway that had opened in the late 1940s. Most of its route through the Third Ward was completed by 1965, remaining at-grade for most of its path. Only a six-lane elevated section running between Dowling Street on the east and Allen Parkway on the west, known as the Pierce Elevated, and the interchange with US 59 were constructed after 1965. The Pierce Elevated opened to traffic in 1967 and for the first time allowed highway users to go east-west through Houston without driving on city streets. At just over three miles long, the stretch of I-45 that included Pierce Elevated and ran from downtown to Scott Street on the east side of the Third Ward displaced nearly 560 residences and businesses.[16]

These four projects exemplify the divergent experiences of Houstonians with road construction. Each of the four examples highlights how residents turned to transportation activism and broader infrastructural citizenship as tools to help shape their neighborhoods. The examples also show, though, how very different the outcome from such attempts could be, depending upon who was making the demands. Through the late 1960s, when it came to highway decisions the city and county governments prioritized official plans and the desires of development and real estate interests over the concerns of nearly all other private citizens. Although Houstonians from across the metropolitan area rallied against the consequences of such top-down planning in their communities, the groups were too small and the projects moved too quickly for them to be successful. The actions residents took, though, would change the nature and outcomes of later fights over invasive infrastructure, setting the stage for later victories amid their defeat.

THE OUTER BELT

Construction on the Outer Belt was not to begin until future suburban growth demanded it. Only a small number of homeowners in the right-of-way saw their homes immediately taken, so while the threat of the road was real for most residents, it was also distant. Despite these tempered effects, suburbanites in areas such as Memorial Bend considered the placement of the road to be onerous and unfair. The residents of Memorial Bend had moved there with the goal of finding a peaceful neighborhood far from the noise and traffic of the central city. The projected road thwarted this vision. The residents complained that the projected highway threatened to change the character of their community by enticing commercial businesses into the area and giving residents fewer reasons to maintain the condition of their homes. They argued that underdeveloped land farther to the west along what was then Houston's urban fringe offered a number of adequate alternative routes that would not displace settled subdivisions. Significantly, Memorial Bend residents were not anti-road as a rule; instead they were simply against the road cutting through their community. Whatever their larger position on roads, Memorial Bend residents protested the official and developer-driven growth model that had for so long determined the city's direction.

Immediately after the Outer Belt's appearance on the City of Houston's Major Thoroughfare and Freeway Plan in 1952, officials began tinkering with its size and path to contend with Houston's population and territorial growth.[17] The route ran a total of 87.6 miles and sat 6 miles farther out from the first ring road, Loop 610.[18] In its first iteration, the road only took a 120-foot right-of-way. However, Houston officials, led by the director of city planning, Ralph Ellifrit, worried that this width would "get us into difficulties later," as it may not permit engineers to keep up with traffic demand as the city grew. While the initial width was being discussed, several pending housing developments along the route, including the Memorial Bend Addition, awaited platting approval. This logjam forced officials to make a decision about the right-of-way. Ellifrit insisted that the right-of-way expand to 150 feet before platting occurred. The Harris County Commissioners Court and the City of Houston agreed to do so in late 1954.[19]

Between 1954 and 1960, real estate developers built seven subdivisions along the Outer Belt's route between Buffalo Bayou and the Katy Freeway (Interstate 10). In the space of a few years, developers converted agricultural lands and forests into homes and created street grids.[20] Following the "leapfrog" tendencies of developers, Memorial Bend and other subdivisions had been located adjacent to undeveloped tracts of agricultural and wooded land. A 1955 fire hydrant map by the Zingery Map Company shows the nature of the landscape surrounding Memorial Bend during its platting (fig. 2.1).[21] Memorial Bend's rural setting—vacant fields, a still-wooded bayou, and few roads—had allowed developers to sell the community as a

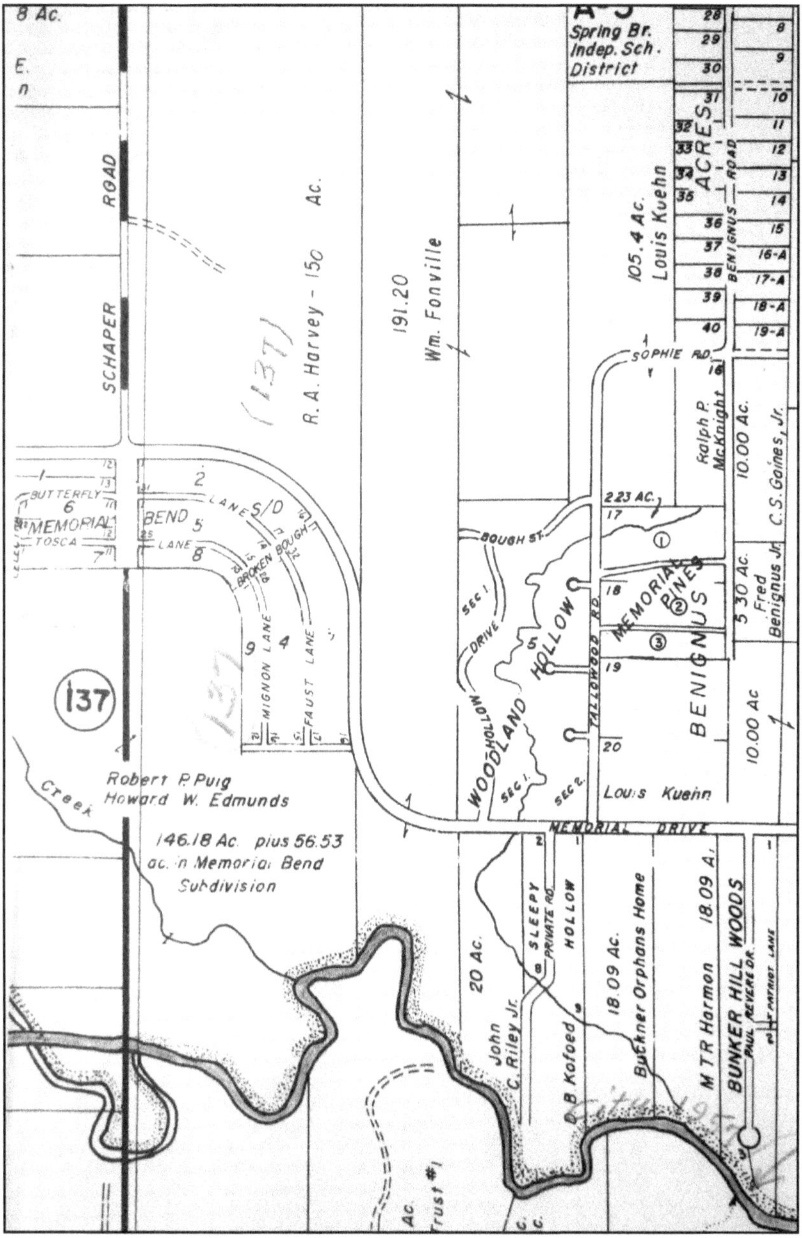

Fig. 2.1. 1955 Zingery Fire Hydrant Map

The map shows Memorial Bend near the upper left corner. Note the empty land both north and south of the community. At its inception it was one of the westernmost developments in Houston. Houston Metropolitan Research Center.

"Scenic Wooded Wonderland" where one could find "Country Living in a Metropolitan Area."[22]

Promoters also sold the subdivision as luxurious, affordable, and desirable. Advertisements pointed to its award-winning architecture, its location on the prestigious Memorial Drive, and its proximity to good schools, country clubs, and other amenities.[23] The promotions also made it clear that Memorial Bend did not suffer from any of the numerous service problems that plagued other area developments: "Memorial Bend is one of the highest points in Harris County, insuring every homeowner of excellent drainage, plus every block has storm sewers, curbs, and gutters."[24] Unlike the slapdash developments popping up across Harris County, Memorial Bend came with all the trappings of a modern subdivision. Despite these selling points, developers recognized that they would have little success if they could not convince potential buyers that their homes would remain connected to the city through area roadways. For this reason, developers prominently remarked on the community's connections to Houston via the Katy Freeway and Memorial Drive. Almost every advertisement listed the driving time to downtown Houston or to other prominent amenities. Because of the existing roadways, the Memorial Bend Development Company could sell the fact that the community offered residents enough distance to escape Houston's problems, yet was close enough to the city to access its resources and employment opportunities. Allusions to the development of the Outer Loop, however, remained absent in the advertisements, because developers, operating under the earlier right-of-way decision, did not expect more than a thoroughfare to come through the area.

Developers of Memorial Bend and nearby subdivisions aimed to attract middle- to upper-class white Houstonians and white-collar migrants as buyers. Between 1954 and 1960, Robert Puig, the developer of Memorial Bend, succeeded in bringing dozens of such families to his development. By mid-1955, 48 of 202 planned homes had been built and sold, with another 50 under construction. The Gregorys, a white, middle-class couple, bought the first home. Appropriately for Houston, both Mr. and Mrs. Gregory worked at energy companies downtown, driving about half an hour each way.[25] The census tract encompassing Memorial Bend reflected the success that Puig and other developers had in recruiting their target buyers. In 1960, the tract was 99.3 percent white, and 87 percent of the households made more than $8,000 a year, the equivalent of nearly $64,000 in 2015.[26] Promoters trumpeted the fact that most of the residents were people of "high standing," with "engineers, lawyers," and architects buying homes. Such neighbors promised higher home values and offered the chance to raise one's children among "good associates." These statements gave the implicit promise of a racially exclusive neighborhood. Houston's long history of racially homogeneous settlement patterns, discriminatory lending practices that benefited whites over other racial groups, and high-priced homes helped to make this insinuation a reality.[27]

When Puig and the Memorial Bend Development Company filed their subdivision plan with Harris County in December 1954, they made room for the Outer Belt's 150-foot right-of-way. The open strip of land split the J-curved subdivision in two, bisecting Butterfly and Tosca Lanes, before meeting Memorial Drive at its northern end (fig. 2.2). Although 150 feet

Fig. 2.2. 1954 Memorial Bend Subdivision Map

The original 1954 platting map for Memorial Bend shows the Outer Belt as the wide road running bottom to top. Its right-of-way is listed at 150 feet. Each of the homes on the sides has an additional 20 feet built in case the right-of-way expanded. Box 4, MSS 118, Houston Subdivision Collection, Houston Metropolitan Research Center.

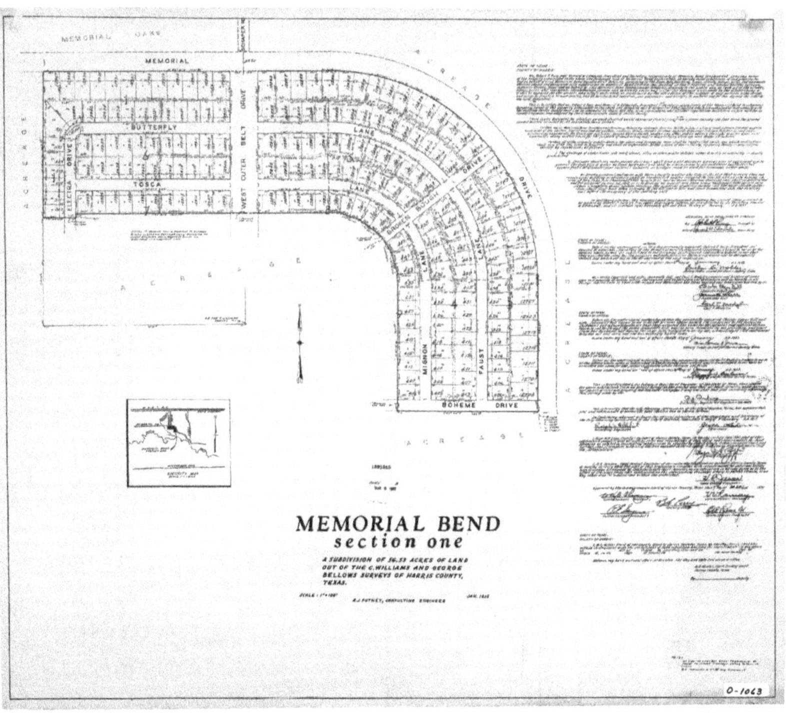

represented the typical highway right-of-way at that time, developers nonetheless left extra room on both sides by restricting structures from an additional 20 feet on lots that bordered the road's path.[28] Given this buffer and the established 150-foot right-of-way, the Houstonians who bought homes in the subdivision over the next five years felt secure in their purchases. Like the developers themselves, they anticipated that, at most, a divided four-lane highway with a grassy median would replace the existing two-lane road. The new residents believed that the platting of their subdivision set the right-of-way in stone. However, neither city nor county leaders had formally approved the final building lines for the Outer Belt, leaving routing decisions unsettled.[29]

The unfinished road plans allowed officials to declare in 1960 that the Outer Belt required another 150 feet of right-of-way to accommodate future traffic. Such an adjustment meant the road would claim nearly thirty developed lots in Memorial Bend. Residential and commercial developers who had not yet built their projects in West Houston strongly supported the push to widen the Outer Belt. Led by Roy Hofheinz, these developers argued that taking a wider right-of-way before construction made economic sense for the city. They also recognized that altering the right-of-way would open the door to other alterations and aimed to influence the routing of the road to serve their interests. Residents of Memorial Bend, however, responded to the news with outrage and fear. Between 1960 and 1963, homeowners like Robert McNair and H. P. Powell, both respected white businessmen, peppered the Houston City Council with complaints. The choice that officials made during the ensuing conflict reflected the city's growth priorities in the early 1960s.

In March 1960, Hofheinz and one of his employees, Fernando Williams, came before the Houston Planning Commission to ask that the body widen the Outer Belt's right-of-way. Hofheinz stood before the commission as the prototypical Houston developer—wealthy, male, white, and politically connected. Hofheinz and R. E. Smith owned thousands of acres throughout the Houston metropolitan area, with numerous tracts in West Houston.[30] Williams had worked for the planning department for nearly a decade before joining Hofheinz in the private sector, and Hofheinz, of course, had served as both mayor and county commissioner. Like many other developers, they held therefore a number of advantages that typical Houstonians, including Memorial Bend homeowners, did not. They knew the commissioners personally. They understood the complicated process of city planning and how to navigate the different levels of government involved. And, finally, they recognized the vital importance of connecting residential and commercial developments to highways.

In their proposal to widen the Outer Belt, Hofheinz and Williams recounted the mistakes the city had made during the right-of-way acquisitions that had occurred during Hofheinz's time as mayor. While buying land for the first loop project, the city had encountered "delay and expense that resulted from increasing the standards for the development of the North Loop and consequent renegotiation with the same owners for wider and wider right-of-way." To avoid repeating this mistake, Hofheinz said, the commission should preemptively widen the right-of-way and buy all the required land before construction started. Expanding the road plans to three hundred feet, he reminded the commission, would also make it wide enough for the Texas Highway Department to add the road to its formal state highway system in the future, saving local governments the millions in maintenance costs that the state would take on.[31]

The questions that members of the planning commission put to Hofheinz reflected the central role developers played in Houston's growth politics. When asked if he was concerned about the right-of-way because of his own real estate interests in West Houston, Hofheinz responded that far from an attempt to secure a financial windfall for himself, his presence at the meeting and interest in the widening project were motivated by civic concerns. He insisted that he did not own right-of-way that he intended to sell along the route. He did, though, have land he would willingly donate for the road to the county or city, if officials created tax deductions for such gifts. One can infer, however, that Hofheinz's hope that running the road near his property would raise its value gave rise to his willingness to facilitate its construction.[32] The Houston Planning Commission approved the widening just after the Harris County Commissioners Court, which Hofheinz also lobbied, voted the same way in December 1960.[33]

Over the next several years, residents of Memorial Bend challenged the validity of the change, while developers continued to back it. The fight pitted two sets of property rights against one another. Given that land ownership was nearly sacrosanct in Texas, the fact that homes were being taken, especially the homes of white suburbanites, was quite problematic. However, as with the homes of African Americans and other Houstonians downtown, the claiming of property was justified by promises of greater total growth. This selling point justified many of the choices Houston officials made in the 1950s and 1960s. Most visible in the building of infrastructure, this line of reasoning also appeared in the construction of the Astrodome, the expansion of the Texas Medical Center within the city, and the embrace of suburbanization. Houstonians whose homes were not affected by these or other projects bought this justification, leaving those who experienced displacement or discomfort out in the cold. Furthermore, in the Memorial Bend case, the influence of the developers led to their property rights being treated with greater weight. The idea of private land ownership remained sacred, but only political influence kept it that way.

Testifying before the planning commission, Memorial Bend residents Robert McNair and H. P. Powell forwarded an argument that reflected ideas of infrastructural citizenship. They contended that altering the right-of-way after the original platting was completed represented an egregious violation of their property rights and threatened to destroy their "excellent residential area" with "commercial and industrial development."[34] By the time they appeared in front of the commission, however, the county had already begun protective buying—purchasing several homes along the right-of-way in Memorial Bend and slotting them for demolition. Undeterred, residents accelerated their campaign against the road. McNair and others organized the petition against the road and urged immediate action by their neighbors to "stop this foolishness." The petition organizers focused on the threat of dropping property values and a transitioning neighborhood, saying, for example, "Do you have any idea what [the highway] will do to the value of your property? Have you noticed the large number of FOR SALE signs recently?"[35] Residents believed that the road negated the very reasons they had purchased their homes in Memorial Bend—the promise of growing property values and country-like seclusion. When residents presented the petition to the planning commission in 1962, they called for the entire Outer Belt to be moved several miles west, beyond the reach of current residential development.[36]

In his initial response to the residents' complaints, Director of Planning Ellifrit attempted to calm nerves by explaining that the construction of the road would not be immediate, but rather done in stages spread over several years. On the subject of moving the highway to the west, he pointed out that a shift of one branch of the ring road would require the rerouting of the entire circuit, likely making the suggestion untenable. The chair of the Houston Planning Commission, Milton McGinty, also weighed in to ease worries about creeping commercialization and the physical toll the road would take on Memorial Bend. He argued that leaving the road in its current state would exacerbate, not prevent, detrimental development, because cars and trucks would use the route more as the city expanded. Wary of seeing their plans derailed or delayed, however, officials attempted to calm the fears of residents by agreeing to study the proposed reroute.[37] Even if the study was an appeasement, it represented an unprecedented acquiescence to citizen demands.

City and county officials conducted the reroute study and presented their findings to the planning commission two weeks after the initial request. They concluded that while a functional substitute route existed to the west along Dairy-Ashford Road, the current alignment remained preferable because of its significantly lower costs and connection to other roads. The reroute would push the Outer Belt 2.75 miles farther west and require nearly two times the number of grade separations. Furthermore, estimates projected that while the new route would save approximately $900,000 in right-of-way costs, it would increase overall costs by $4.5 million. Officials used the cost difference as justification to end consideration of an adjusted route. Although they ultimately rejected residents' requests, officials did attempt to appease some concerns by agreeing not to buy properties in the expanded right-of-way until construction was imminent. Additionally, they agreed to rent out already purchased properties to the former owners, rather than demolishing them immediately. Although residents were disappointed in the overall outcome, they saw these two concessions as important to maintaining a semblance of normal life until construction began.[38]

That residents of Memorial Bend could not alter the highway plans despite their relative social and political power demonstrated that transportation decision-making was not simply a process of catering to the interests of suburban whites. Indeed, the Houston Planning Commission and Harris County Commissioners Court did likely respond to the request to consider a reroute because those making it were wealthy, white homeowners in the path of a road that officials projected would be built twenty years in the future, but even this group could not stop the project. The complaints of Memorial Bend residents proved, too, that not all white suburbanites wholeheartedly supported highways. And the ultimate decision showed that the effects of road construction were not restricted to the central city. For all the concessions they gained, the white suburbanites along the Outer Belt witnessed the disruptive nature of infrastructure planning, and in the future they would have a major highway run through their subdivision.

After helping to usher through the wider right-of-way, Roy Hofheinz and Fernando Williams continued to lobby the Houston Planning Commission. Throughout the late 1950s and early 1960s, the developers worked to secure several realignments and adjustments to the Outer Loop. Although they were smaller in scale and were expected to cost less than the wholesale reroute proposed by Memorial Bend residents, Hofheinz and Williams's requests for changes were not inconsequential. Their success in securing the alterations demonstrated the influence that developers held in Houston's transportation decision-making.

The majority of the property Hofheinz and Smith owned in West Houston lay at or just to the north of the planned intersection of the Outer Belt and US 59. As route plans were solidifying in the late 1950s, the developers asked the planning commission to tweak the route to accommodate their developments. Williams wrote to the commission in December 1958 suggesting a number of changes that would keep Smith and Hofheinz's land as contiguous, and therefore as developable, as possible.[39] In one proposed alteration, near the intersection of Beechnut Street and the Outer Loop, the developers asked that the road follow a straight trajectory rather than curve. This change, Williams argued, would allow a number of developments blocked by the current alignment to go forward.[40] With another request, the developers sought to move the Outer Belt at Richmond Avenue 400 feet farther west to create more than 200 feet of developable property. In his letter, Williams made it clear that he had also contacted county officials who "had no objections to the revisions as long as they are requested by the Houston City Planning Commission."[41] Both government bodies implemented the requests.

The 1958 reroute request was just one of several that developers like Hofheinz, Smith, and Williams made for the route of the Outer Belt. In 1963, Williams returned to secure a smaller reroute. The request focused on the Outer Belt from Beechnut Street to Bellfort Drive. The developers sought a new alignment for this 2.1-mile section of road that would add 1,200 feet to the route. They wanted the Outer Loop to follow an existing road instead of cutting through unimproved land they owned, arguing that building atop an established road would lower construction and right-of-way costs. As with earlier suggestions, Williams made it explicitly clear that the change would leave more developable land on their properties. In the case of this realignment, the new route would "cross their property at a more desirable angle," keeping the property connected and viable for development.[42]

As Hofheinz had shown during the Outer Belt–widening debate, developers and landowners often affected the outcome of planning decisions by donating property along routes to guarantee that highways would follow paths that met their interests. Such actions negated the costs associated with realignment and made officials much more amenable to plan changes. In the case of the Bellfort Road request, city and county officials approved the shift after Hofheinz and Smith donated land that made it possible to alter the alignment at no extra cost.[43]

While the requests made by these and other developers in the early 1960s did not ask officials to move entire highways, they nonetheless represented significant changes to proposed routes. Other West Houston stakeholders did not have the ability to sweeten their requests with donated land; nor did their properties hold the same potential for increased tax revenues that undeveloped land did.[44] The extended timeline of the Outer Belt's construction and the relatively undeveloped nature of the landscape through which it ran made the road a uniquely negotiable project, but officials only truly negotiated with developers.

The Outer Belt projects captured the contentious nature of infrastructure development, even on the still developing edges of the city. Officials justified rejecting citizen complaints by asserting that they did not want to establish damaging precedents. Ralph Ellifrit maintained that if the city gave in to unhappy residents, even once, it would complicate long-range planning, stymie suburban growth, and open the floodgates to future challenges.[45] At a time when Houston officials prioritized economic and territorial expansion, embracing such a risk was far too dangerous.

Given the amount of opposition and negotiation attached to the planning of a future roadway, one might expect that the two major interstates coming through downtown Houston would have fostered even greater debate. As the next section will show, however, officials approached these projects in a very different manner from the way in which they approached the Outer Belt project, and the residents most affected by the roadways did not organize against the routes until it was too late to block construction.

THE INTERSTATES AND THE WARDS

Most Houstonians shared a sense that roads and personal cars enabled access to broader forms of freedom. The meaning and definition of that freedom, though, was where black and white Houstonians most diverged in their thinking about highways. For many black Houstonians, who were embroiled in campaigns against segregation in public spaces and on public transportation, and well aware of similar drives across the nation, personal automobiles represented a chance to escape the discrimination and stress attached to a daily commute on public transit. The ease of movement that automobiles afforded all drivers gave African-American motorists a sense of freedom of choice and control when they were driving that was not available to them on other modes of transportation or on city streets, where segregation laws governed their seat or step.[46]

Yet the physical consequences wrought by the imposition of highways onto black neighborhoods stood in tension with this freedom. During the city's booming 1950s, parts of the Third, Fourth, and Fifth Wards still lacked adequate paving and drainage, suffered frequent service outages, and received little public support for improvements to parks, schools, or hospitals (fig. 2.3). The interstates came directly through the Third and Fifth Wards, causing hundreds of residential and commercial displacements and wholesale turnover of neighborhood land uses. The physical transformation of neighborhoods caused significant shifts in how residents conceptualized and moved through their communities.[47] As they considered their stance toward the city's highways, African Americans had no unified response. By the late 1960s, an accrual of negative consequences led many of those residents who lived in areas directly affected by the presence of highways to vocalize their discontent and to place transportation issues at the center of a broader push for civil rights.

A number of factors limited the efficacy of African-American resistance to the interstates. Chief among them was the fact that the political and economic limitations they faced made any fight of that sort an uphill battle.[48] During the late 1950s and early 1960s, black Houstonians still could not count on influencing the Houston City Council or Harris County officials. The roads ran through neighborhoods that were overwhelmingly black and with residents, on average, who had significantly lower income levels than residents in the predominantly white areas of the city. In 1960, the Third Ward was 98.7 percent black, and only 2.8 percent of its households matched or surpassed the $8,000 ($64,000 in 2015) annual income held by 87 percent of Memorial Bend residents. The Fifth Ward was 98.4 percent black, and only 2.4 percent of its households matched or surpassed that income level.[49] In addition, most of the residents were renters with little legal power to contest eminent domain takings.[50] Facing a politically marginalized population with limited economic means, elected officials had little reason to cater to their concerns. Further, the Houston NAACP chapter, historically one of the city's most powerful civil rights entities and one of the nation's largest chapters in the 1950s, experienced a lull in membership in the early 1960s that reduced the likelihood of citywide organization against the roadways.[51] Moreover, what civil rights momentum did exist in the early 1960s centered mainly on voting rights, integration, and labor rights, not

Fig. 2.3. Fifth Ward Street, 1961
This image shows the conditions of many of Houston's African-American communities. African Americans hoped that development might lead to improvements, but instead such physical issues allowed city and highway officials to justify building roads through these areas. Owen Johnson, photographer, *Houston Post*, December 4, 1961, Houston Post Collection, RG D0006, 284, Houston Metropolitan Research Center.

large-scale infrastructure issues. Finally, the disruptive nature of the highway projects made organizing against them very difficult. The planning and construction of the projects occurred quickly, and when highways bisected neighborhoods, they dispersed residents throughout the city, breaking community networks that might have helped organize resistance.[52]

The first interstate section that threatened downtown black communities was the Pierce Elevated, a six-lane elevated freeway through downtown and part of the Third Ward, for which officials inaugurated a regimen of protective buying and condemnation in 1957.[53] Plans called for the project to claim half a block of property along a 1.25-mile stretch of Pierce Avenue and to cost a total of $8 million, the equivalent of more than $65 million in 2013. Ninety percent of that total came from the federal government through the

Federal-Aid Highway Act. A. C. Kyser, the engineer manager for Houston freeway projects, believed that the route would prevent a traffic crisis downtown.[54] Just as opinions on the Outer Belt depended upon one's connection to the space through which it ran, opinions on the Pierce Elevated varied, with Houstonians who lived and worked along the proposed route expressing different thoughts on the project.

For many white Houstonians, the building of the Pierce Elevated offered the opportunity to remove the eyesore of dilapidated housing and undesirable businesses in the northwest corner of the Third Ward. A 1958 article in the *Houston Post* urged the city to take advantage of the redevelopment opportunities created by highway building. The article, like many before it, embraced the new roads. It contended that Houstonians should celebrate the city's march "into the prairie about it" through its growing network of highways. Elements of the system, "the multi-million dollar expanses of the Gulf Freeway, Eastex Freeway, or Hardy Street Bridge," were modern marvels of engineering that reflected Houston's growing significance and the great capabilities of its citizens. Yet, as drivers cruised along these new routes, they witnessed "the relentless spread of slums" just beyond the business district.[55]

The idea of using highways as a spur for redevelopment and an excuse for removing undesirable populations or structures from the downtown area was not unique to Houston. In many American cities, the construction of roadways occurred simultaneously with other urban renewal projects, such as public housing. Despite being depicted as positive, these contemporaneous strategies most often resulted in the creation of "second ghettos," as African Americans and other impoverished residents were displaced into increasingly segregated and under-supported pockets of the city. In Houston, a dearth of support for public housing and the rejection of federal funds for urban renewal led to an uneven process of displacement and resettling, but areas of concentrated poverty were created nonetheless. The construction of highways contributed to this problem by displacing residents, and many of them resettled into already dense parts of the Third and Fifth Wards, overtaxing their services and resources. The highways also blocked off those neighborhoods with new boundaries, physically defining the de facto second ghettos.[56]

As the route of the Pierce Elevated ran away from the Third Ward toward the heart of downtown Houston, the highway threatened more than homes of African Americans and the small businesses they patronized. Closer to the center of the city, the road necessitated the claiming of properties owned by several prominent white businessmen and corporations. The leaders of these companies were among the first to question the merits of the road. The politics involved with their dissent once again magnified the differences between elite and nonelite citizen complaints and reconfirmed the difficulty of changing road plans. Although none of the corporate leaders who protested were from the topmost echelons of the Houston elite, their economic and political power was certainly not trivial. In the late 1950s, Oscar Weyrich, the president of Houston Bank and Trust Company, waged a campaign to stop the construction of the elevated section of the road because it threatened his bank's expansion plans. Joined by other landowners on the western edge of the route, Weyrich sued the state and city for illegal takings. In 1957, it appeared that the landowners might win as the City Council contemplated removing the building lines and rerouting the road. But, as they had with the Memorial Bend decision, the officials ultimately decided that removing established plans because of an upset minority would set a poor precedent. Instead, they compromised with the majority of the landowning businessmen and agreed to pay higher prices for key plots of land.[57]

Weyrich continued to resist the plan, laying out the consequences he believed would occur in a 1959 letter to Texas Highway Department engineer A. C. Kyser. Weyrich argued that the road meant "the abandonment of plans for office buildings, stores and similar improvements" along Pierce that would have produced tax revenue for the city. Furthermore, he predicted that the displacement caused by the road would not be limited to properties within the right-of-way; instead its influence would ripple outward, and the road would act as "a Chinese Wall to normal development," causing blight for several blocks both north and south of the freeway. Weyrich criticized the highway department for lack of transparency and asked why no public meetings had been held to determine the routing or form the road would take.[58]

Kyser responded directly to Weyrich with several justifications for the route. Kyser argued that growing downtown congestion necessitated a limited-access, interstate-standard roadway. The Texas Highway Department estimated that the new road would increase traffic capacity to 75,000 vehicles a day. Kyser also pointed out that the section was essential to the success of the entire highway system, as it represented the only link between the roads that, at that point, ended on either side of downtown. As far as the blight concerns went, Kyser assured Weyrich that the Pierce Elevated would not cause the same problems that elevated roadways in other cities had caused because it was an "open-type construction with modern, pleasing, architectural lines." Far from hurting the community, the road would promote commerce by removing freeway traffic from local streets and creating a pleasing visual form. In the end, Kyser thanked Weyrich for his input, but asserted that the road plan remained the same.[59]

Unlike the patience they showed with Weyrich's complaints, when officials began work on the interstate projects near downtown and in the Third and Fifth Wards they showed little concern for potential political fallout and moved quickly to purchase and build the roads.[60] As interstate plans took shape and right-of-way clearance began for I-45, the physical consequences of construction—displacements and the reshaping of the neighborhood—became apparent in the Third Ward. Texas Highway Department photographs capture the stark physical changes made by I-45 as it cut through the ward. The Texas Highway Department photographs show the clearing that occurred downtown and in the northern Third Ward (fig. 2.4 and 2.5). With the building of the road, entire parts of the Third Ward disappeared, and the absences forced residents to redefine their daily lives and movements.[61]

As Weyrich predicted, the consequences of construction were not limited to the immediate vicinity of the road. Instead, the effects of the highway rippled outward. The changes to Dowling Street reflect this process. In 1960, seventy-four black-owned and black-patronized businesses operated between the 1800 block and the 2300 block of Dowling Street.[62] The businesses on this stretch demonstrated the centrality of Dowling's involvement in the economy of the Third Ward and wider Houston: fourteen beauty salons and barber shops, eleven restaurants and cafés, five gas stations, three pharmacies, one movie theater, two African-American insurance companies, seven dentists' or doctors' offices, the headquarters of the Houston chapter of the NAACP, and the headquarters of the student-led Progressive Youth Association, another civil rights group.[63] Not only did these businesses provide black patrons with a welcoming place to shop in segregated Houston, but they employed a number of local residents and kept the wealth of the Third Ward within the community.[64] By 1964, when I-45 cut Dowling in half between the 1800 and 2000 blocks, the number of businesses along that same stretch of road dwindled to forty-nine. By 1970, the number had dropped once more, falling to only forty-two businesses.[65] The road's construction corresponded to a marked change in the character of the Dowling Street business district and exacerbated a decline in the economic power of the Third Ward.

The roadway hit the residential sections of the Third Ward particularly hard as well. The ward was about twice as dense as other parts of the city in

1960, ensuring that any roads that ran through it would cause disruption to a larger number of people than it would have elsewhere. Prior to the eminent domain takings for Interstate 45 and State Highway 288, the neighborhood held nearly 17,000 dwellings. By 1966, the community had only 15,000 dwellings. The twin road projects resulted in the removal of over 2,000 homes and put pressure on housing stock in other parts of the ward as they became even more densely populated.[66] The physical toll the roadways took on both businesses and homes does not capture the attached psychological impact they caused for ward residents. Just as the road physically reshaped the neighborhood, it also shifted residents' cognitive ideas of the neighborhood, creating an unrecognizable Third Ward.

Ernie Attwell, a longtime Third Ward resident and city planner, recalled the physical and mental costs of the highways. When an oral history interviewer asked about the interstate's impact, Attwell responded with a question of his own: "What was on the land" in the Third Ward before the roads ran over it? Not waiting for an answer from his interviewer, he continued, "Human beings, houses, businesses were on the land." The roads "about killed" the Fifth and Third Wards because displacement and its aftereffects, which Attwell estimated to have driven away as many as 30,000 people, drained the customer base of businesses. "If you own the hair style place, you have no people coming to your hair style place, right, you moved 30,000 people. You have nobody coming to your grocery store," Attwell said. He also remembered the ripple effects of the road's presence. As the road was built and people moved away, a "knock down, and abandoning of many houses and many buildings" outside of the right-of-way occurred, changing the neighborhood from vibrant, livable space into a shell of its former self.[67]

Residents and outside observers also found fault with the raised form of the Pierce Elevated. Critics singled out the spaces created underneath the road as problematic. To many, the looming structure widened the divide between sections of the neighborhood and created dark, seemingly useless spaces below the road. Prominent architect Patrick Horsburgh disliked the aesthetic effects elevated roadways had on cities and neighborhoods. Writing about the Pierce Elevated, Horsburgh argued that the road's demarcation of central business district boundaries aided long-term planning, but also created "cavernous spaces beneath the highways" that were "psychologically intolerable." The "sheer un-neighborliness" and "drafty dankness" of the road were "detrimental to housing and to other domestic land uses."[68]

Horsburgh's critique highlighted the physical changes the road created in the neighborhood. Rather than productive city blocks lined by businesses

Figs. 2.4 and 2.5. Pierce Elevated

Two views of the Pierce Elevated under construction through downtown Houston. The left photo shows the end of the Pierce just after its opening, but before the interchange with US 59 was constructed. Note the cleared lots on the right side of the picture in the northern Third Ward. On the right side is a view of the road through downtown. Texas Department of Transportation, Communications Division, Media Production, Photo Library. Left photo by F. W. Brown, August 30, 1967. Right photo by Jack Lewis, December 3, 1964.

and private homes, the Third Ward now possessed an elevated freeway with blocks of underutilized space beneath it. The city attempted to retrofit the empty space almost immediately. In 1968, within a year of the road's opening, the Houston Planning Department and the Houston Municipal Art Commission released a report titled "Beautification Study: Freeways." It suggested that the areas underneath the road be developed into a mix of "playgrounds, plazas, and parking" and included a number of illustrations depicting children playing basketball and office workers enjoying a break beneath six lanes of traffic. The northern Third Ward's residential character made it the perfect location "for children's playgrounds . . . basketball courts, game floors, and various forms of play equipment" (fig. 2.6). The report, however, ignored the fact that to access these play areas children would need to cross high-speed frontage roads.[69] While the Texas Highway Department showed a willingness to work with localities on such improvements, aside from a few trails along the bayous north of downtown the effort fell flat. By the mid-1970s, nearly all the areas underneath Houston's elevated highways held parking lots.[70]

Newspaper accounts of the opening of the Pierce Elevated in August 1967 avoided any mention of the controversial and disruptive nature of the project. The *Houston Chronicle* applauded the opening of the road and anticipated

Fig. 2.6. Under Pierce Elevated

Artist's rendition of recreational possibilities below the Pierce Elevated along the Third Ward. Houston Municipal Art Commission, City of Houston, Department of Planning, "Beautification Study: Freeways," 1968, Box 5, City of Houston Planning Department Collection, RG A 004, Houston Metropolitan Research Center.

a significant easing of congestion downtown, as through-drivers could now avoid the "tortuous 23 blocks of street level traffic" they had faced prior to the highway.[71] Echoing the earlier *Houston Post* article that touted the roads and sought a modern downtown to match them, columnists celebrated the fact that drivers no longer saw slums and battered buildings as they drove the Pierce Elevated. Instead the road lifted drivers up and provided a "scenic . . . magnificent view of the business district . . . almost like going up in a cable car."[72] Such celebratory accounts of the Pierce Elevated made it easier for the Houstonians who drove above the Third Ward to ignore the negative consequences of the road on the communities that rested in its shadows.

At the same time that Third Warders were dealing with the construction of I-45 and the Pierce Elevated, residents of the Fifth Ward and the neighborhood just to the east, Denver Harbor, were dealing with the construction of Interstate 10 through their communities. Unlike I-45, I-10 ran below grade through the Fifth Ward. Highway planners viewed depressed routes as less disruptive to surrounding neighborhoods, yet, in the Fifth Ward, this configuration added additional concerns about pedestrian safety to continuing complaints about abuse of eminent domain and a lack of citizen input. The interstate took a huge swath of homes and businesses from the neighborhoods alongside the route. The interchange between I-10 and the Eastex Freeway (US 59) demonstrates the toll the twin roadways took on the Fifth Ward. The combination of fire insurance maps from 1950 and 1970 published by the Sanborn Map Company into one map paints a stark picture of the displacement and destruction the highways caused in the Fifth Ward (fig. 2.7). The map paints a compelling picture. The interchange alone claimed 890 structures. Of those nearly 900 buildings, 686 were homes, 101 were businesses, 11 were churches, 5 were schools, and 2 were hospitals. The roads clearly severed portions of the neighborhood and disconnected longtime mobility and social patterns. Part of the reason why this construction was so disruptive was that the road did not just claim isolated buildings, but instead took well-functioning, essential parts of the community, such as the two business corridors along Jensen Drive and Nance Street, which together housed almost 40 businesses. Residents of the Kelly Homes public housing (the repeated patterned footprints in the upper left of the image) went from being bordered by neighborhood streets and fellow residents to having high-speed highways and frontage roads on two sides. Finally, the highways severed many of the former routes that residents took to get to other parts of the community and city. A number of streets were dead-ended,

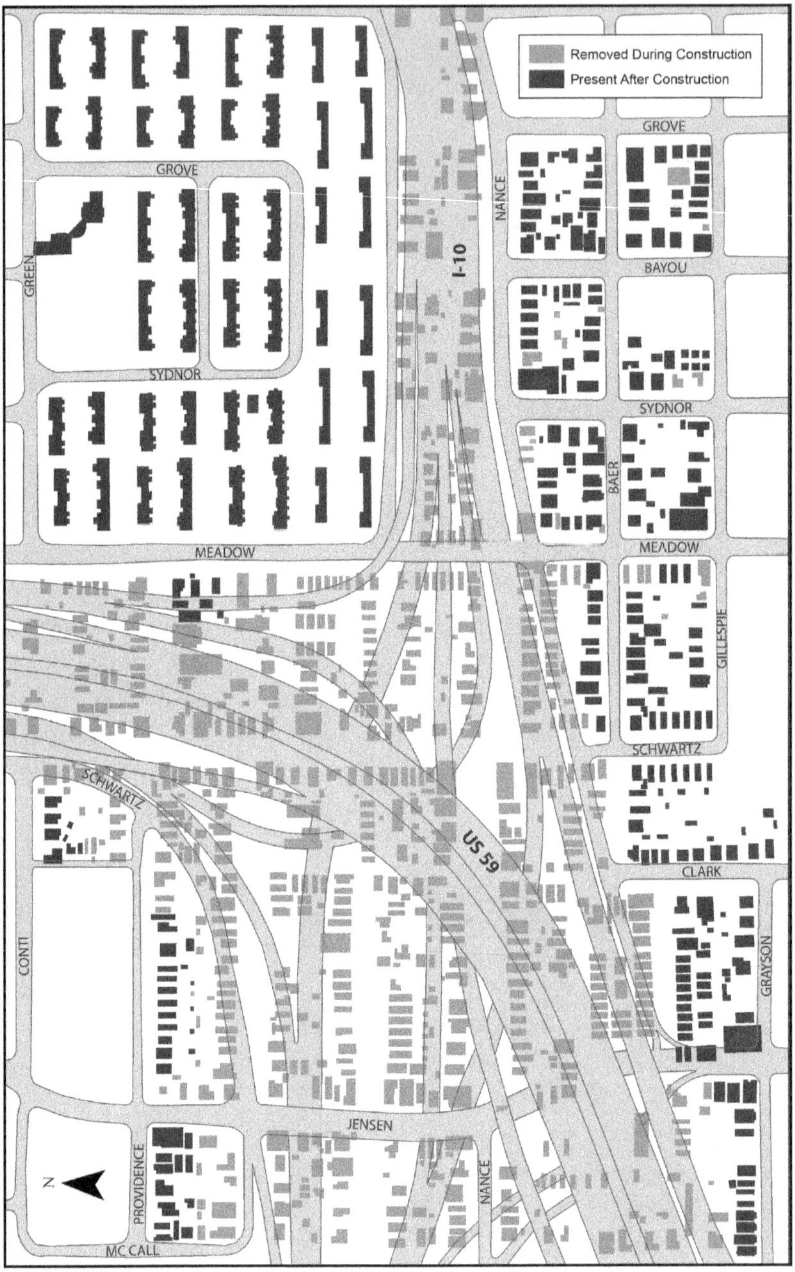

Fig. 2.7. Interchange of I-10 and US 59 in the Fifth Ward

For this image, 1950 and 1970 Sanborn Fire Insurance Company maps were overlayed in a geographic information system (GIS) program. The highways shown are the current expanse of the highways, not the historical boundaries of the roadways, so some differences in routing may exist. The buildings in light gray were demolished by the construction of the highway. The maps from the Sanborn collection are from the Houston Metropolitan Research Center. Map overlay by Kyle Shelton.

further isolating both the northern and southern ends of the Fifth Ward behind walls of infrastructure.

Ramona Toliver, whose story opened the chapter, purchased a house on Tremper Street in the Fifth Ward in the late 1950s. And her experience with the impact of highway construction sheds light on the nature of the road construction and its toll on the neighborhood. When Toliver moved into her home, many black professionals populated the immediate neighborhood. The majority of the schoolteachers and the principal of Wheatley High School, which sat a few blocks to the south, lived nearby. Toliver recalled that other middle-class black residents settled in her part of the ward to take advantage of the updated infrastructure, especially the sewer system, which came with the construction of the school and was lacking in other parts of the ward. Despite access to some amenities, similar to other predominantly black neighborhoods across Houston, Toliver's area of the Fifth Ward lacked paved streets and adequate street lighting and had poor drainage. Some avenues, such as the one that paralleled her home to the south, were not even organized city streets, but rather informal lanes created by residents. Despite the challenges presented by the area's uneven mix of informal, underdeveloped, and developed infrastructure, Toliver remembered the area as a welcoming and desirable place to live.[73]

This version of the ward, however, would not survive the construction of I-10. Toliver's surprise the morning she confronted the state highway employee in her yard indicated how unaware many black residents were of the pending construction of the interstate. According to Toliver, neither she nor her neighbors were notified of the road prior to the appearance of the Texas Highway Department. Toliver prevented the loss of her property only by vociferously resisting the plans, and she benefited from the fact that officials had erred with their first survey. The highway department wanted to build the road as fast as possible and to avoid conflicts with residents that might bog down the process or organize their neighbors against the road. When they resurveyed Toliver's property, the department concluded that the frontage route needed only to run along the edge of her property, rather than through her garage, and moved their staves. Other African-American residents whose homes were within the route of the interstate or frontage were not able to stop the state from taking their property. Some on Tremper saw their entire homes taken; others lost their backyards. The informal road below Toliver's home became the main route for the freeway.[74]

To Toliver and other residents, the interstate accelerated a transition within the ward. By the end of the 1960s, shifts in population, land use, and housing quality had given the Fifth Ward a very different demographic and physical landscape than it had possessed in the previous decade. Once the Texas Highway Department established building lines, homeowners within them were prevented from improving their homes in order to keep property values low ahead of state purchase. This prohibition contributed to the physical deterioration of many structures.[75] Coupled with a decline in housing stock, in the early 1960s better-off African Americans were beginning to leave the ward, as the repeal of segregation made formerly all-white areas of the city, such as MacGregor, available to blacks. Many of those displaced by the interstate joined these residents in the exodus from the community. An absentee owner of several Fifth Ward properties, E. Smith, recalled that even with relocation support, most of her renters resettled outside of the Fifth Ward because of the high prices and intense competition for housing within the ward caused by the displaced scrambling to find shelter.[76] The departure of these residents drastically reshaped the demographics of the ward, which became skewed toward lower-income residents. In addition, the flight of consumers and loss of their spending power—and a lack of exits off the freeway—combined to threaten the ward's once vibrant business community along Lyons Avenue.[77]

The construction of the interstate also redefined the way residents moved through the neighborhood. Prior to the interstate, walking represented a major form of travel in the Fifth Ward. Ramona Toliver recalled that throughout the 1950s her side yard operated as a thoroughfare for students walking to Wheatley High School. Algenita Scott Davis and Beneva Williams, who were children during the construction of the interstate, likewise recalled the prevalence of walking in the ward and discussed the disruptions the road caused. Williams, who was also the plaintiff for one of Houston's first integration lawsuits, remembered the Fifth Ward of the early 1950s as "open and free" with calm neighborhood streets.[78] She herself walked the length of the neighborhood each morning to get to junior high school at E. O. Smith on the west side of the ward. The interstate, Williams said, changed all that. It "busted up" the community, making travel from one end to the other more difficult.[79] The construction of the interstate cut the Fifth Ward in half, separating residents from community institutions on the opposite side of the road. Davis recalled that unlike the wealthy areas along US 59, which were served by ample overpasses, the Fifth Ward "didn't get any cute little bridges . . . we just got a complete wipeout"[80] (fig. 2.8). Because it took several years for adequate pedestrian bridges to be added, walking became more difficult and residents took to automobiles even for

Fig. 2.8. I-10 and the Fifth Ward
View of I-10 through the Fifth Ward looking west. The location is unspecified, but it appears to be the intersection of Schweikhardt Street and I-10, putting Toliver's home on Tremper Street on the left side near the crane. Note the wide swath taken from the neighborhood and the paucity of crossings. One pedestrian bridge and one overpass are pictured here. Texas Department of Transportation, Communications Division, Media Production, Photo Library, December 3, 1964, photographer unknown.

routine neighborhood trips. The road thus changed a primary mode of mobility and altered interactions within the community and city.[81]

The shortage of safe crossings over the interstate did more than force residents into cars and split the neighborhood; it also contributed to several pedestrian deaths.[82] After a number of accidents, including several that resulted in the deaths of local children, residents vocally advocated for the city to construct pedestrian bridges over the interstate. This effort was one of the first instances of collective action aimed at altering the highways and a dire expression of infrastructural citizenship.[83] The *Houston Informer* drew attention to the issue by pointing out that most of the dangerous infrastructure appeared in black communities, suggesting that in the eyes of the City of Houston, "traffic safety [was] still for whites" alone.[84] In April 1970, after

Fig. 2.9. Aerial Photograph of the Fifth Ward
This 1964 photo shows the ward boundaries created by transportation structures. The cleared area on the left is the construction of I-10. The intersection is of I-10 and US 59, which runs left to right in the middle of the picture. Train tracks cut across the north of the community. TxDOT Can 230/SRN006411, February 19, 1964, I-10/1-45-57, Texas Department of Transportation, Aerial Photo Library, Austin, Texas.

years of pressing officials to build walkways over the road, residents of Denver Harbor, a working-class, mostly Mexican-American community adjacent to the Fifth Ward, finally assembled along the frontage roads of the interstate to cut the ribbon on that community's first pedestrian bridge.[85]

I-10 completely boxed in the Fifth Ward with transportation infrastructure. The absence of pedestrian and street overpasses added to an already established collection of structures that cut the ward off from the rest of the city. Significant rail yards had been a part of the neighborhood for decades and marked its northern boundary. I-10 and US 59 created new southern and western borders for the ward (fig. 2.9). The interchange for these two roads destroyed thirty-six square blocks of the Fifth Ward near downtown.[86] Residents on the north side of I-10 recalled feeling more cut off than ever from the rest of the city.[87] In Denver Harbor, congestion from commercial trucks serving the ship channel, the body of water itself, the presence of I-10 to the north, and rail tracks to the east boxed in that community and limited movement. To top it off, neither community would be served by meaningful public transportation until well into the 1970s.[88] As in the Third Ward, the changes came so quickly that residents had little time to form arguments against the roads, much less put those expressions of discontent into action. Before most could move to protect their homes, they were already gone.

CONCLUSION

Citizens' experiences with Houston's nonstop highway building in the wards and Memorial Bend signaled the beginning of a shift in their ideas about the place of highways in their lives—and for many, also led to more organized, longer-lasting infrastructural activism against official-driven planning. During the mid-1960s, the physical problems faced by African-American and Mexican-American neighborhoods piled up, and the consequences of interstate construction magnified the importance of controlling community-level development. In response, some African-American and Mexican-American activists pivoted their civil rights actions toward opposing the adverse effects of infrastructure construction and addressing service shortcomings in their neighborhoods.[89] White Houstonians throughout the region also continued to encounter infrastructure projects in their neighborhoods during the late 1960s and attempted to broker outcomes that served their interests.

Changes in how African-American Houstonians framed highways before and after their construction demonstrated the switch of transportation issues from the political back burner to the fore of civil rights campaigns. Transportation activism became key to these Houstonians' efforts to gain a larger say in how the city operated. In the early 1960s, black leaders used highways as a rhetorical tool, labeling them harbingers of progress that could be used to illustrate broader civil rights goals. A 1960 article in the black-owned *Forward Times* described the struggle for racial equality as a "muddy road" and called on black Houstonians to "start draining off the water of poverty, filling in the low spots of dissoluteness and bringing the bulldozer of unity to scrape off the mud of ignorance." Every resident needed to "pitch in and help with the paving."[90] The article depicted roads, both physically and metaphorically, as crucial to the overall advancement of the city's black population, as a path toward modernity. Just five years later, after the construction of I-10 through the Fifth Ward and I-45 through the Third, Algenita Scott Davis, Beneva Williams, and Ernie Attwell expressed just the opposite sentiments, with each lamenting the destruction the roads had brought. They framed highways not as progress, but as regression. The consequences of highway construction galvanized African Americans to forward a full-throated demand for improved infrastructure and participation in civic decision-making. By attempting to improve the physical conditions of their communities, these Houstonians opened a new iteration of civil rights struggle, one rooted in the equal dispersal of infrastructural benefits and consequences. This demand persisted well into the 1980s and in fact still persists today.[91]

Black Houstonians were not the only ones who continued to encounter problems with road infrastructure during the mid- to late 1960s. White suburban residents, learning from the experience of protesters in Memorial Bend, also articulated arguments of infrastructural citizenship to fight disruptive projects. Residents in the predominantly white and wealthy near-downtown subdivision of Indian Trail, for example, fought against the routing of a major thoroughfare, Chimney Rock Road, through their community from 1963 until 1967. Although the road's impact on the neighborhood would be a far cry from the effects of the Outer Loop or the interstates on other communities, the active resistance of Indian Trail residents demonstrated the growing resolve of citizens not to be forced into accepting official infrastructure decisions. The road, a bridge over Buffalo Bayou, had been on the Houston's Major Thoroughfare and Freeway Plan since the 1950s.[92] Planners saw the bridge as particularly important to metropolitan traffic flow, because, aside from the Inner Loop's bridge over the bayou, no local streets crossed the water between Shepherd Drive in downtown Houston and Voss Road to the west, a distance of almost 5.5 miles.[93] Despite officials' assertions that the road was essential, a group of residents from Indian Trail solicited the support of the Houston City Council to stop the extension.

Articulating many of the same arguments as the Memorial Bend residents, Indian Trail homeowners argued that the road would lower their property values and turn their neighborhood into a strip mall. Because the residents possessed significant economic and political resources, City Council members listened to their demands and requested that the city attorney draw up an ordinance removing the extension of Chimney Rock from plans.[94] The planning commission scrambled to respond to what they believed was an unprecedented and unwise action. Ralph Ellifrit cautioned that the council's choice set a dangerous precedent. Caving to the Chimney Rock residents, Ellifrit believed, made the entire "major thoroughfare system . . . vulnerable" to citizen resistance. Furthermore, it threatened the city's ability to engage in "long-range planning," because fears "of continuing defeats" at the hands of residents might limit the options available to officials.[95] With the Memorial Bend dispute fresh in his mind, Ellifrit worried that altering the major street plan because of complaints from a small group of residents would foster hundreds of other such complaints and hamstring movement throughout the city. After the council passed the removal ordinance, the planning commission announced that it would not remove the extension from its thoroughfare plan. This disagreement led to a legal battle over which entity could impel the actions of the other, and which had the ultimate say in directing Houston's growth.[96] When Louie Welch took over as mayor in 1964, he announced that his administration would back the planning commission and construction plans went forward.

As the impact of highway construction started to become clear, Houstonians from across the region began to resist the locating of roads through their communities. In subsequent debates, such as the Indian Trail fight, residents turned to the rhetoric and actions of infrastructural citizenship to try to derail the top-down, official-driven highway planning and construction. As Houston moved forward, future debates would increasingly revolve around this rhetoric. As citizens became progressively more involved with decisions about the city's transportation network, officials worked to keep the city growing. This change, however, did not represent the end of unequal decision-making in Houston. Wealthy developers, such as Roy Hofheinz, still possessed a great deal of sway, and white suburbanites continued to succeed in getting their complaints aired with local officials more easily than their black neighbors could. Yet, by the end of the decade, it was clear that Houstonians from across the city were no longer willing to absorb the consequences of construction without at least some say in its foundational decisions.[97]

Taken together, protests from African Americans in the wards and the fight by Indian Trail residents against Chimney Rock Road represented fundamental challenges to the city's development status quo. Each of these fights was a reaction to the ignored protests and destruction wrought by earlier road projects. Between 1945 and 1960, city officials dealt with the region's rapid expansion by building the systems they needed and expecting residents to accept them. When the required structures reached the size of interstates and major highways, though, citizens could no longer ignore the impact. Like Ralph Ellifrit, many officials worried that the pushback would derail long-range growth plans and threaten Houston's connection to its growing suburban fringe.[98] Citizen action raised the stakes on such concerns over the coming years. Houstonians' encounters with the consequences of transportation-related construction and structures in the 1960s led many to form new ideas about the place of major highway infrastructure in the city and inspired many nonelite and nonprofessional Houstonians to participate in the planning of the city as transportation activists. And this participation provided quintessential examples of infrastructural citizenship.

CHAPTER 3

"ONLY YOU CAN PREVENT ANOTHER FREEWAY"[1]

The Harrisburg Freeway and the Struggle to Shape a Neighborhood

In the mid-1960s Richard Holgin was sitting on the front porch of his family's Avenue L home in Magnolia Park when his teenage nephew ran up to share some disturbing news. A rumor was floating around the community that the Texas Highway Department planned to "build a freeway through" Magnolia Park. In fact, according to his nephew, the road would run "right over [Holgin's] house" on its way through Houston's East End neighborhoods toward downtown. Looking out at the streets of the tight-knit, predominantly Mexican-American community in which he grew up, Holgin feared that such a project would tear it apart. Shortly after speaking with his nephew, Holgin confirmed the veracity of the rumor: since the early 1960s, officials from the city and the Houston office of the state highway department had been steadily working on plans to run a highway through the East End.[2] Aware of the destruction that had been brought to other central city neighborhoods by the ongoing construction of Interstate 10 and US 59, Holgin, one of a small minority of Mexican-American East Enders with a college education, led several of his neighbors in a struggle to halt the project.[3]

Over the subsequent decade, the contest around the Harrisburg Freeway proposal saw a mainly working-class, predominantly Mexican-American group of protesters resist the plans of authorities from both local and state government.[4] The protesters turned to transportation activism and made claims of infrastructural citizenship to protest the project. In addition to the panoply of typical protest tactics geared around slowing the planning and construction of the roadway, opponents also benefited from shifts in federal highway policy and regulation, a national upsurge in resistance against urban highways, and a timely state-level budget crunch. The coalescence of these factors prevented the road's construction and resulted in its eventual removal from the State Highway Plan. Although the conflict was ostensibly about the roadway, it came to represent a larger struggle that pitted two visions for the future of East Houston against one another. As officials tried to shape the community into a form they believed could best facilitate central city and suburban growth, resident opponents articulated alternative visions to maintain the integrity of their neighborhoods and stop discriminatory decision-making.[5] The struggle increasingly fomented questions about civil rights, political power, and the meaning of place. Infrastructure, both planned and imagined, stood at the center of this struggle.

Added to Houston's Major Thoroughfare and Freeway Plan in 1963 and to the State Highway Plan in 1969, the route for the proposed Harrisburg Freeway connected with State Highway 225 on the east side of Loop 610 and ran to downtown Houston, cutting through the predominantly Mexican-American, working-class neighborhoods of Harrisburg, Magnolia Park, and the Second Ward along the way (fig. 3.1).[6] As planning for the route progressed in the late 1960s, the process threatened to cause heavy displacements, repeating the same pattern that earlier road projects, such as Interstate 10, had produced in the Fifth Ward. And just as they had with earlier projects, city and state officials hoped the new route would alleviate traffic problems on the city's highways and improve the mobility of Houston's growing suburban population. Aware of, but not overly sympathetic to, the disruption caused by displacing hundreds of Houstonians, officials argued that some uprooting was inevitable in the burgeoning city. Officials explained to frustrated residents that unlike projects started at a time when Houston was so "spread out" that planners had "been able to find holes" through which to run roads, by the 1960s the city's rapidly filling urban landscape meant that "there [were] just no holes" for new roadways, so they needed to be created.[7] Officials told East End residents whose homes lay within the potential rights-of-way that such plans needed to be implemented for the greater good of the city.

While, overall, residents of the East End generally approved of the freeway, many Mexican-American residents of Magnolia Park and Harrisburg did not accept that their homes would be cleared in the name of progress. Those who saw the road in a positive light believed it would shorten their daily commutes into downtown Houston and make travel to other parts of the city easier. The push the group of residents made against the highway represented a very different vision of the role of infrastructure to the community and of who had the right to determine its shape. That East Enders like Holgin willingly articulated their vision in opposition to that offered by officials definitively altered the fate of the project.[8]

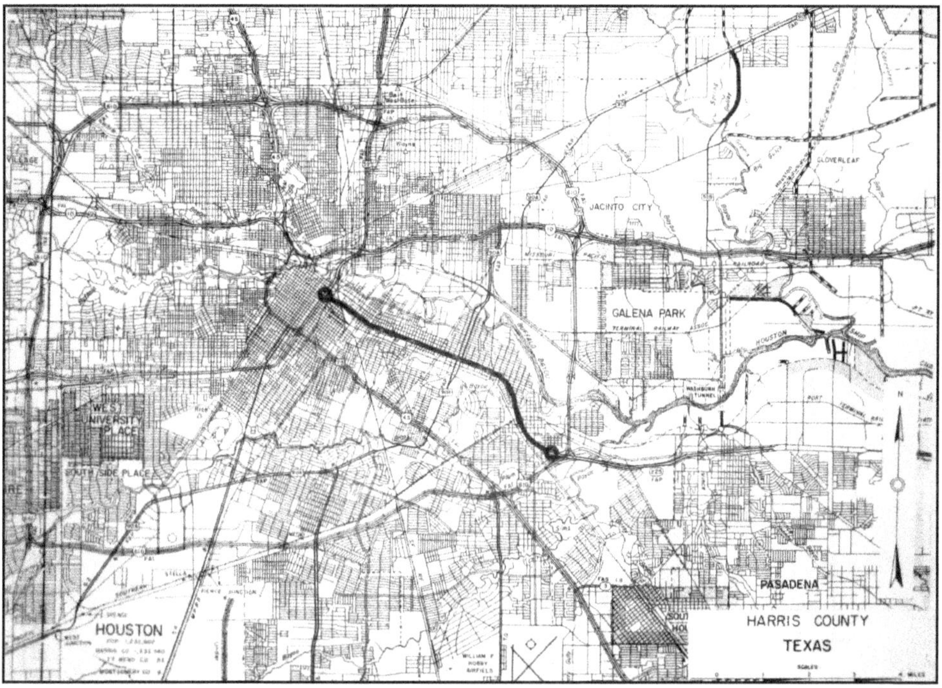

Fig. 3.1. Harrisburg Freeway Proposal
The proposed route of the Harrisburg Freeway extension, the bold black line above, ran from the intersection of SH 225 and Interstate 610 to downtown crossing through Harrisburg, Magnolia Park, and the Second Ward. Texas Highway Department, "Draft Environmental Impact Statement for State Highway 225," FHWA-TEX_EIS-730977-D, 21.

Road opponents in the East End argued that the highway was another abusive infrastructure project that benefited the wealthier parts of the metropolitan area while foisting the consequences of construction onto African-American and Mexican-American communities. By voicing dissent to what they saw as discriminatory planning methods, Mexican-American East Enders challenged the lack of citizen input involved in civic decision-making. This opposition made it clear that a uniform definition of "good" mobility did not exist. Furthermore, the conflict demonstrated that the building of infrastructure was far from a neutral act. The planning, construction, and use of infrastructure created sides and engendered debate among those with competing ideas in Houston. Indeed, the campaign against the road illustrated that various groups possessed divergent, and often contradictory, understandings of the concept and its role in daily life. During the Harrisburg fight, Mexican-American Houstonians forced their visions for the future of their neighborhoods and for the city into public view, in the process changing the nature of Houston's transportation infrastructure development.

The actions taken by Mexican-American highway opponents overlapped with and built upon ongoing civil rights struggles and earlier infrastructural activism in which Houstonians of color advocated for greater control over and access to economic, political, and mobility rights. By the 1970s, Mexican Americans in the East End, like African Americans in the city's Third and Fifth Wards, had been engaged in campaigns for civil rights for several decades. In the Mexican-American East End, those campaigns centered mainly on education, employment, and voting rights.[9] In the late 1960s and early 1970s, a conflict over school integration erupted in the city's Mexican-American neighborhoods. For decades, Houstonians of Mexican origin had been considered white, and during school desegregation efforts Houston leaders had used this categorization to place African-American and Mexican-American children in the same schools and claim that such actions represented black-white integration. Mexican-American Houstonians responded by insisting that they belonged to a separate racial category and that the school district needed to fully integrate black, brown, and white children in city schools.[10] Many of the actors involved in the Harrisburg Freeway fight participated in these other civil rights campaigns. These overlapping battles helped to push a large number of Mexican-American Houstonians into civil rights organizations and public protests. These fights empowered them to voice their shared frustrations about education, police brutality, poor city services, and discrimination.

While the act of moving through the city may seem secondary to the essential political and social rights pursued by more recognized civil rights campaigns, those Houstonians who pushed against the Harrisburg plan came to believe that unhindered and equal access to systems of mobility represented an important piece of the larger push for civil rights. Mexican-American protesters—who urged the city to consider alternative infrastructural and transportation futures, sought the just distribution of the physical costs of transportation systems, and demanded a local voice in planning efforts—made the Harrisburg fight into an important iteration of the local civil rights struggle. And, as a result of the city's multifaceted civil rights actions and changing federal laws, by the mid-1970s Houston's Mexican-American and African-American citizens constituted a much more significant electoral bloc than they had a decade earlier. This growing political influence gave their transportation activism greater weight.

Beyond fighting over the roadway, officials and residents also sparred for the power to define and control the parts of the city through which the road would run. Each side attempted to characterize the landscapes of the East End in ways that best suited their desired ends. Two reports—a required environmental impact statement (EIS) produced by state and city officials for the road project and a Model Cities publication issued by Houston's Neighborhood Improvement Program about neighborhood renovation—captured the very different perspectives of the community held by Texas Highway Department officials and residents of the East End. As products produced by public entities, each of the reports also reflected changes to federal participation in the governance of major public works projects and cities.

Environmental impact statements for all federally funded projects were required by the National Environmental Policy Act of 1969. This requirement was one of the biggest changes the act had introduced. Any agency proposing a project had to put out an EIS giving a breakdown of the social, cultural, and environmental impacts of several alternative designs. In weighing impact, officials had to account for public opinion and consider more than just direct environmental issues, such as air pollution; they had to also look at elements such as the continuity of the fabric of affected neighborhoods. Final decisions about which alternative to pursue were to consider the weight of negative impacts. The documents gave residents a formal record of issues associated with a project and often offered an important tool in fights to resist them. However, in most cases, the EIS became just another step that officials and agencies had to overcome in order to complete a project. Only in moments where intense public scrutiny was brought to bear on the document did the EIS process tend to serve as a helpful tool for citizens.

Model Cities was a federal program initiated during the War on Poverty to get funds to poverty-stricken neighborhoods. The program started as an attempt to address the failures of the push for urban renewal under the Housing Acts of 1949 and 1954 and aimed to bring meaningful, community-directed investment into the task of rebuilding urban centers. A part of the fledgling US Department of Housing and Urban Development (HUD), the program promised to bring substantial funding to city governments for a wide range of projects. Houston began to pursue Model Cities funding seriously in 1968, and much of the funding the city received went toward revitalization efforts like those that were occurring in the East End. While the funding came with attendant participation requirements, counterintuitively, many local officials saw it as a way to circumvent the confrontational local politics of earlier War on Poverty programs, because Model Cities vested most of the decision-making power related to the projects in cities and city officials. Despite its limitations, the program brought a great deal of attention to the areas that it funded.[11]

The two documents on the East End conceived of the community in starkly different terms. The EIS depicted the East End, particularly Magnolia Park and Harrisburg, as rundown and outdated. It claimed that the roadway could encourage urban renewal in the East End. Residents, however, fought to maintain the residential nature of their neighborhoods. In the Model Cities report and in their public comments about the road, they argued that their communities were viable and productive parts of the city. They feared that the road's construction would render their streets unrecognizable, disrupt their patterns of living, disconnect them from the city at large, and accelerate the environmental breakdown of their already stressed landscape.[12] Like suburban Houstonians nervous about the impact of Beltway 8 on their homes and lives, Mexican-American activists articulated their concerns about the road through arguments that focused on issues of mobility, place, and the environment.[13] Transportation activists opposed to the freeway practiced infrastructural citizenship at community meetings, in conversations with their elected officials, and among their neighbors. Their actions made it clear that never again would infrastructure decisions emerge solely from a room of officials poring over maps in search of "holes" through which to run roads.

SITUATING THE DEBATE: A BRIEF HISTORY OF EAST HOUSTON COMMUNITIES

Real estate developers came to East Houston in the early 1900s and conceived of the area as a potential suburban haven in the shadow of downtown. However, due to its position on the edge of the Houston Ship Channel, East Houston had been transformed by the 1920s into one of the leading industrial areas in the city. Shipping companies, cotton compresses, and manufacturing centers clustered along the ship channel seeking easy access to the Gulf of Mexico. At the same time, residential communities such as Magnolia Park and the Second Ward grew up alongside this industry, housing the laborers who flocked to the area in search of jobs, or because of connections with already settled families and friends.[14] Magnolia Park became one of

Houston's earliest Mexican-American barrios. By the end of World War II, as the area's industries began transitioning to the petrochemical and heavy manufacturing interests that would drive Houston's postwar expansion, the residential communities continued to grow apace.

By the beginning of the Harrisburg Freeway debate in the mid-1960s, East Houston communities featured factories, warehouses, and train tracks interspersed with homes, schools, and churches. The factories projected a decidedly industrial landscape dominated by commercial infrastructure and facilities, relegating the residential and natural elements of the area to the background. By the 1970s, industrial land use in a corridor that encompassed both Magnolia Park and Harrisburg stood at 21 percent, which was more than 5 percent higher than the city average. The communities' commercial usage stood at 16 percent.[15] Beyond the physical presence of the factories and shops, the industrial landscape—its processes, infrastructure requirements, and detritus—also left unseen marks upon the area in the form of pollution and toxicity. It was this legacy, as much as the buildings themselves, with which residents contended on a daily basis.

The area's industry served as the foundation for the social and economic activity of the area. In East Houston communities, almost a third of adult residents worked at either one of the numerous factories on Seventy-Sixth Street or along the docks.[16] And just as industrial by-products seeped into the landscape, so, too, did the patterns of industrial life ingrain themselves into every facet of life. Residents timed their daily commutes around slow-moving freight trains; they avoided impromptu garbage dumps outside of factories; they awoke to the foghorns of oil barges and container ships. Unlike Houstonians whose homes sat in the shadows of the growing downtown, East Houston's residents experienced the extreme nature of the city's economic growth firsthand. Although they benefited from the many opportunities created by the city's burgeoning economy, they also absorbed—physically and cognitively—the negative aspects of living in an industrial neighborhood.[17] For residents whose homes rested among and behind the walls of factories and warehouses, the surrounding landscape shaped the way they lived their lives and affected how they interpreted their places within the city.

People, not just landscapes, defined these communities. At the time of the freeway fight, Mexican Americans dominated the demographics of both the Second Ward and Magnolia Park, while Harrisburg and Manchester saw a closer split between Mexican-American and white Houstonians. Other East End neighborhoods, such as Lawndale, Eastwood, and Pecan Park, were predominantly white.[18] Chinese-American and African-American Houstonians had a small but meaningful presence in the neighborhoods as well, particularly in Magnolia Park. Chinese Americans operated several grocery stores there, and African-American laborers and their families clustered near the union hall of the all-black International Longshoremen's Association Local 872.[19] Neither group participated vocally in the Harrisburg Freeway fight. East Houston communities were especially dense as well. In 1970 the citywide average density was 14.4 people per acre. In the East Houston corridor from Magnolia Park to Harrisburg, the density stood at 23.4 people per acre.[20] This statistic guaranteed that any major infrastructure projects in the area would displace a large number of residents.

East Houston—an industrial-residential world, populated by working-class Houstonians from a variety of backgrounds—became the site of the fight over the Harrisburg Freeway. East End residents—who alternately tolerated, benefited from, and complained about their landscape—approached the highway project with a mix of opinions, ranging from acceptance, to resignation, to indignation.[21] No matter how they viewed the road itself, what became clear was that each resident possessed a preconceived notion of the neighborhood and its landscape, one tied to existing infrastructure and threatened by the new. Each resident held his or her own idea about what a highway might mean to movements through the city and the community. From this diverse array of opinions, a solid knot of Mexican-American residents—linked by a mutual fear of the highway and a distrust of the city's power brokers—emerged to resist the highway's construction.

EARLIER COMMUNITY CONFLICTS

The area's industry-centric makeup provides a clue to the opposition of many residents to the Harrisburg Freeway. Well before the fight against the highway began, East Enders had tested the power of infrastructural citizenship, taking stands against toxic pollutants, poor city services, and dangerous transportation crossings. Therefore, they had already shown a desire not only to remove hazards from their communities but also to define the shape of their neighborhoods. Although East Enders became divided over the proposed highway, in earlier fights they had presented a united front against their mutual problems. For some residents, prior experiences with industrial and infrastructural issues influenced the decision to resist the freeway; an awareness of the destructive nature of Interstate 10 through the Fifth Ward also contributed. Furthermore, many residents who opposed the freeway had been prepared for the struggle against it by earlier struggles to shape the neighborhood and to curtail damaging practices.[22]

One major conflict that had arisen from the industrial-residential nature of the East End centered on the near constant movement of train and truck traffic around the Houston Ship Channel's industrial complexes. In 1960, white and Mexican-American residents from the Harrisburg area complained to the Houston City Council about a traffic problem caused by a long line of idling semis in the community. Vehicles came and went at all hours of the day—disrupting sleep, straining infrastructure, and filling the communities with dangerous traffic. In an attempt to exert some control over their neighborhood, residents asked the City Council to pass regulations that prevented trucks from clogging their streets at all hours of the day.[23] They also issued complaints about high train volume, which likewise disrupted easy movement in the communities, and fourteen at-grade train crossings that snarled traffic during the peak hours.[24] The complaints against truck and train traffic centered not just on the disruptions caused by the presence of the two systems, but also on the limitations they imposed onto the daily movements of East End residents. Influenced by these earlier experiences, many residents worried that the construction of the road would worsen, not improve, traffic in their community.

On top of facing the logistical costs of living within an industrial landscape, East End residents also had to contend with some of the worst provision of public services in the entire city. Due to Houston's territorial and demographic growth in the postwar period, the city struggled to provide basic services. The shortfalls in service fell onto the newest of suburbs and the oldest, poorest central city neighborhoods. So, while wealthier central-city neighborhoods had better maintained roadways and received the bulk of drainage work, well into the 1960s working-class, predominantly minority communities struggled with unpaved or poorly maintained roads, faced dire problems during times of floods, and saw their communities fall into disrepair.[25] Facing these issues head-on, Mexican-American East Enders attended Houston City Council meetings and implored council members to help them rid their community of trash, rats, and vacant homes so they could "pursue decent and healthy lives." Pointing to a disparity in services between wealthy and impoverished neighborhoods, these residents lamented the fact that they were "last on the totem pole" for services, arguing that, as taxpayers, they deserved adequate and equal service. They were "not asking them [the council] to do something for us that they are not doing for the whole city."[26]

Residents feared that the new road would add to already significant levels of water and air pollution in the community. By 1970, the ship channel—which East Houston residents lived along, worked near, and, at one time, swam and fished in—was one of the most polluted waterways in the nation.[27] Opponents of the road also worried that the highway would compound the already dangerous air pollution levels experienced in the densely packed industrial neighborhoods. Emissions from industrial vehicles and factories left East Houston communities covered in a haze of "fumes, odors, dirt, and smut," and residents were concerned that a highway would intensify these problems.[28] Providing concrete justification for these misgivings, in 1970 residents of Harrisburg noticed a massive die-off of birds in their community. Residents immediately blamed air pollution as the cause of the bird-kill. After city officials failed to take action, numerous residents, led by a contingent of children ranging from age five to thirteen, marched to the gates of one of the worst polluting companies, blocked a number of trucks from entering the facility, and demanded the company decrease the amount of pollution it created.[29]

This small sample of the struggles captures the infrastructural fights that East Houston residents waged in their communities prior to the one against the freeway. At the most basic level, each of these fights originated in the desires of residents to maintain or improve the character of their communities and the health of their families. When plans for the Harrisburg Freeway were announced, many residents viewed the proposal through a lens colored by these previous experiences and did not like what they saw. Grappling with the environmental problems their communities faced allowed them to articulate their own approach to creating a healthy and productive neighborhood. Their infrastructural activism provided them with an entrée into the larger conversation about the city and its future. With highway construction looming, residents who saw the road as yet another threat to their communities responded, as they had numerous times before, by organizing against the project and asserting themselves within metropolitan politics.

THE FREEWAY PLAN

Texas Highway Department officials took a different view of the Harrisburg Freeway project. In the initial planning stages, they believed the roadway would meet the two primary goals the agency hoped to achieve with each of its new highway projects: supporting suburban mobility, and stimulating citywide economic growth. Specifically, officials thought the freeway would ease traffic problems between downtown Houston and the quickly growing southeastern suburbs. In addition, they believed the roadway would encourage the continued industrial and commercial development of the city's ship channel. Before local opposition to the road coalesced, officials and city boosters promoted suburban mobility and economic growth as arguments for the proposed freeway.[30]

As a result of wartime production demands, the industrial suburbs of Pasadena and La Porte had experienced massive economic and population growth beginning in the early 1940s. This expansion continued after the war, and officials in Houston and its satellite towns moved to control it by linking industrial areas with the larger city. In the early 1950s, the major east-west link between Houston and its eastern suburbs was the locally dubbed La Porte–Houston Highway (later State Highway 225), a small road ill-suited to the high volumes of traffic officials believed continued growth would soon bring.[31] In order to provide better road access to the ship channel, Houston officials called for the construction of a spur road to connect the Gulf Freeway and the La Porte–Houston Highway. At a meeting of the Texas Highway Commission in July 1950, leaders from the Houston Chamber of Commerce, joined by elected officials from Houston and Harris County, went further by lobbying for the expansion of southeastern Harris County's roadways.[32] The desired spur was constructed, but soon thereafter it became clear that a more permanent and higher-capacity road would be required. In 1953, at the urging of local officials, the Texas Highway Commission designated Highway 225 as an official state highway. The original iteration of the road stretched from the outskirts of East Houston to Highway 146 in eastern Harris County.[33] Markedly absent from this designation, however, was a connection between downtown Houston and the end of the road.

As construction of Highway 225 between Houston's Loop 610 and its eastern suburbs began in the 1960s, a simultaneous push for the extension of the road into the heart of Houston picked up speed. In 1961, a report by the Texas Highway Department titled "Preliminary Freeway Phase" first suggested the idea of running a freeway from the western terminus of 225 into the heart of downtown.[34] The report highlighted several yet-to-be-designated projects that the city would need to execute in order to grow, including the Harrisburg Freeway extension.[35] Officials hoped that a downtown-225 link could relieve the growing traffic problems of the Gulf Freeway by shunting the LaPorte/Pasadena commuters off of the Gulf Freeway and onto 225.[36] Because of the hefty financial commitments already given to the interstate system and its priority level, the Texas Highway

Department did not immediately adopt the Harrisburg extension. Despite this inaction, local officials, confident that in due time the route would be added to the state plan, continued to clear the way, conducting feasibility studies and planning possible routes.

Almost immediately upon making plans for the Harrisburg extension public, city and state officials started receiving inquiries about the road from anxious Houstonians. Some wanted the construction to begin; others were wary of its costs. Some Houstonians, including Richard Holgin from the opening anecdote of this chapter, contacted both the Texas Highway Department and the City of Houston when they heard about the plans, wanting to learn the details. As early as 1963, so many inquiries were coming into the highway department's offices that department officials asked the Houston City Planning Department to stop forwarding the calls to them until it was officially a state highway project. In an interoffice memo, the city planning department told employees to ensure callers that, far from having set its plans in stone, Houston had only just begun a "number of alignment studies." To those who were nervous about their homes, the city would offer assurances that construction was "at least eight to ten years in the future." In the same memo, however, officials noted that a general alignment had already been selected running just north of Harrisburg Boulevard through the Second Ward and Magnolia Park before cutting down through Harrisburg and joining up with State Highway 225, which was already under construction.[37]

The fact that the local officials continued to make plans for the highway despite a lack of commitment from the highway department demonstrates the momentum of road projects during the 1950s and 1960s. It also hints at the task facing those who hoped to stop them. Road planning often began ten years before any construction took place. As officials committed resources and planning toward the project, its completion became more and more likely. Even if they conducted public hearings or sought feedback from the public, these activities rarely resulted in changes to the entrenched plans, and no such meetings were required. This practice made the alteration or rollback of projects difficult, if not impossible. The city and county began the planning steps early in hopes of having the required infrastructure in place when the Texas Highway Commission finally moved on the route. This approach precluded the incorporation of citizen feedback and resulted in a muddled public picture of the project and its timeline. The relative lack of transparency stoked the anxiety of residents like Holgin who heard rumors of potential plans, but lacked access to concrete details.

The City of Houston was one of the main actors in preparing the foundation for the extension prior to the announcement of any official plans. In addition to settling on a preliminary location for the route, the City Council instructed numerous departments to take the initial steps required to prepare for construction. In 1963, the director of city planning, Ralph Ellifrit, asked the real estate department to investigate the required right-of-way purchases along the proposed route and to begin making those purchases.[38] In 1964, the City Council established building lines, which restricted property owners from building new structures or making significant improvements to existing structures, in hopes of keeping right-of-way costs down.[39] To residents and business owners in the area, this move signaled that the road really would be coming through their neighborhood and that their homes and their neighborhood were at risk.

As officials laid the groundwork for the extension into downtown, they continued to lobby the Texas Highway Commission to designate it as a state highway route. The Houston Chamber of Commerce worked closely with city and county officials in their efforts to gain the designation, which would bring significant state assistance to the project. At a Chamber meeting attended by A. C. Kyser, the head engineer of the Texas Highway Department's Houston Urban Project, Chamber, city, and county leaders pitched the importance of beginning the route as soon as possible. Houston's director of transportation, Eugene Maier, pointed out that the southeastern parts of the city and county were "seriously deficient in freeway facilities," a problem that would result in "major congestion unless immediate plans are developed for the construction of additional freeways." Chamber members from Humble Oil and Foley's Department Store supported the extension plan in hopes that it would lower shipping costs and offer commercial access to the burgeoning markets of the eastern suburbs.[40]

Texas Highway Department officials clearly supported the plan for extending Highway 225 into the city, but they remained hesitant to add to the state's program of work until more funds could be secured. Thus, they once again delayed the designation.[41] In yet another appearance before the Texas Highway Commission in 1969, local officials used the amount of work and resources that local entities had put into preparing the ground for the road as a justification for state aid. Harris County Judge Bill Elliot pointed out that the city, the county, and the Harris County Navigation District had already spent "some $7 million for construction of connecting roads" and the elimination of at-grade railroad crossings. Officials forecasted that the right-of-way costs for the extension would amount to approximately $16 million, and warned that if the commission did not act quickly, that figure would skyrocket, owing to speculation along the routes.[42] The commitment of city and county officials to the extension project paid off when the Texas Highway Commission made the 225 extension a part of the state highway system in April 1969.[43] The state highway department projected the cost of the highway to be approximately $40 million for right-of-way and construction. Not measured in this cost, however, were the changes that residents believed such a road would bring to their lives.[44]

PUSHING BACK THE INEVITABLE: THE FIRST PHASE OF FREEWAY OPPOSITION

When the Texas Highway Commission brought the Harrisburg Freeway extension into the State Highway Plan, opposition to the roadway began in earnest. Led by Mexican-American residents of Magnolia Park and Harrisburg, opponents attacked the plan for the road from several angles. They condemned the lack of input allowed residents, argued that any roadway would drastically damage the environment and character of the neighborhood, and asserted that the roadway was not the best form of transportation for the neighborhood or the city. While in the early stages it seemed the anti-freeway group was doomed in their battle against the long-planned project, during the debate members received several boosts from changes to federal policy that helped them slow the road-building process considerably.

In response to both the national environmental movement and a growing number of protests against urban highway projects, the federal government altered many of the oversight requirements on major public works projects between 1962 and 1970. One of the most crucial of these changes for the purposes of the Harrisburg Freeway fight was the passage in 1969 of the National Environmental Policy Act. Just as important was the institution of rules by the Federal Highway Administration (FHWA) requiring local agencies to present more opportunities for citizen feedback through public meetings. Finally, because of ongoing resistance to controversial sections of the Interstate Highway System, the federal government decided to back away from contentious road projects.[45]

The National Environmental Policy Act required that the agencies responsible for projects receiving federal funding produce an environmental impact statement for approval by federal administrators. The statement, based on studies of the project area, estimated the negative consequences a project would have on the environment, economy, and residents of its covered area. The law gave the Environmental Protection Agency, which began operation in 1970, the power to reject submitted plans that were deemed to have an overly negative outcome for project areas or require changes to them. The new FHWA standards established a public hearing process specifically for roadway projects that received federal monies that was much more democratic than what had existed previously. Finally, the lack of US Department of Transportation and FHWA support for divisive highway projects made it difficult for state and local officials to push road projects through opposition.[46] The Harrisburg Freeway was the first major roadway in Houston to face this new federal scrutiny. Unlike earlier projects, where public meetings served as little more than a formal rubber stamp, the elongated feedback processes slowed the momentum for highway projects and provided citizens with an additional outlet for critique.[47] East Houston residents who opposed the highway used these new requirements to voice disapproval of the road to the same officials who had earlier ignored them.

Significantly, not all residents of East Houston saw the roadway as a negative. But regardless of their stance toward the road itself, throughout the debate nearly all the residents supported the changes that allowed for more democratic decision-making. Many, including the East End Progress Association, a business-oriented neighborhood group, argued that a road would help develop East Houston. In addition, many white residents who lived in neighborhoods that would not be bisected by the highway supported construction.[48] In the early stages of the debate, city and state officials who wanted to maintain control of development responded to this challenge by alternately trying to circumvent, appease, encourage, or ignore the concerns and thoughts of residents. From 1970 to 1974, the peak of the Harrisburg debate, both residents who opposed the road and local officials who backed it attempted to gain the upper hand.

In a series of articles published in the early months of 1970, Harrisburg resident and Mexican-American community journalist Maggie Landron laid out her case, and that of many of her fellow East Enders, against the Harrisburg Freeway. At a time when debates about mass transit were gaining steam across the nation, she accused local and state officials of tunnel vision when it came to building highways instead of mass transit.[49] Landron argued that in touting the newest highway plans as the "end to all our traffic problems," officials were ignoring the fact that "freeways are out-of-date before they are finished." Landron asserted that "no freeway has solved the traffic problems of Houston," and that the "proposed Harrisburg Freeway will be no exception." Pivoting from here, she articulated an alternative vision of mobility, one that she believed expressed the desire of most of East Houston's Mexican-American residents. Instead of trying to force East Houston into a suburban model of mobility, Landron said, the city should invest in mass transit. Roads, she pointed out, could not serve a community where at least half the residents were either "without cars completely; have ancient, undependable cars that would gladly be gotten rid of; or are too elderly to drive." Labeling the highway plans short-sighted, she argued that a mass transit system would be "transportation for residents within the city for fifty and seventy-five years from now, not just tomorrow." Cognizant of the challenge of breaking Houston's highway monopoly, Landron called on residents to demand the implementation of mass transit and to articulate their own ideas of the politics of mobility. "It is up to you to make the city use their head," she said. With this call to action, Landron vocalized the intention of an active constituency of central city residents to enter into the planning process of the city through an infrastructural debate.[50]

Landron's articles, published in the Harrisburg community newspaper *Papel Chicano*, served as the public voice to freeway opposition in East Houston's Mexican-American neighborhoods. Broadly, Landron and *Papel Chicano* reflected the youth-led Chicano movement that was central to several civil rights campaigns in Houston during the late 1960s and early 1970s. Chicano-identified groups such as the Mexican-American Youth Association represented a mainly younger subset of Mexican-American Houstonians who were unsatisfied with the actions of mainline Mexican-American organizations like the League of United Latin American Citizens. In this way they played a role in the Mexican-American community that was similar to the role played by the Progressive Youth Association in the African-American community. These activists led the push for Mexican Americans to be identified as a racial group separate from whites and to celebrate that heritage. They also employed much more confrontational strategies of protest than most of the highway adversaries, organizing, for example, Huelga (Spanish for "strike") schools during their protests against the Houston Independent School District's desegregation practices. The fact that Landron and *Papel Chicano* covered and participated in the Harrisburg Freeway debate showed that worries about the shape of the community and access to political power were concerns that many generations of Mexican Americans shared.[51]

While other activists, such as Richard Holgin, brought the struggle to the halls of the city and state government, Landron articulated the motivations of their opposition. Harkening back to the industrial and pollution problems that East Houston had faced for decades, she asserted that Mexican-American residents were "fed up choking on our own exhaust fumes; fed up looking at cement ribbons crisscrossing our cities; fed up with homes and people being destroyed to build more and more freeways; and fed up with others determining what is good for us."[52] Landron's words acted as a rallying cry for many in East Houston. Her articles in *Papel Chicano* spurred residents to action and redoubled efforts to drum up support from those who were not yet engaged. Activists strove to learn from their community's damaging experiences with infrastructure projects and pollution. They also advocated for their own ideas about the neighborhoods and the city's mobility.

Mexican-American activists first broached their resistance to the highway by attending a March 1970 public meeting, one required by the new FHWA meeting guidelines. At the meeting, highway department engineer A. C. Kyser revealed three potential corridors—A, B, and C—for the Harrisburg extension, each of which ran through a different part of East Houston and threatened the homes and businesses of residents (fig. 3.2). Kyser said the department believed that Corridor A, which would run between Canal Street and Harrisburg, represented the best potential route. The official count recorded that this path would require the destruction of 1,125 homes. The highway department concluded that this loss represented a lesser cost than the other two proposed corridors because it would not threaten any businesses along the ship channel. Corridor C would displace 330 homes and 70 businesses, whereas Corridor B would remove 775 homes and 110 businesses. While Kyser noted that Corridor A was the odds on favorite, he refused to name any specific route information, instead offering assurances that resident removal remained at least "three or four years" away. According to newspaper accounts, 500 people attended the meeting, most of them concerned that the highway would take their homes.[53]

Opposition activists possessed a very different memory of this meeting, arguing that officials dismissed citizen concerns and made the process seem like a done deal. Holgin recalled the overarching message as an assertion that "this thing was going to go through whether you [the residents] like it or not. It's already set." In his eyes, the department's stance toward residents at the meeting was "you just got to get out of the way, we're going to do this."[54] Holgin and others disliked what they saw as a done-deal-attitude and asserted that, in the opinion of many residents, "no freeway was desirable."[55] Holgin believed that the dismissive attitude of officials at the first meeting helped to galvanize the opposition. At future public forums,

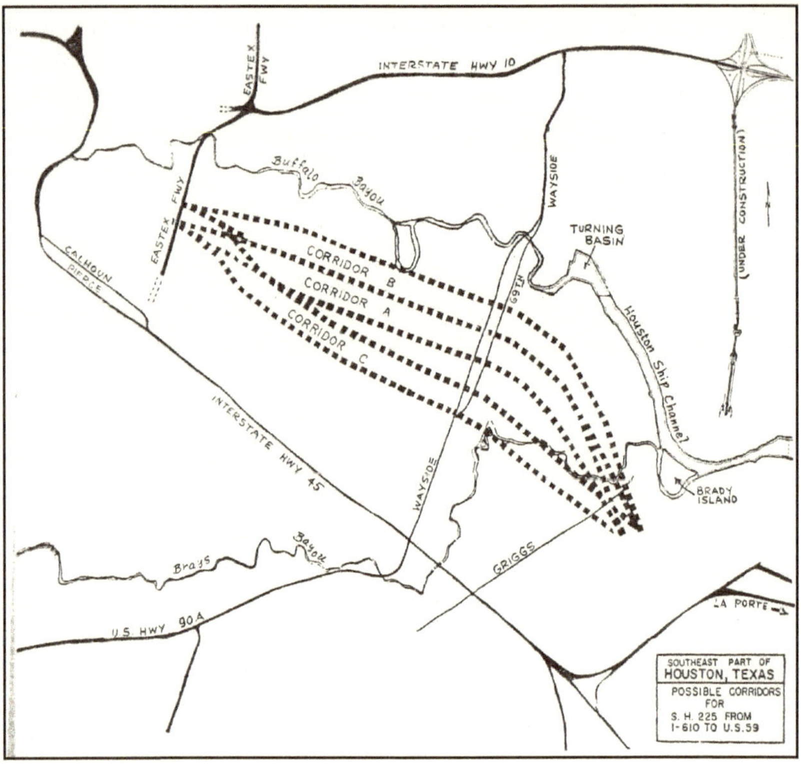

Fig. 3.2. Harrisburg Freeway Alternatives

Three proposed corridors for the Harrisburg Freeway extension presented by the Texas Highway Department at the March 1970 meeting. "Residents on Right-of-Way Safe for 3–4 Years," *Houston Post*, March 10, 1970.

opponents offered much stiffer resistance to the assertions of the highway officials than they had at the March meeting. According to Holgin, officials facing tough audience inquiries at these meetings avoided providing answers by concluding their discussions in a rushed manner and departing without taking questions.[56]

In May 1970, to raise further awareness of the highway department plans and to encourage greater resistance, Holgin organized a meeting at the Ripley House, a community center in the Second Ward that for many years had served as a central social and political site for Houston's Mexican Americans.[57] At this meeting, Holgin and Al Davey, a consulting planner who agreed to work with the residents on their fight against the road, presented a slideshow of community homes and businesses that would be destroyed by the proposed highway if the Corridor A plan was constructed. They also proposed the idea of routing the highway along the ship channel instead of through the neighborhood itself (fig. 3.3). Holgin recalled that the slideshow was particularly effective. It "really woke them [the residents] up." It alerted them to the reality that "all this stuff [was] going to be gone. All these homes and businesses are going to be gone." The slideshow reminded residents of the power of the existing infrastructure, of what they stood to lose if they did not act. Holgin recalled that opposition leaders channeled the momentum of this meeting into greater organization against the highway. He

Fig. 3.3. Locally Preferred Alternative

The preferred Harrisburg Freeway options presented by Richard Holgin and Al Davey at the May 1970 community meeting. Routes 2, 3, and 4 correspond to corridors A, B, and C, from the Texas Highway Department map. Route 1 is the Houston Ship Channel route promoted most heavily by Holgin and other anti-road activists for its avoidance of residential areas. Mark Madera et al., *The Barrios: Mexican-Americans in Houston* (Houston: Magnolia Business Center, a Model Cities Agency, January 1971), 41.

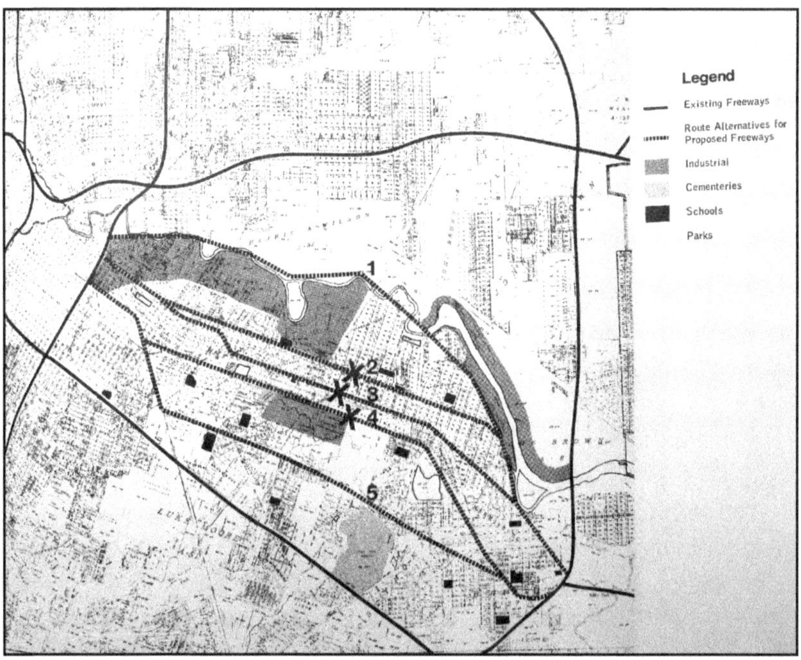

encouraged attendees to come to future meetings, write to officials, and ask questions of the Texas Highway Department.[58]

If this meeting functioned to coalesce opposition to the highway, it also elicited a strong response from highway department officials and other city leaders who hoped to head off the resistance before it could stymie the highway plans. In a letter to Holgin written the day after the May Ripley House meeting, A. C. Kyser chastised opposition leaders, saying they had deliberately misled attendees. Kyser conveyed exasperation over the fact that the "meeting obviously resulted in leaving many of the people with the impression that the bayou location was a feasible alternate and the option was whether the freeway is to be built in Corridor A or along Buffalo Bayou." He asked Holgin to "submit the Davey scheme to a competent, qualified engineer for review," and to limit future discussion to "pertinent matters rather than unworkable schemes proposed by self appointed experts." Kyser dismissed the idea that most of the residents opposed the freeway, asserting that "interested citizens and the government of Houston and Harris County" had solicited the freeway in the first place. He contended that the department was doing its utmost to "build the best facility possible with the least amount of disruption of the neighborhood." While he acknowledged that the highway department stood ready to "listen to constructive suggestions," he chided Holgin and other highway opponents for taking a limited view of the project and its benefits. Although "it was not surprising that some . . . would oppose the project," he argued, the state needed to account for "the desires and interests of the rest of the people of the sector and the entire community," not just those who opposed the plans.[59]

Despite the hopes of A. C. Kyser and other city officials for a smooth highway construction process, the neighborhood's opposition could not be easily dismissed. Responding to residents' complaints about the lack of citizen input and potential disruptions, the Texas Highway Department delayed the initial phase of the project and in July 1970 commissioned the Harrisburg Freeway Study Team to reexamine the routing of the roadway.[60] In creating this group, the highway department clearly intended to assuage the concerns of residents by articulating the "rational objectives and detailed alternatives" of the project and by promising to consider "the social, economic, and physical implications" of the road's presence in the neighborhoods.[61] Despite the goal of establishing a working relationship with the communities through which the road would run, the study team did not include a single community member outside of highway department project engineer Dexter Jones, who had been born in Harrisburg; nor did it have a single local political representative.[62] Instead, the team consisted of twelve white men, ten of whom worked for the highway department. The other two, a sociologist and an economist, worked for Texas A&M—a school intimately connected to the department.[63] Aiming to get command of the various actors and demands involved in the freeway debate, the team began their work in the summer of 1970.

At one of the first official meetings of the Harrisburg Freeway Study Team, Chairman Phil Wilson told state highway and Houston officials that the team's main goal was to prevent the road planning process from becoming a full-blown "controversy." The team hoped that they were entering into the process early enough to combat the "bad feelings" that often arose as these debates dragged on. They thought that such problems could be avoided if they could "meet with everyone involved," shore up supporters, and find "offsets to the objections of the people."[64] Although the team knew that numerous groups and many residents of East Houston supported the roadway, they also recognized the reality that new federal regulations made it so that "one person can stop a freeway" by raising questions through the EIS process and public hearings. In the first months of its existence, the team believed that the freeway would ultimately succeed because, with the exception of Holgin's anti-freeway group, "all of the civic groups and virtually all of the private citizens who have contacted the team have expressed a pressing need for a freeway." Despite this strong support, the study team intended to educate residents about the freeway plans in order to dispel the "rumors" that had been swirling around about the freeway plans ever since the meetings of March and May.[65]

In hopes of promoting the official image of the roadway, the Harrisburg Freeway Study Team began by distributing an informational packet and offering quarterly progress reports on the freeway. The information pamphlet made the case for the freeway through the same celebratory, growth-driven language that had been used to sell earlier highway projects. Published in both English and Spanish, the pamphlet told residents that building the Harrisburg Freeway would put the community on "the road to better living." It would replace the accidents, noise, and exhaust fumes that came from crowded surface streets with better access to jobs, education, and a higher quality of life. Showing their determination to get the input of citizens, the pamphlet asked residents to share information with the team about "where you live, where you work, where you shop, where your children go to school, what church you attend, what parks you have or need," so that it could find the best location for the road.[66] The study team and its community survey resulted directly from the opposition of Mexican-American East Enders. Opposition to the roadway caused a delay in the project and led to a study that promised to include greater citizen feedback. This must be considered a victory for anti-freeway advocates, given the nature of decision-making in the city up until this point.

"HIGHWAYS ARE NO LONGER GODS": CONTINUED FREEWAY OPPOSITION[67]

Building upon their earlier efforts, the Texas Highway Department and the Harrisburg Freeway Study Team wasted no time in attempting to move forward. In a move intended to assuage the demands of residents both for and against the route, government officials shifted their pitch for the project away from the "greater good," suburb-oriented strain of the previous months and replaced it with language that put the affected residents and their concerns at its core. At a February 1971 meeting attended by at least six hundred people, the Harrisburg Freeway Study Team informed residents that the route for the freeway would be chosen by the end of the year.[68] A few weeks later, Dexter Jones attended another information session at the Magnolia Community Center in the heart of Magnolia Park. Here, he faced a number of community activists who opposed the highway. These residents reasserted their demand that the state build no road, no matter the type, through their community. The residents told Jones that they feared "a wide ribbon of concrete will ruin their neighborhoods and scatter residents" across the city, destroying their community. Apparently tone-deaf to these concerns, Jones replied, "The freeway is necessary and it will be built. We don't know how, where, or when, but it will be built." Jones continued, saying that the highway department would consider the ship channel route, but he gave no promises. To Holgin, Jones's assertion that the department was considering the ship channel struck a false note. It seemed simply to be the department's way of trying to "pacify people."[69]

These two meetings signaled that the debate around the Harrisburg Freeway extension was far from over. Undeterred and unwilling to abandon ten years of planning and expense, officials took new steps to try to get the project back on track. In January 1973, the Harrisburg Freeway Study Team announced its conclusion: Corridor A, the route through the heart of Harrisburg and Magnolia Park, was the best route for the roadway.[70] The highway department accepted the study team's conclusion, and, having held the required public meetings, settled the route. Initial construction was still years away, however, and many residents continued to vocally object to the highway. After the route was decided upon, the terrain of the debate shifted once again, centering this time on the definition of the communities through which the road would run.

In the early 1970s, the Texas Highway Department released the draft environmental impact statement for the Harrisburg extension, and the Neighborhood Improvement Program of the Houston Department of Planning released its plan for Magnolia Park. The reports placed the character of East End neighborhoods at their center and pushed a debate about the future of the area to the fore of the freeway debate. The reports offered competing infrastructural visions for the community. In their depictions of Magnolia Park, the Second Ward, and Harrisburg, each report provided evidence for readers looking either for justification to build or reasons to repudiate the freeway, and each was fraught with a political agenda of its own. On one hand, both reports highlighted the institutionalized problems and underserved populations of the East End, seemingly corroborating residents' complaints about the struggles their neighborhoods had faced as a result of underinvestment from the city and the concentration of industry. On the other hand, they both also substantiated some of the claims that proponents of the road had made when they had said that the freeway would not greatly change residents' lives, and painted most of the East End as already dilapidated. To freeway advocates, the problems highlighted in the reports legitimated the proposed destruction of the section of the neighborhoods needed for the freeway. The opponents felt the reports misrepresented their communities. Residents asserted that, far from neglected, their neighborhoods were vital and functional. While acknowledging that the East End had problems, they argued that finding solutions to those problems was within reach; it simply required an increase in resources, not wholesale destruction. This clash over how to perceive and improve the East End would dominate the remainder of the debate around the Harrisburg Freeway extension. The two reports held the spotlight, with both sides exerting a great deal of effort to bend the reports to meet their ends.

Supported by Model Cities funding, Houston's Neighborhood Improvement Program aimed to better the lives of the poorest residents of the city by upgrading their homes and neighborhoods. The program began in the early 1970s and was directed by the Houston Department of Planning. Like the Harrisburg Freeway Study Team, the department conducted neighborhood surveys as part of its planning process. In this case, the planners solicited residents' opinions about the problems they faced in a variety of areas.

The Magnolia Park survey reported that residents were concerned about issues such as poor drainage, too few streetlights, and a lack of parking spaces. The pending highway loomed over the Magnolia Park plan of work and became one of the major issues the program attempted to address. Meanwhile, highway officials wrote their environmental impact statement in order to satisfy the requirements of the National Environmental Policy Act. The document detailed the plans for the Harrisburg Freeway and demonstrated how officials viewed the communities abutting the proposed road. Both the Neighborhood Improvement Program report and the EIS highlighted the arguments that activists and officials had used in their attempts to influence the outcome of the debate and shed light on the ways in which the potential highway was influencing the shape and meaning of the communities that it would run through.

In their delineation of the boundaries of East Houston, both the Neighborhood Improvement Program's plan of work and the EIS demonstrated how the proposed freeway might alter the definition of the neighborhoods. The Neighborhood Improvement Program defined Magnolia Park using one natural boundary, Brays Bayou; two manmade boundaries, the ship channel and the Houston Belt & Terminal railroad tracks; and one imagined boundary, the proposed Harrisburg Freeway.[71] The EIS acknowledged the same boundaries and asserted that because of these preexisting borders, the roadway's route would not cause "any division or disruption of established communities."[72] Even as ink, then, the route that highway officials drew on official maps restructured the communities and landscapes it would eventually disrupt.

The two reports captured the contradictory understandings of the road's proponents and opponents about East Houston. When highway and development proponents looked at East Houston communities, they saw, just as they had with the Third and Fifth Wards, ample chunks of land covered by decrepit or abandoned structures.[73] When East Houston residents looked, they saw their homes. Maggie Landron once again articulated the viewpoint of many Mexican-American residents when she claimed, in a *Papel Chicano* article, that while the "second ward barrios may not mean much to the Anglos of East End or to Mayor Welch . . . they are home to those Chicanos living there."[74] These clashing conceptions of the same landscape and of the potential changes the freeway could bring show how the debate surrounding it quickly became about the future shape of East Houston.

Given that its mission was to find ways to improve the neighborhood it studied, it should perhaps not be surprising that the Neighborhood Improvement Program's findings corroborated the perceptions of community members themselves about their neighborhoods and diverged from the picture of the East End projected by the highway department's rhetoric. The report stated that 72 percent of homes in Magnolia Park were either in excellent condition or needed only minor repairs. Of the remaining 28 percent, only 27 percent required some form of major repair, and just 1 percent were completely unsound.[75] Given that Magnolia Park, as a stable Mexican-American, working-class community, was representative of the neighborhoods that surrounded it, it can be assumed that similar conditions existed in those communities.

Despite the study's conclusion that Magnolia Park and its surrounding communities were far from decrepit, highway officials continued to argue that the road was needed to revitalize a downtrodden neighborhood. In the EIS, officials asserted that the route they had chosen would "enable the parks, playgrounds, historic sites, churches and other community facilities to be utilized more fully."[76] To residents whose homes stood alongside the proposed route, who worked in one of the soon-to-be-razed businesses, or worshiped at one of the two churches in the highway's path, the neighborhood was already used "fully."[77] Once again led by Richard Holgin, these residents would make another push against the freeway plans, gaining a substantial assist from federal regulators and a stagnating state and national economy along the way.

While the Neighborhood Improvement Program's conclusions were encouraging for highway proponents, the federal oversight involved with the EIS made the document the most significant remaining opportunity to slow the freeway's construction. Aware that the requirements of the National Environmental Policy Act made it harder to get projects approved, Richard Holgin moved to make the regulations work in the opposition's favor. He knew the EIS would face federal scrutiny and planned to jump on any errors that federal regulators highlighted. Holgin linked the Harrisburg fight to other freeway revolts taking place across the country. Pointing to the contemporary North Expressway fight in San Antonio as well as similar battles in Boston, Miami, Baltimore, and San Francisco, he announced at one public meeting that the national mood toward highways had shifted: citizen resistance efforts across the nation meant that "highways are no longer gods."[78]

The Environmental Protection Agency's rejection of the Harrisburg Freeway EIS in September 1973 gave anti-freeway activists their best chance to stop the road.[79] Holgin, in a speech before the City Council in October 1973, pointed out that between the release of the routing information and the publication of the EIS, the displacement projections had increased considerably. The original estimate of 900 homes had increased to 1,244 in the EIS, with a final displacement of 4,000 residents.[80] Holgin also lambasted a comment that William Ward, a state highway engineer, had made after the EPA ruling had been announced. In response to the ruling, Ward had commented that the Texas Highway Department was not "too sure how displacing people would have an impact on the environment. We [the highway department] tend to think along the lines of air, noise and water having an environmental impact." In his testimony, Holgin said residents of East Houston disagreed with both Ward and the Texas Highway Department; they believed that "uprooting and displacing 4,000 persons will have an adverse effect on our community—as a total living organ."[81] Holgin's words illustrated how residents connected the highway fight to the very essence of their neighborhoods. For him, the fight against the highway was not just a conflict over whose view of the road would win out, but also a conflict over who possessed the right to interpret the value of the homes and lives that residents had built in East Houston. Holgin's words also spoke to the fact that Americans held competing ideas about the environment in the 1970s. What was once solely a scientific term was quickly taking on political import as Americans applied it to questions about their immediate surroundings in ways that went beyond just the natural setting.

Continuing to rely on the idea that the highway could run through the East End community without causing major disruption, city and state officials maintained their support for the Harrisburg project. The members of the Harrisburg Freeway Study Team vowed to work closely with the EPA to address the shortcomings with the EIS.[82] The City Council continued to follow the advice of the planning department, which echoed the EIS in asserting that the proposed highway would split two drastically different neighborhoods with different racial, ethnic, and socioeconomic characteristics. The planning department explained that the natural split between the communities on the north and south sides of the route meant that the "logical location of a freeway" was right between them.[83] The continued support of the freeway from highway and city authorities—despite the opposition of Mexican-American citizens in the Second Ward, Magnolia Park, and Harrisburg, in addition to the EPA's rejection of the EIS—showed that even when residents articulated their ideas about the politics of mobility openly and repeatedly, they remained subordinate to the planning priorities of officials into the early 1970s.

Six months after the rejection of the EIS, Richard Holgin appeared once again in front of City Council to protest the highway plans. He noted that the plans continued apace and once more asked the City Council to stop them. Mayor Fred Hofheinz and other council members, perhaps to deflate or at least redirect Holgin's complaints, told him that the Texas Highway Department, not the City Council, was the venue through which he needed to voice his complaints. They told Holgin that any role the council played in routing had occurred much earlier in the process and that any future problems would be handled by the state.[84] In a memo he sent to the City Council the day after Holgin's final appearance there, Roscoe Jones, the director of the Houston Planning Department, recounted the history of the development of Highway 225 and his department's ongoing support for the project. Jones, echoing state highway officials, pointed out that in all such projects, "some objections . . . will be voiced," but that such resistance should not discount the "considerable public funds and planning efforts" that had already gone into the project or displace the needs of the city as a whole.[85] Holgin received a copy of this letter and responded to Mayor Hofheinz. Frustrated, Holgin wrote: "It is clear to us that you, as well as your departments, are in favor of building this freeway through our community." He ended the note by telling Hofheinz that he would no longer look to the city for support, now that he knew "what to expect from the Hofheinz Freeway Administration."[86]

CONCLUSION

At the end of 1974, it appeared that the Harrisburg Freeway would be built, despite years of protest from the Mexican-American residents of East Houston. The route still enjoyed the support of the Texas Highway Department, the Houston City Council, and the majority of white citizens in East Houston. The first stages of construction at the west end of Highway 225 resulted in a cloverleaf to connect 225 with the extension, and several acres of land on the right-of-way through the East End were cleared in preparation for building. However, by 1976, larger economic forces had entered into the decision-making process, and ultimately these served as the tipping point for the abandonment of the route. Because of a stagnating state and national economy in the mid-1970s, the amount of federal and state funds available for road construction fell dramatically short of the demand and the need for new roads. When the Texas Highway Commission decided to mothball several projects in 1976 in order to focus on those of the highest priority, the Harrisburg Freeway was among those placed on the back burner.[87]

Despite the indefinite delay caused by the funding crisis, the Harrisburg Freeway did not disappear. In the late 1970s, Texas State Representative Ben Reyes, who represented much of East Houston, wrote to the state highway officials because of continued questions from constituents about the status of the road. Reyes and his aides expressed doubts to highway engineer William Ward about the wisdom of continuing with the highway plan. By Reyes's count, the number of houses that would have to be removed along the route of the highway was now 2,200, almost 1,000 more than the EIS had estimated.[88] Reyes worried that removing that many homes would magnify overcrowding issues and raise rents on Houstonians from the lowest socioeconomic echelon. Reyes and his staff argued that when one took the "cost of replacement housing, the cost of right of way, the city's investment in capital facilities and the pressure on the housing market" into consideration, the project was unviable. Reyes asked the city planning commission and the highway department to remove the road from the Major Thoroughfare and Freeway Plan.[89] Reyes's rhetoric may have been very different from Holgin's, but the gist remained: East Enders did not want the road.

The financial crunch of the mid-1970s, along with continued questioning of the project by elected officials such as Reyes, marked the death knell for the Harrisburg Freeway. But although state highway and city planners turned their attention toward other routes and needs, the project did not completely disappear. Richard Holgin remembers occasionally checking up on its position through local representatives. In one such check-in, in the early 1980s, Lauro Cruz, a three-term state representative, reported back to Holgin that "the line" remained on Texas Highway Department maps. Holgin also continued to seek definitive answers about the road from highway officials, asking why it had not been "done away with." The only answer he remembers receiving in response was, "Well, it's on hold."[90] In fact, as late as 1989, regional planning maps listed the Harrisburg Freeway, and its provisional Corridor A route, as a site of potential future construction. It was not until 1992 that the route was finally excised from all local, regional, and state highway plans.[91] Even with its erasure from the plans, community members have not forgotten the threat of its construction. Holgin, who left Houston around 2000, returned at one point to visit with friends and former neighbors in the East End. As they caught up, Holgin later recalled, "always, behind their mind, they used to ask, 'When are we having that freeway?' . . . They did not want that freeway to come through there."[92]

Ultimately, the combination of the opposition from Holgin and his neighbors, federal regulations, and the financial crises of roadway funding did in the Harrisburg Freeway. But regulation and financing issues represented ongoing problems for many large construction projects. The unique variable in this equation, then, was the infrastructural activism of East Houston's Mexican-American communities.[93] Without their prolonged opposition, the road most likely would have been started well before the funding crises came to pass. By asserting their desire to control the image and definition of their neighborhoods, anti-freeway activists pushed against the established power structures of Houston and Texas. In the end, their view won out. While a victory of this type seemed unlikely when the fight began in the late 1960s, as the debate progressed into the 1970s the previously marginalized residents of East Houston flexed the political muscle they had gained through transportation activism and other parallel movements, demanding that their ideas of the politics of mobility be taken into account.

Houstonians displayed this new political power on the ground both in the projects that came to their neighborhoods and in citywide politics. As residents, community groups, and Mexican-American elected officials gained a larger say in the shaping and planning of their communities, they also called for a wider role in directing the growth of the city. Here, Houston's transportation choices rose to the fore. In the early 1970s, as citizens from across the city and its environs clamored for better, faster, smoother transportation into and out of the city, residents of Central Houston, ignored through most of the postwar period, built upon the Harrisburg Freeway opposition and made their voices and votes heard with more authority than ever before. It is to those voices, and the mobility debates in which they rose in volume, to which we turn in chapter 4.

CHAPTER 4

INFRASTRUCTURAL ELECTIONS

Transit Referenda in the 1970s

In January 1976, just after taking the oath of office for the second time, Mayor Fred Hofheinz reflected upon Houston's place in the hierarchy of American cities at the middle of a tumultuous decade. "America is moving away from the older, more established centers of industry," he intoned; it was shifting instead toward "the younger, newer cities; to the frontier; to the places where America's dreams still can be a reality; to the South, the Southwest and to Houston."[1] During the 1970s the city's growing stature and economic strength amid a national recession gave Hofheinz reason to be optimistic about the future. Yet, for its many advantages, the mayor also knew that the city faced a number of challenges. Throughout the decade and into the early 1980s, leaders and citizens across the region contended with one such obstacle—the city's essential, yet volatile growth.

Increases in Houston's territorial size and population at once drove the region's economy and caused its most pressing problems. The city's at-capacity sewer system, its congested highways, and its diminishing air quality all signaled the strain of five decades of explosive development. Reflecting on the rampant expansion of the first half of the 1970s, Hofheinz maintained that despite the economic increases that accompanied it, untrammeled growth represented "the greatest hazard which lies ahead for Houston." Without proper planning and "the expenditure of funds now to avoid problems then," he warned, the city would crumple under the pressure of its own expansion.[2] No issue better captured the double-edged nature of Houston's growth than the region's attempts to solve its transportation problems during the decade.

The warnings in Hofheinz's speech resonated with many Houstonians who were likewise concerned with the issues caused by the city's growth. By the end of the decade, citizen action on a number of fronts aimed to address the negative consequences of expansion. In many of these efforts, such as the prolonged fight to stop the channelization of the city's bayou river system, infrastructure held a central role.[3] Transportation issues—congested traffic, crumbling and at-capacity highways, and air pollution—presented some of the most visible and dire problems facing the city. Although building more highways remained an option, a decade of contested construction in Harrisburg, an increase in oversight and public-involvement requirements at the federal level, and the potential of new funding channels for mass transit compelled officials to consider bringing public transit to Houston for the first time.

Debates around transit proved to be among the most divisive topics in the city during the 1970s. Houstonians considered two referenda to create a publicly funded transit authority in less than five years. The first, in 1973, asked voters to approve the Houston Area Rapid Transit Authority (HARTA). This plan called for a heavy rail system through the central city and had the backing of corporate and political leaders. It was defeated. The second vote, in 1978, was seen as a restart after HARTA's defeat. A rechristened agency, called the Metropolitan Transit Authority of Houston and Harris County (METRO), offered citizens a plan that called for a mix of road-based and transit improvements. This plan was approved, and METRO began operation in 1979.

As with the earlier highway projects, during the planning and debate of both referenda citizens used the language of infrastructural citizenship to challenge the decision-making power of elected officials and to push for greater community control. Houstonians committed to bringing public transit to the city pressured officials to support new forms of transportation. But the voices of transit advocates did not rise alone. Many Houstonians living on the growing outskirts of the region pushed for more highways and often opposed investments in transit. Because the passage of bonds for a transit authority required voter approval, unlike most highway decisions, Houstonians possessed a direct voice in mass transit planning. During the referenda campaigns, metropolitan citizens put this political leverage to work by advocating for systems that best served their mobility needs, protected their homes and families, and emulated their vision for the future of the city.

Unexpected political alignments bubbled up and dissolved among metropolitan residents during the transit debates. In the lead-up to the HARTA referendum, city officials, elite white Houstonians, and the Chamber of Commerce all promoted the Authority, and mostly white residents in the city supported its creation. In previous decisions, such a collection of backers would have nearly guaranteed a proposal's passage. However, in a rare political configuration that began with the HARTA debate and continued into the 1978 METRO campaign, many white suburbanites found themselves voting in the same manner as African-American and Mexican-American Houstonians. The Houstonians who comprised the opposing sides of these transportation debates were not monolithic; nor were they naturally disposed to form alliances with those who voted similarly to them. Working-class white suburbanites expressed different opinions on transit from their wealthier neighbors in other suburban municipalities. Despite their recent history of cooperation during statewide campaigns for labor rights in the 1960s, African Americans and Mexican Americans did not have an innate connection.[4] Although this grouping did not arise from a formalized alliance, or extend beyond the issue of transportation, it nonetheless shaped the transit proposals in Houston, influenced outcomes of elections, and changed the political geometry of the region.

While these alignments proved ephemeral, the transit elections marked yet another example of the emerging political power of Houston's African-American and Mexican-American population during the 1960s and 1970s. Even as transportation activists gained access to traditional avenues of political power in the form of representative officials, they continued to augment those tools with traditional, less formal approaches to exerting influence—creating strategic alliances with more politically powerful groups, using public protest to draw attention to concerns, and using federal regulations to slow decision-making. The city's transportation fights, starting with the Harrisburg Freeway conflict, gave African-American and Mexican-American activists another venue through which to claim and exercise a role in metropolitan governance. The assertions of non-electoral political power key to the successes of the civil rights movement rolled into fights around transportation in Houston and elsewhere. Even with formalized electoral power slowly coming to pass, in Houston African-American and Mexican-American residents only gained traction at the state level in 1972, when Texas began to transition to single-member state districts and residents built upon earlier campaigns for human and democratic rights.[5] The HARTA vote was one of the first political moments where a combination of formal electoral power and nonelectoral political actions helped African-American and Mexican-American Houstonians shape the result.

The way the HARTA debate played out—and the subsequent political recalibration by white officials to the city's adjusted racial dynamics ahead of the 1978 METRO vote—illustrate how black, Mexican-American, and white Americans were able to negotiate political decisions amid the rapidly changing political atmosphere of cities in the 1970s. The manner in which elected officials responded—or failed to respond—to the transportation activism of African-American and Mexican-American residents directly altered the outcome of both votes. In 1973, the two populations felt ignored and voted against the proposal. In 1978, officials adjusted, working closely with leaders and citizens from each voting bloc to bring the proposal in line with their expectations. The effort was a clear nod to the ascendant political power of each group.

LOCAL ROUTES, NATIONAL CONNECTIONS

The Houston transit debates, similar to parallel conversations in other growing Sunbelt metro areas, brought infrastructural and transportation issues to the fore of urban politics. These debates seeped into countless elements of metropolitan development. Transportation tied into issues from local control and civil rights, to environmental protection and energy issues, to fights over taxation and economic growth. The transit debates in Houston and other cities force our view of metro regions beyond a suburban-urban binary. Divisions between suburb and city cannot be ignored, especially given the rancor with which suburban residents pulled themselves out of cities through tax revolts and metropolitan fragmentation. Yet transportation debates cut across regions, and the choices regions made about transportation pulled suburb and city together. Messy alignments, and even messier antagonisms, emerged. And in Houston's case a somewhat remarkable, if tenuous, suburb-city alliance came together around the topic of transportation.

In the early 1970s, cities across the southern and southwestern United States, including Houston, Atlanta, and Los Angeles, considered or began to implement mass transit systems. These cities each possessed growing populations, increasing traffic congestion, and expansive metropolitan territories with a jumble of political jurisdictions. Although officials in each city built more highways in an attempt to ease congestion, public mass transit gained traction as a possible way to address traffic and lessen pollution. These conversations presented car-bound citizens and cities with an opportunity to embrace, even if on a limited scale, a non-road-centric transportation practice for the first time since the streetcar era. Despite this opportunity, leaders in all three cities struggled to inaugurate transit authorities that could compete with automobiles and serve both the historical core of the city and its ever-growing suburban fringe. The choices citizens and officials in all three metro regions made in the 1970s influenced their approach to transportation for decades to come.

Voters in Atlanta and Los Angeles approved authorities and initial transit plans earlier than Houston, but only after officials developed multifaceted systems that assuaged the concerns of as wide a collection of voters as possible. Selling transit proved to be the most difficult step in both regions. Many suburbanites doubted that the systems would serve them and feared that they would undercut highway development. Some suburban whites also worried that public transit systems would bring nonwhite residents into their communities, a concern that was blatant in Atlanta but underlay transit opposition in a number of cities.[6] Central city residents, however, were not automatic supporters. Some feared renewed displacements and, inverting suburban doubts, thought transit routes might prioritize suburban service at the expense of their own mobility. The passage of transit referenda required advocates to navigate a sea of often countervailing concerns.

Los Angeles's first consolidated public authority formed in 1964, but metropolitan political divides kept service confined to buses into the 1980s. In both 1970 and 1976, leaders attempted to pass rail plans, but these first iterations scared off many voters with definitive route plans that showed whose homes and communities would be affected by construction and who would not be served. Further complicating matters, the spread-out nature of the city and its conflicting jurisdictions made building broad-based political support nearly impossible. Only after offering a general plan of "corridors" that showed a wide service area, and that did not definitively lay out where lines would run, did the plan gain approval. LA's efforts also benefited from the political leadership of Mayor Tom Bradley. During his time in office Bradley worked diligently to negotiate with many jurisdictions and interest groups. He convinced many white, black, and Latino residents of the system's importance and laid the groundwork for what would become the built-out, multimodal transit network seen in the city today.[7]

Atlanta's system, while lacking a single iconic political backer, had the support of both the city's nascent African-American political leadership, including that of soon-to-be mayor Maynard Jackson, under whom the system would be built and expanded, and that of its traditional leading corporate citizens, particularly Coca Cola and the powerful Atlanta Chamber of Commerce. Atlanta, though, could not overcome the class and race divides that separated voters from urban and suburban counties. After a 1969 vote failed, the city's leadership redoubled efforts and painted the system as vital to remaking Atlanta into a modern American metropolis.

Although a new 1971 plan included both commuter lines and central city service, three suburban counties still completely rejected inclusion. Despite this opposition, the two counties that contain Atlanta overwhelmingly approved the Metropolitan Atlanta Rapid Transit Authority, and it became a primarily city-based service when its trains began operation in 1979.[8] Today, Atlanta's transportation system still struggles to overcome the racially motivated divisions of its origin and serve the whole metro region.[9]

As the latest of the three to attempt to form an agency, Houston could have drawn lessons for its 1973 vote from the transit efforts of both LA and Atlanta. Instead, officials in Houston fell back onto the same process of elite political decision-making that they had relied on since the city's founding. Leaders trusted that any proposal created by planning professionals and backed by the city's political and corporate elite would have the support of voters. Officials underestimated how the political balance had shifted, however, ignoring citizens' growing insistence on participating in infrastructure decisions. Because they did not engage deeply with a wide range of citizens in 1973, the vote failed. By 1978, in order to get approval for a transit program, officials had learned to offer a broad-based plan shaped by citizen input that appealed to central city residents and suburbanites alike.[10] That Houston did not have a public authority until 1978, though, allowed for highway expansion to take root, which kept the region from creating positive transit momentum for several decades.

The transportation votes in Houston, Atlanta, and Los Angeles did not occur in a vacuum and were not solely influenced by mobility concerns. Rather, they were tied to national economic, environmental, and political trends that influenced local decisions and reflected a broader push for citizen control over decisions at a variety of levels. Building from the momentum created in previous decades, the 1970s witnessed the crest of a wave of citizen engagement within urban politics. In many metropolitan areas, demands from nonwhite Americans for political power overlapped with campaigns led by middle- and upper-class whites for environmental protection and alterations to local, state, and national tax structures.[11] While the motivations for such campaigns originated from different circumstances, each helped remake American metropolitan areas and influenced citizens' choices toward transportation.

In late 1973, just days after the HARTA vote, the oil crisis began, worsening an already stagnant national economy and contributing to the start of a nearly decade-long national recession. Compared to Midwestern and northeastern cities, which were hit hard by deindustrialization and the recession, Sunbelt cities fared relatively well during the decade, bestowed with the moniker of Sunbelt as a foil to the struggling Midwestern Rustbelt.[12] Sunbelt cities saw an increase of migrants during the 1970s as many Americans moved south and west in search of work. High oil prices allowed Houston to ride through the national recession on a wave of growth, with the oil industry and secondary suppliers providing a wealth of job opportunities throughout the Houston metropolitan area.[13] The oil crisis and other national economic issues elevated debates about automobiles and mass transit to a national topic of conversation, one that reached even relatively economically insulated Houston.

The environmental movement grasped this momentum to push for investment in transit across the nation and build on the string of national environmental protection victories in the early 1970s. In Houston, groups like the Citizens' Environmental Coalition (CEC), the League of Women Voters, and the Bayou Preservation Association advocated for the conservation of natural areas in and around Houston and pushed for lowering pollution in the city.[14] Mass transit held a central place in these efforts, as it could help lower air pollution and ease the demand for new road construction. African-American Houstonians waded into environmental issues as they struggled to address infrastructural inequalities within their neighborhoods.[15] Several large dumps and incinerators operated within the city's black neighborhoods. The fight to have those locations shuttered and the burden of their outputs spread across the region, rather than concentrated within black communities, was one of the city's earliest environmental justice campaigns and represented another iteration of infrastructural activism.[16]

Taxation fights across the nation in the 1970s also seeped into transportation debates. Citizen-led antitax movements, so central to our understanding of the rise of American conservatism and the empowerment of suburban voters in the 1970s, found a perfect outlet for arguments about excessive spending in transportation debates. In Houston and other cities, suburbanites who resisted transit systems disdained the idea of financially supporting a system that only served the city. This opposition echoed the national tax revolt that reached its zenith among America's white-dominated suburbs with the passage of Proposition 13 in California in 1978. In that vote, suburban, predominantly white municipalities removed their tax revenues from central cities like Oakland that were increasingly run by nonwhite politicians.[17] It is likely that the resistance of some suburban Houstonians stemmed from a hesitance to subsidize nonwhite mobility, but Houston officials' control over the Authority and its tax revenue represented an even larger problem for most suburbanites. Taxes proved to be a large issue for African-American and Mexican-American Houstonians during the HARTA campaign, as both groups attacked the regressive emission tax that would have funded the system.

Finally, while Houston's debate served as a connection between some suburban and urban voters, overall, transit debates laid bare growing levels of jurisdictional fragmentation in metropolitan areas throughout the United States.[18] This was most clearly seen in suburban municipalities voting their way out of authorities for either financial, service, or, as Atlanta made abundantly clear, racial reasons. In Houston, suburbanites from across the region resented that the HARTA plan gave the City of Houston complete control of the Authority. As chapter 1 demonstrated, suburban elected officials already disliked the power Houston officials exerted through the city's expansive annexation rights, and they did not want to create another system that Houston could use as a cudgel in metropolitan debates.

The transit votes, then, reverberated both locally and nationally. They meshed with common patterns of urban development and metropolitan political shifts that were occurring across the country. At the same time they reflected unique political realities of the Houston region. Understanding both of these scales is important. The politics of the region, the mobility needs of its residents, and the realities of the city's growth contributed to the surprising defeat of the 1973 vote and the approval of the 1978 proposal. These votes likewise influenced subsequent decisions. Like the Harrisburg Freeway fight, the transit votes were linchpin moments in the city's development history. If the Harrisburg conflict marked an apex of Houstonians' steady attempts to gain influence over city decisions by contesting transportation planning and construction, the transit votes represented that newly secured power and its quickly changing place within metropolitan politics. Before the 1973 vote, the city's leaders confidently laid out the routes of the region's future in any direction they saw fit. Afterward, many voices clamored to shape the way forward.

CONSIDERING TRANSIT: CROWDED HIGHWAYS AND THE SEARCH FOR SOLUTIONS

In the two decades leading up to the HARTA vote, Houston officials diligently constructed an infrastructure network for a city that "grew up with the automobile."[19] Common wisdom dictated that cities would have to make way for personal cars well into the future. Entities such as the Houston

Chamber of Commerce, which considered itself one of the "prime movers for a mobile city," promoted the personal automobile and saw highway development as critical to keeping Houston on the go.[20] Many remained skeptical of public transit, doubting that any system could solve Houston's transportation problems if even an "intensive road program" would be "hard-pressed to keep pace" with the growth of the city.[21]

Much of the optimism around the mobility offered by highways dissipated by the late 1960s, however, as Houston's growth strained the limits of the city's existing transportation system. This stress was especially visible on the city's first-generation highways. Between 1950 and 1969, vehicle registrations in Harris County more than tripled, rising from 306,870 to 1,035,346.[22] Despite opening more miles of highway during the decade than any that preceded it, the city faced worsening congestion levels in the late 1960s.[23] Recognizing that "an adequate and efficient transportation system [was] vitally important to the economy and welfare of the Houston Metropolitan Area," and no longer confident that roadways would provide the answer, city and regional leaders, Chamber of Commerce officials among them, began to search for solutions.[24]

Despite the increasingly dire situation on the area's roadways, to many Houstonians, especially suburban commuters, the suggestion that individuals would have to give up their vehicles to ride transit or have their movements determined by the routes of a fixed system seemed to be un-Houstonian, if not undemocratic. Many tied highways and automobiles to the free-market, nonregulatory attitude so closely linked with the identities of both Houstonians and Texans. As U. C. Waigand, a resident of Brazoria County south of Houston, told Thomas Tyson, head of the city's Public Service Department, Houstonians would choose private automobiles over transit even if the city offered "diamond-studded, fur-upholstered coaches running on gold and silver rails," because they "have no desire to travel in herds."[25]

While some leaders echoed the sentiments, if not the rhetoric, of residents like Waigand in their support of the city's auto-centric transportation system, those tasked with preserving the city's efficient movement recognized the limits of the current highway system. As city leaders began to discuss transit options, though, they also made it clear that any such system would complement, not replace, the city's road network. Officials pitched transit as part of a balanced system, with most plans including an improved bus system or limited rail as well as continued significant investment in roadways.[26] This balanced approach, less ambitious than a wholesale support of mass transit, stemmed from two factors: officials did not wish to alienate politically powerful road proponents; nor did they want to push too hard and cause voters to become oriented against the concept of mass transit itself. With each step toward transit, leaders acknowledged that "a rare level of foresightedness and cooperation" among "both public and private segments of the regional community" remained necessary to create a system.[27]

The careful work to couch transit within a larger transportation system did not prevent road proponents from critiquing early proposals. Eugene Maier, the longtime director of city planning for Houston and a supporter of continued road building, for example, attacked what he perceived as a lack of respect from transit advocates toward America's roadways. In a speech to the Houston Chamber of Commerce in 1971, Maier lamented that "as completion of man's greatest engineering achievement—the Interstate Highway System—draws near, we [planners and engineers] find no general recognition or applause for a job well done." Instead, "ecologists, environmentalists, conservationists, and a growing number of average citizens" attacked the roadways. Maier contended that the preferred transit proposals of these citizens walked a thin line "between possible success and certain failure," a risk that Houston and Texas could not afford as they continued to grow.[28]

Much of the vitriol directed against transit in Houston and across the country in the early 1970s stemmed from tension over the fate of the national Highway Trust Fund. The topic boiled over when the Nixon administration's Department of Transportation, led by Secretary John Volpe, called for using part of the fund to pay for transit projects.[29] Nationwide highway revolts, growing public interest in mass transit, and pressure from leaders of large cities to allow funds to be used beyond highways propelled the administration's shift.[30] The issue came to Houston when Mayor Louie Welch joined the campaign to use the federal gas tax, which supported the Highway Trust Fund, for both road and transit projects. In a 1970 speech, Welch maintained that it was a waste that "the money must be spent for freeways, or not at all," especially given the reality that "the need for new freeway and improved freeways varie[d] from city to city."[31] Rather than relying on a one-size-fits-all approach, he said, the nation should adopt a more open-ended view of the use of funds that would allow money to be spent on transit.

Although Houston's leaders viewed mass transit as a potential salve for the city's immobility, they also hoped that a cutting-edge system would allow the city to keep up with its rivals. They commonly discussed the decisions made by other growing cities, such as Dallas, Los Angeles, and Atlanta.

As cities competed with one another to draw workers, businesses, and investment from across the nation, Houston's officials worked to outpace their rivals. When it came to transit, Atlanta and San Francisco garnered much of Houston's attention, given the successful implementation of the Bay Area Rapid Transit and the Metropolitan Atlanta Rapid Transit Authority, the rail systems in those cities. In 1972, prominent Houston real estate developer Gerald Hines wrote to Houston City Council member Frank Mancuso to lament that, whereas Houston had yet to take action on transit, "Atlanta is a forward thinking, forward moving city that is far ahead of Houston in implementing mass transit." Hines urged Mancuso to recognize that in the future, "the survival of the city is only going to be related primarily to the strength of its total transportation system."[32]

Despite resistance from road proponents, the expansion of federal involvement in mass transit and state-level support via the newly created Texas Metropolitan Transportation Commission made more funds then ever available to local governments in the early 1970s.[33] On the heels of the locally funded "Road and Transit Study," the city applied to the Urban Mass Transportation Administration in 1970 for a technical study grant to create a mass transit plan for the region. The city received a grant for $516,000 in October 1970 and commissioned Alan M. Voorhees & Associates to begin work on a regional transit plan.[34]

With the Voorhees study underway, Houston elected officials began the campaign to create HARTA and to convince residents that the region needed alternatives to the personal automobile. To sell the idea of transit authority, city leaders established the Transit Action Program (TAP) in 1971. Mayor Welch appointed thirteen prominent Houstonians to the TAP's steering committee and tasked the group with creating a system "desirable enough that we, ourselves, use it. We want a system that will be for everybody, not just a system to stop the other guy from gumming up the freeway for us."[35] Wary of public criticism about a lack of citizen involvement, the TAP plan included the creation of the Citizen's Advisory Committee (CAC), which began to operate in early 1972 and purported to offer citizens entrée into the planning process. Welch believed the diversity of the CAC, which consisted of one hundred Houstonians from across "the city's business, industrial, professional and socio-economic segments," would help spread the transit program to a wide range of Houstonians.[36] By attempting to include a broad slice of the population, transit planners and officials tried to spin the roiling debate around the topic in the region as a productive part of the planning process. Welch also hoped that including broader participation, even nominal participation through a group with no binding power, such as the CAC, would help him avoid the kind of criticism his administration had received for not including public input into other efforts, such as the implementation of War on Poverty programs.[37]

Non-government groups that supported transit also helped to sell the system. Beginning in 1971, the Houston chapter of the League of Women Voters began to publicly advocate for mass transit.[38] In a March 1971 press release, the League argued that the costs of highways outweighed their mobility benefits. The system the city possessed, they said, was "congested; it perpetuates pollution; not everyone can use it; it is becoming unsafe; it is costly; it is not always a thing of beauty—and with our present system of development by land speculation, the freeway perpetuates itself." Despite this dim outlook, the League pointed out that Houstonians were lucky, because the city still had a choice to make about its future transportation networks. The choice was simple: Houstonians could "either continue to accommodate our automobiles by expansion of the present freeway systems," and compound the issues this system created, or the city could "balance our system with rapid transit."[39]

In October 1972, the CEC hosted an "inquiry" into the mass transit debate. The group was Houston's leading environmental advocacy organization and a primary driver behind many environmental reforms in Houston during the 1970s.[40] Although the CEC supported transit, the event offered both sides of the debate a public platform from which to broadcast their perspectives on draft plans. A number of supporters testified to the merits of transit for the region. Charles Trost, the director of planning for the Houston-Galveston Area Council, the region's metropolitan planning organization, supported the system because, in his experience, "what you can afford is what gets done and we cannot afford to widen our freeways, widen our major thoroughfares, or live with accumulative vehicles producing air pollution." In his eyes, the only option was to build a rapid transit system.[41]

The efficacy of the balanced road-transit rhetoric and the clearly shifting momentum toward transit led even some earlier opponents of mass transit to express guarded support for transit in the forum. The executive secretary of the Texas Good Roads Association, Gene Robbins, for example, said his organization could approve of a transit plan as long as road building continued to be an equal priority, and if funding for transit came "from sources other than the Highway Trust Fund."[42] Even with these qualifications, it seemed the association accepted the idea of transit coming to Houston only grudgingly. The only voice of dissent, or, perhaps more accurately, of doubt, came from Dr. George Strong, assistant director of Rice University's Southwest Center for Urban Research. Strong raised questions about the practicalities of any plan, specifically about the cost of the proposal, access to the system by the poorer residents of the city, and the makeup of the future Authority itself. Voorhees planners assured him that the plan would adequately address each of these concerns, but Strong's comments would echo through the later debate and prove critical to the outcome of the election.

Support for transit at the local, state, and national levels seemed to preordain the successful creation of HARTA in the pending referendum. On March 2, 1973, Voorhees & Associates released its much-anticipated final report. Two weeks after the plan came out, the Houston City Council adopted it as the city's official transit plan and called for the formation of a provisional HARTA board and for a public referendum. One week after that, the Houston-Galveston Area Council did as well.[43] Then, in what Texas State Representative Kay Bailey called a "surprise," the Houston Chamber of Commerce announced its support for HARTA and for the enabling legislation then under consideration at the state level.[44] In May 1973, shepherded by Houston-area representatives Hawkins Menafee and Bailey, the Texas Legislature passed Senate Bill 642, which allowed major cities to form public transit authorities after approval by their citizens.[45] Houston planned to place HARTA before the voters in the fall of 1973.

A PLAN AND ITS DISCONTENTS

Upon the Voorhees plan's release in mid-1973, the city announced its intentions to implement the full two-stage proposal (fig. 4.1). In the first stage, forty miles of new system—both fixed guideway transit and express bus routes—would be created. The paths of two primary guideways, which would be heavy rail lines similar to those on Chicago's El, hugged close to existing highways between downtown and the first ring road, Interstate 610. One ran along US 59 to the southwest of downtown, and the other along Interstate 10 west from downtown. Two spurs shot off the Highway 59 route. One linked the University of Houston, Texas Southern University, and the Third Ward area to downtown. This route also contained a planned extension to Hobby Airport. The other ran north and served as the first leg of a route toward the Intercontinental Airport. Any major travel corridors not served by rail would receive busways—planned as elevated, separate lanes similar to today's existing High-Occupancy Vehicle (HOV) lanes. Busways would run on both the northern and southern sections of Interstate 45

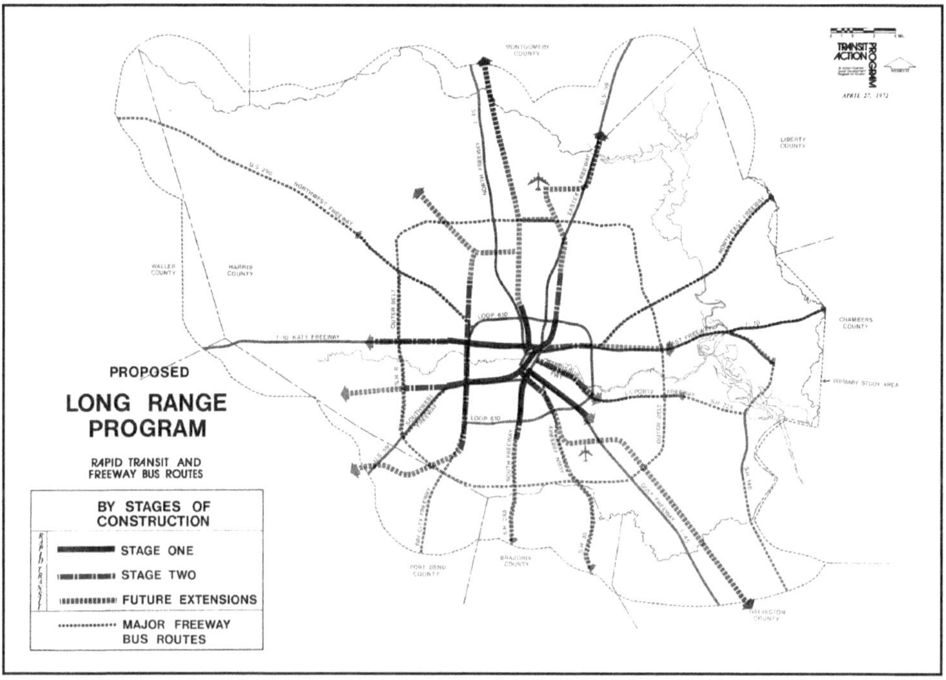

Fig. 4.1. HARTA Plan

The proposed rapid transit plan of the Voorhees and Associates shows the first and second stages of rapid transit, fixed guideway construction, and potential expansions of that system and of freeway busways. The plan was contentious for many Houstonians because of a perceived lack of service to minority and working-class suburban areas. Transit Action Program, "Long Range Program," 1973, Folder 6, Box 49, City of Houston Public Service Department Collection, RG A 20, Houston Metropolitan Research Center.

as well as on State Highway 288. The first stage came with a $795 million price tag. The second stage extensions, which would add another forty-one miles of rapid transit, would cost an additional $655 million. Together, the plan called for a total of $1.45 billion in spending.[46]

Critics of the plan immediately questioned its limited footprint within the sprawling region. Communities of color outside of the Third Ward saw that no part of the system would immediately serve them, and suburbanites to the southeast saw a plan with no concrete timeline for service to their communities. City officials responded to these worries by touting the economic impacts of the system, arguing that positive growth would improve even those areas not touched by the system. This approach, though, opened officials to accusations that they were more concerned with buttressing the economic strength of the central business district and improving the mobility of wealthier white residents in the city and northern suburbs than with serving the whole region.

The makeup of the Authority's provisional board led to further questions about who would have a role in directing the transit effort. Although the plan called for a regional board that included "representation from all local governments," with membership based "either on population, annual costs of transit to each represented government or the amount of transit service rendered," few doubted that Houston would dominate its governance.[47] How the board was assembled would go a long way toward determining whether some outlying areas would support the Authority. Ultimately, regional and state officials decided that the board would consist of nine members—five appointed by the Houston City Council, two appointed by the mayors of the surrounding municipalities within the HARTA territory, and two appointed by Harris County commissioners. This arrangement did not quell suburban doubts about Houston having too much power. Nonetheless, the appointing entities convened the provisional HARTA board on August 23, 1973.[48] Officials tasked the board with selling the Authority and its plan. Appointed with just over a month to go before the election, the nine board members took over the public relations push from city officials and attempted to navigate the debate surrounding the vote.[49]

Given the roiling national debate about the Highway Trust Fund, questions also arose about how the system would be financed. A variety of funding mechanisms supported existing transit authorities across the nation: Baltimore employed a gasoline tax, Atlanta a sales tax, San Francisco a property tax.[50] Texas's long history with regressive taxes led Houston officials to worry that the electorate would object to any progressive schemes. They also recognized, however, that the system required significant local financing to qualify for matching federal funds. Officials settled on a vehicle emissions tax, which the enabling legislation explicitly permitted, and sold the tax as a user fee. Those who drove on, and clogged, the roads, they argued, should pay for the system that would bring them respite. The proposed tax rate ranged from $4 to $15 a year based on engine size—the larger the engine, the higher the rate.[51] In his public pitch to Houstonians ahead of the vote, Mayor Welch reminded people that the "local tax dollar will be matched by up to four federal dollars" and that all the taxes paid "should be more than refunded through time saved due to reduced congestion and in gas saved from avoiding longer and longer waits in traffic."[52] Despite these assurances, as the HARTA debate heated up, this tax received a great deal of criticism.

A final point many observers questioned concerned the governing powers given to the HARTA board. The state legislation allowed transit authorities to levy the vehicle emissions tax, gave them the power of eminent domain, and declared that "the use of property for other public purposes by the State of Texas, its municipal corporations and political subdivisions, and by public utilities and public service corporations, are subordinate and inferior to the higher use of such property for rapid transit purposes in metropolitan areas."[53] Although the emissions tax raised the eyebrows of many Houstonians, it was the rights of eminent domain and the subordination of all other public entities to the land usage needs of the transit authority that became a primary reason for many Houstonians' opposition to HARTA.

With the HARTA proposal in the open, Houstonians began to debate the merits and drawbacks of a definitive plan. Reflecting on the importance of the moment, and advocating for HARTA, the *Houston Post* called for "a countywide educational campaign" to "inform the voters on what needs to be done, on why it must be done, on how it will be financed and on the benefits to be gained." The *Post* article noted that in order to ensure success, leaders needed to "undertake a thorough, comprehensive, neighborhood-by-neighborhood" approach, bringing the details of HARTA to "public hearings . . . schools, civic clubs, and community centers."[54] Transit advocates expected an easy sell, given the pro-transit momentum of the previous years, but nonetheless began a strong push for the system. City officials, members of the TAP steering committee, and the provisional HARTA board led the charge for approval. Transit advocates would not be alone at the community institutions at which they spoke, however. Nor would their opinions be the only ones heeded by voters. As the days crept toward the October election, more and more opponents emerged to challenge the HARTA plan.

The African-American and Mexican-American Houstonians who opposed HARTA—and the elected officials that represented them—voiced two major complaints. First, they argued that the planning effort ignored their communities. Citing their experiences with the building of the city's highways, many publicly doubted that transit would serve their neighborhoods. Second, many considered the emissions tax regressive and called for a different financing vehicle. Importantly, the opposition from the city's communities of color focused on the details of the HARTA plan, not the idea of mass transit in general. Indeed, both before and after the vote, African-American and Mexican-American leaders advocated for an appropriate transit system. As far back as 1969, Quentin Mease, the director of the YMCA in the predominantly black Third Ward, had written to City Council member Frank Mann encouraging the city to address "the plight of the urban poor" by installing "a comprehensive mass transit system" that could provide "all the necessary mobility to ensure equal employment."[55] The nuanced resistance to HARTA of many African-American and Mexican-American Houstonians demonstrated a carefully moderated expression of infrastructural citizenship. They wanted transit, but insisted that it meet the needs of their communities and that it not bring the destructive consequences that highway construction had wrought.

For working- and middle-class white suburbanites, worries that service would be confined to Houston and that Houstonians would dictate policy to other regional residents drove resistance. Only in the close-in northern suburbs did suburbanites feel that the system might serve them. Although suburban opponents echoed concerns about a lack of service and the emissions tax, most questioned the representation on the board and the powers that it possessed. These complaints, too, were expressions of infrastructural citizenship. White suburbanites vested the idea of transit with larger political and social significance. At a time when metropolitan politics were shifting, these residents wanted a say. In addition, though, their view of the proposal remained tied to the concrete details of mobility. They wanted to be immediately served by whatever systems were built.

One of the earliest signs of trouble for HARTA came when the League of Women Voters renounced the findings of a 1972 transit opinion survey it had helped to conduct, which had found overwhelming support for transit. League president Laura Keever announced that the organization needed "to disassociate the League from the survey" because of the "underrepresentation of blacks and Mexican-Americans in the survey sample."[56] In a letter to Mayor Welch, Keever outlined the survey's problems. In 1973, whites made up 61 percent of Houston's population, African Americans totaled 26 percent, and Mexican Americans made up roughly 12 percent. The survey, however, took 80 percent of its responses from white Houstonians, 12 percent from African Americans, and 7 percent from Mexican Americans.[57] The League's withdrawal stemmed less from a concern about equal input from minority Houstonians and more from apprehension that such an obvious problem could weaken the city's overall push toward transit.

Keever worried that the flawed survey afforded communities of color evidence for the "contention that current mass transit plans are designed primarily to serve white, middle-class citizens"; she thought that abandoning the results might undermine this criticism before it damaged the prospects of the vote.[58]

The concerns raised by the League foreshadowed protests that would emerge closer to the election; however, the early summer of 1973 saw few disruptions to the steady drumbeat of transit proponents' arguments.[59] In the June issue of *Houston*, the Chamber of Commerce's in-house publication, president Bernard Sakowitz gave his and the Chamber's reasons for supporting HARTA. In his editorial, Sakowitz lauded the fact that HARTA gave officials a chance to plan for the region's growth. He argued that acting on HARTA in 1973, before traffic became intolerable, could ensure that the city had "the answer available . . . when the real crunch comes." He called on Houstonians to give their support to the Authority.[60]

The League of Women Voters, despite backing away from the opinion survey, maintained their push for a successful transit vote. Led by HARTA board member Mary Rollins and Laura Keever, the organization continued to sell the concept of transit to Houstonians. In an appearance before the Houston City Council, Keever pointed out that Houstonians, whether "housewives whose days are spent chauffeuring children because bike riding is unsafe; workers who must be paid higher wages in order to buy and maintain the car to get to work," or "shoppers who cannot find a parking place," two constants united them: all wanted easier ways of getting where they were going and wanted the right infrastructure in place to make it possible. Keever framed HARTA as an entity that could "save the city from choking on pollution, [and] strangling in vehicle tie-ups," and would also "guarantee to each citizen the basic right of mobility."[61] Keever's words not only supported arguments about congestion and the environment but also acknowledged the importance of accounting for the needs of lower-class, transit-dependent, and minority Houstonians.

The same day that Keever addressed the Houston City Council, the first real signs of opposition and a potential, if unexpected, political alignment surfaced in surrounding suburban communities and among some leaders of Houston's African-American communities. In Pasadena, the City Council voted to oppose HARTA, because they saw "nothing that [would] serve Pasadena," and therefore could not justify "levying a tax on Pasadena people . . . until such time as it [the HARTA plan] has been adjusted to render service to this area." In addition, the community's leaders found it unfathomable that the HARTA board be dominated as it was by Houstonians.[62] Addressing the same council meeting as Keever, Pluria Marshall, a black civil rights leader, said that he and other African Americans could not support HARTA because they feared that the system "would turn out to be a high-class system for affluent suburbanites that would further isolate inner city areas."[63] The participation of Houstonians such as Marshall, who was heavily involved with earlier civil rights and War on Poverty programs, showed that Houstonians saw transportation debates as interconnected with topics such as economic opportunity and racial equality. Furthermore, Marshall's involvement demonstrated that the debates around transportation were connected to years of earlier fights over greater community involvement in decision-making.[64]

These trickles of resistance quickly turned into a stream as other suburban communities began to back Pasadena. One by one, outlying municipalities demanded that they be left out of the proposed taxing district or that they receive a greater say in the planning of the system's services. Some of the wealthier, almost exclusively white suburban municipalities in the northern and northwestern parts of Harris County supported HARTA because the leaders of these growing areas secured service promises—mostly rapid bus service—from the board.[65] However, by the end of July 1973, the larger working-class municipalities to the city's southeast, including Pasadena, Baytown, La Porte, Deer Park, and South Houston, stood staunchly opposed to a system that would take "10 years to get to Pasadena" and "25 to get to La Porte."[66]

Piling on to the opposition act, Leonel Castillo, a prominent Mexican-American leader and Houston's city controller, and Harris County commissioner Tom Bass both announced their opposition to HARTA. In his complaints against the Authority, Castillo criticized the system's financing plan as "the imposition of an unfair and phony tax" on Houstonians and argued that HARTA would just become "another huge bureaucracy for citizens to cope with."[67] Commissioner Bass, who represented many suburban residents in unincorporated Harris County, announced his long-held "private reservations" about the vote just two weeks before the election. Bass insinuated that transit supporters purposefully made the referendum into a special election to avoid the high voter turnout of a November vote. He believed this epitomized an unfortunate "'public be damned' attitude" on the part of transit advocates in the debate. He also worried that the HARTA board would become a "super government," with unlimited taxing powers and no one to hold it accountable.[68]

Transit advocates responded to this growing opposition by ramping up their campaign and shifting their tactics. In order to deflate criticisms against the details of the Voorhees plan, elected officials and even the HARTA board began to distance themselves from it, intimating that the Authority would not have to follow all the plan's details. Willoughby Williams, a HARTA board member, assured Houstonians that, once permanently in place, the board would start "compiling a list of as many alternative" plans as could be found "and communicating with the community about those alternatives."[69] HARTA board members and other transit supporters hoped that acknowledging the complaints of critics and opening the possibility of a different plan would appease voters; the Authority could sort out the details later.

African-American and Mexican-American opposition to HARTA came to a head in September, when, with just two weeks remaining before the election, recently elected African-American and Mexican-American state representatives Mickey Leland, Craig Washington, Senfronia Thompson, Anthony Hall, and Ben Reyes jointly announced that they could no longer back HARTA. Transit backers had banked on the support of the city's communities of color to secure passage of the referendum. Channeling their constituents' concerns that a transit system might re-create the displacements of the highway-building era, the representatives discussed their worries that the board could abuse its power to "levy taxes, issues bonds, condemn private homes and businesses and employ its own police force." Leland and the other representatives wondered whether the oft-ignored central city communities would have to "wait 10 years before they see any benefit" from the system.[70] This concern paralleled the concerns of the suburbanites who worried about how long it would take to see service in their communities.

The effect that such visible and vocal opposition from the leaders of Houston's African-American and Mexican-American communities had on the electorate was unmistakable. In an article published a few days after the announcement, the *Houston Informer*, one of the city's largest African-American newspapers, lauded the representatives for their courage in "acting on behalf of the people" they represented. The officials' actions captured the ongoing undercurrent of mistrust that many African-American and Mexican-American Houstonians felt toward the city and state officials who made infrastructural decisions. Because of their earlier negative experiences with destructive infrastructure projects and their long-running issues with the city's police force, many Houstonians of color feared lawful seizure of property and untrammeled political and police power.[71] The final straw for both the legislators and their supporters, though, was the lack of "commitment to any plan whatsoever in structuring the system" after the abandonment of the Voorhees plan.[72] The Authority's inability to present a definite plan amplified feelings of mistrust, because voters wanted to see concrete details in order to guarantee that "transit lines will not be detrimental to minority neighborhoods."[73]

HARTA board member Carole Pinkett recalled that the effort to convince African Americans to support the proposal suffered greatly because of the lack of a plan. In the public meetings she attended, Pinkett witnessed countless Houstonians ask important questions about details that she and other board members could not address. Pinkett also believed that the HARTA board had failed to connect with the right power brokers among nonwhite Houstonians. The board had made connections with traditional institutions and leaders, especially church leaders and black business leaders, but it had failed to connect with new leaders such as Leland and Thompson. The leaders the board members had relied upon were failing to convince other African Americans to support HARTA.[74] The board also failed to secure the backing of major black civil rights groups or labor groups. The AFL-CIO opposed the system. The leader of the city's NAACP argued that although the city needed transit, it could not risk creating "a Frankenstein over which the people have no control."[75] The Political Association of Spanish-Speaking Organizations (PASO) announced its opposition on October 1, 1973, arguing that although the Mexican-American community "desperately needed mass transit," the HARTA plan was a "shoddy piece of legislation" that failed "to provide adequate public participation, has no defined plan, yet . . . can impose a tax burden upon its entire community without being responsible to a single voter."[76]

The opposition of the five state representatives and the evaporation of support among Houston's African-American and Mexican-American populations, coupled with announcements of opposition from the remainder of the Harris County commissioners and the Harris County Mayors and Councilmen's Association, dissolved momentum for passage of the system.[77] In the summer of 1973, it appeared to the HARTA board and its supporters that they possessed a united political front that all but guaranteed a victory. That united front instead appeared in the unexpected form of the alignment of African-American, Mexican-American, and suburban voters against the system.

In the final days of the campaign, hoping to garner just enough support to succeed, HARTA backers released a final public relations push through the newspapers. The *Houston Chronicle* reminded readers that "it has taken us years to get into our present transportation mess—and it is a mess—and only by starting now can we extract ourselves without bogging down." It warned that either "the Authority is approved Saturday or we will continue to stew for additional years in our traffic jams" and watch as "federal funds now offered pour out of our city."[78] The attempt to link the Authority to the wider acquisition of mobility, though, could not overcome the snowballing opposition and the concerns of HARTA's critics.

COUNTING VOTES

Well before officials tallied the final votes on the evening of October 6, the results were clear—local voters had rejected the HARTA referendum by a three-to-one margin. In the end, despite months of lead-up and constant media coverage, only 16 percent of the registered voters in the proposed taxing district cast a ballot. In areas of substantial opposition, such as the southeastern suburbs of Pasadena, Deer Park, and South Houston, the margin of defeat was closer to four-to-one. The same ratio held in predominantly African-American and Mexican-American precincts as well. In total, 98,457 people voted against the referendum and only 35,680 approved it.[79]

The postmortem dissection of the vote's failure began almost immediately. HARTA member Willoughby Williams placed most of the blame on working-class suburban opponents. Newspaper accounts also chalked the defeat up to the resistance by liberal and minority leaders, including Leonel Castillo and the five state legislators.[80] Thomas Tyson believed that the city had not been given enough time to sell Houstonians on the concept. Writing to inform Jerome Premo of the Urban Mass Transportation Administration about the results of the vote a few days after the defeat, Tyson said that the major flaw lay in giving the HARTA board only five weeks "to educate the public to the need of mass transit in the area and the associated need for the regional authority."[81]

Reflecting on the vote, HARTA board member Carole Pinkett now believes that officials saw the HARTA attempt not as a realistic opportunity for transit, but as a test case for the concept of transit in the city. Pinkett believes that from early on, few higher-up officials actually thought the vote would pass on its first attempt, but that they simply wanted to start the transit conversation.[82] While the previous years of activity around transit in the city contradict Pinkett's perspective, what is undeniable is that after the defeat transit proponents quickly began using language that described the HARTA vote not as a failure but rather as a stepping-stone for later transit development. Mayor Welch, referring to Atlanta's numerous unsuccessful referenda before the creation of that city's transit authority, pointed out that "sometimes it takes two or three times to get" a transit authority established.[83]

The narrative of looking forward to a new plan coalesced quickly, even among former opponents. Newspaper editorials echoed Welch, insisting that "opponents and supporters must close rank . . . regroup and restart."[84] County Judge Bill Elliot, who had opposed the HARTA plan, did not dismiss future transit, but instead called for a plan "acceptable to the people."[85] Clearly Houstonians on both sides of the HARTA debate recognized that the city needed some sort of solution to its traffic and mobility problems. Moving forward from that common recognition, however, proved difficult. Despite the seemingly widespread support for a "new plan" on the heels of the 1973 vote, conflicts around the region's mobility system did not become any easier to resolve. Furthermore, the emergence of white working-class suburbanites, African Americans, and Mexican Americans into regional infrastructural debates meant that new constituencies had to be considered during ensuing debates.

Discussing the HARTA vote, a KXYZ radio editorial pointed out that never before had a measure with the backing of the "Houston Establishment" been defeated, much less defeated three-to-one. Exploring the vote's results in more detail, Houstonians noticed that while most middle- to upper-class whites had supported the referendum, "Blacks, Mexican-Americans, lower-income whites, young people and many other groups" had rejected it. Whereas earlier in Houston's political history, a supporting group could have successfully stifled turnout, or simply expected low turnout, by 1973 "too many Blacks and Mexican-Americans vote to discount their importance." Although the editorial bemoaned the fact that this new political reality had coalesced in the defeat of what in KXYZ's eyes was a much-needed referendum, it concluded that something positive had come from the defeat. No longer would the establishment alone be able to simply decide what was best for Houston and institute it through a nominal vote. Rather, after 1973, political aspirants would need to "go to the many groups who compose our population, [and] involve them in the planning process." And, in the case of a future transit network, they would have to "convince each [group] of the importance of mass transit, both to them and to the city."[86]

REBUILDING A TRANSIT CONSTITUENCY

The defeat of the HARTA referendum forced the city to start from square one in its attempts to augment its jammed highway network with rapid transit. In the first months of his administration, the new Houston mayor, Fred Hofheinz, focused on bringing attainable improvements to the bus system and easing road congestion. The city purchased the failing private bus company in early 1974 and created HouTran to run the system.[87] Hofheinz also inaugurated the Office of Public Transportation in January 1975 to plan and construct an effective system.[88] These steps were limited by a lack of funds. Without a transit authority collecting money earmarked for large-scale improvements or new infrastructure, meaningful work was hard to pursue. However, rather than rushing into a new referendum campaign, officials carefully rebuilt a transit consensus and worked to create a plan that could gain regional approval.

That Mayor Hofheinz was in office confirmed that the role Houston's African-American and Mexican-American citizens played in the HARTA defeat was no fluke. The influence of these constituencies continued into the 1974 mayoral race, as Hofheinz, a young candidate from outside the city's political order running against a handpicked successor to Louie Welch, garnered greater support and turnout in the black community than any other white candidate before him on his way to victory.[89] The embrace of Hofheinz by these citizens mirrored the rationale of the same groups for rejecting HARTA. African Americans and Mexican Americans voted against HARTA because they saw it as a top-down proposal, not because they disliked or did not desire transit. In 1974, they backed Hofheinz because his campaign had worked more than any before it to incorporate their concerns and their leaders into his plans for the city. The same would be true for Hofheinz's efforts to create METRO.

Demographic transitions between 1970 and 1980 cemented the importance of African-American and Mexican-American voters to decisions in Houston and made it clear that white, non-Houston voters would be central in regional choices. By 1980, Houston was nearly a majority-minority city. Over the previous decade, the city's black population had grown from 316,551 to 436,392, the latter number representing 27 percent of the city's total. Over the same period, the number of Houstonians of Mexican origin in the city had increased from 150,000 to 281,331, representing 18 percent of the city's total.[90] White Houstonians dominated growth outside of Houston. The population of suburbanites in Harris County and its four neighboring counties had grown by 912,624. Of those, 695,879, or 76 percent, were white.

Nearly two-thirds of the newcomers to the area had settled outside of Houston, but within Harris County. Another one-quarter had moved to the four surrounding counties. The remainder, just over a tenth of the total, came to Houston. The African-American and Mexican-American populations also grew in non-Houston areas, increasing by about 120,000, with most of those represented by this number settling in Harris County.[91] Houston's leaders recognized that the alignment of these three major constituencies against HARTA had sealed its defeat. They also saw that if a new proposal could hold these disparate groups together, it would almost surely pass.[92]

In the months after the HARTA defeat, the Citizens' Environmental Coalition again hosted a forum on transit with the goal of putting the many ideas for transit and mobility on the table. "'A Fresh Look' at Mass Transit" included actors from both sides of the HARTA debate. City officials, for their part, used the forum to recalibrate their transit sales pitch. Jerry King, executive secretary to Mayor Hofheinz, told listeners that the city had learned a great deal from the HARTA outcome, especially from critiques about the proposal's opaqueness and lack of detail. King guaranteed that "any future authority will actively include and involve representatives from all political subdivisions," whose opinions "relative to mass transit are many and varied."[93] By acknowledging the diverse set of expectations that Houstonians brought to transportation debates and insisting that the city would not fail to account for this diversity in the future, the city began the work of building METRO's constituency well in advance of the Authority's birth.

Addressing citizen concerns about the lack of public input that went into HARTA became a primary focus. Barry Goodman, the inaugural director of the Office of Public Transportation, explained the importance of this task when he asserted that only by cultivating "public awareness and participation in the planning and development" of any proposed new system could officials guarantee its passage.[94] Officials attempted to incorporate Houstonians into the transit planning process by soliciting feedback. A 1976 survey conducted for the Office of Public Transportation found that nearly 50 percent of Houstonians saw transportation as a serious problem. The survey also showed that residents knew of the city's ongoing efforts to confront transportation problems—nearly 84 percent of respondents were able to name an active Office of Public Transportation initiative, such as CarShare.[95] Officials took these responses as a sign that Houstonians were willing to support transit if the right system could be built.

As officials laid the groundwork for that system, they remained keenly aware that they would need to market the new plan to constituencies with very different mobility expectations. The 1976 survey gave officials advice on how to best run such a campaign. The survey concluded that the "affluent, 'enlightened,' suburban segments" of the city were populated by residents who were "most interested in the issue of transportation, and most critical of efforts to date." For this population what was needed was an "ongoing outreach program . . . conveyed by means of a number of imaginative forums and techniques" that would demonstrate the wisdom of transit. The authors pitched an entirely different approach for lower-income citizens. These Houstonians, the survey claimed, would respond best to plans that included "near-term service improvements, new buses and routes and other innovations expanding current public transit service" in their parts of the city.[96] While the veiled racism and classist essentialism found in the descriptions of these groups is problematic, the survey authors clearly saw that no single approach would ensure success.

To get citizens and their disparate visions for the city's mobility systems onto the same page, the City of Houston created the Transportation Advisory Group (TAG). This organ allowed citizens who were interested in shaping transportation priorities to engage directly with the city. An Office of Public Transportation–produced newsletter, *TransPlan*, published in both English and Spanish, documented the group's actions. The newsletter's earliest issue called on suburban and city residents to participate in the creation of a system that addressed the needs of the entire region. TAG members acknowledged that many suburban Houstonians relied almost exclusively on cars for transportation, so they planned for a transit system that could draw drivers off the road and onto buses. At the same time, they argued that any new system needed to account for those without vehicles by making sure bus routes served the areas of the city where this population lived, mainly the lower-income East End and central city wards.[97]

Prominent African Americans and Mexican Americans expressed support for mechanisms like the Transportation Advisory Group, which allowed Houstonians to directly share their visions for the city's transportation future. Dr. Gurney Pearsall, an African American, and Robert Rodrigues, a Mexican-American businessman, both participated in the TAG meetings and lauded the effort. Rodrigues urged all Houstonians to see the transit discussion as a "time for each community to identify and vocalize its needs."[98] By legitimizing these public participation mechanisms, leaders from these two important political constituencies helped draw citizens to TAG meetings, effectively promoting transportation activism. The Houstonians who attended brought with them their personal knowledge of the city's transportation situation and a number of ideas about how to improve it.[99]

By the summer of 1977, the Office of Public Transportation and the city bus service, HouTran, had successfully implemented a number of small-scale but effective transit improvements, ranging from Park-and-Ride lots to a pilot run of contraflow lanes. Goodman and other officials from the office believed these efforts proved to area residents that the city was serious about, and capable of building, an effective transportation system.[100] Using its growing services as justification, the Office of Public Transportation pushed the City of Houston to pursue the creation of a public transit authority. In August 1977, Mayor Hofheinz acted on the suggestion, announcing his intention to form an interim board that could campaign for passage of a countywide referendum and create an authority with taxing powers.[101] By October 1977, the proposed authority had a name: the Metropolitan Transit Authority of Houston and Harris County (METRO). Between METRO's formation and the release of its official plan in July 1978, supportive citizens and officials worked together to form a proposal they hoped would win over the majority of regional residents.

"NO TRANSPORTATION WITHOUT REPRESENTATION": SELLING THE REGION'S TRANSIT AUTHORITY[102]

Continuing the effort of making the process transparent and participatory, and hoping to head off complications that derailed HARTA, Mayor Hofheinz promised that the proposed Authority would "be of benefit to persons and property situated within" its boundaries and that it would serve the "public interest" above those of any single group.[103] Despite these assurances, lingering questions from the HARTA debate about the Authority's boundaries and the position of suburban communities within the agency once again emerged. Most leaders glossed over these issues by insisting that in its final form METRO would cater to the entire region. Warren Henry of the Houston Chamber of Commerce argued that success for transit would be ensured by a "system that is deserving of the support of the voices of this region." Henry lauded the broad-based efforts at citizen participation already put in as "democracy in action."[104]

Buoyed by their previous successes and the initial positive response, the Office of Public Transportation and city moved forward by authorizing the formation of an interim METRO board on October 5, 1977.[105] METRO's enabling legislation gave the mayor of Houston the power to select five of the seven interim board members; the Harris County Commissioners Court would select the sixth for the unincorporated parts of Harris County, and the mayors of all non-Houston cities within Harris County would select the seventh. Hofheinz made his selections with an eye toward building a coalition of support. He named leaders who could speak to "the black community, the Mexican-Americans, the urbanites, the suburbanites—all of Houston." Clearly, Hofheinz planned to use members of the board to convince voters of every class and race to support the Authority. He appointed Albert Hopkins Sr., an African-American pharmacy owner, and Frumencio Reyes, a Mexican-American lawyer and civic leader, to lead the push among the cities two largest minorities. Because he possessed a confrontational political history, Reyes was not confirmed by the City Council, so Hofheinz chose Ninfa Laurenzo, a Mexican-American restaurateur and one of the highest-profile Mexican-American women in the city, to take his place.[106] Hofheinz appointed three white men with his remaining selections: E. L. Oakes, a labor leader, would work with Houston's labor organizations and blue-collar workers in suburbs such as Pasadena. Howard Horne, a businessman and Houston Chamber of Commerce member, would chair the board. And John Butler Jr., another Houston-area business leader, would serve as well. The outlying cities and county court would add two more white men to the board—George DeMontrond, a North Houston car dealer and businessman; and William Black, the former mayor of suburban Deer Park.[107]

The Chamber of Commerce acted as a mouthpiece for the Authority, its leaders proving to be even more supportive of METRO than they had been of HARTA. The Chamber urged Houstonians to recognize that congestion and immobility were crippling problems, not simply inconveniences. The group highlighted what it saw as the democratic and transparent nature of the board itself and the ongoing citizen input processes. It also noted key differences between METRO and HARTA, such as the built-in checks on the board's authority and predetermined dissolution dates if a referendum failed. Furthermore, the Chamber reiterated that the METRO plan intended to bring a metropolitan solution to transportation problems. "Houston is a region, not just the nation's fifth most populous city. . . . We are a community of communities," the Chamber's *Houston* said, and the extent to which residents embraced METRO's plan would "be a measure of their foresight."[108]

With support for some form of a new proposal in place, the superstructure of the Authority began to take shape. Hoping to disassociate the

METRO proposal from the disastrous emissions tax plan of the HARTA vote, officials embraced a sales tax plan as the financial mechanism to support the Authority. The Authority also decided to purchase the existing HouTran buses from the city, rather than starting from scratch.[109] These decisions and other ongoing debates shaped the plan released by the METRO board in July 1978, a three-stage, twenty-year, $3.1 billion regional transit program that would serve the entire region.[110] Continuing to promote the broad and inclusive approach taken during the crafting of the proposal, the cover of the plan trumpeted the fact that the METRO board members had "listened to planners, engineers, other transit professionals . . . and to thousands of Harris County residents" as they outlined the plan.[111] The same day that they released the plan, officials set a public referendum for August 12, 1978.[112]

Wanting to avoid the stigma of unchecked authority that negatively affected HARTA, the METRO board brought citizen input from TAG and public meetings directly into the formal proposal. By folding citizen thoughts into its founding document, board members showed they were taking Houstonians' views of mobility seriously, not simply collecting and ignoring citizens' suggestions.[113] In addition, the plan called for the creation of a group called the Citizen Advisory Board, which would take over for TAG and hold monthly meetings with the METRO board to advise the latter about ongoing user concerns.[114]

The plan itself consisted of three stages that reflected the mix of realism, hope, and caution that planners and the METRO board brought to the process. The first stage promised a continuation of the improvements that the city had started to implement in previous years. Among these were expanded and timely bus service, more crosstown routes, improved bus maintenance facilities, expanded Park-and-Rides, and the continued improvement of carpooling, carsharing, and vanpooling systems. The second stage aimed to ease general congestion through a series of infrastructural improvements and more advanced traffic management practices. This step revolved mainly around the construction of High-Occupancy Vehicle and contraflow lanes on area highways, but also covered improving traffic light systems on main arterials and making grade-separation improvements at some of the city's most congested intersections. The third stage in the proposed plan, which was the most ambitious and the most long-term, called for construction of dedicated, separated transitways on most major highways. According to the plan these routes would begin as dedicated busways but transition to rail or other larger-capacity transit systems when ridership merited such a shift.[115]

METRO officials' attempts to cater to the region's various political constituencies clearly shaped the final proposal. The slow, cautious approach of the first two stages reflected official fears that voters might reject a plan that was too ambitious. The bus system and grade separation improvements aimed to satisfy the demands of intracity transit users—mostly lower-income African Americans and Mexican Americans who did not own cars, but also, increasingly, white-collar Houstonians who commuted by bus from wealthier, predominantly white suburbs to the north and northwest of the city. The HOV lanes, Park-and-Rides, and contraflow lanes appealed to automobile commuters.

COLLECTING VOTES

In the summer of 1978, with the plan circulating, the METRO board and its supporters shifted their attention from collecting feedback to lining up voters. Officials aimed to reconstruct the organic alliance that had derailed HARTA in 1973, but to deploy the alliance in transit's favor this time around. During the campaign, the board experienced success with the city's minority populations but continued to flounder in attempts to gather broad suburban support. Whether they could strike and maintain a balance between large slices of these constituencies while still holding on to supporters in the city would prove to be the difference between a second straight defeat for transit or a resounding, metropolitan victory. The METRO board approached each group with different selling points. When speaking with African Americans and Mexican Americans, board members linked the METRO program with job creation, political access, and improved mobility in the city's core. When talking with white-collar car commuters both inside and outside the city limits, they highlighted the economic promise the initiative brought to the region and the mobility improvements for drivers. To further woo suburbanites, they pushed the fact that the more incorporated cities that voted for METRO, the greater their representation would be on the inaugural board.

Unlike the HARTA campaign, where mostly white city officials and prominent transit proponents had tried to secure the backing of community leaders from the African-American and Mexican-American communities, during the METRO push the board tasked members Ninfa Laurenzo and

Albert Hopkins Sr. with winning over the two important constituencies. Laurenzo and Hopkins did more than discuss the plan with the leaders from the two groups. They engaged with the public through the TAG meetings and held public information sessions throughout the city. Laurenzo also adroitly secured the backing of prominent minority-owned media outlets and employed the pages of *El Sol*, a Mexican-American newspaper based in the Second Ward, to tout the merits and need for METRO to the newspaper's readers.[116]

Despite going to great lengths to avoid many of the criticisms Houstonians had leveled at the HARTA plan, METRO still faced significant opposition. The Authority's proposed powers of eminent domain and taxation, its service area projections, and its structure proved particularly problematic. Even before the release of the full METRO proposal, some suburban mayors resurrected the rhetoric of the HARTA debate and began throwing barbs in the direction of the Authority. Mayor John Harrison, of suburban Pasadena, rehashed a refrain commonly heard during the 1973 campaign when he insisted that "what's good for Houston is not necessarily good for the suburban cities." To Harrison, any tax dollars his community put into the METRO coffers would benefit Houston and not Pasadena, reason enough for his city to reject the Authority.[117] Harrison was not alone in his skepticism toward the METRO plan.

Unlike the HARTA plan, however, the METRO plan was backed by some suburban leaders. One interim METRO board member, the mayor of Deer Park, Bill Black, worked hard for the plan in Houston's suburbs. Likewise, Katy mayor Dan Cox jumped to the METRO side of the debate and argued that suburban cities needed to do all they could to support the economic viability of Houston, because a healthy city meant healthy suburbs.[118] In addition to the backing of Cox, Black, and several other suburban leaders, the proposed Authority had the strong endorsement of leaders from enclave cities such as Bellaire and West University Place. These non-Houston supporters gave METRO officials hope that the initiative would succeed. Officials particularly coveted enclave support, knowing that passage of the referendum within these communities would demonstrate that, at least in Houston, a mandate for improved transportation existed.

The involvement of prominent Mexican-American leaders, such as Houston state representative Ben Reyes, showed that many viewed the METRO debate as an opportunity to improve the quality of life for Houstonians of Mexican origin. At the outset of the METRO discussion, many Mexican Americans doubted that a transit plan would benefit them either in terms of service provision or employment. Reyes asserted that others in the city would be greatly benefiting from the system, noting that "the downtown corporations are going to be making plenty of money out of the $2 billion cost of the system." He did not begrudge them that, but wanted to ensure that his constituents got "their fair share" in the form of jobs. Leaders from the Political Association of Spanish-Speaking Organizations, in contrast, were concerned that "two-thirds of the routing . . . benefitted southwest Houston," and wanted expanded service in and near downtown. Only after METRO officials assured Reyes and PASO that planned improvements and expanded transit routes would be geared toward all Houstonians—and that jobs and construction contracts would come to Mexican Americans—did the leaders give the plan their endorsement.[119]

African-American leaders such as US Congresswoman Barbara Jordan and State Representative Mickey Leland also elicited promises of minority hiring and service to predominantly black neighborhoods prior to expressing their support. Jordan urged voters to "help initiate a new era by voting for the transit plan," touting the access the system could provide to jobs throughout the region. Leland critiqued the Authority's proposed sales tax, but he also admitted that access to transit was so important to his constituents that it was time "to bite the bullet."[120] These officials broadcast their support by lending their images to METRO advertisements run in black newspapers (fig. 4.2).[121] The Authority's openness to citizen feedback and the support of key elected officials pushed hesitant voters and groups to endorse the plan. Despite lingering concerns, after African-American politicians announced their support, a number of black religious groups did as well.[122]

In addition to running advertisements for the approval of METRO, African-American newspapers ran several editorials asking readers to support the referendum. A *Houston Forward Times* article published prior to the referendum announced the newspaper's endorsement of METRO. The newspaper appreciated the fact that "the METRO plan places immediate and heavy emphasis on expanding and improving the present bus service" and that officials intended to direct this improvement toward "the inner-city." The editors of the *Forward Times* told Houston's African-American population to "take a special interest in the August 12 election," because "we will be voting for an issue that will affect our way of life—our very survival—for years to come."[123] The *Forward Times* recognized an essential fact about infrastructure—that it would be around for a long time to come—and that weighing in on its shape meant influencing the future of the city.

Fig. 4.2. METRO Advertisement

This advertisement, run in the *Houston Informer* two days before the METRO vote, trumpeted the endorsement of local black politicians Anthony Hall, Senfronia Thompson, Mickey Leland, and Andrew Jefferson. *Houston Informer*, August 5, 1978, Houston Metropolitan Research Center.

Mexican-American Houstonians celebrated the political empowerment they felt during the METRO debate. Yet another infrastructural fight was now giving Mexican-American Houstonians an opportunity to consolidate the growing political power they had earlier exhibited during the Harrisburg Freeway and HARTA debates. *El Sol* editorials noted that the METRO discussions were expanding the role that Mexican Americans played in city politics. In articles published in the weeks prior to the referendum, the newspaper marked each new endorsement from a community organization as an indication of the population's growing political power. The paper framed the active support of Mexican-American groups from across the political spectrum as a significant statement of unity in the community. When PASO, one of the more politically progressive Mexican-American political groups, endorsed the plan, *El Sol* asserted that its move represented "the frosting on the cake of the growing political awareness and clout" of Houston's Mexican-American population.[124] The decade of infrastructural fights permitted Houston's Mexican-American residents to claim citizenship in direct, tangible ways.

In a piece written in support of METRO two days before the referendum, Laurenzo reflected on the fact that participating in the infrastructural discussions had improved both the community's political standing and the daily mobility of many individuals. Laurenzo complimented the input processes, pointing out that the METRO board had "addressed itself to what the community wants and, more importantly, what the community needs." This engagement with the community's mobility expectations, she argued, was a result of citizen protests against being "excluded from the planning stage and the subsequent development steps of programs that affect us the most." Laurenzo lauded the Mexican-American community for acting as one interest group and displaying "a critical and progressive level of social and political maturity." She asked that, as voters, they not let those gains disappear. She encouraged readers to go to the polls on August 12 to "speak out as a community and demonstrate our concerns and our responsibility" by voting for the creation of METRO.[125]

A cartoon (fig. 4.3) published in *El Sol* the same day as Laurenzo's editorial reinforced many of her points. Drawn by Alfonzo Vazquez, the image juxtaposed two Mexican-American men. The first, intended to represent either a working-class Mexican American or a recent Mexican immigrant, is clearly the butt of the joke. Wearing a T-shirt proclaiming "I do not vote" in Spanish, he is riding a stressed-out donkey. Meanwhile, he is telling his "compadre" that his burro, not the bus the other man is about to board, is the answer to the transportation problem. The second man, dressed in a suit, looks back at the man in exasperation, clearly disregarding his advice, and boards the bus, which is plastered with pro-METRO campaign materials. The cartoon critiqued Mexican Americans who did not support METRO as backward and comically, if not dangerously, anti-modern. Such people, the comic intimated, damaged the reputation of all of Houston's Mexican Americans. Not only is the man a buffoon for riding a donkey, but he is proclaiming that he will not vote, an even more damning fact for readers of *El Sol* who so celebrated their growing influence in city politics.

Fig. 4.3. *El Sol* METRO Cartoon

This cartoon ran the day before the METRO referendum and suggested to Houston's Mexican Americans that in order to be forward thinking they needed to support the Authority. *El Sol*, August 10, 1978, Houston Metropolitan Research Center, 3.

Beyond the two actors, the cartoon also hinted at the economic and mobility benefits the creation of METRO could provide. "Your jobs depend on transportation," a poster on the front of the bus proclaimed. The statement could be read as a reference to the maintenance, driver, and administrative jobs that were promised to Mexican Americans during the METRO campaign or as a reminder of the fact that many Mexican Americans depended on transit to reach their workplaces. Either way, the message was clear—vote for METRO or risk hurting the members of the Mexican-American community who would have found, or kept, employment because of METRO. Finally, the donkey, and the suggestion that a four-legged ride might be an easier way to navigate the city's gridlocked traffic was a reminder of the growing immobility facing the region.[126]

As the day of the election drew near, *El Sol* continued its full-court press with a final endorsement—its own. The paper declared, in a clear generalization of suburban attitudes, that most suburbanites dismissed transit as a service for "the black, the Mexican-American and the poor white communities within the inner city." Because of this negative perception, the paper argued, it was essential for a majority of city residents to support METRO's creation and counterbalance the suburbanites voting against it. The editorial asserted that this would mean more than Mexican Americans voting; indeed, only an alliance between African Americans, Mexican Americans, and working-class whites within the city could cement the referendum's success. In fact, the newspaper noted, such a bloc "pulling together can determine the outcome of the [METRO] election or any election in Harris County and most certainly in Houston." Just as Laurenzo had in her editorial, *El Sol* urged voters to use the referendum as a signal of minority political power.[127] The suggestion of interracial coalition built on the alignment that had emerged with the HARTA vote, and *El Sol* encouraged formalizing it. Although it became increasingly obvious by the end of the METRO debate that working-class suburban whites would not be joining Houston's African-American and Mexican-American populations in a political alliance, working-class and middle-class whites within Houston would act on similar calls.

Suburbanites and central city African-American and Mexican-American voters were not the only groups wooed by METRO officials. Transit officials also worked to gain the votes of white Houstonians who were generally supportive of the transit plan. These Houstonians did not possess the same ideas about or needs for transit as lower-income or transit-dependent Houstonians. But, having faced two decades of worsening traffic, many hoped that the Authority could offer relief. Since this group of Houstonians seemed to at least tacitly back the METRO plan, they did not receive as much direct attention during the campaign. What pitches the board did direct toward this group recycled those offered to suburban whites. The roads would be less congested; the region's economy would grow; Houston would secure its position as a world-class city. The METRO board recognized that while this group was not the most likely to use a public transit system, they would embrace the peripheral benefits it could bring them, and most essentially, were likely to vote.

Nonelected, pro-transit organizations contributed mightily to selling METRO. These transit backers, a loose collection of mostly white Houstonians from the Citizens' Environmental Coalition and the League of Women Voters, worked diligently to promote the new plan, forming a political action group called Citizens for Better Transit. These Houstonians focused a great deal of their attention on the metropolitan nature of transportation decisions and on the environmental benefits of mass transit. Citizens for Better Transit made an explicit, powerful metropolitan argument that "transit problems and needs do not stop at City Lines. The future of every community, every neighborhood in Harris County is at stake. The day we no longer can get around is the day we cease to grow, to prosper." The group countered suburban criticisms of onerous taxation by asserting that sharing the tax burden would lighten the hit to any one group or municipality: "We share the burden; we share the benefits."[128] Having these groups advocate directly for passage greatly aided the efforts of the board and city officials.

In the final weeks before the vote, the board and the plan's supporters attempted to address the remaining questions about METRO. Responding to the backseat planners, those with plans of their own, officials gently chided: "Each of us goes somewhere in Harris County each day. Each of us is a transit expert. Each of us know [*sic*] some improvement that needs to be made . . . but remember: a lot of people put this plan together."[129] The message from the interim board and city officials was clear: the plan is solid, the plan is vetted, and you should support it. In its final editorial before the vote, the *Houston Post* echoed the thoughts of city officials. It told readers the referendum would provide an answer to whether residents wanted to bring "Mass or Mess?" to the city. There were a number of factors to consider, the paper admitted, but, in the end, there was "only one practical, sensible, forward-looking choice. We must vote for mass transit."[130]

METRO board members worked for months to build support for their plan. They elicited citizen feedback, developed arguments aimed at particular groups, and added protections and guarantees to the plan to appease the voters they most coveted. This strategy demonstrated how assertions of transportation activism and infrastructural citizenship had changed the political landscape of the city. Learning from HARTA's defeat and the outcomes of the Harrisburg Freeway fight, officials knew they could not afford to ignore minority voters. On August 12, voters would cast their ballots. The results would show the efficacy of the broad-based campaign and test the strength of minority voting power.

MOVING FORWARD

On August 12, 1978, some 231 residents from the tiny suburban community of El Lago approved METRO by a single vote—116 to 115. In Jersey Village, the results broke the other way. Out of the 233 voters, 117 voted METRO down, beating 116 supporters by a single vote. The razor-thin margins and opposite outcomes in the results of these two suburban cities spoke to a split among suburban voters over the need for the Authority. Despite a lack of cohesion, a large enough minority of suburban voters supported the referendum that, when their votes were tallied and combined with the votes of a majority of Houstonians, the measure passed. Voters moved Houston into to the public transit business for the first time.

Voters in the twenty-four incorporated cities at least partially within Harris County and those from the five districts that made up the unincorporated remainder of the county cast ballots on August 12. Houston, which, for the purposes of the vote, included its enclave cities, passed the referendum by a nearly 16,000-vote margin, 63,510 to 47,596. The results outside of Houston reflected a continued hesitancy toward transit in working-class suburbs and those areas to which METRO offered no immediate services. Of the twenty-four incorporated Harris County cities and five unincorporated sections of the county, a minority of nine approved the Authority. Friendswood, Missouri City, Katy, and the North Harris County unincorporated area led this contingent. All four of these locations were among the metropolitan area's fastest growing and most desirous of easier mobility. Of the fifteen entities that rejected METRO, the working-class suburbs of Pasadena, Deer Park, and South Houston did so by the largest margins. The final regional tally was 80,219 for and 65,883 against, with 12 percent of the electorate, average for a countywide election, casting votes.[131]

The results reflected the divisions apparent during the campaign, but they also demonstrated how political lines had shifted in the city since 1973. In the HARTA campaign, a similar proportion of suburban voters had rejected the system, and, joined by African-American and Mexican-American voters, doomed that proposal. On METRO's go-round, hesitant working-class suburban voters stood alone, and the city's African-American and Mexican-American voters felt assured that METRO would meet their mobility needs. For the second straight transportation election, African-American and Mexican-American voters played a prominent role in the outcome. In addition, the fact that a minority of suburban voters supported the referendum provided METRO with an ostensibly metropolitan mandate and inaugurated one of the region's earliest and most powerful metropolitan governance bodies. The city and its now-fully-employed transit officials hoped that METRO would grow to have a strong presence in the region over the coming years. The results of the vote encouraged officials to maintain the balanced approach between city and suburbs. Officials also quickly realized that passage of the vote would not mean an end to opposition.

The election results determined the structure of the METRO board and shaped the Authority's service area. With only a few suburban areas approving the Authority, the board's makeup would remain the same as before the election. It would consist of seven people—five appointed by the mayor of Houston, one by the Harris County commissioners, and one by the mayors of the participating suburbs. In terms of service area, the Authority would eventually bring transit to every approving entity, practicing "a closed-door policy" in those areas that had rejected the proposal. This meant that even if a route crossed through a nonparticipating community on its way to a part of the service area beyond it, buses could not stop to pick up or drop off passengers. Communities that had rejected the proposal could join the Authority in the future if they passed enabling legislation. If abstaining cities joined the Authority, the METRO board would grow in proportion, to a maximum of eleven members. After choosing to join the Authority, though, communities were bound to remain within it unless state law changed membership protocols. METRO officials were confident that within a few years of service those who voted against its creation would be clamoring to join.[132]

Many commentators remarked that the timing of METRO's approval, in the midst of a nationwide tax revolt, spoke to the depth of the city's mobility problem and the resolve of area voters to address it. One *Houston Post* columnist chalked up the results of the vote to Houston's tradition of biting the bullet and embracing necessary improvements, "even if there was a price tag attached." Almost every commentator noted the importance of the coalescence of black, Mexican-American, and white voters into a winning constituency.[133] For many, the voter breakdown mattered much less than the simple fact that METRO now existed. Whereas a week earlier Houston "had a huge traffic problem and no machinery to deal with" it, upon passage of METRO "the machinery" was in place, "thanks to citizens who rose to the occasion" and supported the plan.[134] For Ninfa Laurenzo, who feted supporters with "margaritas and a mariachi band" at her Navigation Boulevard restaurant, the night was a "double victory," with METRO's successful creation and "an impressive showing of Mexican-American vote-getting," each counting as major accomplishments.[135]

The results within Houston highlighted METRO's patchwork constituency. Election results showed that African-American voters from every economic level had approved METRO, with middle- and upper-class African Americans overwhelmingly supporting the system. The same pattern held true for Mexican-American voters. Middle- and upper-class whites, who represented the largest slice of voters, had passed the referendum by the largest margin, reaching nearly a 70–30 breakdown in support. Although working-class and poor Houstonians from all racial backgrounds were more hesitant to support the system, with margins of approval hovering around the 51–49 range, the results were most likely close because of a less than 10 percent turnout rate for these groups and a persistent skepticism that the city's systems would serve their needs.[136]

CONCLUSION

The passage of the METRO referendum signaled the success of officials' campaign strategy and marked the second time in five years that a majority of Houston's African-American and Mexican-American citizens had joined a plurality of white suburbanites to shape a key moment in the city's infrastructural development. The METRO coalition had one key change from HARTA. Unlike the earlier referendum, in the 1978 vote wealthier white suburbanites replaced working-class whites as the allies of nonwhite Houstonians. This switch occurred because Houston's fast-growing northern and northwestern suburbs all hoped METRO would improve their mobility. White working-class suburbanites maintained their disdain for new taxes and mass transit systems that could not guarantee service. Despite the change, the alignment of these blocs remained unique. That city and suburban residents combined to support METRO differentiated Houston's metropolitan politics from those of its national peers, at least momentarily. Owing partly to Houston's expansive political reach and to the fact that neither city residents nor suburbanites possessed the power to dictate terms to the other, the region did not descend into fragmentation in the late 1970s.

Unlike the earlier highway fights, where physical structures focused political debate and neighborhood streets and homes became the site of conflict, the 1973 and 1978 votes were purely political. The metropolitan discourse served as the arena for the fight. Residents debated infrastructure, yes, but in the referenda they considered structures that did not have a concrete shape. The transit plans, unlike the fully formed highway plans laid down throughout the region by highway officials, presented Houstonians with an entry into metropolitan decision-making. And Houstonians from across the region took that opportunity. In 1973, citizens had rejected yet another official-generated plan. In 1978, they approved one that they had played a major role in crafting. Their approval of METRO gave Houston its first public transit system and presented city officials with a new weapon in the fight to address the city's mobility problems.

The outcomes of both votes followed unexpected paths. The loose coalition of blacks, white working-class suburbanites, and Mexican-American Houstonians who had voted together to reject HARTA reconfigured themselves in 1978, with wealthier white suburbanites replacing their working-class neighbors. To African-American and Mexican-American leaders like Mickey Leland and Ninfa Laurenzo, the role that their constituencies played in the creation of METRO, coming as it did on the heels of their position in the HARTA rejection, proved their indispensable position within metropolitan politics. The votes suggested that African-American and Mexican-American Houstonians could form a potent political constituency in the future. If they incorporated working-class and middle-class white residents from within Houston into a coalition, such a bloc would represent a formidable political voice in city and metropolitan politics, one that could protect and project city residents' interests onto debates about transportation and a host of other issues.

Not all Houstonians understood the creation of METRO as a political watershed, however. Many framed the Authority's approval as an opportunity for the city to extricate itself from increasing immobility, or saw its embrace of mass transit as an important sign that Houston could choose new forms of growth and mobility. Others, mainly suburban opponents of its creation, continued to view the Authority as a colossal waste of money and as an abusive agency of an overly powerful central city. No matter how Houstonians understood the METRO vote, its contestation had provided residents of the region with yet another opportunity to use transportation debates as a means to assert broader political and social expectations into metropolitan discussions.

In its first years of operation, METRO faced a number of problems that slowed the implementation of its systems and opened the agency up to criticism. Opponents of METRO seized upon the Authority's operational difficulties in order to convince residents throughout the region that transit was taking the city in the wrong direction. Accusing METRO of financial mismanagement and criticizing its service failures, opponents drummed up popular opposition to the Authority. METRO survived this early storm and improved its services by 1980. If METRO's approval captured a moment of metropolitan compromise, its implementation contained the roots of division. Officials intended for the 1978 plan to address the region's transportation needs for the foreseeable future, but suburb-heavy metropolitan growth upset Houston's fragile political balance and complicated METRO's attempts to spread resources evenly across the metro area. Houston's relatively peaceful metropolitan equilibrium broke into broader conflicts as suburb-city tensions and disagreements among residents of different economic and racial categories boiled over. These disputes manifested in a 1983 transportation debate, with METRO once again at its center. The results of this debate would reshape the region's transportation system, shuffle the locus of regional political power, and undermine the unique voter alignment that had helped to defeat HARTA and create METRO.

CHAPTER 5

BY ROAD OR BY RAIL?

The 1983 Transit Debate

The scene from the public forum that opened this book occurred five years after the creation of METRO. The forum, and the broader discussion of which it was a part, occurred at the same time that the Authority's suburban constituency was fracturing. That night at St. Patrick's Catholic Church, a divided citizenry from across the region debated the merits of proposals for the Harris County Toll Road Authority (HCTRA) and METRO's heavy rail system. Planning for both systems began in 1979, and the debate around them dominated metropolitan politics between 1980 and 1983. Local officials placed the final decision in the hands of regional voters through two referenda: the first, in June 1983, would consider METRO's proposal, and the second, in September 1983, would deal with the HCTRA plan. The level of citizen input that went into the proposals reflected the influence that the two-decade struggle over transportation issues had given Houstonians in metropolitan debates.

Amid the crowd at the church, a white Catholic priest held a hand-painted sign aloft that read, "Surely, Houston, more imagination than another 20-mile parking lot" (fig. 5.1).[1] The message not only conveyed many Houstonians' doubts that more roads could solve the city's congestion problems but also hinted at the deeper stakes of the 1983 debates. The priest, a member of a citywide, multiracial, interfaith community organization called The Metropolitan Organization (TMO), was there with several dozen fellow members to advocate for the rail plan. TMO turned out in such force because its membership voted to make infrastructural issues, particularly transportation and the fight against the toll road, a priority. For many members, including dozens who lived within the corridor that housed key parts of each proposed system, the debate revolved around protecting their homes, not transportation. For more than two years, the organization and other pro-rail Houstonians had debated a population of mostly white suburban Houstonians and elected officials who supported toll roads. This group believed the roads would provide for suburban mobility and growth. Moreover, most remained wary of METRO and its mass transit plans. Prior to the referenda, pro-toll-road citizens blanketed the region with door hangers and mailings calling METRO's plan "A Colossal Boondoggle," and urging Houstonians to "Vote no [on] METRO Bonds . . . Don't be fooled by more empty promises" (fig. 5.2).[2] These opposing groups and the tense atmosphere of the public forum illustrated how transportation decisions came to engulf Houston politics for much of the early 1980s.

The clashing of plans, and of Houstonians, pushed the region away from the fragile coalition of suburban and urban residents that ushered in METRO in 1978. As Houstonians articulated their positions on the transportation proposals, they posited incompatible visions for the city's future and its future mobility. This divergence made conflict seemingly unavoidable. Suburban Houstonians not only desired easier commutes, but also hoped to improve and sustain the economically and racially exclusive neighborhoods and suburban lifestyle that automobiles and roadways had helped to perpetuate. This divergence reflected a natural limitation of alliances born from transportation activism. The alignments formed around particular projects and their specific impacts, not long-term, interest-based partnerships. When projects finished, or more pressing issues arose, the alliances easily faltered.

While the majority of residents within the city also sought projects that provided them easy movement, they also fiercely resisted projects that threatened to damage their communities. During the 1983 fight, city and suburban officials and residents abandoned rhetoric about balancing metropolitan transportation needs and backed the plan they believed best matched their interests. In the end, the rail plan was defeated by more than 40 percent. A few months later, the creation of the HCTRA was approved by nearly the same margin.[3] The results of the votes led regional officials to orient the development of transportation systems toward the suburban fringe, a return in function, if not exact form, to the infrastructure priorities of the 1950s and 1960s. The lopsided defeat of the rail plan signaled that the influence of suburban voters had eclipsed that of city residents on regional issues. Furthermore, it represented a setback for African-American and Mexican-American political power within the region, which, during the decade preceding the votes, had been on the rise and central to Houston's transportation decisions.

Figs. 5.1 and 5.2. Hardy Corridor Images

These images demonstrate competing thoughts about the toll road and rail proposals put before Houstonians in 1983. Fig. 5.1 shows anti-tollway Houstonians protesting at a Houston City Council meeting. Fig. 5.2 is the front side of an anti-rail door hanger. Fig. 5.1, *Northeast News*, April 26, 1983, Central Chancery Files, Archives of the Archdiocese of Galveston-Houston, Houston, Texas. Fig. 5.2, Box 4, Michael Berryhill Collection, MSS 074, Woodson Research Center, Rice University.

Changes in the federal government's stance toward transportation and urban policy during the early 1980s also affected the outcome of Houston's debates. Under President Ronald Reagan, federal highway officials devolved decision-making power to the state and local levels and deregulated a number of transportation industries. Although federal officials maintained control over the amount of money devoted to transportation, they deferred to their state-level counterparts in project priorities and allocation. State officials, in turn, relied more on local actors, giving Houstonians and their elected officials more power than ever to shape their city. Devolution also strengthened citizen oversight and environmental protection measures that were put into place in the late 1960s and early 1970s by giving citizens even more direct input into infrastructure decisions.[4]

Not all federal policies benefited local decision-makers and citizens, however. The Reagan administration drastically cut back on funds devoted to mass transit, for example. METRO's rail project only progressed after intense lobbying by leaders at the national level succeeded in securing earmarks. Cuts and realignments to streams of federal money for social programs sent officials and citizens scrambling as well. Federal support for community development initiatives that had survived intact through the 1970s declined in the 1980s. The Community Action Program and the agencies it supported, which were popular during Lyndon B. Johnson's presidency, were reshuffled into the Community Block Grant Program under President Richard Nixon, and in the 1980s that modest support was removed.[5] In response to these changes, a new generation of community organizations, such as TMO, emerged that relied less on federal dollars.[6]

Beyond these changes, two other major trends shaped Houston and the decisions residents made in the transportation debates. When oil prices reached an all-time high in 1980, Houston stood at the peak of a wave of petroleum-based prosperity that had been surging for nearly seventy years. In 1981, however, a double blow of national recession and dropping oil prices crippled the city's economy. The price of oil plummeted from $31 a barrel ($81 in 2016) in 1980 to just over $12 a barrel ($31 in 2016) by 1986.[7] Fifty-five percent of the city's workforce was either directly or indirectly connected to the oil industry, and the drop in prices led to massive layoffs.[8] In 1982–1983, the city lost 160,000 jobs and the unemployment rate rose to 9.8 percent. By 1986, the rate had grown to 15 percent, higher than during the Great Depression.[9] The economic decline affected Houstonians' perspectives of the city. According to the Kinder Houston Area Survey, a yearly study of attitudes and beliefs of Houstonians conducted since 1982, the number of Houstonians who believed that Houston offered excellent job prospects dropped from 76 percent in 1982 to 11 percent by 1986.[10] More than just perception, however, businesses, residents, and the city and state governments struggled to pay their bills without the profits, economic growth, and taxes that came with elevated oil prices. Bankruptcies and foreclosures were commonplace. In 1986, some 25,000 homes and businesses were foreclosed upon. Bankruptcies, which in 1980 occurred at the rate of twenty-five per month, rose to ninety-three a month by 1984, with retail, real estate, and energy businesses the hardest hit.[11]

On top of the economic changes, a massive influx of immigrants from Central American and Asian countries altered the demographic makeup of the city and reshaped its settlement patterns. Approximately 100,000 Central Americans and 50,000 Southeast Asians came to the city during the 1980s.[12] Because of their larger number, Central American immigrants were most directly linked with the shifts occurring throughout the metropolitan area. Predominantly from the war-torn countries of El Salvador and Guatemala, these immigrants settled outside of traditional Mexican-American neighborhoods on Houston's east side, giving Houston a diverse Latino population. Both Central American and Asian immigrants moved into West Houston apartment complexes originally constructed to house white-collar workers prior to the economic bust. Seemingly overnight, the ethnic makeup of entire sections of the city changed.[13] The combination of economic uncertainty and new residents increased competition for resources and raised the stakes of regional debates.[14]

Despite their connections to national and international trends, most Houstonians framed the transportation debates in decidedly local, infrastructural terms. A close examination of Houstonians' participation in the contests shows that many citizens dealt with the city's uncertain future by attempting to exert control over their immediate surroundings. In that vein, while this chapter considers how the argument played out across the city, it will also look closely at its contestation within the Hardy corridor, a four-hundred-foot-wide swath of land that ran for several miles from downtown Houston north toward Montgomery County. This area was slated to house either one or both of the rail and toll road networks, which placed it at the center of the broader struggle over the systems. Defined here as the land that falls in the rough triangle made by I-45, SH 59, and current-day Beltway 8, the corridor contained just under 180,000 Houstonians in 1980. White residents made up 66 percent of that number. African Americans represented 15 percent, and Latino citizens made up an additional 17 percent.

White residents dominated the northern parts of the corridor, while black and Latino residents made up majorities in several downtown census tracts. The median income of households in the corridor was $21,266 ($56,000 in 2016), making it a solidly middle-class section of the city.[15]

As previous chapters have shown, Houstonians' understandings of place often shaped their reactions to infrastructure projects. Just as conflicting perspectives about the Fifth Ward influenced decisions about the interstates, so, too, did competing meanings predicate the discussion around the Hardy corridor. Many residents of the racially and economically mixed corridor area belonged to TMO. With the help of the organization, these citizens resisted the toll road plan because it threatened their neighborhoods with displacement and increasing pollution. Non-corridor residents, too, held strong notions of place, but because they did not identify with the corridor beyond seeing it as a possible congestion relief valve, Houstonians from outside the area did not worry about the potential negative effects that toll road construction might have on residents who lived near it. In the end, the way many Houstonians voted in the two 1983 referenda boiled down to where they lived and how they perceived the places where they did not live.[16]

Given the political, social, and economic situation that swirled around the 1983 transportation debates, framing the conflict as one between suburbanites and city residents, or blacks and whites, will not suffice. A diverse collection of actors from Houston and its environs participated in the dispute and held varying understandings of mobility and about how the decision would affect the future of the region. Houston's 1983 debate was hard to define. At one moment, it concentrated on a single right-of-way; at the next, it connected with national-level policy debates. Other cities confronted transportation problems that were similar to Houston's in the 1980s and did so within the same national framework. Yet citizens in each locale made choices unique to their circumstances.[17] The plasticity of these debates not only altered the way citizens discussed and understood the contests but also helped determine their outcomes, illustrating how patterns of metropolitan development in American cities were shaped by both national frameworks and local peculiarities.

THE PRIMARY ACTORS

As details of the toll road and rail proposals emerged beginning in 1979 and 1980, it became clear that there would be friction owing to their overlapping routes. At one point, it appeared possible that the rail and toll systems could be built on shared rights-of-way, but divisions soon emerged that scuttled possible compromises.[18] When the city's economic prospects nose-dived, the projects, and their massive price tags, became all the more contentious. Given the see-sawing nature of the region's political balance between suburban and city interests and the gamut of attitudes about METRO, the transportation debates quickly morphed into a skirmish in the larger fight to control political power in the region. The battle lines of the 1983 debates were not clean, however. Some suburban residents supported rail. Some city residents clamored for toll roads. While the opposing sides were not monolithic, on the whole the contest pitted mainly residents from within the city limits against those from beyond them. Many from each group had, just five years earlier, joined forces to create METRO. This alliance dissolved at the precise moment that citizens—especially suburban whites, African Americans, and Latinos—gained greater decision-making power in American urban politics. In Houston, these groups found themselves embroiled in a clash over who possessed the power to determine the city's future.[19]

RAIL SUPPORTERS

In April 1982, METRO made a splashy hire. The Authority tapped Alan Kiepper, one of the nation's leading experts on and managers of public mass transportation systems, to head the agency.[20] Hiring Kiepper, the man who had steered the construction of the Metropolitan Atlanta Rapid Transit Authority in the 1970s, sent an obvious signal to Houstonians: METRO was serious about building a rail system.[21] Kiepper and METRO argued that a train system would cement Houston's place in the pantheon of the nation's elite cities. Houston officials pushed the rail plan, worried that the city would fall behind its peers if they did not.[22] This trope—the idea that a city's transportation structures equated to or reflected its progress and growth—held a central place in the rhetoric of both sides during the debates.[23] With the backing of city leaders, Kiepper and the staff of transit veterans he imported from Atlanta expanded and accelerated the development of the rail plan that METRO began formulating in 1980.[24]

METRO's rail proposal walked the line of balanced suburb-city service that the agency had promised during the 1978 campaign. As we saw in chapter 4, in an effort to garner the support of residents in both areas, METRO officials had embraced approaches that evenly distributed the consequences and benefits of transportation structures across both the city and its suburbs. METRO sold rail to suburban voters by touting the plan's intention to connect the job centers of West Houston to the homes of commuters north of the city. For city residents, METRO echoed its 1978 campaign, promising that the line would provide improved movement for all city dwellers, especially transit-dependent residents from the near north side.[25]

Impressed by the balanced elements of the rail plan and convinced that such a system offered the best way forward, TMO became one of the staunchest supporters of METRO's rail efforts. The organization modeled itself on the San Antonio–based Communities Organized for Public Service (COPS) and its umbrella organization the Industrial Areas Foundations (IAF).[26] It also directly built upon the successes of community organizations and the citizen empowerment efforts of the civil rights movement and the War on Poverty.[27] TMO and COPS departed from the course set by IAF founder Saul Alinsky by depending less on direct confrontation and civil disobedience and more on working to cultivate local leadership, create long-term connections between organizers and members, and foster close relationships with church groups. They also used a process called relational organization—which empowered residents and members to create the group's agenda—to address the multifaceted issues facing member communities.[28] Building as it did on so many influential precursors, TMO's work represented a culmination of citizen participation efforts in local governance. The group aimed to meaningfully incorporate marginalized Houstonians into civic governance by systematizing political action, carefully organizing communities, and directly acting on the concerns of members. The Hardy corridor and road-rail debate became one venue through which TMO would take these actions.

TMO's emphasis on citizen participation and empowerment echoed earlier actions in Houston that offset official-driven planning. Rather than act as advocates for Houstonians, TMO organizers aimed to cultivate leaders from among the group's membership and empower them to create the group's agenda.[29] Ramona Toliver, whose experiences with the interstate were explored in chapter 2, belonged to the organization in the 1980s and recalled that the group encouraged members to act on their own behalf. TMO taught Toliver to remember "that whatever you stand for, you stand for. You don't change."[30] Having members in leadership roles meant that TMO was intimately connected to its constituents and their immediate concerns.

A majority of TMO's membership consisted of poor and working-class Latino and black citizens from Catholic churches across the city. A significant minority of working-class and middle-class white Catholics also belonged to the group, as did congregants from a handful of black and white

Protestant churches and Jewish synagogues. Similar to COPS, TMO secured financial support through dues paid by member congregations, which gave the groups an independence that previous community organizations had not possessed.[31] TMO's relational organization strived to bring marginalized Houstonians into civic discourse by empowering them as leaders and by acting on the issues members identified as most pressing. In its first years of organizing, TMO tackled a disparate slate of topics, including immigration reform, voting rights, transportation, and government accountability. The approach allowed the organization to quickly assemble a large constituency. At its peak in 1980, TMO brought members together from nearly eighty religious congregations.[32]

TMO appealed to many Houstonians of faith because of its emphasis on self-help, citizen empowerment, and mission for social good. These tenets meshed particularly well with Catholic beliefs that touted service to the poor and personal liberation.[33] The city had a diverse Catholic population that included African Americans from Louisiana, Mexican Americans, white Houstonians, and, increasingly during the early 1980s, Central American immigrants.[34] TMO's rise coincided with a moment when the broader Catholic Church and the leaders of the Archdiocese of Galveston-Houston were confronting two decades of immense change and theological revolution. Vatican II, the rise of liberation theology in Latin America, and the social action demands of the civil rights and Chicano movements all challenged the church to help alleviate poverty and inequality.[35]

During the late 1960s and 1970s, many Catholic leaders in Texas, including those in Houston, had responded to the desires of their lay members by offering support for the social causes pushed by Mexican-American and African-American congregants. While Catholic Church officials in Houston and Texas had reacted strongly against the radical actions by some congregants during the Chicano movement, by the mid-1970s most Catholic leaders had begun to support campaigns for social justice.[36] In the mid-1970s, John Morkovsky, bishop of the Archdiocese of Galveston-Houston, had backed the formation of the Metropolitan Ministries, a predecessor to TMO.[37] Morkovsky, his auxiliary bishop, John McCarthy, and several prominent priests had backed TMO from its inception.[38] These leaders recognized that such organizations not only adhered to Catholic teachings, but improved the communities of their congregants and brought Catholics from across the city together. In addition, they served to shore up loyalty to the Catholic Church. The early 1980s was a time when Pentecostal churches were gaining ground on the Catholic Church in Latin America and within immigrant populations in the United States. Catholic Church leaders recognized that supporting groups like TMO might help keep parishioners content and prevent an exodus to other Christian denominations.[39]

The fact that TMO consisted of mainly Catholics and received such support from the Catholic Church differentiates the group from other community organizations that were shaped by the leadership of other Christian churches. In the South, African-American churches had a long history of participation in a variety of political causes, none more prominent than their leadership during the civil rights movement. These denominations had different interactions with and perspectives toward the activism of their congregants than the Catholic Church. Houston's Protestant and Jewish congregations did get involved with the group, but did so to a lesser extent than the city's Catholics. Although both traditions had long histories of engagement with social justice causes, the decentralized structure of Protestant congregations—and TMO's struggles to convince non-Catholic groups that their interests would be valued in a group dominated by Catholics and Latinos—made recruiting these congregations difficult. Once the balanced, participatory methods of TMO and the power of citywide collective action became clear, several synagogues and Protestant congregations joined the group.[40]

TMO's effectiveness as a political organization rested on the religious institutions from which it drew its members. As stable community anchors with dedicated members and deep connections to distinct parts of the city, church communities provided many resources from which TMO could draw. The knitting together of religious institutions cultivated a network of racially and economically diverse residents from across the city, forming a formidable political coalition. Unlike the neighborhood-level resistance of the Houstonians who had organized against the Outer Belt or the Harrisburg Freeway, TMO's citywide constituency had a broader set of concerns and could bring greater pressure to bear on politicians.

TMO combined traditional electoral significance—its role as a mouthpiece for thousands of religious Houstonians—with progressive, often confrontational political tactics to bring attention to the issues it wanted to address. Once members identified transportation as a major topic of interest, TMO engaged deeply with debates and forwarded members' perspectives on the region's infrastructural choices. The group advocated for the provision of adequate access to mobility systems for all the city's residents and called for greater citizen input in the transportation decision-making process. Propelled by the concerns of its members, TMO became one of the main combatants in the 1983 debates. Residents of the Hardy corridor wanted to protect their homes. Black and Latino members living in neighborhoods underserved by buses hoped the rail plan would make their daily movements less stressful. TMO campaigned to secure each of these outcomes, and in the process a diverse constituency of Houstonians worked together to shape the city's future. The group invested a good deal of its political capital into the rail plan and pressured local, county, and state leaders to reject toll roads.

As groups like TMO joined METRO and other city officials in backing the rail plan, they elevated the stakes of the transportation debate. The involvement of TMO and other citizens made it clear that, like the HARTA and METRO decisions, the 1983 debates would not be settled by officials alone. Residents took full advantage of federal devolution and citizen oversight mechanisms to participate in the debates.[41] Rail proponents argued that the system could solve the metropolitan area's traffic problems, vault Houston into the national elite, and balance the needs of both the central core and the booming suburbs. Just as pro-rail citizens felt strongly about rail and exercised their right to participate in the decision-making process, however, so, too, did supporters of the toll system feel warranted in pushing back against the rail plan and advocating for toll roads.

TOLL ROAD SUPPORTERS

As Kiepper and his METRO staff busily drew up rail plans and consolidated support, toll road proponents promoted their system. Offered first by the Texas Turnpike Authority (TTA) in 1979, the toll road plan took off after Harris County Judge Jon Lindsay proposed the creation of a county-run toll system. County officials, including Lindsay, recognized that metropolitan-level decisions offered an avenue through which they could attain more political power. Buoyed by burgeoning suburban populations and the defection of these communities from METRO, county politicians strengthened their hold on power by catering to non-city voters and vesting themselves with greater governing authority through metropolitan bodies like the HCTRA.[42] In selling the toll road plan, promoters argued that a user-fee approach would provide funding for infrastructure at a time of shrinking federal budgets and ballooning local needs.[43] Furthermore, HCTRA backers pointed out, creating a toll road authority would put control of the metropolitan area's roadways into local hands.

Structured to benefit the political aims of county officials and the transportation needs of suburban residents, the toll road proposal scrapped the balanced approach to metropolitan transportation. It offered few projects that aided the central city, focusing instead on facilitating the movement of suburban residents into and out of downtown. Despite the fact that the toll roads would only reach certain sections of the city, just like the rail system, Lindsay shrewdly sold the toll roads as something that would improve the mobility of the entire metropolitan area. This tactic allowed the HCTRA to gain broad support, unlike METRO, which failed to convince voters that the rail system would be a metropolitan solution. Pitching the system as a whole, rather than attempting to fight over its individual parts, also allowed supporters to avoid becoming mired in particularly divisive debates, such as those around the Hardy corridor.

White suburbanites took an active role in the debates, most often supporting the toll road plan because they felt it would be cheaper than rail, and doubted that METRO and Houston officials had their best interests at heart. Some suburbanites, and many city residents, for that manner, did not support transit because they feared allowing systems into the suburbs and exclusive neighborhoods would lead to nonwhite and poorer citizens moving into those areas. The actions suburbanites took in the debates demonstrated that the region was becoming increasingly fragmented. While Houston officials effectively avoided this problem during the METRO decision, city leaders could no longer ignore the demands of increasingly powerful suburban constituencies and jurisdictions. As they grew in population and political power, these entities threatened to separate themselves from Houston's control.[44] In hopes of stemming some of the calls for autonomy, Houston officials catered more and more to suburban voters and their officials.

Beyond suburban politicians and residents, the most politically influential promoter of the toll road plan was the Houston Chamber of Commerce. Although the organization gave tacit support to the rail referendum, it wholeheartedly embraced the toll roads and clearly preferred them to mass transit. The Chamber's feeble support for rail signaled a shift from a Houston-oriented group to a metropolitan-focused one.[45] Like Harris County officials, Chamber officials recognized that Houston's incredible outward growth made broadening its message and focus essential. They believed that because roads encouraged development along the suburban fringe, these systems could do more to promote the region's economic growth than rail. The backing of this powerful interest group, one that had influenced Houston policy for decades, played a big role in convincing many Houstonians to support the toll road plan.

As earlier chapters showed, few Houstonians who found their homes and neighborhoods within the projected routes of transportation systems viewed this position as a positive. Indeed, both toll road and rail plans elicited a number of not-in-my-backyard (NIMBY) reactions from residents across the city. Outside of TMO member objections about the tollway in the Hardy corridor, some of the loudest complaints came from elite Houstonians who lived along the southwestern leg of the proposed rail system in the Rice University, Bellaire, and Montrose areas. While NIMBY responses to infrastructure projects were by no means new, as land for rights-of-way became increasingly difficult to secure in Houston, officials confronted greater citizen pushback than ever before.[46] In the lead-up to the 1983 votes, most Houstonians agreed that something needed to be done about the city's traffic problems, but no one—not the working-class residents of the northern Fifth Ward nor the middle- to upper-class residents of Bellaire—wanted the solution to run through their communities.

THE HARDY CORRIDOR AND THE ROOTS OF DEBATE

The roots of the 1983 transportation referenda can be traced to 1979 and 1980, when the TTA first proposed a regional toll system with a leg running through the Hardy corridor, and METRO proposed a plan for a West Houston rail line that would later expand to include a line through the Hardy corridor. The announcements instigated a metropolitan-wide debate that persisted until the day came to vote. TMO, led by white, Latino, and black members who lived in the corridor, rose to prominence during these initial discussions and objected to the TTA's plans by articulating a place-based defense of their neighborhoods. This opening salvo defined the actors, rhetoric, and parameters of the 1983 referendum campaigns.

In early 1979, when the TTA announced that it would study the possibility of bringing toll roads to Houston, it initiated studies for three possible routes—one along Hardy Street, one through the Westpark corridor, and one that followed the much-contested Harrisburg route.[47] Given the tensions around highways in East Houston, the Harrisburg route was quickly dismissed, leaving only the Hardy and Westpark routes as possibilities. Eventually, the TTA concluded that the Hardy corridor presented the most feasible option for the first arm of a broader toll road network. With the support of Houston officials, the TTA conducted a feasibility study on the Hardy Toll

Road near the end of 1979.[48] In its final assessment of the corridor's suitability, the TTA asserted that a toll road could only succeed in the corridor if "no directly competing toll road or other expressway-type facilities . . . or mass transit projects" were built in or near the area.[49] This conclusion made the stakes over controlling the corridor's future obvious. The construction of one transportation system would likely prevent the building of others.

METRO forwarded a plan for the Westpark corridor in a September 1980 draft environmental impact statement. The Authority called for the construction of a heavy rail system, similar to Chicago's El or New York's subway, which would run from the western suburbs into downtown.[50] TMO and other rail proponents immediately asked METRO to expand its proposal to include the Hardy corridor. At this initial stage, Harris County officials, the Chamber of Commerce, and the Houston City Council all expressed support for the Westpark plan, but none of them openly called for its expansion.[51] At a public hearing on the rail line, Judge Lindsay happily reported the county's backing. In his remarks he lauded rail as an important first step in addressing the region's mobility problems. He pointed out, though, that "we have a very complex transportation problem in Harris County. It's not only a rail system that's needed, but all facets of transportation." In order to address the region's traffic problems, Lindsay concluded, "we need to work together."[52] Although this cooperative approach seemed possible for a brief moment, conflicts emerged as the details of the plans solidified and expanded.

A rift between the road and rail proposals emerged when TMO and other pro-transit Houstonians refused to give the same support to the toll roads that county and suburban officials had given to rail. TMO immediately criticized the toll road proposal's potential impact on the Hardy corridor and called for extending the rail line into the corridor. Well aware of earlier damaging highway projects, TMO argued that a toll road would create long-term problems for residents in the area. The road would bring "increased air pollution, wasteful energy use . . . increased runoff and flooding, and aesthetic blight" to the neighborhoods through which it ran. TMO called upon citizens to embrace the "cleaner, safer, and more efficient" option of mass transit, insisting that the "primary concern for transportation in Houston in the next twenty to thirty years" needed to be a "focus on how best to move more people, not more automobiles."[53]

TMO also contended that the Hardy Toll Road's true purpose was to benefit a small cohort of builders and developers with vested interests along and at the end of the route. As we saw in chapters 1 and 2, developers possessed significant power in directing, and benefiting from, Houston's growth. This reality had not disappeared by the 1980s. The Houston Planning Commission still consisted mainly of men with direct ties to construction industries. In addition, Houston mayor Jim McConn and Harris County Judge Jon Lindsay owned construction firms involved in suburban development, and both received campaign support from development interests.[54] Many residents from the Hardy corridor believed the road was planned only as a way to benefit these developers and the communities they built north of the city, such as the Woodlands.[55] By highlighting what they saw as insider politics, TMO and other rail advocates hoped to dispel the "regional good" rhetoric of the toll road's proponents.

Finally, TMO asserted that the TTA was downplaying the actual costs—both financial and physical—of their plans. TMO leader Brian McCann, a white resident of the Hardy corridor, argued that descriptions of the toll road plan purposefully underestimated the footprint the road would leave on the surrounding areas. According to Louie Welch, Houston's onetime mayor and Chamber of Commerce president during the debate, the toll road's right-of-way would be approximately 135 feet. McCann, looking at other area highways and consulting the engineering standards of the Texas Highway Department, concluded that when all was said and done, the actual right-of-way would come in at more than 550 feet. Such a right-of-way, McCann argued, meant that parts of the bordering communities "would be wiped out."[56]

Despite TMO's formation just two years earlier, the response of local politicians to its protest of the Hardy Toll Road plan demonstrated the group's tangible political power. Many officials whose districts overlapped with the Hardy corridor came out against the toll road. US Representative Bob Eckhardt, who had also opposed the proposed Harrisburg Tollway in the 1970s, derided the potential road as "the same old worn-out solution" to Houston's congestion problems.[57] Dale Gorczynski, a member of the Houston City Council and a former member of TMO, argued that although the toll road would benefit "the trucking industry and Montgomery County," he could not envision any benefits for those "residents living along it."[58] Council member Ernest McGowen joined Gorczynski in opposition and pledged at the annual TMO meeting to defeat the tollway "even if it means lying down in the street." McGowen lauded the hard work of TMO, telling its members that they were "talking loud enough for City Hall to hear you."[59] Because TMO mobilized a vocal set of citywide voters, local officials clamored to support the group's agenda in the early 1980s.

The furious pushback by TMO and its political backers against the toll road plan nearly led to the TTA abandoning the proposal. TMO tried to ensure this outcome by convincing the Harris County Commissioners Court to withdraw its support for the plan. Although TMO representatives made a withering presentation against the toll road plan at an August 1980 Commissioners Court meeting, Judge Lindsay convinced his fellow commissioners to maintain their support for it.[60] Undeterred by this setback, rail advocates turned their attention to the Houston City Council. Hundreds of TMO members converged on a September 1980 meeting. The speakers represented TMO's diverse membership—a priest, a labor leader, a pharmacist, a teacher, and a neighborhood association president all spoke against the toll road plan.[61] In front of the roiling crowd, the City Council passed a resolution that established "rail as a preferred mode of mass transportation for the Hardy Road corridor," but took no definitive action.[62] It was not a complete victory, but the resolution gave TMO and its allies momentum in their fight to stop the toll road plan.

Not convinced that local resolutions alone could protect corridor residents, TMO members redoubled their efforts against the toll road project by joining METRO officials on a trip to promote the city's rail proposal in Washington, DC. Along with Representative Eckhardt, TMO representatives and METRO officials met with the US secretary of transportation, Neil Goldschmidt, in October 1980.[63] METRO officials likewise continued to lobby the recalcitrant Reagan administration for federal support.[64] By joining with local officials and taking the METRO plan before federal officials, TMO actively participated in the national conversation surrounding transit. Though no funds were guaranteed at the original meeting, the lobbying efforts brought Houston's plans to federal attention, and by 1983 a large chunk of funds were earmarked for Houston.[65] Buoyed by federal support, the METRO board fulfilled TMO's hopes and broadened its rail plans by designating the Hardy corridor as a path for a future rail line.[66] The announcement marked a victory for TMO and other rail advocates. It also ensured that the corridor, now home to two transit proposals, would hold a central place in the contest to shape the city's transportation decisions.

TMO's success during the early stages of the debate irked its opposition. Numerous public officials who found their views or themselves the target of TMO critiques expressed concern about the group's agenda and tactics. TMO used direct confrontation—attending meetings en masse, putting tough questions to officials, and demanding that promises be put down in writing—among other methods. Texas Highway Commissioner Ray Barnhart accused

TMO of using scare tactics to drum up opposition to the toll road plans. Barnhart said TMO "mobilized blacks, browns, and the elderly and then invaded city hall saying 'they're going to destroy our neighborhoods,'" without truly considering the importance of the highway.[67] Barnhart's overtly racist critique showed that some white Texans, including many traditional power brokers, still dismissed the political action of African Americans and Latinos as a nuisance and as illegitimate. The motivation for such attacks stemmed from the reality that TMO, with its multiracial, broad constituency, was making real political waves. With his blustering, Barnhart tried to cover up and dismiss the efficacy of the group, but his comments belied the fact that officials were both aware and wary of the growing political influence of TMO.

Leaders of the Archdiocese of Galveston-Houston and TMO staff members responded to such expressions of hostility by arguing that the organization provided an essential organ for confronting the pressing problems of life in urban America. Joseph Fiorenza, the Galveston-Houston diocesan director for social action, urged church leaders to resist allowing the criticisms to corral or cajole the church into denying support to TMO.[68] Auxiliary Bishop John McCarthy responded directly to the criticisms in a letter to TMO member churches. McCarthy told TMO leaders to continue their work with the organization, reminding them that "religiously committed people struggling for social justice have always encountered criticism, slander and worse. Continue your noble efforts to develop a strong multi-issued, ethnically diverse, widely based community organization."[69] The responses of Catholic officials to these critiques strengthened the resolve of TMO members and emboldened them to continue the fight for the future of the Hardy corridor.

The corridor debate became a key part of the 1982 mayoral election. The election marked an end to the first stage of the city's transportation debate and served as a launching pad for discussion of the 1983 referenda. It also represented the high point of TMO's influence and political power in the city. Amplified by the group's involvement with the corridor fight, TMO's agenda received a huge amount of attention during the election, leading to promises ranging from service improvement in black and Latino neighborhoods to immigration reform from candidates.[70] The group's participation in the race and the vocal role of its members in the transit debate mirrored the actions of African-American and Mexican-American residents during the Harrisburg, HARTA, and METRO fights. In all four of these campaigns, Houstonians challenged political officials and forwarded their own visions about the city's transportation structures. In the November election, Houstonians elected Kathy Whitmire, whom TMO endorsed. Whitmire, the city's first female mayor, represented a significant departure from Houston's typical politics. Many viewed Whitmire's election as the end of Houston's "old boys' club" of political leadership, and in that role she echoed TMO's challenge to the status quo. After the election, TMO continued to push its agenda upon the mayor they had helped elect, putting special emphasis on their concerns about the Hardy corridor.

THE ACCELERATING DEBATE

If the 1982 mayoral election signaled the peak of TMO's influence, the ensuing transit debate marked its waning. After Whitmire's election, Houstonians who felt the rail program would hurt the city's growth refused to let TMO, mass transit advocates, and METRO dictate regional transportation policy. Suburban officials and residents, the Houston Chamber of Commerce, and other toll road advocates began to push back against the early momentum enjoyed by rail backers.

The Houston Chamber of Commerce waded into the transit debate with the release of its Regional Mobility Plan just weeks after Kathy Whitmire's election. Given Houston's lack of zoning and subsequently weak planning department, the reports of groups like the Chamber held great weight in city discussions.[71] The plan called for a $16.2 billion program that, while not directly dismissing rail, clearly emphasized road-based improvements on the grounds that such projects were far cheaper and could be built faster than higher-cost rail projects. The plan called for the construction of almost 300 miles of new freeways, 1,400 miles of new arterial streets, and 30 miles of transitways. It also sought an expansion of the bus fleet, the widening of nearly 200 miles of existing freeways, and the resurfacing of older roadways.[72] It conceded that rail and other high-cost projects could eventually be built, but only once "travel demands cannot be met by lower cost options," i.e., roads.[73] Initially the report garnered support, or at least praise, from many groups, including TMO, for bringing the thoughts of almost all the major transportation agencies and advocates into one document.[74]

Despite these plaudits, however, TMO harbored a number of concerns about the Regional Mobility Plan. As with its attacks on the TTA, TMO wasted no time in laying out its critiques of the report. Most of its objections related to the broad "financial, social, and environmental problems they believed would result" from the program. Unsurprisingly, TMO offered particularly strong criticism of the plan's pro-toll-road stance for the Hardy corridor, its general road-based emphasis, and its apparent lack of citizen input. They lamented its continued reliance on automobiles and again called for a system that could "begin now to provide alternatives" to roads and cars.[75]

In response to the TMO's criticism, the Houston Chamber of Commerce and pro-toll-road Houstonians defiantly championed the Hardy Toll Road and the wider road network. In a supplemental report to the Regional Mobility Plan, the Chamber concluded that toll roads were the most economically viable choice, maintaining that the Hardy route would result in fewer displacements than earlier road projects.[76] In the eyes of Chamber leaders, the benefits of the road outweighed the costs it would engender. Citizens for Better Transportation, a coalition of suburban residents and businesses that sprouted up during the debate (different from the similarly named group that supported METRO's initial creation), joined the Chamber in supporting the toll roads. The group played a major role in the referendum debates, often directly engaging with TMO in exchanges that displayed the growing antagonism between suburban and city residents.[77]

The Regional Mobility Plan accelerated METRO's rail plans. Hoping to act before road construction could impede its agenda, METRO announced a new rail plan in September 1982. The updated proposal called for an 18.2-mile heavy rail line to run through both the Westpark and Hardy corridors along what the agency called the "spine corridor." The plan was the brainchild of Alan Kiepper, who quietly commissioned a feasibility study for the broader system using $28 million in federal funding shortly after his arrival in Houston. Only after the METRO board released the plan did Kiepper make the work his agency conducted public.[78] METRO moved toward implementation immediately, beginning the process of right-of-way purchasing and preparing for the first stage of construction, which together would cost $190 million.[79]

Rail opponents criticized METRO's adjusted proposal and scrambled to respond. Jon Lindsay accused the agency of overreaching its authority, ignoring the Regional Mobility Plan, and unilaterally forcing an expensive project upon residents. METRO's actions spurred suburbanites from North Houston, backed by some of the largest developers and corporations of the area, to form the North Houston Association in November 1982, in order to oppose the expanded rail plan. Citizens for Better Transportation and the North Houston Association together claimed 250,000 members and put that constituency to work pressuring the Houston City Council and Mayor Kathy Whitmire to support the toll road proposal.[80]

While neither the City Council nor Whitmire took definitive action on the toll road plan, the political pressure exerted by the road supporters did secure a guarantee that the rail plan would be put before voters. The 1973 and 1978 votes provided precedent for such a referendum. Given the results of the 1978 election, and despite its early hiccups, METRO officials felt confident that a vote would result in the passage of the rail plan. Surveys the Authority conducted during the debate corroborated this confidence, with as many as 77 percent of Houstonians saying they supported the rail system.[81] As 1982 came to a close, Whitmire called for a referendum on the rail plan to be scheduled. Kiepper assented, despite his own desire to begin construction immediately.[82]

METRO's announcement prompted Jon Lindsay to take action on formally creating the HCTRA. Working with State Representative Erwin Barton, Lindsay submitted a bill to the Texas Legislature that gave Harris County permission to form a toll road agency.[83] As his plan moved through the legislature, Lindsay wrote to Houston City Council member Dale Gorczynski to convince him of the merits of the HCTRA and to seek a compromise between tollway and rail supporters. Lindsay promised that the county did not intend to ride roughshod over the city or its citizens. Furthermore, he reiterated that METRO and the HCTRA could work together to improve the metropolitan area's transportation network. After offering these conciliations, however, Lindsay made it clear that he would not let TMO or pro-rail opposition spoil his toll road plans. The region's "rapidly deteriorating traffic situation indicates it's past time for plans and studies," he wrote. "It's time for someone to pour concrete."[84]

SETTLING THE DEBATE: THE REFERENDA

With Lindsay's HCTRA proposal out in the open, the 1983 transit debates assumed their final form. Once again, a public forum sheds light on how this debate was joined. At an April 1983 meeting, the rail and toll road proponents openly clashed. Each side accused the council of catering to the interests of the other. Addressing the meeting, one TMO member and Hardy corridor resident asserted that far from anti-progress "vigilantes," he and his neighbors were "citizens, taxpayers, and voters" who simply did not want the toll road to "uproot homes for the benefit of just a few people." Another corridor resident, Ramiro Villareal, promised to support any proposal that did not force him and his family to "find new homes, new churches, new friends, and new ways of life." Road proponents responded to this passionate plea by reiterating that Hardy Street presented "a natural corridor coming out of central Houston," and that the toll road plan presented "a once in a lifetime opportunity."[85]

The two perspectives presented in the breakout session demonstrated the deep divide between suburban and corridor residents over the future shape of the area and its meaning in their lives. Supporters of each system possessed wholly different conceptions of the Hardy corridor as a physical landscape. To area residents, the debate concerned the future of their homes. To suburban commuters, the corridor simply presented an "opportunity" for improved mobility. For the remainder of the debate, corridor residents focused on preventing negative physical changes to their communities, while suburbanites concentrated on easing their commute. When METRO released a supplemental draft environmental impact statement on the rail system, corridor residents celebrated its conclusion that rail rapid transit represented the best path forward. The report stated that a rail line would result in less air pollution and necessitate fewer displacements than the toll road.[86] Much of the transit debate pivoted on these hyper-local concerns. Houstonians supported the system they felt best matched their individual interests.

"JUST A RAIL BAD DAY FOR METRO"[87]

Although METRO officials would have preferred to start construction on the rail system without a vote, Kiepper and others did not want to jeopardize the agency's steadily improving reputation. Begrudgingly, the agency scheduled the vote for June 11, 1983. The referendum potentially represented a clear path for the construction of the system, but it also placed the fate of the plan solely in the hands of voters. The risk for METRO was clear. As agency leaders acknowledged, if the vote failed, they had no financial backup plan and would be left adrift.[88]

During the lead-up to the June referendum, it became clear that no matter the outcome, the balanced transportation approach of the previous decade would be abandoned. Given the growing city-suburb divide, only one side would get what it wanted. Local officials, community groups, and voters lined up behind the rail proposal or made their opposition clear. The makeup of the two sides held few surprises. City leaders mostly backed the rail plan, and many county officials stood firmly in opposition. The majority of city residents, mainly working- and middle-class Houstonians of all races, expressed support for rail. Many elite white Houstonians and most white suburbanites did not. Two interesting exceptions to expected allegiances did emerge. First was the West Houston Association (WHA), a consortium of businesses located near the western terminus of the proposed rail line in the Galleria area, which supported the rail. While the rationale for the WHA's support was clearly economically motivated, it was nonetheless one of the few business groups to support the system. On the anti-rail side, the most unexpected development was Judge Lindsay's relative silence. Despite the energy he had poured into pushing against the plan, Lindsay refused to endorse or oppose the referendum after its announcement, choosing to remain apart from a vote that did not directly involve his jurisdiction. Lindsay did make it known, however, that he remained focused on forming the HCTRA and pushing for its passage, a tacit statement of disapproval.[89]

Although METRO campaigned throughout the region and aimed to convince a wide range of citizens to support the rail, just as with the 1973 and 1978 referenda, Authority officials believed that the support of the city's African-American and Latino voters and politicians would be key to the success of the election. After working closely with METRO and TMO throughout the process, most of the region's black and Latino politicians came out in support of the referendum. State Representative Anthony Hall voiced his approval once METRO forwarded a plan to bring rail to his Southeast Houston district. State Representative Ben Reyes of East Houston pointed specifically to the jobs that the construction of the system would bring to many of his constituents as the primary rationale for his support.[90] METRO took these endorsements as a positive omen for the referendum's result.

African-American and Latino Houstonians who supported the rail proposal also promoted the system independent of their political leaders. Many members of these groups who were also active in TMO had campaigned against the Hardy Toll Road and likewise threw their support behind the rail plan. Black, white, and Latino TMO members kept up a constant stream of editorials, attended meetings, and held rallies to encourage Houstonians to vote for rail. The Second Ward's Mexican-American newspaper, *El Sol*, much as it had during the 1978 METRO debate, endorsed the proposal after Alan Kiepper and other METRO officials held a meeting with Latino community leaders in May 1983.[91] The paper appealed to Houston's Latino residents to "turn out to the ballot box and vote." Echoing TMO's arguments against the toll road plan, *El Sol*'s editorial team pleaded that voters not let the "small but potent self-interest groups that oppose its passage" win the day. The paper urged its readers to "show Houston what the Hispanic and Mexican-American community can do in unison" and vote for the referendum.[92]

Pro-rail groups also targeted black and Latino constituencies with advertisements in *El Sol*, the *Houston Defender*, and the *Houston Informer*. In *El Sol*, The Committee for Houston Bus and Rail—a consortium of rail supporters that came together to campaign for the referendum—talked up the positive economic benefit the project would have in terms of both jobs and growth. It promised more buses, better service, and revamped facilities. It also warned voters that "the problems of transit are worse than we can Imagine!" and asserted that "Houston needs to plan—now!" Demonstrating the importance of local power brokers, the advertisements also listed the prominent leaders and politicians supporting the referendum.[93] Ads placed in the *Informer* and *Defender* took the same approach (figs. 5.3 and 5.4).[94]

While rail supporters campaigned for passage of the rail bonds, opponents sharpened their critiques. If many pro-tollway politicians refrained from directly criticizing the rail plan, their supporters did not. White suburban community groups, such as the Cypress Creek United Civic Association and Meyerland Community Improvement Association, initiated letter-writing campaigns and published editorials attacking the rail plans.[95] Playing on the self-governing ethos of both Houston and Texas, David Legge, the editor of *Houston City Magazine*, also criticized the rail plan. Legge argued that "Houston . . . is the least likely candidate for heavy rail in America. It's spread out, free-spirited, and independent-minded."[96] Legge went on to suggest that support for the rail plan was tantamount to supporting the infringement of the individual rights so sacred to many Texans. Through this tactic Legge changed the nature of the vote from METRO's vision of freedom via a new transport mode into one that represented rail as a power grab by a government agency. For many, especially those still unconvinced by METRO's overall effort, this tactic proved convincing.

Despite this vocal criticism, in the days before the election, the momentum, as it did in 1973, appeared to be on the side of passage. A *Houston Chronicle* article pointed out that proponents of the rail plan had outspent their opponents by a wide margin. With three days remaining before the election, the Committee for Houston Bus and Rail had spent $114,657 of an estimated $185,000 raised on the campaign. In comparison, two opposition groups—The Neighborhood Forum and Citizens for Better Transportation—reported expenditures of little more than $15,000.[97] Given this financial advantage, along with the support of many prominent Houstonians, such as Bus and

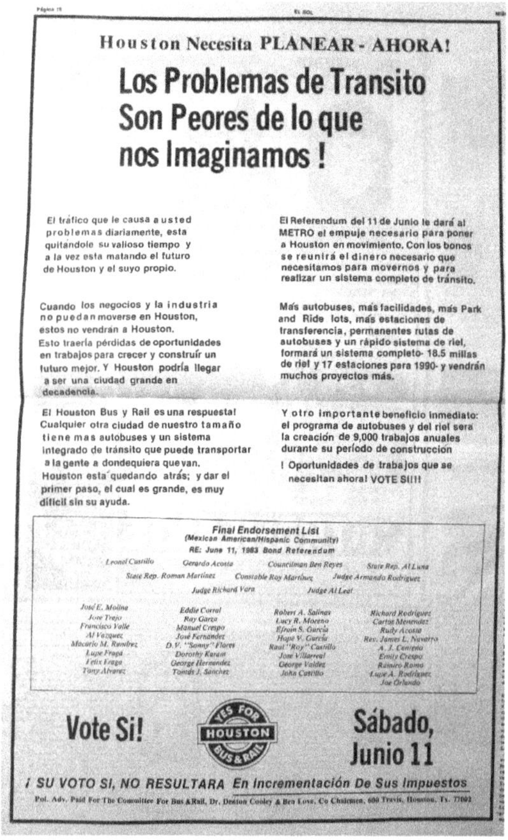

Figs. 5.3 and 5.4. Pro-Rail Advertisements

Ads in support of rail taken out in African-American and Latino community newspapers. Fig. 5.3, *El Sol*, June 8, 1983, Houston Metropolitan Research Center. Fig. 5.4, *Houston Defender*, May 20, 1983, Houston Metropolitan Research Center.

Rail Committee chair Ben Love, and a commitment by many black, Latino, and white city residents, METRO officials felt optimistic about the chances of the referendum's passage.

Writing on the day of the rail referendum, *Houston Post* columnist Lynn Ashby defended METRO's efforts during its first four years of existence and urged voters to support the rail plan. Although the opposition had a right to ask questions of METRO and its plans, Ashby said, he feared they had gone too far—becoming impediments to progress rather than paragons of the democratic process. Inverting Legge's version of Texas self-governance, he reminded fellow Houstonians that their city "was not turned from a backwater village on an unknown bayou into the fastest-growing city in the nation by a bunch of whiners and naysayers. It was built by doers." After delivering this admonition, Ashby called on voters to go to the polls and support the referendum.[98]

To any Houstonian who could remember the 1973 HARTA election, June 12, 1983, must have dawned with an extreme sense of déjà vu. Just as in 1973, nearly two-thirds of voters rejected a transit referendum that just weeks earlier had seemed destined to pass. METRO officials expressed shock and disappointment, with many blaming low voter turnout in areas of expected support and a lack of voter understanding as the root causes of the referendum's defeat. Just 110,978 voters, approximately 12 percent of those Houstonians who lived within the Authority's jurisdiction, cast ballots.[99] Unfortunately for supporters of transit, those who turned out overwhelmingly opposed the rail. The geographic distribution of "no" votes reflected continued suburban disdain for "Houston-centric" transit plans, as suburban precincts such as those in Fort Bend County rejected the referendum by ratios approaching 3 to 1. In addition, the vote expressed the trepidation held by the wealthier residents who lived along the proposed Westpark segment of the system and likewise voted down the proposal.[100]

The rejection of the rail plan led to three major outcomes. First, it vaulted the HCTRA agenda to the fore of metropolitan transportation politics. Second, it resulted in the loss of federal funding for mass transit in Houston. Third, it shifted METRO's agenda toward meeting suburban mobility needs. Furthermore, given the fact that African American and Latino Houstonians had given the referendum staunch backing, its failure marked the first time in nearly a decade that minority votes had failed to swing a regional transportation vote. The fact that these voters had combined their votes with many white rail supporters and still lost also demonstrated the limits of city-based political power in the increasingly suburbanizing region.

The rejection of the referendum almost immediately resulted in a redistribution of earmarked federal transportation funds. Members of the committee in the US House of Representatives that had promised Houston the money for the project if the referendum succeeded announced that they would be sending the $110 million meant for Houston to other cities. They lamented the fact that "one of the nation's most promising" transit projects had fallen apart. Houston-area national politicians also began to back away from their efforts to secure transit dollars. Congressman Jack Fields, who represented a Houston district and was one of the leaders who helped bring money to the project, announced that he would cease all efforts to attain federal funding.[101] Senators Lloyd Bentsen and John Tower, who were both instrumental in convincing the US Department of Transportation to keep some mass transit funding in its budget, expressed disappointment at the defeat and the wasted allocation.[102] The rejection of the rail referendum made it unlikely that national leaders would support such an ambitious plan in Houston anytime soon.

After the referendum defeat, METRO faced, as one newspaper article put it, "soul-searching time."[103] Having invested between $50 million and $90 million into planning, preparation, and engineering, the agency stood at a crossroads, faced with several ways forward.[104] Even as Authority officials shut down the preliminary work that had been started in anticipation of the referendum's passage, they weighed the possibility of returning to voters with a different plan in the coming months. Regardless of how they moved forward, Alan Kiepper acknowledged, the defeat "shot us [METRO] down pretty solidly. . . . We are eating Humble Pie. . . . We thought we had a good plan, but we'll have to come up with another one."[105] METRO responded by announcing that it would start long-term transit planning anew, with a special focus on bringing citizen feedback into any new proposal.[106] METRO's next transit proposal, which took more than a year to create, oriented the agency in a new direction—toward the suburbs. Because of the sound defeat of the 1983 rail plan, the agency conceded that it needed to account for suburban needs, a decision that caused shifts to the region's mobility choices for the next twenty years.

TOLL ROADS RUSH IN

Two days after the rail referendum, Jon Lindsay asserted that "the METRO bond election is now history" and asked Houstonians to support the creation of the HCTRA.[107] "The community is hungry for a solution to its traffic problems," Lindsay insisted, and toll roads represented the only feasible answer.[108] HCTRA supporters, learning from the defeat of the rail vote, painted the plan and its proposed system as one for the entire metropolitan area (fig. 5.5). This tactic allowed the HCTRA to insulate the proposal from the fractious Hardy Toll Road debate. Lindsay and other officials recognized that, given the significant opposition that remained from groups like TMO, they might not be able to pass a stand-alone, yes/no referendum on the Hardy Toll Road. Instead, they lumped all of the proposed roads into one ballot measure, thereby ensuring wider support and capitalizing on Houstonians' general frustrations with traffic.[109]

Many Houston officials came over to the toll road camp after the rail defeat. Several former supporters of the rail plan realized that they would have to take a position on the toll road proposal, and more and more expressed support owing to their doubts that another transit plan would emerge.[110] Officials who had opposed the rail plan, including John Goodner, a member of the Houston City Council, lauded this embrace of the HCTRA plan and hoped that its quick passage might prove that Houston was not "negative on transportation."[111] Goodner's line once more hinted at the fear among Houstonians that continued problems with traffic, or even just the bad publicity of a divisive debate, could damage Houston's national reputation.

Despite the defeat of the rail plan, opponents of the toll road refused to allow the HCTRA's creation without a fight. Gorczynski, ignoring Judge Lindsay's earlier olive branch, helped to form an anti-tollway group, Taxpayers Against Toll Road Bonds, which consisted of several TMO-supported politicians and other civic organizations sympathetic to the anti-tollway cause.[112] The group and TMO offered the most cohesive resistance to the HCTRA in the lead-up to the September 13 election day. Taxpayers Against Toll Road Bonds grounded most of its attacks in financial concerns about the system and the risks it brought to county taxpayers. The group projected that, with interest included, the actual cost of the toll system would be $2.35 billion, not the $900 million that county leaders estimated.[113]

TMO, which, like METRO, was reeling after the defeat of the rail referendum, once again focused on the Hardy corridor and attacked the developers and wealthy Houstonians who, in their view, would benefit most directly from the Hardy Toll Road. During the HCTRA debate, the organization asked the Houston Conduct Review Board to initiate an official inquiry into possible conflicts of interest that Houston City Council members might have

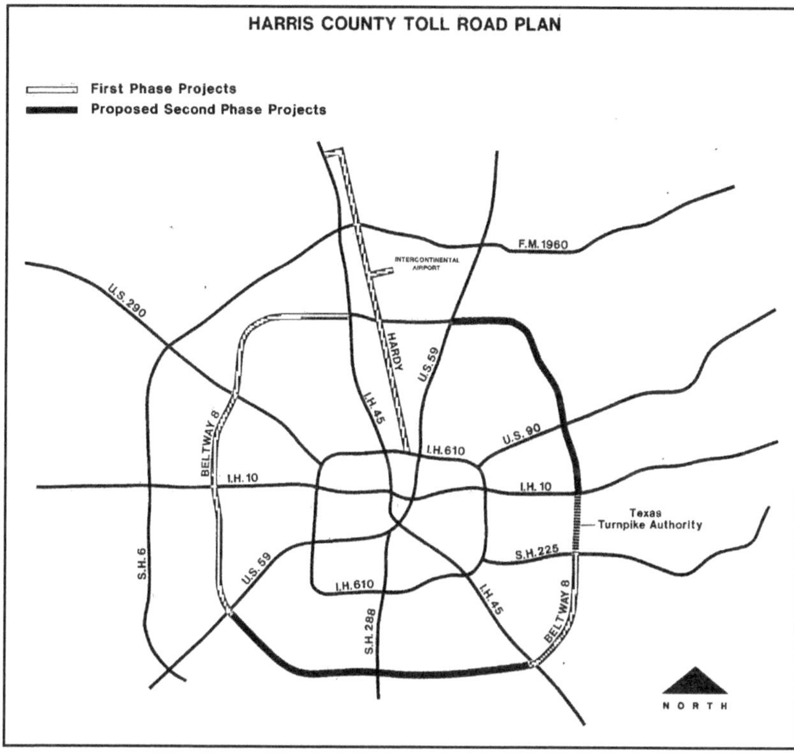

Fig. 5.5. The HCTRA Toll Road Proposal

The outlined roads represent the toll routes that would be built after the proposal's passage; the thick black lines depict future routes. Absent from this early rendition is the Westpark toll road. Houston-Galveston Regional Transportation Study, October 1983, Michael Berryhill Collection, Woodson Research Center, 5.

with the Hardy corridor proposal. TMO argued that the fact that developer Walter Mischer Sr. owned significant acreage along the corridor—and had donated money to twelve of the fifteen council members—constituted a conflict.[114] TMO's accusation infuriated the City Council. Although the review board quickly dismissed TMO's complaint, the fact that it was levied at all stoked criticism of the group.[115] Several members of the council who were Catholic wrote a public letter to Bishop John Morkovsky of the Archdiocese of Galveston-Houston, questioning TMO's role in city politics and the church's support of the organization. Labeling TMO's paid staff "outside agitators," the letter's authors suggested that the group exploited poorer churches.[116] Bishop Morkovsky responded to their questions with unwavering support for TMO. He assured council members that funding for TMO had been secured voluntarily through member congregations' fees and donations.[117] Despite ongoing support for TMO, especially from the churches, the group's critiques failed to gain traction and its political influence declined.

As TMO and toll road opponents searched for arguments that could cut into the HCTRA's momentum, the vote approached. Pro-toll-road citizens helped form the Harris County Citizens for the Toll Road Alternative and released a pamphlet titled "Restoring Mobility" arguing that the passage of the referendum would create regional mobility and that its failure would mean continued congestion.[118]

Toll road proponents trumpeted the system's ability to bring mobility to the entire city. The Chamber of Commerce stumped hard for the referendum, highlighting the promises of the Regional Mobility Plan and telling voters that a "yes" vote for toll roads was a "vote for mobility."[119] Toll road proponents' focus on easing congestion hit a chord with many Houstonians who were sick of sitting in traffic. Even those who did not feel strongly about the toll road plan leaned toward supporting it simply to see some sort of action take place. In the days before the election, *Houston Post* columnist Lynn Ashby, who had also supported the rail referendum, reflected this attitude when he wrote a column supporting the toll road plan. Though he continued to lament the missed opportunity represented by the failure of the rail referendum, Ashby, nearly parroting the toll road proponents, asserted that the plan at least gave the city "a second chance to do something about our traffic." Ashby concluded that in the face of feeble state and federal funding, the user-fee model of the plan was a necessary evil. Summing up the situation, he concluded, "We either build these needed roads ourselves or the job doesn't get done."[120]

On September 13, 1983, the Harris County electorate, which was 100,000 people larger than the METRO electorate, overwhelmingly approved the HCTRA. In an inversion of the rail referendum results, 95,524 (70 percent) county residents approved the bonds and 40,055 (30 percent) voted against. With 12 percent of eligible county voters weighing in, more than double other contemporary county elections, the importance of the vote was clear.[121] Judge Lindsay said the victory showed that Harris County was not going to sit idle as its traffic piled up. Suburban civic groups and officials that supported the bonds celebrated their victory.[122]

The result of the toll referendum highlighted the efficacy of both the metropolitan mobility pitch of the plan's proponents and the limitations of place-based political stances. The defeated TMO begrudgingly admitted that its singular focus on the Hardy corridor during both referenda had hurt its chances in each.[123] The toll road vote was yet another blow to TMO. Its inability to muster much of a turnout and the sound defeat of its preferred action were signs of its waning influence.[124] Furthermore, the success of the referendum meant that the communities of many corridor residents would soon be changed forever. If passage of the HCTRA presaged TMO's decline, it signified the arrival of suburban residents and business leaders as new regional powers. Nothing made these political shifts as clear as the financial details of the HCTRA campaigns. Pro-toll-road groups had raised more than $400,000 to support the referendum, whereas the toll road's opponents could muster no outside funding for their campaign against the proposal, a significant shift from the support they had found during the rail push, and a signal, perhaps, that most Houstonians wanted to move forward with some form of solution.[125]

Harris County moved quickly on the toll roads after the vote. The Commissioners Court created the Authority on September 22.[126] By early 1984, plans for acquiring right-of-way in the Hardy corridor were underway. Ultimately, the county removed seventy homes and fifty-four businesses and another five hundred properties were affected.[127] Hoping to accelerate the acquisition process and speed construction, a number of developers and landowners along the Hardy corridor donated nearly 14 percent of the total right-of-way, land valued at $6 million, to the county.[128] The alacrity with which the county moved to build the toll system was a product of Houstonians' intense demand for a resolution to the city's congestion. Ground was broken on the Hardy Toll Road in September 1984. On the same day that bulldozers made the ceremonial cuts in the earth, the HCTRA announced that it would be accelerating the construction process. Officials aimed to have the Hardy Toll Road opened to traffic, and collecting fares, by July 1988.[129]

CONCLUSION

Hundreds of bicycles rushed down the smooth lanes of the Hardy Toll Road in September 1987. Almost exactly four years after the passage of the inaugural HCTRA bonds, the northern section of the roadway opened to great fanfare: a parade, marching bands, and a bike race took over the road during the celebrations.[130] Two years later, the pop band the Bangles headlined a concert from a stage built across the surface of the new Sam Houston Tollway (Beltway 8) in celebration of that road's official opening, playing for 25,000 people.[131]

These celebrations announced more than just the completion of two toll roads. To many, the opening of the roads represented the attainment of relief from congestion, a decades-long goal in Houston. To others, especially those Houstonians who had engaged in the heated 1983 debates, the inauguration of the roads marked a significant place in the struggle to influence the growth of the city. For those on the winning side of the debates, the roads represented the embrace of their hopes for the city. For those who had resisted the highways, the opening was a reminder of their inability to see their visions for the future upheld. No matter how one framed its significance, though, the opening of the toll roads undeniably marked the continuation of Houston's highway-centric development pattern and its suburb-first transportation planning.

After 1983, TMO's influence in city politics declined precipitously for reasons that went beyond the ability of suburban areas to outvote the city in metropolitan debates. The oil bust of the 1980s crippled Houston's economy and left many Houstonians unemployed, and the city's poverty rate grew in concert. The pressures of poverty undoubtedly affected the ability of some TMO members to devote time and money to the organization. In addition to personal circumstances, the recession exacerbated many of the problems that TMO had tried to address within the city during the early 1980s. However, because the city now possessed so few resources to devote to social programs, or with which to try to improve the condition of schools, streets, and police service anywhere, TMO's complaints were simply added to the long list of problems the city faced during the 1980s that ended up on the back burner. The recession also accelerated the flight of white-collar workers of all races out of Houston and helped re-inscribe segregation across the region based on both income and race. The economic and social distance these processes placed between working-class and middle-class Houstonians of all races made coalitions like TMO increasingly harder to build. Finally, the rise of suburbs and conservative politics cannot be underestimated. The ascent of the Republican Party to power in suburban Houston and Texas led to increased animosity between cities and suburbs. Newly elected Republican leaders and the constituencies that supported them maintained their resistance to supporting projects in the City of Houston, often preventing county and state funds from being spent in the city. Weakened by political defeat, the economic struggles of its membership and of

Houston itself, and challenged by the conservative politics of the Houston suburbs and the federal government, TMO, like community organizations across the country, shifted away from direct confrontational tactics to embrace new forms of organization that meshed more easily with the political moment.[132] Although city residents by no means stopped participating in metropolitan debates, all of these factors gave their suburban neighbors the upper hand.

Given this new metropolitan political order, METRO, county, and city officials increasingly catered to the needs of suburban residents.[133] Because they often ignored jurisdictional lines, transportation decisions illustrated this reality better than most other metropolitan topics. The creation of the HCTRA so quickly after the rejection of the rail plan forced METRO officials to reevaluate their future plans. In line with the region's car-centric growth and realigning political realities, the Authority embraced a suburb-focused system. METRO continued the improvement plan it had begun in the early 1980s: increasing bus service, reducing maintenance problems, and improving safety. In addition, the agency prioritized travel between the central city and the suburbs. To meet this goal METRO built more Park-and-Ride lots and opened High-Occupancy Vehicle lanes on almost every highway.

After spending the first year after the referenda implementing changes intended to meet suburban mobility needs, METRO unveiled three potential options for its mass transit program in 1984. The options put forward, however, reflected the agency's suburban orientation, as none of the proposals aimed to improve transit service to the central city residential communities most in need of it. Further establishing its commuter focus and exacerbating service shortages in the city, all three plans centered on express busways that ran entirely on highways and provided no local service. The transit elements in one proposal serviced only employment centers and Park-and-Ride lots.[134] METRO's suburban orientation emerged even in its rhetoric. The agency no longer aimed to provide basic mobility to all Houstonians; rather, it hoped to give commuters "an attractive alternative to the automobile," a goal clearly attainable only by convincing suburban drivers to convert their daily journey from car to transit.[135] It was not until Mayor Lee Brown, the city's first black mayor, successfully combined METRO, Houston, and federal funds to open the first leg of a proposed light rail system in 2004 that METRO reestablished a semblance of city-suburb balance to its system. This suburban reorientation intensified the immobility of Houston's poorest residents. As jobs, resources, and services moved out of many parts of the city, those without access to cars or public transportation found themselves stuck.[136]

METRO's approach to transportation after the 1983 transit debates confirmed the city's embrace—physically and cognitively—of a car-centric landscape.[137] On top of the HCTRA's and the Texas Highway Department's continued construction of highways, Houston's development continued to decentralize, and automobiles and buses became the sole means of movement for most residents.[138] Officials oriented the region's infrastructural decisions around highways. This choice influenced the urban form at every level. Sidewalks were hard to maintain in a spread-out city, and walking became increasingly difficult. Local streets and thoroughfares were built wider and wider to ensure capacity and allow cars to travel faster. Residents of the Hardy corridor, like those before them in the Third and Fifth Wards, swallowed hard as the toll road came through their community. The new road not only reshaped the physical landscape, but also influenced the perceptions of the neighborhoods through which it passed. To most Houstonians, the homes in the Hardy corridor became simply the backdrop to the highway. As with other projects, the erasures brought by the road faded as new developments filled empty lots and the city moved on. Yet the legacies of the fight remained visible in the homes that hung on in the shadows of the toll road and in the minds of displaced residents and those who had fought against its construction.

These changes did not mean that a suburban vision of mobility or the building of highway infrastructure went uncontested after 1983. Although suburban Houstonians had seemingly taken control during the 1983 campaigns, the contentiousness of the debates illustrated the fraught nature of transportation decisions. Infrastructural fights continued, and city residents did not simply cede the political arena. Central city voters could not outvote suburbanites; nor could suburbanites completely ignore the will of city residents. This dynamic became even more complicated as immigration into Houston from Central America, Asia, and the Middle East continued. The diversification of the city's suburbs ensured that no single racial, economic, or political group would be able to dictate regional policy without creating coalitions and compromises.

The 1983 transit debates represented just a fraction of the many factors that influenced the city's continued growth from the 1980s until today. The outcome of the contest ensured that the city's transportation network and future mobility systems would be unique to Houston. Residents from across the metropolitan region—urban and suburban, politician and voter, transit backer or toll road advocate—shaped the terms of the debate and the choices the city made in 1983. Through those choices, they fashioned the city itself. The contest between road and rail captured the thought processes of Houstonians in action and demonstrated the decidedly local flavor of their mobility decisions in the midst of devolution and increasing citizen participation. Struggling to contend with a rapidly changing demography, economy, and metropolitan landscape, Houstonians argued, compromised, and voted their way into Houston's mobility future.

CHAPTER 6

THE LEGACIES AND LIMITS OF INFRASTRUCTURAL CITIZENSHIP

My problem is that y'all's staff is lying to us. Lying to me and probably lying to y'all and making y'all seem that this whole project's a real pretty thing. But we're being hurt, impacted weekly on this. . . . Y'all gave us $25,000 six years ago. This project was supposed to be a three-year project. We've been in here six years. . . . Can I ask something of the Board? How can you be sure that your community outreach is going to actually outreach?

MARK RODRIGUEZ, METRO BOARD MEETING, MAY 2015

Mark Rodriguez, the owner of Gulf Coast Used Cars in Houston's East End and active member of a nearby community association, did not pull his punches when he spoke before the METRO board of directors in May 2015. He directed his ire that day at the delayed construction on the Green Line, the light rail line through the East End that METRO had started building in 2008. Rodriguez blasted the agency's public outreach officials for not adequately informing area businesses about the ongoing construction delays. The interruptions were related to a years-long fight over whether to build an underpass or an overpass at a rail crossing along the line. Furthermore, Rodriguez criticized what he perceived as a lack of empathy from the board, and METRO as an organization, for the hard times that construction had visited on him and other business owners in the Greater East End. Though they might have given him $25,000 in assistance to help with construction-related losses, to Rodriguez that clearly was not enough.

Many of Rodriguez's points were valid. His business likely had suffered from the disruption of traffic on the street in front of his doors. And the overpass debate had contributed to several lengthy delays. Moreover, many residents felt that METRO's outreach and support efforts during the extended process did not meet the expectations of the community. As others had before them, the citizens who spoke to the METRO board that May day focused on elements of infrastructure—the rail line, the street in front of their homes, and their physical businesses—to make their arguments. Rodriguez, and the others who have attended countless public meetings between 2008 and today, engaged in transportation activism and exercised infrastructural citizenship.[1] But the infrastructural citizenship Rodriguez and others expressed in 2015 was far different from that of 1960 or 1980. Rodriguez possessed greater influence over and input into the infrastructural decisions affecting his life than previous generations of Houstonians.

More than forty years after residents of Houston's East End fought and helped prevent the planned Harrisburg Freeway from bisecting their neighborhoods, the Green Line edged its way into the communities. Far from another infrastructural intrusion, however, many East End residents celebrated the rail line as a signal of progress and as a major investment by METRO into their community. East Enders supported a 2003 city referendum that considered a light rail system by 60–40, approving the system by one of the widest margins in the city.[2] Many hoped it would both provide improved transit connections to other parts of Houston and spur development and investment in the area. As planning and construction progressed, the community and its elected officials, a group that looked very different from those of the 1970s, closely monitored the process and forwarded direct input to METRO and other officials, and they saw many of those demands adhered to.

The access that Rodriguez and other residents enjoyed to Houston's decision-makers could trace its roots to the 1960s and 1970s and the fights of those eras around the Harrisburg Freeway. If the community had not demanded better transportation options and greater input into infrastructural decision-making several decades prior, the Green Line might not have existed for Rodriguez and others to give input to at all. More than two decades of transportation activism by East Enders, coupled with broader citywide and national campaigns for greater public access to decision-making, made it possible for Rodriguez to stand in front of the METRO board, speak his mind, and expect to be listened to. Although problems persisted, and the decision-making process remained far from completely democratic, in the twenty-first century, infrastructural citizens such as Rodriguez found themselves more empowered than ever before.

Beyond tying back to earlier activism, Rodriguez's words and the larger debates around the Green Line illustrate the double-edged nature of infrastructural decision-making in the late twentieth and early twenty-first centuries. The discussion around the Green Line's planning and construction highlighted the benefits secured through decades of citizen campaigns. With the line, the East End received the type of direct transit investment, nearly $600 million in local funds, that residents had sought for decades. As we shall see, Rodriguez and his neighbors, still predominantly Latino and mostly working class, also possessed a far larger platform for participating in every step of the planning and construction process than their predecessors. The rail directly displaced only a handful of residents, and the system for their compensation was firmly established. Moreover, unique among major transit agencies at the time, METRO provided direct financial assistance to businesses affected by the construction of its light rail lines in the early 2000s, and again to a select group impacted by the overpass delay. Clearly, the shape of infrastructural decision-making had morphed considerably from the solely elite- and technocrat-driven, nondemocratic practices of the 1950s through the 1970s.

Despite all that has been positive, however, the Green Line's history and present position also show the challenge of building major transportation infrastructure in the United States in the twenty-first century. After the passage of the National Environmental Policy Act in 1970, the planning and construction phases of major projects extended as a result of growing reporting and investigative requirements. Although this due diligence was necessary to ensure an equitable use of resources and to protect neighborhoods and individuals from unfair physical impacts, it also added years to projects. Furthermore, as the transit and tollway fight explored in chapter 5 showed, by the 1980s the leaders of citizen campaigns for infrastructural issues had learned how to manipulate public feedback processes and to lobby their legislators in ways that often slowed or derailed projects. Not-in-my-backyard (NIMBY) attitudes emerged and were empowered by the careful steps put in place to protect residents from abusive projects. The tools that were meant to be used to prevent injustice or unequal impact of infrastructure construction quickly became used as tools to fight off perceived threats to neighborhoods and homes, whether or not the projects served a larger public good or caused any real harm to the objectors. Parsing which objections were rooted in true injustice and which were merely inconvenient became an immense challenge for public officials and agencies.[3] Additionally, the costs of major projects skyrocketed, and little to no political will existed or appears on the horizon to pay for major additions to the transportation systems in most cities. Finally, a great deal of influence over such decisions does remain vested with moneyed and politically empowered citizens and groups. For all the successes that infrastructural citizenship has afforded to lower-class and nonwhite urban residents, it has not yet enabled citizens to overturn a decision-making hierarchy that was carefully crafted over decades to benefit a small slice of society.[4]

Although the entire Green Line project could offer insights into the contemporary place of infrastructural citizenship in metropolitan politics, the debate surrounding the construction of either an underpass or an overpass at a key intersection of that line acts as magnifying glass. During planning and construction, the question of how the light rail line would cross a set of Union Pacific freight rail tracks became a special point of friction. The conflict over this decision raged for six years, and despite the final selection of an overpass and the beginning of construction in 2015, elements of the debate rage on to this day. The fight divided the community, raised old concerns about the level of trust citizens should give to public agencies, and influenced state-level election outcomes. Nearly every step of the process was steeped in expressions of infrastructural citizenship and reverberated with the East End's history of transportation activism. Ultimately, when METRO chose to build an overpass—over many objections—some in the community felt their concerns had been ignored. To opponents, the decision lay bare the reality that historic patterns of decision-making had not been fully abandoned. METRO, for its part, engaged in massive outreach campaigns throughout the process, even as the decisions on the overpass became increasingly acrimonious. Despite the conflict over the freight rail choice, as Rodriguez's testimony and the transcripts of dozens of meetings and presentations showed, East Enders were intimately involved in the choices made throughout the process. The actors who participated did not always agree—nor could the outcomes of the debate serve all sides—but the debate occurred and took place on relatively equal terms. This is perhaps the most tangible legacy of infrastructural citizenship—it has provided a space to be heard.

That we can talk about a light rail in Houston today is in and of itself rather remarkable, given the region's history of highway-first development and its increasingly suburban-dominated regional decision-making. Little changed in the regional transportation trajectory between 1983 and 2000. Houston grew outward along its highways. Congestion crises cropped up, and officials widened roadways in response. All the while, perspectives on transit in Houston were slowly shifting. In the 1990s, METRO improved its Park-and-Ride system and floated a few larger, but unimplemented plans. Finally, through the decisiveness of a single mayoral administration, the long work of dedicated advocates, and a successful transit referendum, Houston approved a light rail system in 2003 and opened its first leg in 2004.[5] The Green Line is the latest iteration of that effort. The system as a whole marked a broader shift in the conversation around how Houston approached transportation and its built environment.

INFRASTRUCTURAL CITIZENSHIP THEN AND NOW

The rail plan is an example of how transportation decision-making has shifted in Houston over the course of the past decades. This transition mirrors that which took place in many other American metro areas as well. The project reflects the swelling tide of citizen participation that began in the 1960s and continues to grow today. But it also illustrates the ongoing competition for resources and decision-making power in metropolitan areas. Communities across the Houston region, their elected officials, and public agencies still engage in a constant tug-of-war over which areas and which projects will receive the most effort and funding. The Green Line is another in a long line of examples of this tension. Beyond the ongoing fight for control, though, this example undeniably shows how the legacies and continued practice of infrastructural citizenship, no matter its contradictions, has helped to shape the current built environment of our cities and will continue to shape them going forward.

Although the Green Line and the larger rail system might seem to be the realization of part of Houston's infrastructural trajectory, as the previous chapters have shown, that path in Houston has hardly been consistent. Metropolitan residents have rarely shared opinions about the best way forward. If transit seems to be ascendant in the central city and METRO's service area, that position is still perilous. Tensions between competing ideas of infrastructural citizenship and over whose conceptions of transportation should take precedent will persist. The infrastructural assertions of transit advocates or central city citizens are not the only opinions in the pile. Suburban residents, anti-transit urbanites, and a whole slew of other metropolitan dwellers possess their own ideas for the future of the city and its transportation systems. Just as in the past, today no single vision for the city exists. Even when road advocates had broad support and political power, there were residents who said no to highways, and the same situation still applies.

The Green Line and its underpass/overpass debate lay bare the struggle to situate the legacy of historical transportation activism and to square it with its present-day iterations. It's a struggle with contradictions. In the

1960s and 1970s, the fights resulted in the establishment of crucial regulations and protections for citizens affected by government projects. Slowdowns in planning and construction meant greater opportunity for public input and empowerment. The Green Line debates, then, are the outcome of a laudable process; at the same time, however, such debates have turned many infrastructural developments into quagmires, contributing to the calcification of highway-oriented planning across the Houston region—a situation mirrored across the nation. When projects become difficult, it is easier to build on what you have than to start anew. Innovation and new direction are political and economic hurdles few cities overcome. The conflict between versions of transportation activism pits changing desires for mobility and public participation against intractable delays and status-quo decision-making. Above all, just as with earlier highway and transit fights, the Green Line shows the ongoing competition of ideas about what our cities should become and whom they should serve.

GETTING TO THE GREEN LINE

The disputed creation of METRO's light rail system was tinged with overtones of both the HARTA and earlier METRO debates. After the defeat of the rail referendum in 1983, transit advocates and METRO floundered from plan to plan in an attempt to find their footing. Another transit deal seemed nearly certain to go through in 1988 before real estate developer, future Houston mayor, and longtime mass-transit skeptic Bob Lanier torpedoed it from his position on the METRO board.[6] Finally, in the late 1990s, METRO announced the adoption of "Horizon 2020," a new long-range plan that made the Main Street corridor into a transit route.[7] Officials planned to use the corridor for the seven-mile Red Line light rail, to be built in time for the 2004 Super Bowl, which the city was already scheduled to host. Mayor Lee Brown, the city's first African-American mayor, who had also been the city's first African-American chief of police, worked with METRO to build the line solely from the agency's local sales tax funds, a move that allowed the city to avoid another referendum. Construction began in 2001, and the Red Line began operating in 2004. While the Red Line was under construction, METRO held a referendum to finance a larger system of light rail with routes that mirrored the proposed legs of the failed 1973 and 1983 rail proposals almost exactly.[8]

The vote for the proposal in 2003 unearthed many of the arguments of the earlier debates, but the city of the early 2000s brought a new context to the conversation around mass transit. Twenty years of suburb-oriented highway development had made Houston synonymous with traffic jams by the first decade of the twenty-first century. Unlike other auto-centric Sunbelt cities, such as Los Angeles, San Diego, and Dallas, Houston could not point to any non-road transit systems as a sign that officials were working on addressing that congestion. What was more, the makeup of the central city was changing, with more and more white-collar Houstonians returning to homes inside the inner loop to be closer to the resources of the city. Central Houston residents sought better transportation options. Significantly, by the 1990s, the Houston City Council reflected the demographic diversity of the city. In 2000, nine of the sixteen council members, counting the mayor and controller, were African American, Latino American, or Asian American.[9] The council and METRO, encouraged by Houston's growing and diversifying central city, chose to buck their suburb-oriented transit practices and embrace the push for light rail.

Proponents of rail pitched the system as a solution to congestion issues, as a way to provide mobility to central city residents, and as a method to encourage the economic and residential development of the Main Street corridor. Learning from the two previous rail debates, supporters also couched the rail system within a package of bus and road improvements to entice broader voter support.[10] Critics once again attacked METRO for spending too much money and argued that rail could not possibly serve the entire region. The vote for light rail passed in 2003. The first line quickly collected a high volume of riders, carrying 32,000 passengers a day between downtown, the medical center, and Reliant (now NRG) Stadium by the end of its first year of operation. Because the line was at-grade, it did have problems with car-train collisions, and critics continued to lambast its small service area and cost, but METRO nonetheless declared its original foray a success.[11] Today the original Red Line segment has the highest number of passengers per mile of all but some of the most established rail lines in eastern American cities.

Light rail remained a controversial topic in the region even as the segments approved in the 2003 referendum began to be built. By 2008, an extension to the Red Line, the Green Line, and the Purple Line were all under construction. However, the crucial Blue Line, a key crosstown connector, faced significant NIMBY pushback in the form of protesting business owners and residents at certain sections along the planned line. Supported by their US congressman, Republican John Culberson, whose 7th congressional district is predominantly suburban, opponents of the Blue

Line succeeded in stymieing its construction.[12] On top of this protest, in November 2012 regional voters drastically altered the rail system's future in a referendum that effectively prevented METRO from funding two planned extensions.[13]

More than just about the extensions, the 2012 vote also reflected the continued contest over the funding of transit at the regional level. After 1988, all METRO jurisdictions received a slice of the Authority's revenue to pay for general mobility projects. This money has become indispensable to the budgets of every city in the METRO service area, including Houston. The 2012 vote would have given control of those funds back to METRO, a result that terrified local officials, who had come to depend on the general mobility money as part of their transportation budgets. The threat of losing this crucial revenue stream led them to campaign against the change. The outcome of the referendum maintained the revenue-sharing system and made the possibility of a full rail system less likely, at least in the short term. Despite this blow, METRO pushed on with the three rail extensions that were under construction. In December 2013, the North Line opened, adding another five miles of track to the original Red Line. In 2015, the Green and Purple Lines began service.[14] While divisions over the place and purpose of rail in the city remain, the new lines offer options that promise to reframe many residents' conceptions of mobility. Not aiming to provide total coverage, but instead seen as part of a larger mobility network, the rail lines are a valuable option for moving through parts of the city. The last planned segment of Houston's light rail system to get under construction opened upon completion of the overpass in January 2017.

BUILDING THE LINE

The Green Line first appeared in METRO's Mobility 2025 plan and was approved by voters as a part of METRO's 2003 referendum—METRO Solutions 2025.[15] During the referendum campaign and initial planning stages, transportation activism by East Enders played a large role in shaping the system. In the original plans, the East End was left out entirely because of low ridership forecasts. However, pressure from residents and the community's heavily transit-dependent population convinced officials to locate a line there despite the low predictions. In 2004, nearly 21 percent of the community had no access to a car, and about the same percentage were reliant on public transit to reach work.[16] In those first plans, the line was supposed to terminate at the Magnolia Park Transit Center, well short of serving the whole East End. Residents again weighed in, threatening to vote against the referendum if the line was not extended several miles farther to the southeast, to Gulfgate Mall and Hobby Airport. The push was a clear sign that many citizens wanted access to the system, and as a result of the pressure, the proposed line was lengthened in the Solutions referendum.[17] Public pressure also helped to keep the transit line a light rail plan despite brief consideration of building a bus rapid transit system instead.[18]

When they sited the route for the Green Line, METRO officials decided to run it down Harrisburg Boulevard—almost directly over the course that would have been taken by the once-planned freeway. While there is likely no connection between the two routes beyond it being a desirable corridor, the irony of one system being built atop the never realized plans of another reflects the success of neighborhood activism. The attitudes in many parts of the East End appeared to be a complete inversion of those which had been forwarded around the highway. Whereas one had been foisted, the other was welcomed, if not demanded. The distance between the realized and planned can be explained by decades of infrastructural activism in the East End.

While the efforts of the community directly shaped the initial plans, several political and financial controversies embroiled METRO between the approval of the plan in 2003 and the beginning of construction on the Green Line in 2008. These issues resulted in the original Solutions plan being significantly cut. The Green Line's route would again terminate at the Magnolia Transit Center. Though this change created frustration among East End residents, the fact that any line existed, when others had been eliminated altogether, prevented many residents from protesting the change. Additionally, METRO officials proved their commitment to the community when they did not abandon the line after it was announced that the low ridership projections meant it did not qualify for federal financing. Initial estimates placed the cost at more than $400 million, and METRO committed to paying for the line out of local funds. The line was by far the largest single investment directly into the streets of the East End in decades.[19]

Further alleviating the sting of having the line changed, and likely in response to the community's constant public pressure, METRO worked diligently to keep East End residents engaged in the planning and construction processes. Working jointly with the local chamber of commerce and several neighborhood associations, METRO formed a Citizens Advisory Board (CAB) to facilitate communication about the line. The CAB pulled together a wide swathe of residents who would be affected by the rail—including many of the wealthier, white residents from the Lawndale and

Eastwood communities. The resulting coalition of Latino and white voters, supported by local businesses and politicians, proved to be central to the conversation around the rail and the overpass/underpass debate. Creating a tie between these communities was particularly important given the fact that Houstonians from Lawndale and Eastwood lined up against the mainly Mexican-American East Enders who fought the Harrisburg Freeway. In addition to convening the CAB, METRO created the business assistance fund to help merchants located along the light rail lines during construction. The assistance fund was one of the first of its kind in the nation and was created in response to merchants' worries about loss of revenue. These two efforts appealed to different, but not mutually exclusive, residents of the Greater East End and helped to create a broad base of support for the rail.[20]

Construction on the Green Line proceeded relatively smoothly in the months after the ground breaking in 2008.[21] As engineering and construction progressed, however, a looming, but expected, problem emerged near the tail end of the route. A little over a mile from the eastern terminus of the Green Line at the Magnolia Transfer Center, Harrisburg Boulevard intersects with a Union Pacific freight rail line that carries more than thirty trains a day. The intersection of road and railway has been a traffic problem since the 1950s, when the City of Houston first considered creating a grade separation. In the first years of the 2000s, both Harris County and the Gulf Coast Rail District recommended building an underpass.[22] Going into construction, METRO knew it would have to contend with the intersection, but the agency did not expect to struggle to find a solution that worked for the community. Residents of the East End, however, empowered by their influence on earlier steps in the process and eager to see the line meet their needs, forwarded strongly held ideas about how the intersection conflict should be solved.

The conflict over the rail intersection began in March 2008, when Union Pacific officials announced that it would not be possible for the light rail line to cross their tracks at-grade. The assertion threatened the final mile of the line. And in hopes of avoiding significant delays, METRO officials announced that they intended to simply end the line at the previous station and create a permanent shuttle service between the transfer station and the last rail stop. Residents who had already seen the line shortened once were not happy with this outcome. Joined by several transit advocates, residents clamored for a solution. The option of building an overpass quickly moved to the fore. The logic of some form of grade separation was clear, as transit advocate and future METRO board member Christof Spieler reflected: "The overpass isn't just needed for trains; it's needed for cars and pedestrians. Harrisburg grinds to a halt whenever a freight train passes; commuters end up late for work, children can't make it to school, fire trucks are delayed. . . . [T]he county, the city, the freight rail district, the railroad, and METRO have an opportunity to get together and improve not just transit service but traffic and public safety."[23] Houston mayor Bill White pledged $10 million to getting the overpass built, and by April, Union Pacific had agreed to help pay for a portion of the construction as well.[24] But the solution did not sit well with residents.

Almost immediately, East Enders organized a push for an underpass. Leaders of this effort highlighted several advantages of the approach that resonated with earlier complaints about intrusive infrastructure. An overpass would be too large. It would hurt businesses and block light. It would attract vagrants and negatively impact the future development prospects of the community. All of these arguments were infrastructural. Each meditated on the role that the built landscape could play in the future of a neighborhood. METRO initially argued that an underpass was too expensive and required far more complex engineering than an overpass. Residents refused to accept this argument. Building on their previous efforts to shape the line, residents quickly mounted a campaign to change the plans.

The range of letters that East End residents sent to Mayor Bill White in January 2009 soliciting the construction of an underpass demonstrated the diversity of opinions among East Enders who invested in shaping the rail's development. Representatives of the Harrisburg Merchant Association and several civic associations urged the mayor to support the underpass. The merchants fretted that the "overpass would convert the area into an undesirable neighborhood as well as destroy the dream of merchants that love this city and are willing to make any sacrifice to see" the community thrive.[25] Marilu De La Fuente, a community leader and head of the Harrisburg Heritage Society, asserted that while residents remained committed "to bring[ing] a mass transit system that will enable visitors to the Harrisburg area we must make sure that we have somewhere for visitors to visit." An overpass would threaten too much of the area's character and history. De La Fuente asked that the mayor and City Council "stand with the East End community to help us preserve Harrisburg Boulevard."[26] A few residents were more direct. "It's going to be just massive," said Robert Gallegos, president of the Houston Country Club Place Civic Club. "It would be a blight for generations to come that live in the East End."[27] Angie Martinez, the president of the Magnolia Park Pineview Civic Club, had already grown tired of the excuses. She pointed out that Harris County engineers had attested to the feasibility of creating an underpass. Martinez contrasted this to METRO's seeming refusal to consider the approach. "Volunteers from the East End have worked tirelessly to address METRO's every excuse for why an underpass is infeasible," she said. "It is time for the engineers at METRO to lend a helping hand to those exhausted volunteers, by using their expertise to solve problems instead of just finding them."[28]

A number of factors fanned the debate between residents and METRO. The divide threatened the careful work the agency had pursued in garnering support from residents. As the struggle over the choice raged, METRO's CEO, Frank Wilson, garnered criticism for what East Enders perceived as dismissive communication. In response to the January letters, Wilson had written to Mayor White as well, pointing to the extra expense and the risk of environmental contamination that might complicate construction. The pollution risk, like the intersection debate, was not a secret. The land in the East End was pockmarked with former industrial sites. The area around the proposed pass had once housed oil storage and a service station. These previous uses had left a variety of chemicals and pollutants in the ground, but the same situation existed across the industrial landscape of the East End. In previous mentions of the pollution, METRO and other agencies had not forwarded concerns about it complicating construction. When Wilson used the threat as a justification for choosing the overpass, residents objected. The CAB requested an independent engineering analysis of the site and pressured Wilson to more clearly communicate the situation to the community.

Wilson remained insistent that the overpass was the only way forward. Community members remained stalwart in their demands for further study and clearer communication. Several active members of the CAB said that Wilson's refusal to listen to community concerns had soured relations between METRO and the East End, allowing years of carefully cultivated cooperation to disappear.[29] When a new mayor, Annise Parker, was elected in 2010, she quickly pressured Wilson from his post as CEO, and the METRO board, made up by a majority of mayoral appointees, chose former City Council member George Greanias as the new CEO. Wilson's final years were embroiled in scandals beyond the overpass fight, and many both outside and inside of the organization viewed the atmosphere as toxic and unproductive. In his comments introducing Greanias, METRO board chair Gilbert Garcia pointed to a need to "improve the morale and the staff, . . . regain the public trust, and work better with our community and neighborhood leaders." All of these comments resonated with the concerns of East Enders. Greanias, in his introduction, likened the past years of the organization to a faulty engine, saying it would "take time to change Metro's internal culture while altering its public image of executive arrogance and unresponsiveness."[30]

The replacement of Wilson signaled a new era of engagement with the East End. Mayor Parker and the two members of the Houston City Council who were from the area, James Rodriguez and Ed Gonzalez, reengaged with the community. After working with Greanias and METRO to connect back to community concerns throughout 2010 and 2011, Parker announced that the city supported an underpass and pledged $20.6 million to make it happen. Parker noted that the "All Under Option" would mean less capital improvement money for other projects in the community, and that it would likely mean a slower construction timeline.[31] She also asked that the METRO board vote to support the underpass, which they did two days after the city's announcement.[32]

To proponents of the underpass, who had worked for years to see this outcome through, the victory was gratifying. Beyond those individual actors, though, the choice of the city and METRO board reflected the genuine influence of infrastructural activism and the power of public participation. East Enders had seemingly secured the right to determine the shape of their neighborhood's transportation system. This success echoed that of the Harrisburg Freeway fight, but moved beyond that struggle by making even more direct and formalized use of the political system. Unlike in the Harrisburg Freeway fight, in the rail line and underpass fight residents had fought and seemed to have won. In 2011, both seemed assured, and both had significant public investment behind them. The East End could thank its active advocates for these results.

However, the total community victory was short-lived. The site of the underpass was put under more environmental scrutiny beginning in early 2012. Several studies looked in closer detail at the pollution plumes that METRO had highlighted during Frank Wilson's tenure. Although many studies concluded that the pollution would not jeopardize the construction or the plans, over time the forecasts worsened, and additional contamination risks were found. These findings, the costs associated with remediating them, and the delays that remediation would cause jeopardized the plans for the underpass and put the successes achieved by the neighborhood activists at risk.

The worst of the environmental issues did not come to the fore until 2014. Between 2012 and 2014, the CAB met regularly with METRO officials, and planning on the underpass proceeded as planned. Since the outset of the intersection planning in 2008, METRO had made no secret of the fact that pollution might be an issue during construction; nor did officials hide the fact that they were studying the problem further. Monthly CAB meetings invariably included updates on plans for the underpass and on pollution remediation. The problem seemed to be solvable. METRO proposed a variety of fixes, such as waterproof retaining walls to keep contamination out of the underpass and the removal of contaminated dirt during construction. The agency wanted to make sure the community was happy with the details of the underpass. Apparently they were successful in easing worries: at a December 2012 public meeting, they collected over forty comments about the design, and not a single participant mentioned the pollution.[33]

Despite the fact that the debate seemed to be dormant, at least when it came to the pollution issue, the overpass became a central part of a closely contested special election for the East End's Texas State Senate seat in early 2013. The candidates, State Representative Carol Alvarado and former Harris County commissioner Sylvia Garcia, each vying to replace the recently deceased incumbent, framed themselves as champions of the community who would listen to their concerns about the rail line. Garcia, in particular, focused attention on the rail debate, framing herself as an advocate of the underpass plan and Alvarado as a proponent of the overpass. This message culminated with a campaign mailer that Garcia produced ahead of the special election on January 26, 2013 (fig. 6.1). The mailer superimposed a large, ominous rail bridge casting dark shadows onto an East End street. The text said that Alvarado had long campaigned for the overpass, and had even been paid by METRO as a consultant in the early stages of the process. The mailer accused her of continuing to support the overpass against the wishes of the community.[34] Alvarado and her surrogates hit back against this accusation, but the overpass mailer was damaging nonetheless.[35] Garcia received about 1,000 more votes than Alvarado in the special election and repeated the performance in the runoff between the two in March 2013.[36] The rail debate was one of several important topics in the campaign, but those involved with the CAB and the conversation remember it as a central and influential topic in the East End. The fact that this infrastructural debate was even part of the election showed the weight it carried for the residents who worked on rail planning.

Fig. 6.1. Sylvia Garcia Election Mailer

This mailer was sent out by the campaign of former county commissioner Sylvia Garcia to paint her opponent, State Representative Carol Alvarado, as pro-overpass during the special election for a Texas State Senate seat. Garcia and Alvarado each claimed to be the best advocate for the community's interest. Copy of mailer accessed through newsletter of then Houston City Council member James Rodriguez, in possession of the author.

Even as the special election trained a spotlight on the overpass debate, several official studies released to METRO during 2013 seemed to corroborate the idea that the construction could proceed without issue. In April, engineering consultants on the project prepared and released the affected property assessment report for the project. This required environmental document laid out all the known containments and evaluated the risk of construction. The consulting firm found several pollutants and even noted that the pollution plume was larger than expected, but classified them all as matters presenting no risk to the project and requiring no major additional costs.[37] In the next monthly meeting, officials introduced METRO's formal remediation plans.[38] In August 2013, a final environmental assessment was released finding the same possibility of remediation.[39] General municipal elections were held in November 2013, and with planning proceeding as expected on the underpass, the project was mostly a nonissue in the campaigns.

In early 2014, after local government officials took office, the rumor began to spread that METRO intended to back out of the underpass plan, on account of higher-than-expected pollution and rising costs. As the rumor fanned out across the East End, all the ill will between residents and METRO that had been buried by the choice to go under the tracks burst to the surface. Even before METRO formally announced the problem, the overpass/underpass debate raged once again into the public eye. Residents accused METRO and the city of withholding news of the problem until after the election. Almost immediately, the CAB fell apart. The final formal meeting had been in November 2013. Underpass proponents protested the backtracking and stopped attending the meeting called by METRO in protest.[40]

METRO officials formally announced their intention to return to the overpass plan in a January 2014 public meeting, pointing to additional testing done by the contractors assigned to the underpass construction that found an even larger plume. The officials worried specifically that the plume of pollution would be displaced by construction onto neighboring properties and that they would be held liable. They estimated that an adequate cleanup would require approximately $8 million to $16 million in additional spending and add five to ten years to construction of the last mile. The agency argued that the costs and risks—in both liability and worker safety—were far too high. The only feasible option was to return to the overpass.[41]

Stunned by the reversal, but not deterred, residents who supported the underpass employed several of the same tactics that previous generations of transportation activists in Houston had used in fighting against seemingly final decisions. They once again wrote letters expressing their opposition. The leaders of the push for the underpass revisited their long involvement with the Green Line in their arguments against the switch back to the overpass:

> The East End carried the METRO referendum by an overwhelmingly 71% while the rest of the city stood at 51%. We helped elect individuals who supported the underpass. We worked tirelessly for five and a half years achieving our vision for Harrisburg. East End Civic leaders were engaged in a process created by METRO through their monthly CAB program. Every month we asked questions of METRO concerning financing and especially about the environmental assessments. Why did METRO suddenly steer away from the very process they established? . . . Community engagement was the cornerstone of the "new" Metro yet the old ways are surfacing once again.[42]

In the eyes of the residents, the decision once again cast mistrust onto METRO. Advocates accused the agency of abandoning the CAB process and the goodwill it had created. Despite the setbacks, though, community leaders assured METRO and city officials that the East End remained ready to "roll up its sleeves . . . and get this done right. We only get one opportunity at making sure that an infrastructure improvement such as light rail is a complement to our community."[43] They only asked that METRO officials once again hear them.

The voices of protest around the overpass reversal echoed those that had come before them in the East End and in wider Houston. Like many infrastructural activists before them, East Enders pointed out that the choice was far from an isolated one; rather, its consequences would ripple forward for decades. And like the East Enders who fought the Harrisburg Freeway, the underpass advocates also enlisted professional help from both inside and outside of their ranks. They asked the University of Houston Law School to prepare briefs dispelling METRO's liability concerns, and they asked one of the primary proponents of the underpass, Dr. John Jacob, a soil scientist and East End resident, to offer his perspective on the situation.[44] The resources that East Enders brought to bear on the process were formidable and professional.

Opponents of the overpass were not the only East End residents weighing in on the debate, however. Many East Enders, some involved with the CAB, and others, such as Mark Rodriguez, who were not, responded to the change of course in a different way. This group of residents, consisting mostly of business owners, argued that the community should cut its losses, accept the overpass, and move on. As community member Yolanda Navarro wrote in an email to METRO chair Gilbert Garcia, clearly criticizing the protesting members of the CAB, the overpass decision "should not be about egos, he said, she said, they lied, it is not true. This is about what is best for the greater good and I am sure we will come up with the best method of assisting businesses."[45] Julio del Carpio, an early supporter of the underpass, wrote the mayor on behalf of the Harrisburg Merchants Association to express concern over continued delays and to ask her to dismiss the arguments of those still pushing the underpass: "We [business owners] are the *ONLY taxpayers* affected by your decision and our livelihood depends on Metro finalizing the rail that is creating severe losses to our businesses. . . . None of these civic leaders [who oppose the overpass] have businesses in the immediate area or are risking any contamination to their property."[46] One local developer, Alan Atkinson, even alluded to the fight over the Harrisburg Freeway in his call for the overpass to move forward. Instead of framing the earlier conflict as a victory for local participation, the developer viewed the highway fight result as a direct cause of the East End's subsequent decline. In his eyes, the failure to bring a highway through the community "further isolate[d] the East End and contribut[ed] to further economic decline in ensuing decades."[47] Clearly, the history of transportation activism could be interpreted in a variety of ways—just like its contemporary iteration.

In the months following the overpass announcement, METRO added the "costly delay" arguments to its liability and safety concerns to buttress its position on the overpass. "The overwhelming sentiment, [Chair Gilbert] Garcia says, is that the line needs to be finished. 'We want to get out of the way.'"[48] METRO convened two special meetings of its board to contend with the issue, each time laying out an argument that the liability, safety, cost, and delays were too much to justify pursuing the underpass. On May 22, the board formally approved the return to an overpass.[49] However, formal METRO board approval did not come with the city's formerly promised funds. Proponents had a final card to play: using their political advocates to attempt to block the overpass from progressing.

Underpass proponents responded to the final push for an overpass with one last public attempt to sway opinion and slow the decision. They, too, embraced the delay rhetoric, in a *Houston Chronicle* op-ed in April 2014, but they put it to different use by arguing that a small delay was worth it if it meant protecting the future of the East End: "The decision about whether to build an underpass or an overpass is an important one that will leave its mark for a hundred years or more into the future. This is a decision that should not be taken lightly. Yes, we all want this process to be finished quickly . . . [but] the East End can wait for the right decision." Proponents also forwarded language tied directly to citywide trends then emerging that reimagined Houston and its built environment. These East Enders employed the language of transportation and smart-growth advocates to argue that the light rail did not represent transportation alone, but a broader idea about what the corridor could become. The light rail line was about a "different pattern of urbanization. . . . This new light-rail will bring about a fine-grained pattern of shops and cafes . . . a pattern that is the very essence of 'walkability,' the new standard for sustainable urbanism. An overpass will break up that pattern right in the heart of Harrisburg."[50] The risk of moving forward with the overpass without delay was too much, opponents argued. Not only did it ignore the years of input, they said, but it threatened one of the best opportunities the community had to reinvent itself as a more desirable urban place.

Political representatives from the community attempted to slow the process and push METRO to reconsider the underpass. Council members Robert Gallegos and Ed Gonzalez withdrew their commitment of capital improvement program (CIP) funds unless the agency reopened the discussion.[51] The push did not dissuade METRO from its course, however.[52] The agency rejected the call for delays, even threatening at one point to move forward without city support and to build an unpopular rail-only overpass.[53] This threat, coupled with continued negotiation that promised direct community input on the bridge, as well as the long delay, helped to slowly erode resistance to the overpass. This reality became apparent in July 2014, when the Houston City Council voted to reinstate its commitment to funding an overpass that could carry both car and light rail traffic.[54] In explaining his vote, Gonzalez, who had threatened to withhold his CIP funds, showed how fatigued many had become by the drawn-out process: "At the end of the day we have to come together as a community. We have to think about what's best for the greater Houston community. And while maybe our position didn't prevail in the end, we still have to stay focused on the end game."[55]

Despite the acrimonious nature of the fight, with the overpass approved, METRO once again reached out to the community in an effort to seek feedback on the shape it would take. This move not only tied back to METRO's long-running attempts to engage with the community, but also reflected once again the major shift in how residents and agencies interacted.

The decision was final. Both the board and the City Council had approved the overpass. METRO could have built whatever it liked, but METRO officials nonetheless reengaged and spent several more months going over designs with the community. Furthermore, the METRO board voted to extend business assistance funds to those businesses directly impacted by the overpass construction, allotting an additional $2.5 million to help defray the costs of delay.[56]

The board held three public meetings in September 2014 to hash out the design with the community. At each, METRO representatives struck a conciliatory, engaged tone. They often rehashed the language of seeing progress on the line and a commitment to bringing service to the community. METRO board chairman Garcia told the community that the board wanted to "make something special" with the overpass, "something unique and special and to almost be a grand entry into the East End." Board member Christof Spieler echoed Garcia, asking for the community to help the agency create something "that really speaks to the East End. That becomes a neighborhood landmark," something that could appear on the cover of community brochures. The agency forwarded a number of ideas in the public meetings on the landscaping, art, and lighting. It also solicited the thoughts of residents on what should be done underneath the overpass in terms of programming or activating the space. At the end of each meeting, Spieler thanked the residents for coming out, and his words once again reflected the changing nature of the relationship between the residents and the decision-makers: "I really appreciate everyone coming," Spieler concluded. "I love seeing this kind of turnout. I love seeing young people. I love seeing people who I know are incredibly committed to this neighborhood." Even after the goal of an underpass had been dashed, many residents continued to engage in the process and offer their perspectives.[57]

CONCLUSION

At the official groundbreaking ceremony for the overpass in March 2015, the conciliatory attitude of the overpass design meetings persisted in the message of public officials. Chairman Garcia lauded the community planning efforts, saying, "We really let the community choose. . . . [T]his bridge belongs to the community; it is their bridge. We heard, we responded and I think we came up with something special." The final designs included soft blue LED lights, art reflecting the area's Hispanic heritage and history, and a planted "green wall" of vegetation leading up the side of the bridge in homage to the Green Line name. Acknowledging ongoing concerns about delays, Garcia committed to building the bridge at "warp speed." METRO board member Diann Lewter ruminated on the battle to get to that moment: "It really is kind of an emotional day for this community," she said, as its members had "fought so hard" to shape the project. In the end, despite the fact that the community's views were not completely adhered to, Lewter concluded, the bridge served as its own metaphor: "This bridge once divided the community, and now it's bringing it together."[58] Whether or not this will hold true will depend upon how the area around the bridge develops in the years after its completion. This outcome will be shaped by the continued efforts of citizens, METRO, and the City of Houston to ensure that the area meets each group's expectations.

Well before the impact of the Green Line and its overpass are known, though, it is pertinent to ponder how the East End fight fits into the larger narrative around infrastructural citizenship in Houston. Should the process, over thirteen years in the making, be considered a success from the point of view of the residents, since the light rail exists? Or does the overpass fight demonstrate the persistent power of public decision-makers? The two outcomes are difficult to separate. Perhaps such choices no longer have cut-and-dried winners and losers as they once did. The Green Line's history demonstrates the significant growth of public access to power, and, simultaneously, lays bare its limits. As a signpost on a broader, shifting spectrum of public participation, the line serves as a marker of the abandonment of the historical patterns of decision-making laid out earlier in this book. The East End in the 1960s and 1970s faced far from democratic processes that aimed to drive a highway through the heart of the community. Only fierce and sustained opposition helped derail that effort. That work informed and strengthened the resolve and power of East Enders during the light rail campaign. They benefited from the accountability that earlier generations had worked to instill into the decision-making process, and they saw many of their desires—most fundamentally, their push for the rail itself—realized.

Although one could argue that the line divided the community—with conflicts around it now ongoing for nearly fifteen years—the energy attached to the debate also reflects a shared commitment to the neighborhood. The residents did not always agree throughout the process, but they were all invested in the project and its results. The infrastructural fight provided a space through which the residents could assert their visions for the community, no matter how disparate. An engaged public worked with METRO and the city to create the final product. No one group got its way entirely.

Fig. 6.2. East End Overpass History Panels
This photograph shows the installation of several of the history panels that make up the side of the overpass. The panels reflect one of the compromises METRO struck with East End residents after the decision to build the overpass was finalized. Photo by Christof Spieler, used with permission.

Indeed, that is an impossibility in truly democratic decisions. The drive to bring effective transportation to the neighborhood also allowed the East End to advocate for and secure its interests at a metropolitan level. Although the allocation of citywide and regional resources continues to be a far from equal practice, the growing power of politicians from traditionally underserved communities like the East End has meant that these parts of the city have seen upticks in investment over previous years. While the East End and other traditionally underfunded communities do not yet receive equal financial support from the city when compared to the most well supported communities, infrastructural spending is beginning to draw closer together. Persistent gaps in investment and the political systems that encourage them are likewise garnering more negative attention in the region.[59]

The Green Line began operation in May 2016.[60] Ridership numbers in the first months were lower than many had hoped it would be, and progress on the overpass had been delayed for a variety of reasons.[61] Testing began on the overpass in October 2016, and the bridge opened in January 2017. Along the sides of the bridge, important dates of Harrisburg's history appear (fig. 6.2). The panels mark the community's founding and give the names and achievements of famous residents, the stuff of memorials and historical markers. Absent from the panels is any mention of a long past freeway fight. Nor does the bridge make mention of the conflict that shaped its very structure and presence. But neither are these fights, one built atop the foundation of the other, entirely absent. The bridge itself, its girders and concrete, reflect the long struggle around its construction. The desires of the community, their views on what the infrastructure could provide or take away, are interwoven into the overpass. The choices the residents made helped to bring rail to the community. They helped bring attention to what they and their neighbors wanted. They articulated a clear vision of what a single infrastructural element could provide. They invested it with their hopes, expectations, and anxieties. This investment, a clear assertion of infrastructural citizenship, vested the rail with significance and turned a transportation line into a venue through which a community organized and articulated its vision for the future.

CONCLUSION

> *A wasteland, exactly at the center of Right-of-Way, Houston, Texas, United States of America, from which her asphalt could stretch and rest and roll and be here and be now with us now. So then in 1975 she came, her parents had only moved 295 as her Uncle Eis would later say, and "no one protested" as they would say. . . . Travelin' Man played because they had made some 295 men and women into traveling men and women and invited them, for soon they could travel up and down her body which would be there to serve them. And they cut ribbon with too large scissors in suits they didn't want to wear in the sweltering heat and underneath the sun that poked them with balls of burning warmth. . . . Nine years later, on this day September 5, 1984, she had grown wide and flat and gray and white the traveling men and women had found her body to take them back and forth and back again.*
>
> CHARISSE WESTON, *TRAVELIN' MAN* EXHIBIT TEXT, PROJECT ROW HOUSE GALLERY, 2014.

In 2014 visual artist and poet Charisse Weston installed an exhibition on the walls of a gallery space at Project Row Houses in Houston's Third Ward. Titled *Travelin' Man*, the combination of block prints and text depicted the construction of State Highway 288 through the middle of South Central Houston between 1974 and 1985. According to the 1974 Environmental Impact Statement, which Weston styled as "Uncle Eis" in the passage above, the roadway displaced 295 households. It also severed the Riverside neighborhood of the Third Ward from the rest of the community.[1] Riverside was a subdivision of middle- to upper-middle-class homes that were only integrated in the mid-1950s. The movement of these black Houstonians into the community had been a point of pride at a time when intimidation and violence directed at the first black families moving into white neighborhoods was the norm in Houston and across the nation. When Highway 288 was planned and built, this group absorbed a great deal of the impacts, losing what some families had fought for decades to achieve.

Weston's exhibit reflected on the legacy of highway construction and the ceremony of constructing mobility in Houston. The image of elected officials and community supporters standing astride a newly poured expanse of highway holding ceremonial scissors reads as a facile recounting of the history laid out in this book. The roadway was progress to many and pain to a few. Within the framework of Houston's car-oriented infrastructure, 288 proved a crucial provider of mobility to a sprawling region. The highway connected the industrial productivity of Freeport to Houston's petrochemical complex. It also linked burgeoning suburban communities, such as Pearland, to downtown Houston. Crucially, it became the primary transportation artery for these suburban communities into the growing Texas Medical Center, now one of the world's largest medical complexes. The celebration of the opening, a cheer for easy mobility and growth, elided the spaces, structures, and lives that populated the landscape prior to the highway. At similar openings across the region, the cheers often outnumbered the laments. The new lane lines and overpasses and traffic replaced the homes and local streets and daily moments that had preceded them. Weston's words and images captured that loss, preserved it and held it aloft, asking the viewer to remember.

Weston's metaphor is powerful. The roadway is a person, a body used for the benefit of others. This image resonates with the experiences of those Houstonians whose lives and homes were impacted by the negative consequences of highway construction. It likewise connects, though, to those who applauded the construction of the road. To some, 288 was a disruption, a sting that persists today, as Weston's art gracefully documents. To others, the road provided an invaluable economic and mobility lifeline for the region. The contemporary and historical viewpoints on this highway project illustrate the multiple, often conflictive meanings that infrastructures hold for urban dwellers. The parsing of those many opinions is difficult. Not every voice of protest can be recorded; nor can every beneficiary be marked. The place and meaning of infrastructures are hard to contend with—both historically and in the present day. That an artist in 2014 chose to focus on the impact of a highway built in the 1980s demonstrates the undeniable staying power and presence that these structures hold in everyday life well after they are built. Although Weston's words were meant to frame one road, similar descriptions could be crafted for countless other projects, past and present.

More than twenty years before Weston installed her show, local state representative and prominent African-American politician Harold Dutton spoke to the seemingly timeless practice of displacements affecting non-white, lower-income areas. Discussing a pending widening of I-45 through Houston's Fifth Ward in 1991, Dutton lamented the impacts of the widening on the community. It might not have been a new highway, but the widening hurt and it signaled the region's ongoing emphasis on ensuring suburban mobility. Dutton argued that the notion that the nature of Houston's infrastructural decision-making had changed much since 1950 was far from accurate. He pointed out that Houston's African-American and Mexican-American communities too often got skipped over when benefits were being passed out. It was only "when it comes to a burden being passed down" that the communities got "more than their fair share."[2] Dutton's words, similar to Weston's art, captured the complicated nature of Houstonians' relationship to their city's transportation network and their understanding of the history that shaped it.

Dutton's lament could have just as easily been lifted from a newspaper in 1950 or 1970 as from its actual source in 1991. Indeed, for all the progress that had occurred since 1950 in terms of democratizing transportation decision-making and dispersing its benefits and consequences equally, much about the region's growth practices appeared, to Dutton and to many others, not to have changed at all. Even today, there is clear evidence that the physical costs of Houston's growth, now most often appearing in the form of under-investment, lack of services, or displacement, continue to fall disproportionately onto working-class and nonwhite populations.[3] However, the fact that Dutton spoke in 1991, and not 1950, mattered a great deal, because the historical context surrounding infrastructure projects had shifted markedly. In the postwar period, black Houstonians from Dutton's Fifth Ward had little formal recourse when highways bore through their neighborhoods. By 1991, however, when Fifth Ward residents faced additional infrastructure challenges, they could expect support from elected officials at the local, state, and national levels, who, like Dutton, came from their neighborhoods and shared their concerns for its future. Dutton's comments illustrated the evolution of Houston's transportation-framed version of infrastructural citizenship over the previous seventy years. That a representative like Dutton could deploy his political weight to express dismay about potential displacements reflected the decades-long efforts of a diverse collection of Houstonians to first demand access to and then claim influence over regional infrastructural debates.

The scope and significance of citizen participation in Houston's transportation debates changed drastically over time. Although a collection of nearly all white and male elected officials, professional planners, and private developers held immense power over the decision-making process in the 1950s and 1960s, they never completely controlled it. The actions of citizens outside of that group—from the protests of white middle- and upper-class suburbanites in Memorial Bend against the Outer Belt to the complaints of African Americans in the Fifth Ward about lack of pedestrian overpasses—at least forced leaders to acknowledge the divergent perspectives citizens held about transportation infrastructure, even if they only rarely embraced them. By the mid-1970s, aided by changes in federal oversight and citizen participation regulations, as well as by their practice of transportation activism, an increasingly diverse set of Houstonians—male and female, African American, Mexican American, and white, urban and suburban, rich and poor—possessed more influence over the city's choices. Simultaneously, residents' competing conceptions of mobility and goals for the region engendered new contests for power in the 1970s and 1980s. These fights included more citizens than ever before and brokered unique metropolitan alliances, but they also highlighted Houstonians' new calculations about how best to defend their homes and promote their interests through infrastructural debates. Today's debates about the city's infrastructure are rooted in these earlier contests, as the East End Green Line fight shows so well.

The practice of infrastructural citizenship in Houston was never static; nor was the makeup of the groups that utilized the rhetoric of transportation activism consistent. Citizen involvement in the city's struggle to shape highways and mass transit projects continually shifted, and individuals' conceptions and expectations for the transportation infrastructure that surrounded their homes changed over time. So, too, did their desire to actively engage in debates around the planning, construction, or presence of infrastructural projects. Often Houstonians expressed the most concern about a project only when it directly affected their daily lives—their property or their commute. Only rarely, as the case of TMO's work against the Hardy Toll Road and the defeat of the HARTA referendum by a broad population of citizens, did Houstonians form coalitions that included more than directly affected neighborhoods.

While the arc of this history shows how much access to participatory mechanisms has changed, the decision-making process has not yet resulted in an equal or consistent distribution of political power. A number of the victories highlighted in this book were short-lived—the alliance between nonwhite voters and suburbanites in 1973 and 1978 had dissipated by 1983, and slowing projects by gumming up federal oversight is a far cry from establishing equal participation and political power. Rather than reflecting a constant arc of progress toward democratization, influence over the transportation choices made in the city has risen and fallen in connection with larger metropolitan and national forces. The growing power of nonwhite voters influenced the outcomes of the referenda in 1973 and 1978. But white suburban backlash against fears of metropolitan taxation and city-based control of the region also influenced these elections. Such national trends, when paired with localized concerns, help explain how unique alliances emerged and declined among Houstonians at these moments. The interplay between the blurred nature of an individual's relationship to particular transportation infrastructures and to broader national trends reverberated on the ground in Houston. Understanding the outcomes of this mixture requires a simultaneous focus on definitive physical structures and the amorphous politics that surrounds them.

Houston was built differently from New York, Chicago, and Philadelphia. Much of that difference rests in the political choices about the built environment that the region's officials and citizens have made over the course of more than seventy years. Houston exemplified the auto-centric development of southwestern and southern cities after World War II—rapid population increase, the embrace of highways by elected officials and citizens, and a resulting proliferation of low-density urbanization. Houstonians' struggle to build and define the city's highways and mass transit system overlapped with other contests concerning metropolitan politics, economic and racial equality, and the growth pressures of a developing metropolis. Although it shared characteristics with other Sunbelt cities, Houston's choices in mass transit debates, the constituencies who participated in the struggles to define the city, and the influence the implemented systems had on the course of Houston's development were uniquely its own. Permutations in socioeconomic, demographic, political, and cultural details in other Sunbelt cities tweaked the shape of infrastructural citizenship and citizens' engagement with the idea. The outlines of these stories are much the same, even if their telling comes in different words. Houston's lessons shed light on the infrastructural past of other Sunbelt cities, but other metro regions possess their own stories and choices. Those, too, must be parsed and recorded.

Houston's version of this mixture, the contours made by the interaction of citizens with built environment and with local, state, and national politics, reflect the legacies of the creation, implementation, and aftereffects of the long-term exercise of infrastructural citizenship. Acknowledging and documenting the efforts of infrastructural citizens over time brings the thoughts, stories, and needs of citizens in American postwar cities to the fore in essential ways. The case study of Houston provides a crucial window into how democratic political participation, mobility, and place intersect in the physical form of infrastructure. Debates about transportation structures—highways and mass transit systems, in particular—are at the core of metropolitan decision-making, yet they remain understudied. This is partly because scholars have a tendency to focus on moments of inflamed conflict. Future work must strive to look beyond moments of infrastructural crisis—the highway revolts, displacements, and transit votes—to consider carefully the context surrounding infrastructural decisions and their impacts on daily mobilities.

HIGHWAYS VS. TRANSIT?

This history is not a diatribe against nondemocratic highways or a paean to the participatory wonders of transit. Instead it should be read as a reflection on the choices that went into the creation of both systems and the choices that continue to be made about each in our cities today. Both modal choices had and have detractors and defenders. And, although regions that rely almost solely on car-based transport modes face a slew of problems, there is no way to refute Houston's infrastructural past. These events and choices happened. The structures were built and their outcomes sown. The regions dominated by highways will continue to be dominated by highways in the foreseeable future. Our roadways can no more disappear than can the impacts and legacies of their construction. Acknowledging that history and likely future allows for a more careful reflection on past choices and provides a chance for officials and citizens alike to consider what practices would best serve the widest population going forward. What should our regions become? Who should have a role in making those decisions? How should the inevitable mix of opinions and ways forward be balanced? Though the effects of previous decisions cannot be removed, their impacts can be moderated and improved. Present-day choices about transportation and other infrastructural systems are integral parts of building our urban future.

No transportation infrastructure exists in a vacuum. Those who choose to continue to support the outward, highway-oriented growth of cities must also acknowledge the historical roots and compounded contemporary consequences of those choices. Several of the systems that allowed Houston to sprawl outward are still in place, including cheap land, cheap gasoline, and cheap automobiles; lax regulation on development; housing policies that prevent meaningful density and promote single-family suburban homes as an American reality and priority; and misconceptions about the social import of mobility and the role that mass transit can play in bringing it to our most pressed citizens. Each of these continues to influence the choices metropolitan citizens make. Certainly, there are tangible benefits to these choices. For many, it has meant cheaper housing, more room, greater control over local governments, and separation from people or forces that many citizens do not wish to encounter in their daily lives. But concrete consequences roll forward with these auto-rooted choices. Reliance on car use has dramatically contributed to climate change. Metropolitan built environments are oriented around cars—wide lanes, few sidewalks, and much-maligned non-drivers. The physical arrangement of the car-based city contributes to higher speeds and daily deadly encounters between cars, bicyclists, and pedestrians. Finally, our collective national health has declined precipitously over the past half-century, and, though it is just one of many factors in the equation, long periods of stationary commuting contribute to the problem.

Transit is not without its problems. Fixed-rail systems can cost just as much as new mega-highways, with some lines reaching into the billions of dollars. They, too, can displace and disconnect. Fear of political defeat and a short-term focus too often lead to the building of transit systems of political expedience, rather than systems that follow the most productive routes or take the most effective forms. Transit-oriented development offers incredible opportunities to build for density and urban activity, but without attendant affordable housing policies, it threatens to become available only for the wealthy. For mass transit proponents, as for road proponents, it is also all too easy to promote only one form or approach to mobility, ignoring the opinions and needs of those who would remain unserved.

Neither approach to mobility is foolproof, and neither can exist in isolation from the other. Cities have always been spaces of messy interaction—whether politically, socially, or infrastructurally. Approaches to transportation must embrace that messiness, at least in the brainstorming stage, and recognize the system-based nature of our choices. Transportation networks are not disconnected from one another. Roadways and transit systems coexist and can be mutually beneficial, if they are planned correctly. Metropolitan regions are increasingly becoming integrated. Lines of division between suburbs and city, jobs and homes, are not as stark as they seemingly once were, or, at least, were perceived to be. The suburban areas of many regions are beginning to look decidedly urban. Both traditional downtown areas—still major economic drivers in most regions—and their satellite suburbs are increasing in density and turning into more walkable environments. Our transportation systems must recalibrate to those realities, with modal choices that work together rather than separately. Highways and transit are not the only answers, whether in isolation or in concert. Biking and walking hold a crucial place in this equation as well. Creating multimodal approaches that allow citizens to shift from one form to the next is crucial.

In Houston, regional leaders, led by Houston's mayor, are beginning to recognize the importance of creating a truly metropolitan approach to transportation. In early 2016, Mayor Sylvester Turner used one of the first speeches of his tenure to ask the Texas Transportation Commission to find ways to support more than just road funding. Turner began his statement to the body by declaring that "the transportation strategies that the Houston region has looked to in the past are increasingly inadequate to sustain regional growth." Continuing, Turner singled out the limitation inherent in the practice of building out roadway capacity for single-occupancy vehicles, pointing to the issue of induced demand on new highways.[4] If you build it, cars will come. Instead of business as usual, Turner called instead for a "paradigm shift" in the funding and planning of transportation infrastructure. He pointed to a need to create more high-occupancy trips on transit and on highways and called for more highway funds to focus on central city highway projects rather than suburban roadways. Turner encouraged greater investment in the local street grid to improve the interface between streets and highways, sidewalks and streets. Turner made it clear that improving the mobile experience of all users, no matter the mode, needed to be paramount.[5] He redoubled this stance in his State of Mobility speech, in May 2016, calling not just for complete streets, but for complete communities, where safe and easy mobility was a right.[6]

Turner's words echoed several broader infrastructural and transportation trends reshaping the Houston region. They were also a call to reflection for those Houstonians still recalcitrant about embracing a networked transportation reality—the idea that highways alone are not enough to move a region effectively and equitably. Today, funding and incentives for roadways cannot outstrip funding and incentives for other modes of transportation as much as they have over the past seventy years. Two in-progress highway projects, each of which are rooted in past choices, shed light on the current state of metropolitan realities in Houston. How each highway fits or breaks with the mold of the city's historical approach to mobility is telling about the current state of the system and about the choices we still face as our cities grow.

Sitting nearly thirty miles from the center of Houston and running for a total length of just over 180 miles, the Grand Parkway, Houston's third ring road, appeared on maps in the 1960s projecting future plans. It remained in the plans until the late 1970s, when officials removed it because ongoing transportation fights made such a long-term project seem untenable. After the creation of the Harris Country Toll Road Authority in the 1980s, when suburb-oriented visions of mobility became ascendant in the choices of the region, the highway reappeared in the plans. Construction began in the 1980s and continues to this day. Since it has been an active project for more than fifty years, the parkway's drawn-out planning and construction process reflects the historical contours of Houston's transportation decision-making process and the ongoing role of land speculation in directing it in ways that other transportation structures do not.

Part of the parkway's significance stems from the public-private partnership that governs the road's routing and fundraising. The Grand Parkway Association was commissioned by the State of Texas to head a public-private initiative that would allow landowners along the route, mostly real estate speculators and developers, to donate the land where the state would build the parkway.[7] To pay for the construction, the state would make the parkway a toll road. This funding structure was crucial given the huge demands placed on Texas's infrastructure budgets by a statewide population increase of more than 4 million people between 1980 and 2000. The Texas Highway Department could barely keep up with maintenance needs on the state's more than 72,000 miles of highway, much less afford to build massive new roads to accommodate burgeoning traffic. Into this space came the parkway's public-private partnership model, which, while allowing developers an inordinate say over the route, also allowed construction to continue in spite of funding difficulties.

Today about half of the Grand Parkway is completed or slated to open soon. The remaining segments are to be constructed in the coming decades.[8]

The route is both an artifact and a product of past transportation debates, a situation that gives the road a complicated position in the region. The parkway, with its roots in the 1960s, hews closer in form to the tenets of an earlier era of planning, when the city and its mobility options were quite different from those of today. Like the majority of Houston's transportation structures, the parkway is based not on decisions made in 2018 to address 2018 problems, but on the choices made over the course of almost sixty years. For this reason it prioritizes outward growth even as the needs and shape of the region have changed.

A radical departure from the planning for the Grand Parkway and the state's historical approach to road building, the so-called North Houston Highway Improvement Project (NHHIP) has the chance to completely reshape downtown Houston. The project proposes to remove the Pierce Elevated section of I-45 through downtown, run two major highways (I-10 and I-45) together along the northern edge of downtown, and then feed them into an existing interchange with I-69. The project also intends to depress major sections of the realigned road below grade, with the option of eventually creating capped greenspaces atop the road, as has been done successfully in Dallas and Boston.[9] The result, according to the Texas Department of Transportation (TxDOT) and the Houston-Galveston Area Council (HGAC), the region's metropolitan planning organization, will be a more rationalized highway system around downtown, freer flowing traffic, and an opportunity to remake Central Houston.

At a surface level, a road project that results in the creation of sections of highway more than twenty lanes across is hard to label as a significant shift away from previous models. And to a great extent, the North Houston Highway is an emulation of older decision-making, a slightly unavoidable outcome, given that its planning has been carried out over more than fifteen years.[10] In the end, there is no denying that the focus of the highway project remains on moving auto traffic through and around the city. However, unlike any other project before it, the highway realignment contains elements—such as the teardown of Pierce and the proposed capped sections—that acknowledge changing public attitudes toward transportation infrastructure and that demonstrate the influence that small groups of committed officials and citizens can play in shaping today's major decisions.[11] For as much as the highway plan seems to be business as usual, the process that shaped its current iteration was much more intimate, informed, and participatory than what occurred in the past.

In the more than a decade of planning, proposals for the new highways have shifted from miles-long tunnels cut under huge sections of Houston, to traditionally widened highways, to the present-day plan. These transitions were shaped by public participation in the process—through organized protest manifested in engaged public comment and complaint at dozens of public meetings, online, and in the press—and through the actions of public agencies and actors with new visions for how downtown Houston might be shaped in the future. When TxDOT and HGAC initially began to study the expansion of I-45 in 2004, they planned a traditional expansion of the freeway. Citizens from communities alongside the highway, including many who remembered a previous round of displacements in the widening that Representative Dutton protested in the early 1990s, objected to this plan. Aided by the passage of SAFETEA-LU, a transportation law that added further reporting requirements, resident groups successfully lobbied for further studies that included the feasibility of bringing mass transit to the corridor and called for considering a tunnel in lieu of widening.[12]

After several plans formed and faded away during the early 2000s, Central Houston, Inc., a public, special district tasked with improving the built environment of downtown, took a leading role formulating the redesign effort. Central Houston coordinated with TxDOT, the City of Houston, residents, other public districts, and advocate groups in an effort to turn the plans into a transformational project. The emergence of this non-agency actor has been key in brokering the visions of the NHHIP. Central Houston and others worked with TxDOT not only to come up with a provisional set of plans that pushed the envelope, but to make the public process of feedback a productive one. How the NNHIP will play out is not yet known, but similar to the Green Line debate, the public conversation around the project has been much more engaged than the discussions of the past.[13]

The two road projects signal the nearly impossible task of coordinating infrastructural needs and visions across a major metropolitan area and across time. The forces contributing to each project are similar—a drive to see Houston grow, for investors in the areas they serve to see profit, and for citizens and goods to move—but the processes used to reach the final product have been quite different. The Grand Parkway is tied to an older model of development in Houston, one that sees outward growth as a given and a positive. The NNHIP offers a shift in vision for downtown highways and potentially for future suburban roadways as well. The simultaneity of the debates within Houston illustrates how difficult it remains to create a system that serves such a large geographic region and the varied needs of a diverse population.

The highway projects are just two examples in the universe of choices that Houstonians have made in recent years about mobility. Although the overwhelming majority of funding continues to flow to more suburban-oriented highway and road projects, Houston's choices for its infrastructure and metropolitan built environment have changed. Houston's light rail system, a revolutionary reimagining of the bus system, the passage of the city's first general plan, massive overhauls to the city's parks, and a new bike master plan are all a part of this transition.[14] So, too, are new ideas for highways, for ride-sharing applications, and on the impact of autonomous cars.[15] Consideration of these systems is the heir to earlier decades of transit advocacy and part of the ongoing debate over what form of transportation can best serve a sprawling metro area.

But legacies of historical decisions are not painlessly overcome. For downtowns that are attempting to shift toward density, overnight revolutions are not possible. The reemergence of support for transit and the goal of reimagining downtowns are happening at a moment when land is more expensive and construction more difficult than in the past. Because of decades of underinvestment, transit makes up far less of the existing infrastructure than road networks, and maintaining what does exist has become a monumental problem.[16] New transit projects mean new disruptions. Highways, in contrast, have had dedicated routes for years, and widening them is often less of an uphill battle. The roadway is received infrastructural wisdom, and its widening an assumed outcome. Cities and communities grappling with transit, especially of the fixed-route variety, are facing new challenges in their effort to plan and construct these systems in increasingly difficult political settings. The same can be said for public officials working to change the development and transit approaches in predominantly single-family, car-dependent suburban areas.[17]

Adding to this challenge is the growing role of residents in asserting or confronting the desirability of any given project. Infrastructural citizenship and public participation in decision-making are double-edged practices. Citizen involvement is essential to democratic participation, but this involvement also means longer processes and higher costs. There are many options for pursuing temporary, experimental changes to city streets and mobility systems—changes that often can be transitioned into permanent alterations over time.[18] But so-called tactical urbanism must also be supported by larger reformulations in how mobility structures look and function.

No greater challenge exists for our changing metropolitan regions, though, than ensuring that mobility is provided equally to all residents and that the consequences of new projects do not fall on the same shoulders as they have historically.

INFRASTRUCTURAL CITIZENSHIP AND EQUITY IN THE TWENTY-FIRST CENTURY

The changing mobility demands and practices of the twenty-first century present Houstonians and other city dwellers with significant challenges. Physical mobility, a concept redefined in the postwar period by its links to automobiles and highways, today encompasses more modes than in the past—including walking, bicycling, and mass transit—and overlaps significantly with broad planning concepts and urban issues, such as transit-oriented development, affordability, sustainability, and immobility. Moreover, the very shape and pattern of urban growth is shifting, and cities are becoming increasingly diverse. In recent years, Houston's outward suburbanization has continued, but that movement has been balanced by the movement into the central city of a wealthier class of former suburbanites and recent arrivals.[19] As central cities gentrify, pushes to improve the livability of these areas dominate planning theory and practice.[20] Working to encourage centralization and quell the adverse ecological effects of expansive urbanization, planning practitioners have attempted to construct neighborhoods that foster greater density and wean Americans off their overreliance on automobiles.[21] These approaches successfully demonstrate that cities can become more sustainable while still developing economically. The simultaneity of continued expansion and recentralization presents Houstonians, and urbanites across the United States, with a difficult set of questions about whether current transportation approaches provide adequate and equal access to mobility for the residents of their metropolitan areas. This problem is particularly acute in southwestern cities, where auto-centric development has created sprawling urban areas and even the best bus and rail systems struggle to meet the needs of transit-dependent riders.

For all their recent accomplishments, most smart growth and livability projects have not adequately addressed the issues of social equity that arose during their implementation. Many have failed to incorporate the perspectives of a wide population of urbanites, especially the opinions and needs of the poor and ethnic minority communities. Resources and consequences are still distributed unevenly, raising concerns about social and environmental justice.[22] Just as suburban areas received more city services in the 1960s, today's gentrifying, higher-income neighborhoods in Houston and other cities have more amenities than lower-income areas. This reality has contributed to a variety of negative health and lifestyle consequences for residents without access to public transportation, walkable spaces, or other "planned" resources.[23]

In some cities and metropolitan regions, planning and governance practices have begun to tackle equity issues. Particularly in cities with progressive planning regimes and tightly controlled land-use regulations, such as Portland, Oregon, discussions of mobility and access are increasingly connected to conversations about housing, infrastructure, and economic development.[24] Houston and other southwestern cities with expansive corporate limits are likewise working to overcome historical barriers and incorporate elements of this type of planning into their cities.[25] In many places, community organizations are helping to fill the gaps left by lacking government policies in transportation and other areas, using meaningful citizen participation and egalitarian decision-making to create and implement plans.[26] Pushes in numerous cities to bring participatory budgeting processes to city governance and infrastructural investments are further reflections of ongoing attempts to more meaningfully incorporate individual desires into how cities operate.[27] That these efforts are being pursued also indicates that current decision-making does not yet adequately incorporate the viewpoints of all citizens.

A great deal of work remains. Problems facing immobile or carless populations—the poor, the transit dependent, the elderly, the disabled, and the young—persist and contribute to issues with unemployment, a lack of education, and poor health. Yet across the nation, governments and planners, often at the insistence of citizens, are working to address these and other interconnected issues, such as air pollution and incompatible land uses. These actions are deepening definitions of mobility and incorporating previously underserved constituencies into the infrastructural planning process. Officials and citizens must strive to make decisions that encourage participatory planning and that reflect urban residents' shifting expectations for mobility.[28] At the same time, they must acknowledge that such planning is not a panacea to injustice; nor is it easily attained. Ongoing discrepancies in citizens' access to political power and social capital make the goal of democratic planning difficult to achieve, but it is a goal that should be pursued nonetheless.[29] In infrastructural decision-making, this task is all the more pressing as a result of the long-lasting legacies of the systems put into place on urban landscapes.[30] Just as the choices Houstonians made in 1950 continue to affect the city today, so will the choices made in 2018 ripple forward for decades.

Viewing infrastructural citizenship not simply as a historical construction, but instead as an actionable, ongoing practice, can teach us how to better recognize the opinions and needs of residents in the future. Citizen advocates have played a growing role in urban transportation since World War II. In many cities, mass transportation advocates in particular have been weighing in on where they want their cities to go—and seeing results in partnership with engaged public officials.[31] But even in cases of relative success, and especially in instances where citizen input and needs are not being recognized, city planners and policy makers should enshrine the process of infrastructural citizenship, bearing the costs and delays and disagreements of daily democratic participation. Public meetings and seemingly uninformed questions may lead to delays, but the structures being built affect real people's lives. They do not exist solely in renderings or as flawlessly engineered structures. Citizens are impacted by them. As Houston's history has shown, those citizens want a voice in how their communities are being built. Sometimes, that requires officials to take the time to answer basic questions. And sometimes it requires slowing down the wheels of decision-making, or even rolling them back.

Nearly every city and every neighborhood contains examples of political and social conflicts that demonstrate the resonance of infrastructural citizenship and its ongoing role in urban politics and planning. Some examples have been localized battles—such as the fight over People's Park in San Francisco in the 1960s, or the debates about the process of redevelopment in Brooklyn in the early 2000s, when the National Basketball Association's Brooklyn Nets built their new stadium in the borough.[32] Others have been metropolitan in scale, such as Los Angeles's long-running debate about the management, financing, and expansion of its transportation system, or Chicago's recent installation of a network of bike lanes.[33] Finally, some assertions of infrastructural citizenship continue to redefine and repurpose existing infrastructures. Citizens contesting police killings of African Americans in a number of US cities in recent years have blocked highways and local streets as a primary protest tactic. This practice allows protesters to assert control over a public right-of-way and to repurpose it for their own ends. Disrupting commerce and daily commutes is an especially impactful approach, as it draws attention to the issue from people who otherwise might have remained removed from the political action.[34] Recognizing and parsing competing examples of infrastructural citizenship in a metropolitan context could help scholars better navigate the sea of interest groups and arguments that have affected metro-level decision-making over the previous seventy years.

In 1973, black residents of the Third Ward in Houston engaged in a failed protest against the expansion of I-45 within the neighborhood. Just before the decision to widen the road was made, state highway engineer Dewitt Greer came to Houston to dedicate the final section of I-10. Running north of downtown and paralleling the Pierce Elevated, the expanse represented the last element of Houston's contribution to the interstate system until a new segment was designated in the 2010s. To Greer, and to other officials standing on the road surface to celebrate the opening, the completion of the highway system was more than "a dream come true" for the city; it was "the realization of many dreams."[35] Greer was only partially correct. The road did meet some Houstonians hopes for mobility. But the fights that predated I-10's dedication and those that came after proved that the "dreams" of which Greer spoke, the notions of mobility he saw represented in the freshly poured concrete, were not universal.[36]

Today, Houston's infrastructural debates remain unsettled. That is, perhaps, the inevitable outcome of a system that is by definition never complete, never adequate. Houstonians have inherited a sprawling, autocentric city that emerged from the contests waged by earlier generations of residents. They have also received a system of participation and governance that affords citizens a greater opportunity to shape the city's future decisions. The challenge for Houston, and for other cities, is to confront the issues created by their historical urban form—continued suburbanization, auto-dependence, and a lack of walkability—while also addressing the mobility needs of residents spread across the region. New coalitions and divisions will surely emerge as residents reevaluate their expectations for transportation and find allies who share those conceptions. New systems will be proposed, debated, dismissed, and embraced as Houstonians jockey to define the future of the city. As they make choices in the coming years about where the city is going and how it should get there, they would be wise to look in their rearview mirror.

ACKNOWLEDGMENTS

A few weeks prior to submitting this manuscript I enjoyed a weekend with friends and family during the American Historical Association's annual meeting. Sitting with these people, folks who had traveled the long road of graduate school as peers or our partners, I was struck by the power and importance that each had played in the formulation of this book. While they may not have all read its earlier iterations, their love, support, laughter, and friendship helped me reach this final stage, even from afar. It was a fitting reminder that book projects are labors of love and that we do not undertake these efforts alone.

I owe a great deal of thanks, therefore, to the many who have helped me travel this path.

This book began with my work as a graduate student in the History Department at the University of Texas at Austin. The financial support I received during my tenure there allowed me to research and write the dissertation from which this book emerged. Fellowships from the Dolph Briscoe Center for American History, the New Orleans Center for the Gulf South, the University of Texas College of Liberal Arts, and the History Department supported me during research and writing. The History Department provided me with an academic home. Professors and peers challenged and nurtured my work, making it better with each step. Staff, especially Marilyn Lehman, helped me navigate the ins and outs of the graduate program.

I owe a special debt to the mentors who served on my dissertation committee. From their comments and critiques at my defense to their ongoing feedback on my work, they have helped bring this book to fruition. Laurie Green has been a mentor since my early days at UT. This book and my own approach to historical scholarship are much stronger thanks to her careful eye and insistence that I produce the best work I can. Jacqueline Jones contributed to every step of my journey at UT. Conversations with Erika Bsumek helped shaped my notions of place, space, and the environment. Working with her on a course about the American built environment pushed me toward studying infrastructure. Steven Hoelscher taught me to view the American landscape as a primary source and first suggested that

I investigate mobility as a historical category. Martin Melosi, after reading an early draft chapter of my dissertation, assured me that I would undoubtedly finish my project (a boon to any graduate student's psyche) and urged me to tackle big ideas. His guidance has continued during my time in Houston as the dissertation morphed into this book. It is my hope that this work lives up to the expectations of these scholars.

Many archivists and librarians assisted my research in Houston and Austin. At the Houston Metropolitan Research Center, Joanna Collier, Joel Draut, Laney Dwyer, Barbara Morales, Erin Norris, Tim Ronk, Elizabeth Sargent, and Aaron Winslow aided my search for sources and made my long days in the archives enjoyable. The entire staff at the University of Houston Special Collections, especially Teresa Tomkins-Walsh, made my visits productive, while Sarah Canby Jackson and Annie Golden at the Harris County Archives helped me negotiate boxes of county appraisals. Oscar Erik Slotboom generously shared documents he collected during his own research on the history and construction of Houston's highways. Staff members of the Woodson Research Collection at Rice University, the Archives of the Archdiocese of Galveston-Houston, and the Texas State Archives also helped me track down essential sources. The staff of the Texas Department of Transportation Houston Branch planning department, aerial photo division, and communications division gave me access to a number of state-held sources, particularly aerial photos. Finally, the Transportation Library of the Houston-Galveston Area Council, the Harris County Clerk's Office, and the Houston City Secretary's Office opened small collections for me that had a large impact on this project.

Friends, colleagues, and mentors have helped make this project a reality. Jim Sidbury played a prominent role in my first years of graduate school and generously allowed me to housesit his Houston home during research. Laurie Green invited me to join a dissertation group of her advisees in my second year. Members of that group—Leah Deane, Deirdre Doughty, Luritta DuBois, Cristina Salinas, and Sarah Steinbock-Pratt—walked with me through dissertation writing, providing an invaluable support network. In the UT History community, Cheasty Miller Anderson, José Barragán, Juandrea Bates, Felipe Cruz, Christopher Heaney, Brian Jones, Renata Keller, Shannon Nagy, Julia Ogden, Rachel Ozanne, Claudia Rueda, and Cameron Strang commiserated, brainstormed, and celebrated with me along the way. Numerous Austin and Houston friends have likewise been by my side and know who they are. Charlene Boyer Lewis and James Lewis stoked my deep love of history and gave me the academic tools to pursue it during my undergraduate study at Kalamazoo College. Kara Schlichting and I traded chapters for years, and some of this book's best parts can find their roots in her suggestions. Andrew Needham, Wes Phelps, and Chris Wells all offered important input along the way. Geoff Carelton, Jerome Gray, Tom Lambert, and Christof Spieler all reviewed sections of this book and offered helpful insights. Jean Aroom helped me navigate the perils of using geographic information system (GIS) technology and took over when my limited skills got in the way.

Conferences and workshops helped to flesh out this project. Alex Byrd and Emily Strauss organized the "Race and Place" conference at Rice University where I first presented this work. The Center for Energy and Environmental Research in the Human Sciences at Rice allowed me to workshop an early book chapter. Tim Cresswell, who served as commentator at the workshop, and each of its participants, but especially Dominic Boyer, Jim Elliott, Randal Hall, and Cymene Howe, pushed me to better articulate my project and its importance. The International Association for the History of Transport, Traffic, and Mobility provided me with an energetic set of peers who were likewise interested in questions of mobility. I would like to particularly thank Gijs Mom and Peter Norton for inviting me into that organization as an editor for *Mobility in History* and helping to shape my ideas of how to study the ways we move.

The Kinder Institute for Urban Research and Rice University have been incredible professional homes for the past three years. It is a pleasure to spend every day working with them to try to make our cities into more equitable, better places.

The entire staff of the University of Texas Press has been incredible. Robert Devens worked with me to bring this book out from the confines of the dissertation. His careful editing, probing suggestions, and commitment to the project helped me to reach the finish. I would also like to thank Sarah McGavick for helping bring the final details, of which they are so many, into place. The reviewers of this work offered important suggestions that strengthened the argument and pushed me to be a better historian.

Finally, the support and love of my family made this book possible. My mother, Chris Shelton, and my father, Terry Shelton, taught me to love reading and writing, to value everyone's stories, and to pursue what moves me. My siblings and their partners—Anna Shelton and Seth Kirby, Cully Shelton and Laura O'Leary—have been welcome company and excellent sounding boards throughout this process. Micheal Vickery and Linda Koebert welcomed me into their family and encouraged Kate and I through every step of our educations. Shirley Smith, members of the extended Krumdieck, Shelton, Vickery, and Koebert families, as well as friends from Madison, Kalamazoo, and too many others to name, have also helped me reach this point.

My wife, Kate Vickery, is my center. Her love, intelligence, sense of humor, and drive have balanced me, taught me, pushed me, and left me breathless. Without her I surely would not have passed page one.

And, as perhaps the ultimate reminder of just how long a book takes to produce, our children, Julius and Etta, were born in years four and six of this project. Their arrivals helped spur me through the process. Their presence brought great energy and joy to my life as I finished the book. I look forward to forcing them to read it.

NOTES

INTRODUCTION

1. *Northeast News*, April 26, 1983, Central Chancery Files (CCF), Archives of the Archdiocese of Galveston-Houston, Houston, Texas (AAGH); "City Council Hearing on Hardy Toll Project Draws 300," *North Freeway Leader*, April 28, 1983, CCF, AAGH.

2. Ibid.

3. This argument builds from Nikhil Anand, "PRESSURE: The PoliTechnics of Water Supply in Mumbai," *Cultural Anthropology* 26, no. 4 (November 2011): 542–564; Gabriel Klaeger, "Dwelling on the Road: Routines, Rituals and Roadblocks in Southern Ghana," *Africa: The Journal of the International African Institute* 83, no. 3 (2013): 446–469, and from James C. Scott's idea of infrapolitics, visible in much of his work, but seen most directly in *Domination and the Arts of Resistance: Hidden Transcripts*, reprint ed. (New Haven, CT: Yale University Press, 1992), and "Beyond the War of Words: Cautious Resistance and Calculated Conformity," in Louise Amoore, ed., *The Global Resistance Reader* (New York: Routledge, 2005).

4. James C. Scott, *Weapons of the Weak: Everyday Forms of Peasant Resistance* (New Haven, CT: Yale University Press, 1987).

5. Eric Avila, *Folklore of the Freeway: Race and Revolt in the Modernist City* (Minneapolis: University of Minnesota Press, 2014); Bruno Latour, *Reassembling the Social: An Introduction to Actor-Network-Theory* (Oxford: Oxford University Press, 2007); Mandi Isaacs Jackson, *Model City Blues: Urban Space and Organized Resistance in New Haven* (Philadelphia: Temple University Press, 2008); Ruth Miller, *Snarl: In Defense of Traffic and Faulty Networks* (Ann Arbor: University of Michigan, 2015), 83–101.

6. Jane Jacobs, *Death and Life of Great American Cities* (New York: Vintage Books, 1961); Robert Bullard, *Dumping in Dixie: Race, Class, and Environmental Quality*, 3rd ed. (Boulder: Westview Press, 2008); Andrew Needham, *Power Lines: Phoenix and the Making of the Modern Southwest* (Princeton, NJ: Princeton University Press, 2014).

7. This idea echoes Kevin Fox Gotham's conception of community identity and notions of place serving as the impetus for protest in "Political Opportunity, Community Identity, and the Emergence of a Local Anti-Expressway Movement," *Social Problems* 46, no. 3 (1999): 332–354. Eduardo Contreras, "Voice and Property: Latinos, White Conservatives, and Urban Renewal in 1960s San Francisco," *Western Historical Quarterly* 45, no. 3 (Autumn 2014): 253–276, shows how Latino actors in San Francisco responded to urban renewal with their own push for citizen participation and decision-making power. Likewise, Lydia Otero, *La Calle: Spatial Conflicts and Urban Renewal in a Southwest City* (Tucson: University of Arizona Press, 2010), 137–188, shows how historical preservation efforts could also help maintain an individual's image of a place's history.

8. There are several seminal works that have explored links between transportation and the urban built environment, but the majority of these focus on the early part of the twentieth century. See Paul Barrett, *The Automobile and Urban Transit: The Formation of Public Policy in Chicago, 1900–1930* (Philadelphia: Temple University Press, 1983); Sam Bass Warner Jr., *Streetcar Suburbs: The Process of Growth in Boston, 1870–1900*, 2nd ed. (Cambridge, MA: Harvard University Press, 1978); Kenneth T. Jackson, *Crabgrass Frontier: The Suburbanization of the United States* (New York: Oxford University Press, 1987). A few works have dealt directly with the topic of transportation systems and the American built environment in the second half of the twentieth century. See, especially, Owen D. Gutfreund, *Twentieth-Century Sprawl: Highways and the Reshaping of the American Landscape* (New York: Oxford University Press, 2005); Christopher Wells, *Car Country: An Environmental History* (Seattle: University of Washington Press, 2013); Joseph DiMento and Cliff Ellis, *Changing Lanes: Visions and Histories of Urban Freeways* (Boston: MIT Press, 2012).

9. Some historians have viewed this transition in urban policy as a shift from "policy for the whole" to policy oriented around individualized political power. See Robert B. Fairbanks, *For the City as a Whole: Planning, Politics and the Public Interest in Dallas, Texas, 1900–1965* (Columbus: Ohio State University Press, 1998), and Robert Fairbanks, *The War on Slums in the Southwest: Public Housing and Slum Clearance in Texas, Arizona, and New Mexico, 1935–1965* (Philadelphia: Temple University Press, 2014). Others have used the transition between government-driven decisions and greater citizen involvement to ask how policy choices can balance the needs of individuals with those of the whole. See Zane Miller and Bruce Tucker, *Changing Plans for American Inner Cities: Cincinnati's Over-the-Rhine Neighborhood and Twentieth-Century Urbanism* (Columbus: Ohio State University Press, 1998).

10. Mark H. Rose and Raymond A. Mohl, *Interstate: Highway Politics and Policy Since 1939*, 3rd ed. (Knoxville: University Tennessee Press, 2012); DiMento and Ellis, *Changing Lanes*; Avila, *Folklore of the Freeway*; Raymond A. Mohl, "Stop the Road: Freeway Revolts in American Cities," *Journal of Urban History* 30, no. 5 (July 2004): 674–706; Zachary M. Schrag, "The Freeway Fight in Washington, DC: The Three Sisters Bridge in Three Administrations," *Journal of Urban History* 30, no. 5 (July 2004): 648–673; Raymond A. Mohl, "The Interstates and the Cities: The US Department of Transportation and the Freeway Revolt, 1966–1973," *Journal of Policy History* 20, no. 2 (April 2008): 193–226; Katherine M. Johnson, "Captain Blake Versus the Highwaymen: Or, How San Francisco Won the Freeway Revolt," *Journal of Planning History* 8, no. 1 (February 2009): 56–83; Christopher W. Wells, "From Freeway to Parkway: Federal Law, Grassroots Environmental Protest, and the Evolving Design of Interstate-35E in Saint Paul, Minnesota," *Journal of Planning History* 11, no. 1 (2012): 8–26; Joshua Cannon, "Huntsville, the Highway, and Urban Redevelopment: The Long Road to Connect

Downtown Huntsville, Alabama to the Interstate Highway System," *Journal of Planning History* 11, no. 1 (February 2012): 27–46; Robert Gioielli, "'We Must Destroy You to Save You': Highway Construction and the City as a Modern Commons," *Radical History Review* 109 (Winter 2011): 62–82.

11. This federal devolution of authority was most apparent in transportation decision-making. See Mohl and Rose, *Interstate*; Mark H. Rose, Bruce E. Seely, and Paul F. Barrett, *The Best Transportation System in the World: Railroads, Trucks, Airlines, and American Public Policy in the Twentieth Century*, 2nd ed. (Philadelphia: University of Pennsylvania Press, 2010).

12. On debate in San Francisco, see Louise Nelson Dyble, *Paying the Toll: Local Power, Regional Politics, and the Golden Gate Bridge* (Philadelphia: University of Pennsylvania Press, 2009). On Washington, DC, see, Zachary M. Schrag, *Great Society Subway: A History of the Washington Metro* (Baltimore: Johns Hopkins University Press, 2006).

13. Kyle Shelton, "What Old Transit Maps Can Teach Us About a City's Future," *CityLab*, October 10, 2014.

14. Matthew Lassiter, *The Silent Majority: Suburban Politics in the Sunbelt South* (Princeton, NJ: Princeton University Press, 2006); Robert O. Self, *American Babylon: Race and the Struggle for Postwar Oakland* (Princeton, NJ: Princeton University Press, 2003); Kevin M. Kruse, *White Flight: Atlanta and the Making of Modern Conservatism* (Princeton, NJ: Princeton University Press, 2005); Lisa McGirr, *Suburban Warriors: The Origins of the New American Right* (Princeton, NJ: Princeton University Press, 2001).

15. In recent years scholars have diversified their understanding of democracy movements in the 1960s and 1970s by looking beyond the activities of the mainstream civil rights movement and focusing intently on local examples. One such work is Wesley Phelps, who looks at how Houstonians used "War on Poverty" programs as a stage to push for the democratizing of local decision-making. See Wesley Phelps, *A People's War on Poverty: Urban Politics, Grassroots Activists, and the Struggle for Democracy in Houston, 1964–1976* (Athens: University of Georgia Press, 2014). In addition, the "front porch" politics of the 1970s and 1980s right and left has been examined in recent years. See Michael Stewart Foley, *Front Porch Politics: The Forgotten Heyday of American Activism in the 1970s and 1980s* (New York: Hill and Wang, 2013).

16. The impact of urban development in southwestern cities has often been framed as less damaging than that which took place in northern and eastern cities. See, for example, John Mollenkopf, *The Contested City* (Princeton, NJ: Princeton University Press, 1983). I join Otero, *La Calle*, in challenging this notion of southwestern redevelopment by showing how impactful major public projects have been on many residents.

17. To augment highway revolt readings, see additional work on the unequal impact of transportation provision, such as Robert D. Bullard, Glenn S. Johnson, and Angel O. Torres, *Highway Robbery: Transportation Racism and New Routes to Equality* (Cambridge, MA: South End Press, 2004); Tom Lewis, *Divided Highways: Building the Interstate Highways, Transforming American Life* (New York: Penguin Books, 1997).

18. And suburbs across the country were becoming increasingly diverse. See Becky

Nicolaides, *My Blue Heaven: Life and Politics in Working-Class Los Angeles, 1920–1965* (Chicago: University of Chicago Press, 2002); Andrew Wiese, *Places of Their Own: African-American Suburbanization in the Twentieth Century* (Chicago: University of Chicago Press, 2004).

19. The connection between infrastructure and politics was importantly called for by a special section of the *International Journal of Urban and Regional Research* in 2008. The section was edited by Colin McFarlane and Jonathan Rutherford and introduced by their piece "Political Infrastructures: Governing and Experiencing the Fabric of the City," *International Journal of Urban and Regional Research* 32, no. 2 (2008): 363–374.

20. Some scholars have already looked closely at the before, during, and after impacts of infrastructure. See Avila, *Folklore of the Freeway*; Rose and Mohl, *Interstate*; DiMento and Ellis, *Changing Lanes*; Jackson, *Model City Blues*; Samuel Zipp, *Manhattan Projects: The Rise and Fall of Urban Renewal in Cold War New York* (New York: Oxford University Press, 2010); Elihu Rubin, *Insuring the City: The Prudential Center and the Postwar Urban Landscape* (New Haven, CT: Yale University Press, 2012); Needham, *Power Lines.*

21. Notable exceptions that include discussions of numerous groups are Avila, *Folklore of the Freeway*, and Contreras, "Voice and Property."

22. Augustus Allen and John Kirby Allen, "The Town of Houston," *Telegraph and Texas Register*, August 30, 1836.

23. On Houston's early history, see David G. McComb, *Houston, a History* (Austin: University of Texas Press, 1981); Harold L. Platt, *City Building in the New South: The Growth of Public Services in Houston, Texas, 1830–1910* (Philadelphia: Temple University Press, 1982); Joe R. Feagin, *Free Enterprise City: Houston in Political and Economic Perspective* (New Brunswick, NJ: Rutgers University Press, 1988); Howard Beeth and Cary D. Wintz, *Black Dixie: Afro-Texan History and Culture in Houston* (College Station: Texas A&M University Press, 1992); Marilyn McAdams Sibley, *The Port of Houston: A History* (Austin: University of Texas Press, 1968); Bernadette Pruitt, *The Other Great Migration: The Movement of Rural African-Americans to Houston, 1900–1941* (College Station: Texas A&M University Press, 2013); Arnoldo De León, *Ethnicity in the Sunbelt: Mexican-Americans in Houston* (College Station: Texas A&M University Press, 2001).

24. Martin V. Melosi, Joseph A. Pratt, and Kathleen A. Brosnan, eds., *Energy Capitals: Local Impact; Global Influence* (Pittsburgh: University of Pittsburgh Press, 2014).

25. Recent scholarship is beginning to rectify this situation. See Pruitt, *The Other Great Migration*; Phelps, *A People's War on Poverty*; Maximilian Krochmal, *Blue Texas: The Making of Multiracial Democratic Coalition in the Civil Rights Era* (Chapel Hill: University of North Carolina Press, 2016); Tyina Steptoe, *Houston Bound: Culture and Color in a Jim Crow City* (Berkeley: University of California Press, 2015); Brian D. Behnken, *Fighting Their Own Battles: Mexican-Americans, African-Americans, and the Struggle for Civil Rights in Texas* (Chapel Hill: University of North Carolina Press, 2011). Social science research is also on the rise; see the work of The Kinder Institute for Urban Research, in particular.

26. PolicyLink and USC Program for Environmental and Regional Equity, "An Equity Profile of the Houston-Galveston Region," Policy Link, 2013, 17.

27. Greater Houston Partnership, "Foreign-Born Population," October 17, 2014, www.houston.org/newgen/09_Demography/09G%2030%20Foreign-Born%20Population%20Major%20MSAs.pdf, accessed September 19, 2015.

28. Greater Houston Partnership, "Social, Economic, and Demographic Characteristics of Metro Houston," October 2014, https://www.houston.org/pdf/research/quickview/Population_Employment_Forecast.pdf, accessed August 5, 2015, 3–5.

29. Leah Binkovitz, "Fort Bend County's Diversity Confirmed by Survey," *Houston Chronicle*, May 1, 2015.

30. Corrie Maclaggan, "What Ethnic Diversity Looks Like: Fort Bend," *New York Times*, November 23, 2013.

31. De León, *Ethnicity in the Sunbelt*, 98; Robert D. Bullard, *Invisible Houston: The Black Experience in Boom and Bust* (College Station: Texas A&M University Press, 1987), 23; Pruitt, *The Other Great Migration*; Stephen Klineberg and the Center for Houston's Future, "An Historical Overview of Immigration in Houston, Based on the Houston Area Survey," Kinder Institute for Urban Research, Rice University, 2008, http://kinder.rice.edu/reports, accessed December 2, 2013.

32. To trace the changing nature of the Houston region's demographic profile and to track how these shifts altered the social and political views of residents, see the Kinder Houston Area Survey, conducted by Stephen Klineberg and the Kinder Institute for Urban Research at Rice University, http://kinder.rice.edu/has.

33. McComb, *Houston*; Platt, *City Building in the New South*; Feagin, *Free Enterprise City*.

34. Martin Melosi, *Effluent America: Cities, Industry, Energy, and the Environment* (Pittsburgh: University of Pittsburgh Press, 2001); Sarah S. Elkind, *How Local Politics Shape Federal Policy: Business, Power, and the Environment in Twentieth-Century Los Angeles* (Chapel Hill: University of North Carolina Press, 2011); Amy Bridges, *Morning Glories* (Princeton, NJ: Princeton University Press, 1997); Feagin, *Free Enterprise City*; Beeth and Wintz, *Black Dixie*; Platt, *City Building in the New South*.

35. C. Wright Mills, *The Power Elite*, rev. ed. (Oxford: Oxford University Press, 2000).

36. Heather O'Connell, "The Shifting City: Houston's History of Unequal Racial Change," Kinder Institute for Urban Research, 2016; Heather O'Connell and Junia Howell, "Disparate City: Understanding Rising Levels of Concentrated Poverty and Affluence in Greater Houston," Kinder Institute for Urban Research, 2016.

37. The historiography on Houston and Texas civil rights fights is long and growing. For works on African-American civil rights struggles, see Merline Pitre, *In Struggle Against Jim Crow: Lulu B. White and the NAACP, 1900–1957* (College Station: Texas A&M University Press, 1999); Darlene Clark Hine, *Black Victory: The Rise and Fall of the White Primary in Texas* (Millwood, NY: KTO Press, 1979); Thomas R. Cole, *No Color Is My Kind: The Life of Eldrewey Stearns and the Integration of Houston* (Austin: University of Texas Press, 1997); Steptoe, *Houston Bound*; Pruitt, *The Other Great Migration*; Wintz and Beeth, *Black Dixie*. For literature dealing mainly with Mexican-American civil rights fights in Houston, see Guadalupe San Miguel, *Brown, Not White: School Integration and* *the Chicano Movement in Houston* (College Station: Texas A&M University Press, 2001); Thomas H. Kreneck, *Mexican-American Odyssey: Felix Tijerina, Entrepreneur & Civic Leader, 1905–1965* (College Station: Texas A&M University Press, 2001); De León, *Ethnicity in the Sunbelt*. For works that deal with both groups and larger racial dynamics in Houston, see William Henry Kellar, *Make Haste Slowly: Moderates, Conservatives, and School Desegregation in Houston* (College Station: Texas A&M University Press, 1999); William S. Clayson, *Freedom Is Not Enough: The War on Poverty and the Civil Rights Movement in Texas* (Austin: University of Texas Press, 2010); Behnken, *Fighting Their Own Battles*; Krochmal, *Blue Texas*; Phelps, *A People's War on Poverty*.

38. A number of foundational works on Sunbelt politics and metropolitan politics focus on the actions of elites. See, for example, John R. Logan and Harvey Molotch, *Urban Fortunes: The Political Economy of Place* (Berkeley: University of California Press, 1987); Bridges, *Morning Glories*; Feagin, *Free Enterprise City*; Elkind, *How Local Politics Shape Federal Policy*. The groundwork laid by these books has opened the door for more zoomed-in looks at the political participation of citizens in Sunbelt cities. See, for example, Michelle Nickerson and Darren Dochuk, eds., *Sunbelt Rising: The Politics of Place, Space, and Region* (Philadelphia: University of Pennsylvania Press, 2011); Otero, *La Calle*; Needham, *Power Lines*.

39. Wells, *Car Country*; Dennis Soron, "Driven to Drive: Cars and the Problem of 'Compulsory Consumption,'" in Jim Conley and Arlene Tigar McLaren, eds., *Car Troubles: Critical Studies of Automobility and Auto-Mobility* (London: Ashgate, 2009).

40. On Houston's geography and environmental history, see Martin V. Melosi and Joseph A. Pratt, *Energy Metropolis: An Environmental History of Houston and the Gulf Coast* (Pittsburgh: University of Pittsburgh Press, 2007).

41. US Department of Agriculture Economic Research Service, "A Case Study of Urban Expansion and Annexation, Harris County, Texas," US Department of Agriculture, 1973.

42. Kyle Shelton, "Houston (Un)Limited: Path Dependent Highway and Annexation in an American Metropolis," *Transfers: Interdisciplinary Journal of Mobility Studies* 4, no. 1 (Spring 2014): 91–115.

43. On characteristics of Sunbelt development, see Carl Abbott, *The New Urban America: Growth and Politics in Sunbelt Cities*, rev. ed. (Chapel Hill: University of North Carolina Press, 1987); David R. Goldfield, *Region, Race, and Cities: Interpreting the Urban South* (Baton Rouge: Louisiana State University Press, 1997); Raymond Mohl, *Searching for the Sunbelt: Historical Perspectives on a Region* (Athens: University of Georgia Press, 1993); Bruce J. Schulman, *From Cotton Belt to Sunbelt: Federal Policy, Economic Development, and the Transformation of the South, 1938–1980* (New York: Oxford University Press, 1991); Nickerson and Dochuk, eds., *Sunbelt Rising*.

44. For the mileage total, see Erik Slotboom, *Houston Freeways: A Historical and Visual Journey* (Cincinnati: C. J. Krehbiel, 2003); Houston Chamber of Commerce, "Houston Facts, 1965," H-Freeways-Gulf Freeway Vertical File (VF), Houston Metropolitan Research Center (HMRC); Houston-Galveston Regional Transportation Study 1980, H-Traffic-1980–1984 VF, HMRC. On registrations, see Houston Chamber of Commerce,

"Motor Vehicle Registrations in Harris County, 1950–1984," H-Chamber of Commerce-Statistics VF, HMRC.

45. Jason Henderson, "The Politics of Mobility: De-essentializing Automobility and Contesting Urban Space," in Conley and McLaren, eds., *Car Troubles*; Peter D. Norton, *Fighting Traffic: The Dawn of the Motor Age in the American City* (Cambridge, MA: MIT Press, 2008); Clay McShane, *Down the Asphalt Path: American Cities and the Coming of the Automobile* (New York: Columbia University Press, 1994); Wells, *Car Country*; Mohl and Rose, *Interstate.*

46. Brian Cudahy, *Cash, Tokens, & Transfers: A History of Urban Mass Transit in North America* (New York: Fordham University Press, 1990).

47. Timothy Cresswell, *On the Move: Mobility in the Modern Western World* (New York: Routledge, 2006), 238–280 (on women and mobility, 312–348); Cotten Seiler, *Republic of Drivers: A Cultural History of Automobility in America* (Chicago: University of Chicago Press, 2008), 69–128; Sarah Frohardt-Lane, "Close Encounters: Interracial Contact and Conflict on Detroit's Public Transit in World War II," *Journal of Transport History* 33, no. 2 (December 1, 2012): 212–227; Deborah Clarke, *Driving Women Fiction and Automobile Culture in Twentieth-Century America* (Baltimore: Johns Hopkins University Press, 2007).

48. Seiler, *Republic of Drivers*, 112–116; Clair Brown, *American Standards of Living: 1918–1988* (Cambridge, MA: Blackwell, 1994), 223–230.

49. For example, car ownership among African Americans has risen from just 57 percent in 1970 to 80 percent in 2013, but white car ownership is still at 93 percent. American Association of State Highway and Transportation Officials, Census Transportation Planning Products Program, "Commuting in America 2013: The National Report on Commuting Patterns and Trends," September 2013, 10, http://traveltrends.transportation.org/Documents/B7_Vehicle%20and%20Transit%20Availability_CA07-4_web.pdf, accessed July 15, 2015.

50. Self, *American Babylon*; Lassiter, *The Silent Majority*; Arnold Hirsch, *Making the Second Ghetto: Race and Housing in Chicago, 1940–1960* (Cambridge: Cambridge University Press, 1983); David P. Fruend, *Colored Property: State Policy and White Racial Politics in Suburban America* (Chicago: University of Chicago Press, 2007); Kruse, *White Flight.*

51. William Fulton, *The Reluctant Metropolis: The Politics of Urban Growth in Los Angeles* (Baltimore: Johns Hopkins University Press, 2001).

52. Jason Henderson, "Secessionist Automobility: Racism, Anti-Urbanism, and the Politics of Automobility in Atlanta, Georgia," *International Journal of Urban and Regional Research* 30, no. 2 (June 1, 2006): 293–307.

53. Shelton, "Houston (Un)Limited."

54. Henry Petroski, *The Road Taken: The History and Future of America's Infrastructure* (New York: Bloomsbury, 2016).

55. Francesca Russello Ammon, *Bulldozer: Demolition and Clearance of the Postwar Landscape* (New Haven, CT: Yale University Press, 2016).

56. Generally, most studies of infrastructure fall into a spectrum of frames, ranging from a macro, large technical systems focus to a focus highlighting individuals' interactions with infrastructure. On macro systems, see Thomas Hughes, *Networks of Power: Electrification in Western Society, 1880–1930* (Baltimore: Johns Hopkins University Press, 1983); Latour, *Reassembling the Social*; Wiebe E. Bijker, Thomas P. Hughes, and Trevor Pinch, *The Social Construction of Technological Systems: New Directions in the Sociology and History of Technology*, anniversary ed. (Cambridge, MA: MIT Press, 2012). For a more individual-level study, see Samer Alatout, "'States' of Scarcity: Water, Space, and Identity Politics in Israel, 1948–1959," *Environment and Planning D: Society and Space* 26 (2008): 959–982; Ashley Carse, "Nature as Infrastructure: Making and Managing the Panama Canal Watershed," *Social Studies of Science* 42, no. 4 (August 2012): 539–563; Anand, "PRESSURE"; and McFarlan and Rutherford's edited section on "Political Infrastructures," *International Journal of Urban and Regional Research* 32, no. 2 (2008).

57. Brian Larkin, "The Politics and Poetics of Infrastructure," *Annual Review of Anthropology* 42, no. 1 (2013): 327–343.

58. Geographer J. B. Jackson argued that roads themselves warranted close study as simultaneously physical, cultural, and technological pieces of the landscape. See John Brinckerhoff Jackson, "Roads Belong in the Landscape," in Jackson, *Discovering the Vernacular Landscape* (New Haven, CT: Yale University Press, 1984).

59. Stephen Collier, *Post-Soviet Social: Neoliberalism, Social Modernity, Biopolitics* (Princeton, NJ: Princeton University Press, 2011); James C. Scott, *Seeing Like a State: How Certain Schemes to Improve the Human Condition Have Failed* (New Haven, CT: Yale University Press, 1999).

60. Larkin, "The Politics and Poetics of Infrastructure"; Avila, *Folklore of the Freeway*; Otero, *La Calle*, 13–58; Cresswell, *On the Move*, 238–280.

61. Avila, *Folklore of the Freeway*; Bruno Latour, *We Have Never Been Modern*, trans. Catherine Porter (Cambridge, MA: Harvard University Press, 1993).

62. Mimi Sheller, "Automotive Emotions: Feeling the Car," *Theory, Culture, and Society* 21, no. 4/5 (2004): 221–242; Wells, *Car Country*; David Nye, "Redefining the American Sublime, from Open Road to Interstate," in Mari Hvattum, Janike Kampevold Larsen, Brita Brenna, and Beate Elvebakk, eds., *Routes, Roads and Landscapes* (Burlington, VT: Ashgate, 2011).

63. Peter Merriman, "Enfolding and Gathering the Landscape: A Geography of England's M1 Corridor," in Hvattum et al., eds., *Routes, Roads, and Landscapes*, 213–228; Jason Henderson, "The Spaces of Parking: Mapping the Politics of Mobility in San Francisco," *Antipode* 41, no. 1 (2009): 70–91.

64. Timothy Cresswell, "Toward a Politics of Mobility," in Hvattum et al., eds., *Routes, Roads and Landscapes*, 163–177.

65. The field of mobility studies has fast become a vibrant and important subfield of several disciplines. Among its foundational documents, see Mimi Sheller and John Urry, "The New Mobilities Paradigm," *Environment and Planning A* 38, no. 2 (2006): 207–226; John Urry, *Mobilities* (Cambridge: Polity Press, 2007); Cresswell, *On the Move*. Within history, mobility is gaining importance within transport, and urban history in particular. See Seiler, *Republic of Drivers*; Norton, *Fighting Traffic*.

66. For the early history of mobility and the shape of the city, see Norton, *Fighting Traffic*; Brian Ladd, *Autophobia: Love and Hate in the Automotive Age* (Chicago: University of Chicago Press, 2008); McShane, *Down the Asphalt Path*; Barrett, *The Automobile and Urban Transit.*

67. Kevin Lynch, *The Image of the City* (Cambridge, MA: MIT Press, 1960).

68. Yi-fu Tuan, *Landscapes of Fear* (New York: Pantheon Books, 1979).

69. Matthew Klingle, *Emerald City: An Environmental History of Seattle* (New Haven, CT: Yale University Press, 2007); Barbara L. Allen, *Uneasy Alchemy: Citizens and Experts in Louisiana's Chemical Corridor Disputes* (Cambridge, MA: MIT Press, 2003); Carse, "Nature as Infrastructure."

70. Otero, *La Calle*; Jackson, *Model City Blues*; Doreen Massey, *Space, Place, and Gender* (Minneapolis: University of Minnesota Press, 1994); Dolores Hayden, *The Power of Place: Urban Landscapes as Public History* (Cambridge, MA: MIT Press, 1995).

71. For a description of the rise of citizen activism, see Harry Boyte, *The Backyard Revolution: Understanding the New Citizen's Movement* (Philadelphia: Temple University Press, 1980).

72. Foley, *Front Porch Politics.*

73. Alan A. Altshuler and David E. Luberoff, *Mega-Projects: The Changing Politics of Urban Public Investment* (Washington, DC: Brookings Institution Press; Cambridge, MA: Lincoln Institute of Land Policy, 2003).

74. Jeremy Korr, "Physical and Social Construction of the Capital Beltway," in Thomas Zeller and Christof Mauch, eds., *The World Beyond the Windshield: Roads and Landscapes in the United States and Europe* (Athens: Ohio University Press, 2008); Mohl, "The Interstates and the Cities"; Altshuler and Luberhoff, *Mega-Projects*, 251–254.

CHAPTER 1

1. Joseph A. Pratt, *The Growth of a Refining Region* (Greenwich, CT: Jai Press, 1980), 99–107. Real estate boomed in the 1950s and 1960s with both residential and commercial construction on the rise in the suburbs and downtown. See Joseph A. Pratt and Walter Buenger, *But Also Good Business: Texas Commerce Banks and the Financing of Houston and Texas, 1886–1986* (College Station: Texas A&M University Press, 1986), 222–226.

2. George Sessions Perry, "Houston," *Saturday Evening Post*, November 29, 1947, Box 35, Folder 12, George Fuermann Collection (GFC), Special Collections Library, University of Houston (SCLUH); "Greater Houston: Its First Million People—and Why," *Newsweek*, July 5, 1954, Box 35, Folder 12, GFC, SCLUH; "Houston Texas: What It's Like to Be New," *Business Week*, January 23, 1953," Box 35, Folder 12, GFC, SCLUH; "The Air-Conditioned Metropolis," *Time*, April 12, 1963; "Houston: Boomingest Town in the US," *Newsweek*, June 11, 1962; "The Houston Complex," *Fortune*, February 1958.

3. Tyina Steptoe, *Houston Bound: Culture and Color in a Jim Crow City* (Berkeley: University of California Press, 2015); Bernadette Pruitt, *The Other Great Migration: The Movement of Rural African-Americans to Houston, 1900–1941* (College Station: Texas A&M University Press, 2013); Cary Wintz and Howard Beeth, eds., *Black Dixie: Afro-Texan History and Culture in Houston* (College Station: Texas A&M University Press,

1992); Arnoldo De León, *Ethnicity in the Sunbelt: Mexican-Americans in Houston* (College Station: Texas A&M University Press, 2001); Guadalupe San Miguel, *Brown, Not White: School Integration and the Chicano Movement in Houston* (College Station: Texas A&M University Press, 2001); Darlene Clark Hine, *Black Victory: The Rise and Fall of the White Primary in Texas* (Millwood, NY: KTO Press, 1979).

4. Joe R. Feagin, *Free-Enterprise City: Houston in Political and Economic Perspective* (New Brunswick, NJ: Rutgers University Press, 1988), 106–148; David McComb, *Houston: The Bayou City* (Austin: University of Texas Press, 1969), 200–240; Chandler Davidson, "Houston: The City Where the Business of Government Is Business," in Wendell Bedichek and Neal Tannahill, eds., *Public Policy in Texas* (Glenview, IL: Scott, Foresman, 1982), 275–288; Craig Smyser, "Houston Power," *Houston Chronicle*, June 29, 30, July 1, 1977; Albert Schaffer, "The Houston Growth Coalition in 'Boom' and 'Bust,'" *Journal of Urban Affairs* 11, no. 1 (March 1989): 21–38; Igor Vojnovic, "Governance in Houston: Growth Theories and Urban Pressures," *Journal of Urban Affairs* 25, no. 5 (December 2003): 589–624; Robert Fisher, "Urban Policy in Houston," *Urban Studies* 26 (1989): 144–154; Richard Murray and Robert Thomas, *Progrowth Politics: Change and Governance in Houston* (Berkeley: Institute of Government Studies Press, University of California, 1991), 95.

5. Martin Melosi, "Houston's Public Sinks: Sanitary Services from Local Concerns to Regional Challenges," in Martin Melosi and Joseph A. Pratt, eds., *Energy Metropolis: An Environmental History of Houston and the Gulf Coast* (Pittsburgh: University of Pittsburgh Press, 2007), 109–147.

6. Kyle Shelton, "Houston (Un)Limited: Path-Dependent Annexation and Highway Practices in an American Metropolis," *Transfers: An Interdisciplinary Journal for Mobility History* 4, no. 1 (March 2014): 97–115.

7. All highway construction decisions during the 1950s and 1960s were made by a combination of local, state, and federal policy makers. See Bruce Seely, *Building the American Highway System: Engineers as Policy Makers* (Philadelphia: Temple University Press, 1988); Joseph DiMento and Cliff Ellis, *Changing Lanes: Visions and Histories of Urban Freeways* (Cambridge, MA: MIT Press, 2013); Mark Rose and Raymond Mohl, *Interstate: Express Highway Politics, 1939–2000*, 3rd ed. (Knoxville: University of Tennessee Press, 2012); Mark Rose, Paul S. Barrett, and Bruce Seely, *The Best Transportation System in the World: Railroads, Trucks, Airlines, and American Public Policy in the Twentieth Century* (Columbus: Ohio State University Press, 2006).

8. For a discussion of Holcombe's approach to politics, which mixed elite friendship with populist appeal, see Amy Bridges, "Boss Tweed and V. O. Key in Texas," in Char Miller and Heywood T. Sanders, eds., *Urban Texas: Politics and Development* (College Station: Texas A&M University Press, 1990), 66–67.

9. McComb, *Houston*, 168–170. For more on Jesse Jones and other elites, see Feagin, *Free Enterprise City*, 106–148; Steven Fenberg, *Unprecedented Power: Jesse Jones, Capitalism, and the Common Good* (College Station: Texas A&M University Press, 2011).

10. Joseph A. Pratt and Christopher J. Castaneda, *Builders: Herman and George R. Brown* (College Station: Texas A&M University Press, 1999), 157–191.

11. Miller and Sanders, eds., *Urban Texas*, xi; Char Miller and David R. Johnson, "The Rise of Urban Texas," in Miller and Sanders, eds., *Urban Texas*, 3–29; Joseph A. Pratt and Kenneth Lipartito, *Baker and Botts in the Development of Modern Houston* (Austin: University of Texas Press, 1991), 47–63; Feagin, *Free Enterprise City*; McComb, *Houston*; Barry J. Kaplan, "Houston: The Golden Buckle of the Sunbelt," in Richard M. Bernard and Bradley R. Rice, eds., *Sunbelt Cities: Politics and Growth Since World War II* (Austin: University of Texas Press, 1983), 196–212.

12. See Joseph Pratt, "8F and Many More: Business and Civic Leadership in Modern Houston," *Houston Review of History and Culture* 2, no. 1 (2004): 2–7, 31–44. Pratt argues that while there is no disputing that these leaders acquired massive power and often supported goals that benefited their interests, they also helped shepherd through a number of essential reforms, policies, and practices that benefited Houston as a whole by facilitating growth and development. Pratt and Lipartito, *Baker and Botts*.

13. Robert B. Fairbanks, *For the City as a Whole: Planning, Politics, and the Public Interest in Dallas, Texas, 1900–1965* (Columbus: Ohio State University Press, 1998); Sarah Elkind, *How Local Politics Shape Federal Policy: Business, Power, and the Environment in Twentieth-Century Los Angeles* (Chapel Hill: University of North Carolina Press, 2011).

14. Amy Bridges, *Morning Glories: Municipal Reforms in the Southwest* (Princeton, NJ: Princeton University Press, 1999); Harold L. Platt, *City Building in the New South: The Growth of Public Services in Houston, Texas, 1830–1910* (Philadelphia: Temple University Press, 1983), 202–208. Platt argues that the shift to commission government in 1905 allowed the city's elites to weaken the political strength of both labor unions and African-American voters. Feagin, *Free Enterprise City*, 118–119.

15. Martin V. Melosi, Joseph A. Pratt, and Kathleen A. Brosnan, *Energy Capitals: Local Impact, Global Influence* (Pittsburgh: University of Pittsburgh Press, 2014); Feagin, *Free Enterprise City*, 4, 20, 43, 70; Platt, *City Building in the New South*, 43; Pratt, *Growth of a Refining Region*, 8–9; Pratt and Lipartito, *Baker and Botts*.

16. For a discussion of Houston's pre-oil economy, see Platt, *City Building in the New South*; Feagin, *Free Enterprise City*; Pratt, *Growth of a Refining Region*.

17. Melosi and Pratt, eds., *Energy Metropolis*, 3. For more information on the hurricane, see David McComb, *Galveston: A History* (Austin: University of Texas Press, 1986), 121–149.

18. For a list of active factories and refineries along the ship channel in 1955, see Houston Port Commission, "Port of Houston Industrial District," Map, Box 36, Folder 9, GFC, SCLUH.

19. For the growth of the petrochemical industry and other secondary economic sectors, see Pratt, *Growth of a Refining Region*, 10, 99–107; McComb, *Houston*, 184–186; Platt, *City Building in the New South*, 177. For discussion of World War II's impact on the city, see Paul Alejandro Levengood, "For the Duration and Beyond: World War II and the Creation of Modern Houston" (PhD diss., Rice University, 1999).

20. Melosi et al., *Energy Capitals*.

21. For early economic history and rail history, see Platt, *City Building in the New South*, 30–33; Feagin, *Free Enterprise City*, 49–50, 112–114.

22. For a general overview of the port's history, see Marilyn Sibley, *The Port of Houston: A History* (Austin: University of Texas Press, 1968); McComb, *Houston*, 93–97; Lynn M. Alperin, *Custodians of the Coast: History of the United States Army Engineers at Galveston* (Galveston, TX: US Army Corps of Engineers, 1977). For the role the city's banks played in financing the port, see Pratt and Buenger, *But Also Good Business*, 23–24.

23. For more information about Houston's earliest commuter transit, see Peter Papademetriou, *Transportation and Urban Development in Houston, 1830–1980* (Houston: Metropolitan Transit Authority of Harris County, 1982); Erik O. Slotboom, *Houston Freeways: A Historical and Visual Journey* (Cincinnati: C. J. Krehbiel, 2003), 4–5; Steven Baron, *Houston Electric: The Street Railways of Houston, Texas* (Lexington, KY: S. M. Baron, 1996). For a discussion of the impact streetcars had on urban areas, see Kenneth Jackson, *Crabgrass Frontier: The Suburbanization of the United States* (New York: Oxford University Press, 1985), 87–125; Sam Bass Warner Jr., *Streetcar Suburbs: The Process of Growth in Boston, 1870–1900* (Cambridge, MA: Harvard University Press, 1962).

24. Char Miller and David R. Johnson, "The Rise of Urban Texas," in Miller and Sanders, eds., *Urban Texas*, 11. On the rise of trucking, see Rose and Mohl, *Interstate*; William Childs, *Trucking and the Public Interest: The Emergence of Federal Regulation, 1914–1940* (Knoxville: University of Tennessee Press, 1985).

25. Neighborhood Improvement Council, "Zoning in History," Pamphlet, Box 39, Folder 9, GFC, SCLUH, 1959. Both the George Fuermann Collection, Box 39, SCLUH, and the V. P. Ringer Collection, Houston Metropolitan Research Center (HMRC), contain the records of the Neighborhood Improvement Council, a pro-zoning organization from the 1959 zoning push. See Barry J. Kaplan, "Urban Development, Economic Growth, and Personal Liberty: The Rhetoric of the Houston Anti-Zoning Movements, 1947–1963," *Southwestern Historical Quarterly* 84 (October 1980): 133–168; Ben Koush, "Houston Lives the Life: Modern Houses in the Suburbs, 1952–1962" (Master's thesis, Rice University, 2002), 17.

26. For more on Houston's zoning policies and the desire of developers to maintain no zoning, see David McComb, *Houston*, 217–220; John Mixon, interview by author, November 11, 2011, Houston, Texas, audio recording. Mixon is a real estate and property law professor at the University of Houston. He was active in the 1989 zoning campaign and possesses an encyclopedic knowledge of earlier efforts. See also Bernard Siegan, *Land Use Without Zoning* (Lexington, MA: Lexington Books, 1972); Kaplan, "Urban Development," 133–168.

27. Wesley Phelps, *A People's War on Poverty: Urban Politics, Grassroots Activists, and the Struggle for Democracy in Houston, 1964–1976* (Athens: University of Georgia Press, 2014): 150–155; Neighborhood Improvement Council, "Zoning Education Committee: Utilities Report," 1960, Box 39, Folder 9, GFC, SCLUH; "Houston: Where Growth Comes Naturally," *Engineering News-Record*, July 20, 1961, Box 39, Folder 9, GFC, SCLUH; Kaplan, "Urban Development."

28. Robert Fisher, *Let the People Decide: Neighborhood Organizing in America* (New York: Twayne, 1994), 87–97; Robert Fisher, "Protecting Community and Property Values:

Civic Clubs in Houston, 1909–70," in Miller and Sanders eds., *Urban Texas*, 128–137; Kaplan, "Urban Development"; Beth Anne Shelton, Nestor Rodriguez, Joe Feagin, Robert Bullard, and Robert Thomas, *Houston: Growth and Decline in a Sunbelt Boomtown* (Philadelphia: Temple University Press, 1989), 55–60.

29. On racial violence directed toward integrating blacks in Houston, see the film *This Is Our Home, It Is Not for Sale*, directed by Jon Schwartz, 1987, which tells the story of the integration of Riverside Terrace.

30. For information about River Oaks' deed restrictions, see Box 4W201, Ima Hogg Papers, Dolph Briscoe Center for American History (DBCAH); Houston Subdivision Collection, Box 4, MSS 118, HMRC; River Oaks Collection, MSS 12, HMRC; Koush, "Houston Lives the Life," 19–26.

31. Feagin, *Free-Enterprise City*.

32. Such attitudes are not unique to Houston. See James Cobb, *The Most Southern Place on Earth: The Mississippi Delta and the Roots of Regional Identity* (Oxford: Oxford University Press, 1992); Bruce J. Schulman, *From Cotton Belt to Sunbelt: Federal Policy, Economic Development, and the Transformation of the South, 1938–1980* (New York: Oxford University Press, 1991).

33. Feagin, *Free Enterprise City*. For Houston's approach to federal urban renewal money, see Susan MacManus, *Federal Aid to Houston* (Washington, DC: Brookings Institution Press, 1983); Shelton et al., *Houston*, 41–47. For discussions of oil regulation, see Melosi and Pratt, eds., *Energy Metropolis*, 9; Joseph A. Pratt, "A Mixed Blessing: Energy, Economic Growth, and Houston's Environment," in Melosi and Pratt, eds., *Energy Metropolis*, 21–51; Hugh S. Gorman, "The Houston Ship Channel and the Changing Landscape of Industrial Pollution," in Melosi and Pratt, eds., *Energy Metropolis*, 52–68.

34. Colin Williams, "Billion Dollar Builder," *Texas Parade*, July 1969, Box 26, Folder 6, GFC, SCLUH, 23–30; Pratt and Castaneda, *Builders*; "Roadbuilders with a Flair for Other Jobs," *Business Week*, May 25, 1957, Box 26, Folder 6, GFC, SCLUH, 90–108.

35. McComb, *Houston*, 189.

36. "Sharp Announces Houston's Biggest Home Project," *Houston Post*, July 3, 1954, Box 34, Folder 1, GFC, SCLUH; "Metropolitan Houston Reaches 1 Million Population Figure" *Houston Post*, July 3, 1954, Box 34, Folder 1, GFC, SCLUH.

37. "Metropolitan Houston Reaches 1 Million."

38. "Greater Houston: Its First Million People—and Why."

39. Melosi and Pratt, eds., *Energy Metropolis*, 10–11. On the oil industry's economic impact on the Houston area, see Pratt, *Growth of a Refining Region*. George Brown, as chair of Rice University's Board of Trustees, played a key role in facilitating the bidding process for the NASA development. Humble Oil, now ExxonMobil, donated a huge chunk of land for the project and began to invest heavily in Houston real estate. On NASA, see Amy L. Bacon, "From West Ranch to Space City: A History of Houston's Growth Revealed Through the Development of Clear Lake" (PhD diss., University of Houston, 1996); Henry C. Dethloff, *Suddenly, Tomorrow Came . . . A History of the*

Johnson Space Center (Washington, DC: NASA History Office, 1993); Kevin Michael Brady, "NASA Launches Houston into Orbit: The Political, Economic, and Social Impact of the Space Agency on Southeast Texas, 1961–1969" (PhD diss., Texas Christian University, 2009). On the role of corporate development visions influencing the growth and shape of an urban area, see Elihu Rubin, *Insuring the City: The Prudential Center and the Postwar Urban Landscape* (New Haven, CT: Yale University Press, 2012), 5. For a discussion of the role Houston's large law firms and banks played in shaping the city's development, see Pratt and Lipartito, *Baker and Botts*; Pratt and Buenger, *But Also Good Business.*

40. For more on the medical center's development, see "Houston: Where Growth Comes Naturally," 32; McComb, *Houston*, 241; Frederick Elliot, *The Birth of the Texas Medical Center: A Personal Account*, William Kellar, ed. (College Station: Texas A&M University Press, 2004). On the building of the Prudential Insurance Houston Regional Home Office, see Rubin, *Insuring the City*, 50–57. In *But Also Good Business*, Pratt and Buenger discuss the high level of real estate investment by banks after World War II. See Carl Abbott, "Real Estate and Race: Imagining the Second Circuit of Capital in Sunbelt Cities," in Darren Dochuk and Michelle Nickerson, eds., *Sunbelt Rising: The Politics of Place, Space, and Region* (Philadelphia: University of Pennsylvania Press, 2011), 265–289.

41. Historical figures from the Port of Houston, "Overview," http://porthouston.com/portweb/about-us, accessed February 8, 2017; "Port That Supports a City," *Houston*, May 1956, HMRC. The ship channel and port were also a part of the federally constructed intercoastal waterway, which allowed barge traffic protection between the Atlantic seaboard and the Gulf of Mexico. See "The Intercoastal Waterway," *Time*, October 1, 1956, Box 36, Folder 7, GFC, SCLUH.

42. Port of Houston, "Welcome to the Port of Houston," 1957, Box 36, Folder 7, GFC, SCLUH. Will Clayton, one of the founding owners of Anderson, Clayton, and Company, a major cotton interest, referred to Houston as the tip of a funnel. See McComb, *Houston*, 112.

43. McComb, *Houston*, 177.

44. For a discussion of the prewar migration to Houston and its causes, see De León, *Ethnicity in the Sunbelt*; Pruitt, *The Other Great Migration*; Thomas Kreneck, *Mexican-American Odyssey: Felix Tijerina, Entrepreneur and Civic Leader, 1905–1965* (College Station: Texas A&M Press, 2001), 3–36; David Montejano, *Anglos and Mexicans in the Making of Texas, 1836–1986* (Austin: University of Texas Press, 1987); Emilio Zamora, *The World of the Mexican Worker in Texas* (College Station: Texas A&M University Press, 1993); Steptoe, "Dixie West."

45. Pratt, *Growth of a Refining Region*, 83–85, 89–99; De León, *Ethnicity in the Sunbelt*, 98–99.

46. Raymond Arsenault, "The End of the Long Hot Summer: The Air Conditioner and Southern Culture," *Journal of Southern History* 50, no. 4 (November 1984): 597–628.

47. De León, *Ethnicity in the Sunbelt*, 98; Robert D. Bullard, *Invisible Houston: The Black Experience in Boom and Bust* (College Station: Texas A&M University Press, 1987), 23; US Census, www.census.gov, accessed December 2, 2013; Stephen Klineberg and the

Center for Houston's Future, "An Historical Overview of Immigration in Houston, Based on the Houston Area Survey," Kinder Institute for Urban Research, Rice University, 2008, http://kinder.rice.edu/reports, accessed December 2, 2013.

48. See Victoria Hyonchu Kwon, *Entrepreneurship and Religion: Korean Immigrants in Houston, Texas* (New York: Garland, 1997); Nestor Rodriguez, "Hispanic and Asian Immigration Waves in Houston," in Helen Rose Ebaugh and Janet Saltzman Chafetz, eds., *Religion and the New Immigrants: Continuities and Adaptations in Immigrant Congregations* (Walnut Creek, CA: Rowman and Littlefield, 2000); Nestor P. Rodriguez and Ximena Urrutia-Rojas, "Impact of Recent Refugee Migration to Texas: A Comparison of Southeast Asian and Central American Newcomers," in Wayne H. Holtzman and Thomas H. Bornemann, eds., *Mental Health of Immigrants and Refugees* (Austin, TX: Hogg Foundation, 1990), 263–278.

49. See US Census data for Houston, 1950 and 1960, available via Social Explorer, www.socialexplorer.com, accessed February 25, 2014.

50. For conditions in African-American and Mexican-American neighborhoods, see Pruitt, *The Other Great Migration*; De León, *Ethnicity in the Sunbelt*; Bullard, *Invisible Houston*; Robert Bullard, *Dumping in Dixie: Race, Class, and Environmental Quality*, 3rd ed. (Boulder: Westview Press, 2008); Robert D. Bullard, "Dumping on Houston's Black Neighborhoods," in Melosi and Pratt, eds., *Energy Metropolis*, 207–223.

51. Jon Teaford, *Metropolitan Revolution: The Rise on Post-Urban America* (New York: Columbia University Press, 2006); Shelton, "Houston (Un)Limited."

52. David Bintliff, interview by Marguerite Johnson Barnes, April 1985, transcript, Box 1, Folder 9, Marguerite Johnson Barnes Collection, MSS 445, Woodson Research Center (WRC), Rice University; Feagin, *Free Enterprise City*; Abbott, "Real Estate and Race."

53. Farm numbers and acreage taken from the US Department of Agriculture's Census of Agriculture for Texas, 1954 and 1974, Census of Agriculture Historical Archive, http://agcensus.mannlib.cornell.edu/AgCensus/homepage.do, accessed November 18, 2013.

54. Square mileage from Houston Planning Department, "Comprehensive Plan, 1959: 1c, Population, Land Use, and Growth," Box 1, Folder 5, City of Houston Planning Department Records (CHPD), RG A 004, HMRC, 106. Population figures from Martin Melosi, *Effluent America: Cities, Industry, Energy, and the Environment* (Pittsburgh: University of Pittsburgh Press, 2001), 161. Parts of the discussion of annexation and territorial expansion in this section are adapted from Shelton, "Houston (Un)Limited."

55. Voisin quoted in McComb, *Houston*, 199.

56. For an exploration of how the interplay between private companies and public officials shaped suburban development, see Paul G. Lewis, *Shaping Suburbia: How Political Institutions Organize Urban Development* (Pittsburgh: University of Pittsburgh Press, 1996).

57. Murray and Thomas, *Progrowth Politics*; John Mixon, interview by author, November 11, 2011.

58. Lars Lerup, *One Million Acres and No Zoning* (London: Architectural Association,

2011), 93–97. This idea meshes with that of Albert Pope, *Ladders* (New York: Princeton Architectural Press, 1997).

59. G. Ross Stephens and Nelson Wikstrom, *Metropolitan Government and Governance: Theoretical Perspectives, Empirical Analysis, and the Future* (New York: Oxford University Press, 2000), 12–13, 19, 129–133; Louise Dyble, *Paying the Toll: Local Power, Regional Politics, and the Golden Gate Bridge* (Philadelphia: University of Pennsylvania Press, 2009); Eric H. Monkkonen, *The Local State: Public Money and American Cities* (Stanford, CA: Stanford University Press, 1995); Alberta Sbragia, *Debt Wish: Entrepreneurial Cities, US Federalism, and Economic Development* (Pittsburgh: University of Pittsburgh Press, 1996). Dyble, Monkkonen, and Sbragia discuss many of the abuses of power and poor planning that stem from extra-governmental entities such as special districts, transit authorities, and utility companies. For a discussion of Houston's experiences with municipal utility districts and the dubious nature of some districts, see John Mixon, interview by author, November 11, 2011.

60. Melosi, *Effluent America*, 161; Houston Planning Department, "Comprehensive Plan, 1959: 1c," 27.

61. Extra-city subdivision statistics from City of Houston Planning Commission, "Planning Commission Annual Report: 1957," Box 1, Folder 2, CHPD, HMRC.

62. Ibid.

63. For a more in-depth discussion of Houston's annexations and the politics surrounding them, see Murray and Thomas, *Progrowth Politics*; Melosi, *Effluent America*, 190–205; McComb, *Houston*, 199–205.

64. James Holley, "Two Cities Annex 7 Chem Plants," *Houston Post*, January 1, 1961, Box 38, Folder 10, GFC, SCLUH.

65. Murray and Thomas, *Progrowth Politics*, 151–158; James Holley, "Pasadena Takes in 78.12 Square Miles," *Houston Post*, December 28, 1960, Box 38, Folder 8, GFC, SCLUH.

66. Murray and Thomas, *Progrowth Politics*, 158; Melosi, *Effluent America*, 194; Stephens and Wikstrom, *Metropolitan Government*, 19, 47. Texas's law was among the most liberal in terms of power given to large municipalities. See M. G. Woodroof III, "Systems and Standards of Municipal Annexation Review: A Comparative Analysis," *Georgetown Law Review* 58 (1970): 743–776.

67. Colin Gordon, *Mapping Decline: St. Louis and the Fate of the American City* (Philadelphia: University of Pennsylvania Press, 2009); Robert O. Self, *American Babylon: Race and the Struggle for Postwar Oakland* (Princeton, NJ: Princeton University Press, 2003). The same is true for Los Angeles. See Juliet F. Gainsborough, "Bridging the City-Suburb Divide: States and the Politics of Regional Cooperation," *Journal of Urban Affairs* 23, no. 5 (2001): 497–512. For a discussion of non-Houston annexation policies in Sunbelt cities, see Olga Smirnova and Jeremy Ingalls, "Influence of State Annexation Laws on the Growth of Selected Southern Cities," *Southern Geographer* 47, no. 11 (May 2007): 83–97. For the importance of flexibility in annexation ability to city development, see David Rusk, *Cities Without Suburbs* (Washington, DC: Woodrow Wilson Center Press, 1993).

68. James Holley, "29 Cities in County—and That May Be All," *Houston Post*, February 10, 1963, Box 38, Folder 5, GFC, SCLUH.

69. Harris County Freeway Committee, "Traffic Jams or Freeways," Pamphlet, H-Freeways-1950 vertical file (VF), HMRC.

70. Jim Mathis, "Flow: Traffic Moves Despite Bottlenecks," *Houston Post*, January 26, 1958, H-Traffic-1950–1979 VF, HMRC.

71. Christopher Wells, *Car Country: An Environmental History* (Seattle: University of Washington Press, 2013).

72. Registration numbers from Slotboom, *Houston Freeways*, 19; Thomas Watson McKinney, "Superhighway Deluxe: Houston's Gulf Freeway" (PhD diss., University of Houston, 2006), 32.

73. Houston Planning Department, "Comprehensive Plan, 1959: 1c," 42–47.

74. Houston Chamber of Commerce, "Houston Highlights #23: Highway System," November 1962, H-Freeways-1960s VF, HMRC.

75. Teaford, *Metropolitan Revolution*, 45–59; Robert Fogelson, *Downtown: Its Rise and Fall, 1880–1950* (New Haven, CT: Yale University Press, 2001), 315–316; Alison Isenberg, *Downtown America: A History of the Place and the People Who Made It* (Chicago, IL: University of Chicago Press, 2004), 166–202.

76. For further information about the origins, construction, and significance of the Gulf Freeway, see McKinney, "Superhighway Deluxe"; Slotboom, *Houston Freeways*, 144–165.

77. Slotboom, *Houston Freeways*, 151.

78. Norris and Elder Consulting Engineers, "A 15-Year Study of Land Values and Land Use Along the Gulf Freeway, Houston, TX 1956," City of Houston Traffic Engineering, City Planning Records—RG 0942, Box 45/75/B, HMRC. Commissioned by the Texas Highway Department, this influential report was instrumental in documenting the value and effect of the freeway on Houston's economic landscape. See also "Prospect of Freeway Causes Property Values to Spurt Up," *Houston Post*, August 11, 1957, H-Freeways-1950s VF, HMRC; "Program to the Formal Opening of the Gulf Freeway, August 2, 1952," Box 29, Folder 1, GFC, SCLUH.

79. McKinney, "Superhighway Deluxe"; "Freeway Guinea Pig for State, US study," *Houston Post*, June 28, 1950, H-Freeways-1950s VF, HMRC.

80. Eugene Maier, "Success Must Be Planned," *Houston*, November 1954, H-Traffic-1950–1979 VF, HMRC.

81. Slotboom, *Houston Freeways*, 11–15; "12 Major Freeways Planned for Houston," *Houston Press*, September 8, 1953, H-Freeways-1950s VF, HMRC.

82. The city passed several bond elections, but bond proposals also failed a number of times. The September 17, 1955, election to create a wheel tax passed only to be deemed unconstitutional. See Oscar Holcombe Collection, MSS 20, Box 6, Folder 10, HMRC. For a full account of the bonds, see Slotboom, *Houston Freeways*, 144–165.

83. McKinney, "Superhighway Deluxe," 14–35.

84. Rose and Mohl, *Interstate*.

85. McComb, *Houston*, 181.

86. Houston Harris County Transportation Plan, Volume 3, Box 16, Folder 26, Foley's Department Store Collection (FDSC), 07/2007–004, SCLUH.

87. Robert Dundas to Mr. Levine, January 7, 1961, Box 19, Folder 25, FDSC, SCLUH.

88. "Office memo," October 11, 1961, Box 17, Folder 22, FDSC, SCLUH; Vance Newell, Max Jacobs Agency, to Max Levine, Foley's President, September 22, 1958, Box 17, Folder 22, FDSC, SCLUH.

89. Charles Florian to Bernard Calkins, July 7, 1961, Box 17, Folder 22, FDSC, SCLUH.

90. KE Antone, Main Street Realty, to Robert W. Dundas, n.d., Box 19, Folder 25, FDSC, SCLUH; Foley's Research Department, "Southeast Houston—Galveston Area," Store Research Report, August 1962, Box 19, Folder 13, FDSC, SCLUH.

91. For more on this fight, see Shelton, "Houston (Un)Limited." For more on the history of Clear Lake and the changes that development brought to the area, see Bacon, "From West Ranch to Space City."

92. "NASA Traffic Crisis," *Houston Post*, January 22, 1963, Box 3K405, Folder 1, DeWitt Greer Papers (DGP), DBCAH.

93. "Houston: Boomingest Town in the US," *Newsweek*, June 11, 1962, Box 35, Folder 12, GFC, SCLUH.

94. Jim Maloney, "People Replace Pastures," *Houston Post*, June 28, 1970, Box 35, Folder 6, GFC, SCLUH.

95. Timber Cove Community Pamphlet, 1958, Timber Cove Collection #2011-0008, University of Houston–Clear Lake Archives.

96. David W. Jones, *Mass Motorization: Mass Motorization + Mass Transit: An American History and Policy Analysis* (Bloomington: University of Indiana Press, 2008), 99–101.

97. Jim Mathis, "Flow: Traffic Moves Despite Bottlenecks," *Houston Post*, January 26, 1958, H-Traffic-1950–1979 VF, HMRC.

98. "Freeways Alone Not the Answer," *Houston Chronicle*, May 27, 1961, H-Transportation-1920–1960s VF, HMRC.

99. Houston Metropolitan Area Transportation Study Office, "Existing Street Network," 1966, City of Houston Traffic Engineering, City Planning Records, RG 0942, Box 45/75/B, HMRC.

CHAPTER 2

1. "Attention Homeowners and Taxpayers," Flyer, May 1962, City of Houston Planning Department Records (CHPD), Erik Slotboom Research Collection (ESRC).

2. Houston City Planning Commission Minutes, June 5, 1962, Box 2, Folder 5, V. P. Ringer Collection (VRC), MSS 143, Houston Metropolitan Research Center (HMRC).

3. Ramona Toliver, interview by author, April 20, 2012, Houston, Texas, audio recording.

4. Joseph DiMento and Cliff Ellis, *Changing Lanes: Visions and Histories of Urban Freeways* (Cambridge, MA: MIT Press, 2013); Amy Finstein, "Lofty Visions: The Architectural Intentions and Contrary Realities of Elevated Urban Highways in America, 1900–1959," (PhD diss., University of Virginia, 2009).

5. Mark Rose and Eric Avila, "Race, Culture, Politics, and Urban Renewal: An Introduction," *Journal of American History* 35, no. 3(March 2009): 335–347; Bruce Seely, *Building the American Highway System: Engineers as Policy Makers* (Philadelphia: Temple University Press, 1987); Mark H. Rose and Bruce E. Seely, "Getting the Interstate System Built: Road Engineers and the Implementation of Public Policy, 1955–1985," *Journal of Policy History* 2, no. 01 (January 1990): 23–55; Paul Barrett and Mark H. Rose, "Street Smarts: The Politics of Transportation Statistics in the American City, 1900–1990," *Journal of Urban History* 25, no. 3 (March 1, 1999): 405–433. Barrett and Rose, as well as Rose and Seely, show how highway planners and engineers consolidated and exercised immense power, becoming nearly independent policy makers in many situations.

6. Seely, *Building the American Highway System*; Mark H. Rose, Paul Barrett, and Bruce Seely, *The Best Transportation System in the World: Railroads, Trucks, Airlines, and American Public Policy in the Twentieth Century* (Columbus: Ohio State University Press, 2006). On Houston power brokers, see Joe R. Feagin, *Free Enterprise City: Houston in Political and Economic Perspective* (New Brunswick, NJ: Rutgers University Press, 1988), 121–133.

7. Carl Abbott, *Metropolitan Frontier: Cities in the Modern American West* (Tucson: University of Arizona Press, 1993); Jon C. Teaford, *Metropolitan Revolution: The Rise of Post-Urban America* (New York: Columbia University Press, 2006). City officials did not want to lose influence over the metro region. One approach to achieving this goal was to create cultural institutions in the downtown area that could draw suburban residents into downtown, see Kyle Shelton, "Culture War in Downtown Houston: Jones Hall and the Postwar Battle over Exclusive Space," *Southwestern Historical Quarterly* 116, no. 1 (July 2012): 1–24.

8. See Mark Rose and Raymond Mohl, *Interstate: Express Highway Politics, 1939–2000*, 3rd ed. (Knoxville: University of Tennessee Press, 2012), 85–111; Tom Watson McKinney, "Superhighway Deluxe: Houston's Gulf Freeway," in Martin Melosi and Joseph A. Pratt, eds., *Energy Metropolis: An Environmental History of Houston and the Gulf Coast* (Pittsburgh: University of Pittsburg Press, 2007), 148–149.

9. Owen Gutfreund, *Twentieth-Century Sprawl: Highways and the Reshaping of the American Landscape* (New York: Oxford University Press, 2004); Kyle Shelton, "Houston (Un)Limited: Path-Dependent Annexation and Highway Practices in an American Metropolis," *Transfers: Interdisciplinary Journal of Mobility Studies* 4, no. 1 (March 2014): 97–115.

10. Jan Lin, "Ethnic Places, Postmodernism, and Urban Change in Houston," *Sociological Quarterly* 36, no. 4 (Autumn 1995): 629–647.

11. On examples of protests about infrastructure problems and unequal access to transportation in Memphis, see Laurie Green, *Battling the Plantation Mentality: Memphis and the Black Freedom Struggle* (Chapel Hill: University of North Carolina Press, 2007): 204–205. On Atlanta, see Ronald H. Bayor, *Race and the Shaping of Twentieth-Century Atlanta* (Chapel Hill: University of North Carolina Press, 1996). On similar earlier fights in Houston, see Guadalupe San Miguel, *Brown, Not White: School Integration and the Chicano Movement in Houston* (College Station: Texas A&M University

Press, 2001); Bernadette Pruitt, *The Other Great Migration: The Movement of Rural African-Americans to Houston, 1900–1941* (College Station: Texas A&M University Press, 2013); Robert D. Bullard, *Invisible Houston: The Black Experience in Boom and Bust* (College Station: Texas A&M University Press, 1987); Arnoldo De León, *Ethnicity in the Sunbelt: Mexican-Americans in Houston* (College Station: Texas A&M University Press, 2001).

12. This push can be seen as the beginning of the environmental justice movement and a shift toward focusing on the physical inequalities that African-American and Mexican-American urban dwellers faced. See Bullard, *Dumping in Dixie*.

13. Kevin Lynch, *The Image of the City* (Cambridge, MA: MIT Press, 1960); Yi-fu Tuan, *Landscapes of Fear* (New York: Pantheon Books, 1979).

14. Many scholars have shown the massive impact infrastructure construction wrought on African-American and Mexican-American neighborhoods. See Eric Avila, *Popular Culture in the Age of White Flight: Fear and Fantasy in Suburban Los Angeles* (Berkeley: University of California Press, 2004); Rose and Mohl, *Interstate*; DiMento and Ellis, *Changing Lanes*; Joshua Cannon, "Huntsville, the Highway, and Urban Redevelopment: The Long Road to Connect Downtown Huntsville, Alabama to the Interstate Highway System," *Journal of Planning History* 11, no. 1 (2012): 27–46. Others have shown the changes brought to white or wealthier neighborhoods. See Jane Jacobs, *Death and Life of Great American Cities* (New York: Vintage Books, 1961); Christopher W. Wells, "From Freeway to Parkway: Federal Law, Grassroots Environmental Protest, and the Evolving Design of Interstate-35E in Saint Paul, Minnesota," *Journal of Planning History* 11, no. 1 (2012): 8–26. Addressing these two focuses together is essential to understanding citywide transportation politics and decision-making. McKinney, in "Superhighway Deluxe," acknowledges the fact that the Gulf Freeway had a negative impact on the property of both wealthy and poorer Houstonians, 158.

15. Bullard, *Invisible Houston*, 30–31. For a discussion of the significance of the Third and Fifth Wards and their main drags to the black community of Houston, see Pruitt, *The Other Great Migration*.

16. Displacement figures from Houston Chamber of Commerce, "Houston's Regional Mobility: Plans into Action; North Corridor and Hardy Road," July 1982, Box 1, Folder 8, RG F 18, Hardy Street Toll Road Controversy Collection (HSTCC), HMRC, 14. For detailed information on the completion dates and projects of the Houston area highways, see Erik Slotboom, *Houston Freeways: A Historical and Visual Journey* (Cincinnati: C. J. Krehbiel, 2003). The figure of 890 comes from GIS map work done by the author and will be explored in more depth later in the chapter.

17. Alfred Knapp, City of Houston Major Thoroughfare and Transportation Committee, "Response to Memorial Bend Movement of Highway Proposal," June 18, 1962, CHPD, ESRC.

18. Texas Highway Commission Public Hearing Docket, March 6, 1969, Box 2002/101–35, Folder "Harris County," Texas State Archives (TSA).

19. Ralph Ellifrit to Kyle Chapman, September 21, 1954, CHPD, ESRC.

20. In 1954 the majority of the county was still classified as agricultural land, according to the US Department of Agriculture's Census of Agriculture for Texas, 1954,

Census of Agriculture Historical Archive, http://agcensus.mannlib.cornell.edu/AgCensus/homepage.do, accessed November 18, 2013.

21. Zingery Map Company, Hydrant Map, 1955, HMRC.

22. Memorial Bend Advertisement, *Houston Chronicle*, November 11, 1957, HMRC. For a discussion of urbanization's impact on Houston's forest and tree cover, see Diane C. Bates, "Urban Sprawl and the Piney Woods: Deforestation in the San Jacinto Watershed," in Melosi and Pratt, eds., *Energy Metropolis*, 173–184.

23. Memorial Bend Advertisement, *Houston Chronicle*, February 15, 1959. Memorial Bend did have several significant modernist architectural designs. See Betty Chapman, "Memorial Bend Subdivision Expanded City Style During 1950s," *Houston Business Journal*, May 27–June 2, 2005; Michael Brichford, "Where the '50's Were Fabulous: A Driving Tour of Memorial Bend," *Cite* 57 (Spring 2003): 10–11. On Houston's modern residential architecture in the 1950s, see Ben Koush, "Houston Lives the Life: Modern Houses in the Suburbs, 1952–1962" (Master's thesis, Rice University, 2002).

24. Memorial Bend Advertisement, *Houston Chronicle*, August 19, 1956, HMRC.

25. "Memorial Bend Builders Push Big Program," *Houston Chronicle*, September 25, 1955, HMRC.

26. Income and racial statistics taken from Social Explorer records for Houston Census Tract 91, 1950 and 1960. See www.socialexplorer.com, accessed October 24, 2013.

27. On lending practices by the Federal Housing Administration, see David P. Fruend, *Colored Property: State Policy and White Racial Politics in Suburban America* (Chicago: University of Chicago Press, 2007); Colin Gordon, *Mapping Decline: St. Louis and the Fate of the American City* (Philadelphia: University of Pennsylvania Press, 2008); Douglas Massey and Nancy Denton, *American Apartheid: Segregation and the Making of the Underclass* (Cambridge, MA: Harvard University Press, 1993); Arnold Hirsch, *Making the Second Ghetto: Race and Housing in Chicago, 1940–1960* (Cambridge: Cambridge University Press, 1983). Houstonians who lived in Memorial Bend included architects and developers, such as prominent architect Bill Caudill and Memorial Bend developer Howard Edmunds, future Houston Texans owner Robert McNair, and other business owners and professionals. For a larger list, see "Memorial Bend: Notable Past Residents," Memorial Bend Architecture, n.d., http://memorialbendarchitecture.com/notable.htm, accessed December 3, 2013.

28. See 1954 plat map of Memorial Bend Subdivision, Box 4, MSS 118, Houston Subdivision Collection, HMRC.

29. Milton McGinty to the Houston Planning Commission, Memo, May 1962, Box 3, Folder 3, VPC, HMRC.

30. The dealings of Smith and Hofheinz were common features in Houston newspapers during the 1950s and 1960s. See, for example, "Smith Tract Sold for $6 Million," *Houston Post*, July 23, 1964, Box 33, Folder 11, George Fuermann Collection (GFC), Special Collections Library, University of Houston (SCLUH). The men also jointly developed the Astrodome area in the early 1960s.

31. Houston Planning Commission Minutes, March 15, 1960, Box 2, Folder 3, VPC, HMRC.

32. Ibid.

33. Houston Planning Commission Minutes, December 20, 1960, Box 2, Folder 3, VPC, HMRC.

34. H. P. Powell to M. A. Walker, May 15, 1962, CHPD, ESRC; Houston Planning Commission Minutes, June 5, 1962, Box 2, Folder 5, VPC, HMRC.

35. "Attention Homeowners and Taxpayers!!" Memorial Bend Protest Flyer, CHPD, ESRC.

36. Houston Planning Commission Minutes, June 5, 1962, Box 2, Folder 5, VPC, HMRC.

37. Ibid.

38. Houston Planning Commission Minutes, June 19, 1962, Box 2, Folder 5, VPC, HMRC.

39. In a Houston Planning Commission meeting, Williams expressly stated that he was addressing the concerns of Smith and Hofheinz and listed the particular changes they wanted to see. Fernando Williams and Roy Hofheinz to Houston Planning Commission, December 22, 1958, CHPD, ESRC.

40. Ibid.

41. Ibid.

42. Houston Planning Commission Minutes, February 6, 1963, Box 2, Folder 6, VPC, HMRC.

43. Ibid.

44. Owen Gutfreund discusses the power that such donations gave developers in several case studies in *Twentieth Century Sprawl*, 107. The relationship between the development of Sharpstown and US 59 was also shaped by land donations of landowners. See "Spiller Enlarges Offer of SW Freeway Right-of-Way," *Houston Post*, September 6, 1957, H-Freeways-1950s Vertical File (VF), HMRC; "Freeway Give-Away," November 1957, *Houston*, H-Freeways-1950s VF, HMRC.

45. Houston City Council Minutes, January 27, 1965, HMRC.

46. On the treatment and discrimination of blacks on public transportation and African-American responses, see Robin D. G. Kelley, "Congested Terrain," in Robin D. G. Kelley, *Race Rebels: Culture, Politics, and the Black Working Class* (New York: Free Press, 1994), 55–75; Blair Kelley, *Right to Ride: Streetcar Boycotts and African-American Citizenship in the Era of "Plessy v Ferguson"* (Chapel Hill: University of North Carolina Press, 2010). On contemporary transportation-oriented protests, see Robert J. Walker, *Let My People Go! The Miracle of the Montgomery Bus Boycott* (Lanham, MD: Hamilton Books, 2007); Raymond Arsenault, *Freedom Riders: 1961 and the Struggle for Racial Justice* (New York: Oxford University Press, 2006); Christina Melton, *Signpost to Freedom: The 1953 Baton Rouge Bus Boycott* (Louisiana Public Broadcasting, 2004), film. Houston had a brief street boycott by black residents in 1903 when the original segregation laws for public transit were passed. See William Henry Kellar, *Make Haste Slowly: Moderates, Conservatives, and School Desegregation in Houston* (College Station: Texas A&M University Press, 1999), 12. On the importance of cars to a Houston African-American man,

Eldrewey Stearns, see Thomas R. Cole, *No Color Is My Kind: The Life of Eldrewey Stearns and the Integration of Houston* (Austin: University of Texas Press, 1997), 14–15, 146, 152. On the freedom automobility provided to African Americans, see Cotten Seiler, *Republic of Drivers: A Cultural History of Automobility in America* (Chicago: University of Chicago Press, 2008), 105–128; Kathleen Franz, "'The Open Road': Automobility and Racial Uplift in the Interwar Years," in Bruce Sinclair, ed., *Technology and the African-American Experience: Needs and Opportunities for Study* (Cambridge, MA: MIT Press, 2004); Mark S. Foster, "In the Face of 'Jim Crow': Prosperous Blacks and Vacations, Travel and Outdoor Leisure, 1890–1945," *Journal of Negro History* 84, no. 2 (1999): 130–149; Paul Gilroy, "Driving While Black," in Daniel Miller, ed., *Car Cultures*, Materializing Culture (Oxford: Berg, 2001), 81–104.

47. The remaking of neighborhoods by highways echoes that caused by urban renewal. For the impacts of those programs on neighborhoods, see Andrew R. Highsmith, *Demolition Means Progress: Flint, Michigan, and the Fate of the American Metropolis* (Chicago: University Of Chicago Press, 2015); Mindy Fullilove, *Root Shock: How Tearing Up City Neighborhoods Hurts America, and What We Can Do About It* (New York: One World/Ballantine, 2004).

48. Even the wealthiest and most influential of Houston's African-American and Mexican-American populations possessed significantly less political power than whites of their equivalent class or social position for most of the twentieth century. See Thomas H. Kreneck, *Mexican-American Odyssey: Felix Tijerina, Entrepreneur & Civic Leader, 1905–1965* (College Station: Texas A&M University Press, 2001), 108–114; Pruitt, *The Other Great Migration*, 246–248.

49. Income and racial statistics taken from Social Explorer records for Houston Census Tracts 37 and 18, 1960, www.socialexplorer.com, accessed October 24, 2013.

50. In 1960, 90 percent of the Third Ward homes in Houston Census Tract 34 were rented; 75 percent of Fifth Ward homes in Houston Census Tract 18 were as well. See Social Explorer, 1960, Houston Census Tracts 18 and 34, www.socialexplorer.com, accessed October 24, 2013.

51. For more on Houston's NAACP activities, see Merline Pitre, *In Struggle Against Jim Crow: Lulu B. White and the NAACP, 1900–1957* (College Station: Texas A&M University Press, 1999), 107, 120–128 (membership); Gary Lavergne, *Before Brown: Heman Marion Sweatt, Thurgood Marshall, and the Long Road To Justice* (Austin: University of Texas Press, 2010); "A Fading Symbol," *Forward Times*, January 12, 1963, HMRC. See also Gloster Current to Earl Boone, November 20, 1962, microfilmed papers of the NAACP Selected Branch Files, 1956–1965, Part 27, Series A, Reel 15 (Bethesda, MD: University Publications of America, 1999). On membership comparison, in 1951 the entire state of Mississippi had a total of 1,303 members, down from 3,540 in 1948. Likewise, the Memphis branch had only 731 members in 1952. Mississippi figures from Patricia Sullivan, *Lift Every Voice: The NAACP and the Making of the Civil Rights Movement* (New York: New Press, 2009), 400. Memphis figures from Green, *Battling the Plantation Mentality*, 190.

52. Alan Altshuler and David Luberoff, *Mega-Projects: The Changing Politics of*

Urban Public Investment (Washington, DC: Brookings Institution Press; Cambridge, MA: Lincoln Institute of Land Policy, 2003); Mandi Isaacs Jackson, *Model City Blues: Urban Space and Organized Resistance in New Haven* (Philadelphia: Temple University Press, 2008).

53. "Big Highways Program in Harris Gets Go Ahead," *Houston Post*, July 17, 1957, H-Freeways-1950 VF, HMRC.

54. "Plan for New Gulf Freeway Feeder Offered," *Houston Chronicle*, October 20, 1956, H-Freeways-Gulf Freeway VF, HMRC.

55. "Core: City's Heart Needs Treatment," from "Houston, 1958," Supplement to *Houston Post*, January 16, 1958, Box 3, Folder 5, VPC, HMRC.

56. For further discussion of the conscious use of roadways by city and state officials as a form of urban renewal, see Rose and Mohl, *Interstate*, 95–111; Martin Anderson, *Federal Bulldozer: A Critical Analysis of Urban Renewal, 1949–1962* (Cambridge, MA: MIT Press, 1964); Bernard Friedan and Lynne Sagalyn, *Downtown Inc.: How America Rebuilds Cities* (Cambridge, MA: MIT Press, 1989). For a description and discussion of the "second ghetto," see Hirsch, *Making the Second Ghetto*. Houston's history with public housing is documented in Bullard, *Invisible Houston*, 41–49.

57. "Tracts Bought for Elevated Roadway Here," *Houston Chronicle*, January 15, 1958, H-Freeways-Gulf Freeway VF, HMRC; "City May Knock Out Pierce Freeway Line," *Houston Chronicle*, April 18, 1957, H-Freeways-Gulf Freeway VF, HMRC.

58. Oscar Weyrich to AC Kyser, October 20, 1959, Weyrich Letters, Box 2002/101–72, Texas Highway Department Historical Records (THDHR), TSA.

59. A. C. Kyser to Oscar Weyrich, October 22, 1959, Weyrich Letters, Box 2002/101–72, THDHR, TSA.

60. "City Seeks Elevated Freeway, *Houston Post*, July 22, 1960, H-Freeways-1950s VF, HMRC.

61. Jacobs, *Death and Life*. Jacobs explores the importance of smaller side streets and cross streets to neighborhood cohesion and health.

62. *Polk's Houston (Harris County) City Directory* (Houston: Polk, 1960), Dolph Briscoe Center for American History (DBCAH).

63. Ibid.

64. For more on the significance of Dowling and its businesses, see Pruitt, *The Other Great Migration*.

65. The 1964 and 1970 numbers are from *Polk's Houston (Harris County) City Directory* (Houston: Polk, 1960), DBCAH.

66. City of Houston Planning Department, "Third Ward Data Book," Box 2, CHPD, RG A 002, HMRC, 1–6.

67. Ernie Attwell, interview by Dorothee Sauter, September 22, 2004, transcript, Box 9, 2006–005, Houston Oral History Project (HPP), SCLUH.

68. Patrick Horsbrugh, "Blight, A Foretold Affliction," *Texas Architect*, May 1966, Box 29, Folder 3, GFC, SCLUH, 7–8. In *City of Quartz: Excavating the Future in Los Angeles*, new ed. (New York: Verso, 2006), Mike Davis makes similar arguments about the built environment in Los Angeles.

69. Houston Municipal Art Commission, City of Houston Department of Planning, "Beautification Study: Freeways," 1968, Box 5, CHPD, RG A 004, HMRC.

70. Texas Highway Commission Minutes, August 5, 1971, Minute Order #65169, Box 1998/69–06 (May 1970–May 1971), THDHR, TSA, 44.

71. "Gulf Freeway Through Town Expected by September 1," *Houston Post*, June 25, 1967, H-Freeways-Gulf Freeway VF, HMRC.

72. "A New, Beautiful Freeway Link," *Houston Chronicle*, August 22, 1967, H-Freeways-1950s VF, HMRC.

73. Ramona Toliver, interview by author, April 20, 2012. Several histories of Houston describe the infrastructural challenges many Houston communities faced. See Feagin, *Free Enterprise City*, 210–264; David G. McComb, *Houston, the Bayou City* (Austin: University of Texas, 1969), 209; Martin Melosi, "Houston's Public Sinks: Sanitary Services from Local Concerns to Regional Challenges," in Melosi and Pratt, *Energy Metropolis*, 109–147.

74. Ramona Toliver, interview by author, April 20, 2012.

75. Algenita Scott Davis, interview by J. R. Wilson, July 19, 2006, interview #00624, transcript, Box 10, Houston History Project Collection (HHP), SCLUH.

76. The Federal-Aid Highway Act of 1962 was the first to mention relocation assistance for displaced residents and businesses.

77. Ramona Toliver, interview by author, April 20, 2012. On lack of freeway exits, see Algenita Scott Davis, interview by J. R. Wilson, July 19, 2006.

78. Beneva Williams, interview by J. R. Wilson, July 13, 2003, interview #00628, transcript, Box 10, HHP, SCLUH. On Williams and the desegregation case, see McComb, *Houston*, 231; Kellar, *Make Haste Slowly*, 89–103.

79. Beneva Williams, interview by J. R. Wilson, July 13, 2003.

80. Algenita Davis, interview by J. R. Wilson, July 19, 2006.

81. Both Toliver and Smith discussed the changes to their personal mobility patterns and the increase in car trips after the construction of the road. See Ramona Toliver, interview by author, April 20, 2012, and E. Smith, interview by author, April 18, 2012, Houston, Texas, audio recording. On the experiential significance of changing mobility modes from walking to driving, especially to interstates, see David Nye, "Redefining the American Sublime, from Open Road to Interstate," in Mari Hvattum, Brita Brenna, Beate Elvebakk, and Janike Kampevold Larsend, eds., *Routes, Roads, and Landscapes* (Farnham, UK: Ashgate, 2011), 99–112.

82. The dangers presented by the location of transportation structures in or around lower-class neighborhoods has been a problem for African Americans for decades. For an example of recent work on this topic, see Mark Fiege, *The Republic of Nature: An Environmental History of the United States* (Seattle: University of Washington Press, 2012), 318–357.

83. Houston City Council Minutes, April 12, 1966, HMRC; Margaret Scanlan, "Boy Fatality of East Freeway," *Denver Harbor News*, May 12, 1970, Box 1, Folder 2, Margaret Scanlan Collection (MSC), MSS 266, HMRC.

84. "Traffic Safety Is Still for Whites," *Houston Informer*, February 10, 1968.

85. Margaret Scanlan, "Denver-Harbor CC Opens Crosswalk," *Denver Harbor News*, April 28, 1970, Box 1, Folder 2, MSC, HMRC.

86. TxDOT Can 230/SRN006411, February 19, 1964, I-10/1–45–57, Texas Department of Transportation Aerial Photo Library, Austin, Texas.

87. Reflections upon the Fifth Ward's physical boundaries come from an informal conversation by the author with longtime Fifth Ward resident Patricia Prather on April 24, 2012.

88. Denver Harbor descriptions from City of Houston Department of Planning, "Denver Harbor/Port Houston Data Book," Box 2, CHPD, RG A 004, HMRC, 11.

89. On the physical conditions facing African-American and Mexican-American communities, see De León, *Ethnicity in the Sunbelt*; Bullard, *Invisible Houston*; Robert Bullard, *Dumping in Dixie: Race, Class, and Environmental Quality*, 3rd ed. (Boulder: Westview Press, 2008); Robert D. Bullard, "Dumping on Houston's Black Neighborhoods," in Melosi and Pratt, eds., *Energy Metropolis*, 207–223. On shifts toward confronting such physical problems and poverty, much of which was rooted in the Community Action Program of the War on Poverty, see William S. Clayson, *Freedom Is Not Enough: The War on Poverty and the Civil Rights Movement in Texas* (Austin: University of Texas Press, 2010), 63–64, 80–83. For more on CAPs across the United States, see Robert Fisher, *Let the People Decide: Neighborhood Organizing in America* (New York: Twayne, 1994), 119–131; Annelise Orleck and Lisa Gayle Hazirjian, eds., *The War on Poverty: A New Grassroots History, 1964–1980* (Athens: University of Georgia Press, 2011).

90. "About Muddy Roads and Men," *Forward Times*, April 16, 1960, DBCAH, 21.

91. This push can be seen as the beginning of the environmental justice movement and a shift toward focusing on the physical inequalities that African-American and Mexican-American urban dwellers faced. See Bullard, *Dumping in Dixie*.

92. See Chamber of Commerce, Master Freeway Plan, March 1954, Box 6, Folder 10, Oscar Holcombe Collection, MSS 20, HMRC; Houston Chamber of Commerce, "1975 Freeways and 1925 Thoroughfares," 1958, HMRC; Houston Planning Commission, "Plan for Major Thoroughfares and Freeways," 1957, Texas Reading Room Map Collection B3, HMRC.

93. Ralph Ellifrit to the Houston Planning Commission, September 25, 1963, Box 3, Folder 4, VRC, MSS 143, HMRC.

94. Houston City Council Minutes, October 2, 1963, HMRC.

95. Ralph Ellifrit to the Houston Planning Commission, September 25, 1963, Box 3, Folder 4, VRC, MSS 143, HMRC.

96. "Planning Board Insisting, Open Chimney Rock: Overrules Council on Thoroughfare, Refusal to OK Subdivision Plat Reopens Fight," *Houston Press*, December 31, 1963, VRC, Box 3, Folder 6, HMRC.

97. For additional examples, see Kyle Shelton, "Building a Better Houston: Highways, Neighborhoods, and Infrastructural Citizenship in the 1970s," *Journal of Urban History*, October 2015, http://journals.sagepub.com/stoken/rbtfl/SYeYrsbwCikwA/full.

98. Houston City Council Minutes, January 27, 1965, HMRC.

CHAPTER 3

1. Maggie Landron, "Freeway Kills—City Thinks," *Papel Chicano*, April 11, 1970, Houston Metropolitan Research Center (HMRC), 7.

2. Richard Holgin, interview by author, February 22, 2012, San Antonio, Texas, audio recording. I define the East End as the combination of the Second Ward, Magnolia Park, Harrisburg, Eastwood, and Lawndale neighborhoods. Holgin confirmed the rumors by attending an early community information meeting about the road at a neighborhood church. He believes it was either 1963 or 1964.

3. According to the 1960 US Census, only 1.6 percent of East End residents had a college degree. See 1960 US Census, Tracts 19, 20, 21, and 22, Social Explorer, www.socialexplorer.com, accessed March 15, 2014.

4. Dock Burke, P. K. Guseman, J. L. Buffington, and D. L. Schafer, "Evaluation of Residents' Attitudes and Expectations of a Planned Freeway," Texas Transportation Institute (TTI), College Station, Texas, and Texas Highway Department (THD), 1974, TTI Report 148–6, THD Study 2-1-71-148, iv; Richard Holgin, interview by author, February 22, 2012.

5. For a discussion of how "community identity" can act both as an internal understanding of a specific place and as a frame for larger political action, see Kevin Gotham, "Political Opportunity, Community Identity, and the Emergence of a local Anti-Expressway Movement," *Social Problems* 46, no. 3 (1999): 332–354.

6. US Department of Transportation (USDOT), Federal Highway Administration (FHA), and Texas Highway Department (THD), "Draft Environmental Impact Statement for State Highway 225 from US 59 to Lawndale Avenue in Houston, Harris County, Texas," FHWA-TEX_EIS-730977-D, 7; Minutes of the Texas Highway Commission, Minute Order 62158, April 2, 1969, Box 1998/069–5, Texas State Archives (TSA).

7. "Houston Most Auto-Dominated City Next to LA," *Houston Chronicle*, February 22, 1972.

8. Burke et al., "Evaluation of Residents' Attitudes," 9–20. Seventy percent of the East End residents surveyed approved of the highway plan, 15 percent opposed it, and 15 percent expressed no opinion. Controlling for Anglo residents, the approval rating rose to 78 percent, but among Mexican Americans it dropped to 66 percent. This difference demonstrates a higher level of skepticism among the East End's Mexican-American population toward the project. The study also concluded that the primary opposition arose from the Mexican-American residents of Harrisburg and Magnolia Park.

9. Raymond Mohl and Mark Rose have argued that many of the national upsurges in highway revolts can be linked with other civil rights victories. See Raymond Mohl and Mark Rose, *Interstate: Highway Politics and Policy Since 1939*, 3rd ed.(Knoxville: University of Tennessee Press, 2012), 113–134. Likewise, Joseph DiMento and Cliff Ellis have argued that the negative impact of urban highways on people's lives in American cities pushed both planning professionals and citizens to react against new road plans by the 1960s. See Joseph DiMento and Cliff Ellis, *Changing Lanes: Visions and Histories of Urban Freeways* (Cambridge, MA: MIT Press, 2012). For a sample of works dealing with Mexican-American civil rights fights in Houston, see Guadalupe San Miguel, *Brown, Not White: School Integration and the Chicano Movement in Houston* (College Station: Texas A&M University Press, 2001); Arnoldo De León, *Ethnicity in the Sunbelt: A History of Mexican-Americans in Houston* (Houston: University of Houston Press, 1989); Brian Behnken, *Fighting Their Own Battles: Mexican-Americans, African-Americans, and the Struggle for Civil Rights in Texas* (Chapel Hill: University of North Carolina Press, 2011); Thomas H. Kreneck, *Mexican-American Odyssey: Felix Tijerina, Entrepreneur & Civic Leader, 1905–1965* (College Station: Texas A&M University Press, 2001); William Henry Kellar, *Make Haste Slowly: Moderates, Conservatives, and School Desegregation in Houston* (College Station: Texas A&M University Press, 1999); Cynthia Orozco, *No Mexicans, Women, or Dogs Allowed: The Rise of the Mexican-American Civil Rights Movement* (Austin: University of Texas Press, 2009).

10. In *Brown, Not White*, San Miguel argues that the fight in Houston around the topic of school integration helped radicalize a vast majority of the city's Mexican-American population. This fight began almost simultaneously with the buildup to the Harrisburg Freeway conflict. See also Behnken, *Fighting Their Own Battles*, 154–194.

11. Wesley Phelps, *A People's War on Poverty: Urban Politics, Grassroots Activists, and the Struggle for Democracy in Houston, 1964–1976* (Athens: University of Georgia Press, 2014), 148–155.

12. Burke et al., "Evaluation of Residents' Attitudes," 43.

13. This chapter's discussion of place-making and resident/official conceptions of landscapes relies greatly on the idea of framing historical work through an "ethic of place," which allows for a given landscape or space to be understood as a collection of definitions and viewpoints from a variety of actors while taking into account the physical, natural landscape itself. This idea comes from Matthew Klingle, *Emerald City: An Environmental History of Seattle* (New Haven, CT: Yale University Press, 2007).

14. De León, *Ethnicity in the Sunbelt*, 3–42.

15. City of Houston Planning Department, "Magnolia Park/Harrisburg-Manchester Data Book, 1976," City of Houston Planning Department Records (CHPD), RG A 004, Box 2, HMRC, 22.

16. USDOT et al., "Draft Environmental Impact Statement for State Highway 225," 7. See also Richard Holgin, interview by author, February 20, 2012; Frank Partida, interview by author, March 5, 2012, Houston, Texas, audio recording.

17. Joseph A. Pratt, "A Mixed Blessing: Energy, Economic Growth, and Houston's Environment," in Martin Melosi and Joseph A. Pratt, eds., *Energy Metropolis: An Environmental History of Houston and the Gulf Region* (Pittsburgh: University of Pittsburgh Press, 2007), 21–51; Hugh S. Gorman, "The Houston Ship Channel and the Changing Landscape of Industrial Pollution," in Melosi and Pratt, eds., *Energy Metropolis*, 52–68. Both Pratt and Gorman discuss the costs and benefits of living along the ship channel. Proximity brought access to jobs, but it also created grave environmental risks.

18. Burke et al., "Evaluations of Residents' Attitudes," 7. See also the census-tract-level data for these neighborhoods, which demonstrate that in 1960 and 1970 the East

End had a mix of white and Mexican-American residents, but that in most census tracts the percentage of Mexican-American residents rose between the decades. Data from Social Explorer, www.socialexplorer.com, accessed November 30, 2012.

19. Frank Partida, interview by author, March 5, 2012; Gordon Quan, informal conversation with author, April 17, 2012. Quan's parents and uncles operated grocery stores in Magnolia Park and lived in the community. For more information about ILA Local 872, see Rebecca Montes, "Working for American Rights: Black, White, and Mexican-American Dockworkers in Texas During the Great Depression" (PhD diss., University of Texas at Austin, 2005).

20. City of Houston Planning Department, "Magnolia Park/Harrisburg-Manchester Data Book," 22.

21. Burke et al., "Evaluations of Residents' Attitudes"; Dock Burke, Jesse Buffington, and Hugo Meuth, "Attitudes, Opinions, and Expectations of Businessmen in a Planned Freeway Corridor," 1972, TTI, Report 148–2.

22. On the lack of public services and the environmental hazards facing the ship channel neighborhoods, see De León, *Ethnicity in the Sunbelt*; Robert D. Bullard, *Invisible Houston: The Black Experience in Boom and Bust* (College Station: Texas A&M University Press, 1987), 60–75; Robert Bullard, *Dumping in Dixie: Race, Class, and Environmental Quality*, 3rd ed. (Boulder: Westview Press, 2008); Robert Bullard, "Dumping on Houston's Black Neighborhoods," in Melosi and Pratt, eds., *Energy Metropolis*, 207–223; David McComb, *Houston: The Bayou City* (Austin: University of Texas Press, 1969), 209; Joe R. Feagin, *Free Enterprise City: Houston in Political and Economic Perspective* (New Brunswick, NJ: Rutgers University Press, 1988), 210–264; Martin Melosi, "Houston's Public Sinks: Sanitary Services from Local Concerns to Regional Challenges," in Melosi and Pratt, eds., *Energy Metropolis*, 109–147.

23. Houston City Council Minutes, September 14, 1960, HMRC.

24. Texas Highway Commission Public Hearing Docket, March 6, 1969, Box 2002/101–35, Folder "Harris County, Re: Highway Matters in the Houston Area," TSA, 44.

25. Problems with service delivery have been discussed in a number of places, including Feagin, *Free Enterprise City*, 210–288; Martin Melosi, *Effluent America: Cities, Industry, Energy, and the Environment* (Pittsburgh: University of Pittsburgh Press, 2001), 158–188; Kyle Shelton, "Houston (Un)Limited: Path-Dependent Annexation and Highway Practices in an American Metropolis," *Transfers: An Interdisciplinary Journal for Mobility History* 4, no. 1 (Spring 2014): 97–115.

26. "Harrisburg Citizens Invite Welch to Live Amidst Trash, Rats," *Houston Chronicle*, February 1, 1970, H-City Council-1970s Vertical File (VF), HMRC. For a breakdown of the poor quality of service provision to minority and lower-income communities, see City of Houston Planning Department, "Magnolia Park/Harrisburg-Manchester Data Book."

27. "US Aide Tours Area: Channel Pollution Rated in 10 Worst," *Houston Post*, January 19, 1970, Box 29, Folder 9, George Fuermann Collection (GFC), Special Collections Library, University of Houston (SCLUH); Frank Partida, interview by author, March 5, 2012; Gorman, "Houston Ship Channel," 52–68.

28. City of Houston Planning Department, "Houston's Neighborhood Improvement Planning Program: Magnolia Park," Box 1, Folder 9, CHPD, RG A 004, HMRC, 30–31.

29. Maggie Landron, "Children March in Manchester," *Papel Chicano*, April 1, 1970, HMRC, 3.

30. The economic growth argument forwarded by Houston officials for infrastructure projects was similar to those used by politicians and officials in other growing American cities at the time, particularly in the Sunbelt, to justify mobility and general infrastructure projects. For examples from Phoenix, see Philip VanderMeer, *Desert Visions and the Making of Phoenix, 1860–2009* (Albuquerque: University of New Mexico Press, 2010). For Los Angeles, see Jonathon Richmond, *Transport of Delight: The Mythical Conception of Rail Transit in Los Angeles* (Akron, OH: University of Akron Press, 2005). For Atlanta, see Miriam Konrad, *Transporting Atlanta: The Mode of Mobility Under Construction* (Albany, NY: SUNY Press, 2009).

31. For a more detailed description of Highway 225's history and construction, see Erik Slotboom, *Houston Freeways: A Historical and Visual Journey* (Cincinnati: C. J. Krehbiel, 2003), 194.

32. Public Hearing Docket, Texas Transportation Commission, July 1, 1950, Box 2002/101–72, Folder "Harris County, 7/1/50, Continued Development of Highways in Houston," TSA; "3,000,000 Addition to Freeway Announced," *Houston*, December 1950, 58, HMRC.

33. Slotboom, *Houston Freeways*, 194; Texas Highway Commission Minute Order 34178, September 23, 1953, TSA.

34. Texas Highway Department, "Preliminary Freeway Phase: Houston Metropolitan Transportation and Transit Study," August 1961, Texas Department of Transportation, Houston Branch, Planning Library Records.

35. City of Houston Planning Commission, "A Study of Thoroughfare Development in Southeast Area of Metropolitan Houston and Harris County," 1963, CHPD, RG A 004, Box 1, Folder 13, HMRC, 1.

36. "Would Ease Traffic," *Houston Chronicle*, July 1961.

37. City of Houston Planning Department, Interoffice Memo, April 5, 1963, La Porte Freeway Extension File (LPFE), CHPD, Erik Slotboom Research Collection (ESRC).

38. Ralph Ellifrit to Earl Martin, August 28, 1963, LPFE, CHPD, ESRC.

39. Houston City Council Minutes, October 13, 1964, HMRC, 23.

40. Minutes of the Highway Committee of the Houston Chamber of Commerce, October 2, 1963, Box 20, Folder 18, Foley's Department Store Collection 03/2007–004, SCLUH, 2.

41. DeWitt C. Greer, State Highway Engineer, to Bob Casey, US Representative, July 29, 1965, Box 2002/101–72, Folder "Harris County Re: State Highway 225," TSA. Greer asserts the THD's commitment to Highway 225, but points to an earlier commitment of resources to NASA-area roads as a priority.

42. Texas Highway Commission Public Hearing Docket, March 6, 1969, Box 2002/101–35, Folder "Harris County, Re: Highway Matters in the Houston Area," TSA, 44.

43. Minutes of the Texas Highway Commission, Minute Order 62158, April 2, 1969, Box 1998/069–5, TSA.

44. W. E. Carmichael, Texas State Highway District 12 Engineer, to Clara Bewie, Secretary Texas Highway Commission, February 26, 1969, Box 2002/101–35, Folder "Harris County, Re: Highway Matters in the Houston Area," TSA.

45. Alan Altshuler and David Luberhoff, *Mega-Projects: The Changing Politics of Urban Public Investment* (Washington, DC: Brookings Institution Press; Cambridge, MA: Lincoln Institute of Land Policy, 2003), 251–254.

46. Raymond A. Mohl, "The Interstates and the Cities: The US Department of Transportation and the Freeway Revolt, 1966–1973," *Journal of Policy History* 20, no. 2 (April 2008): 193–226. Mohl argues that in order to assure the completion of the majority of the interstate system, two US secretaries of transportation, Alan Boyd and John Volpe, began to transition federal dollars and influence away from controversial projects. While the Harrisburg Freeway is not a part of the Interstate Highway System, I would argue that the waning support of divisive projects at the federal level influenced decisions on local highways as well, even if they received little federal funding.

47. Slotboom, in *Houston Freeways*, 200, discusses the role of the National Environmental Policy Act in the Harrisburg fight. See also Jeremy Korr, "Physical and Social Construction of the Capital Beltway," in Thomas Zeller and Christof Mauch, ed., *The World Beyond the Windshield: Roads and Landscapes in the United States and Europe* (Athens: Ohio University Press, 2008), 196. For other examples of how new federal laws affected the highway revolt, see Christopher W. Wells, "From Freeway to Parkway: Federal Law, Grassroots Environmental Protest, and the Evolving Design of Interstate-35E in Saint Paul, Minnesota," *Journal of Planning History* 11, no. 1 (2012): 8–26. See also Joshua Cannon, "Huntsville, the Highway, and Urban Redevelopment: The Long Road to Connect Downtown Huntsville, Alabama to the Interstate Highway System," *Journal of Planning History* 11, no. 1 (2012): 27–46. General sources on the National Environmental Policy Act include Richard A. Liroff, *National Policy for the Environment: N.E.P.A. and Its Aftermath* (Bloomington: Indiana University Press, 1976); Lynton Caldwell, *The National Environmental Policy Act: An Agenda for the Future* (Bloomington: Indiana University Press, 1998); Ray Clark and Larry Canter, eds., *Environmental Policy and NEPA: Past, Present, and Future* (Boca Raton, FL: St. Lucie Press, 1997).

48. Burke et al., "Evaluation of Residents' Attitudes," 9. For a description of the business community's reaction, see Burke et al., "Attitudes, Opinions, and Expectations," 23. See also Richard Holgin, interview by author, February 22, 2012.

49. A variety of cities, including Atlanta, San Francisco, San Diego, Buffalo, Los Angeles, and Washington, DC—were considering or already constructing mass transit systems by this point. Federal funding through the Urban Mass Transit Administration reached its peak in the early 1970s with the opening of the Highway Trust Fund for mass transit projects. See Konrad, *Transporting Atlanta*, 52–56; Richmond, *Transport of Delight*, 149–213; Zachary Scharg, *The Great Society Subway: A History of the Washington Metro* (Baltimore: Johns Hopkins University Press, 2006), 32–195; Louise Nelson Dyble,

Paying the Toll: Local Power, Regional Politics, and the Golden Gate Bridge (Philadelphia: University of Pennsylvania Press, 2009), 125–148.

50. The quotations in this paragraph all come from Maggie Landron, "The Freeway to End All Freeways," *Papel Chicano*, March 12, 1970, HMRC, 6.

51. A number of studies consider the role of Chicano activists in Houston. See De León, *Ethnicity in the Sunbelt*; Behnken, *Fighting Their Own Battles*; Kellar, *Make Haste Slowly*; San Miguel, *Brown, Not White*; Maximilian Krochmal, *Blue Texas: The Making of a Multiracial Democratic Coalition in the Civil Rights Era* (Chapel Hill: University of North Carolina Press, 2016).

52. Maggie Landron, "Freeway Kills—City Thinks," *Papel Chicano*, April 11, 1970, HMRC, 7.

53. "Residents on Right-of-Way Safe for 3–4 Years," *Houston Post*, March 10, 1970, H-Freeways-1970s, HMRC.

54. Richard Holgin, interview by author, February 22, 2012.

55. Mark Madera et al., *The Barrios: Mexican-Americans in Houston* (Houston: Magnolia Business Center, a Model Cities Agency, January 1971), 38–39.

56. Richard Holgin, interview by author, February 22, 2012.

57. For more information about Ripley House and its transition to serving the East End's Mexican-American population, see Felix Fraga, interview by author, February 13, 2012, Houston, Texas, audio recording.

58. See Richard Holgin, interview by author, February 22, 2012. See also Slotboom, *Houston Freeways*, 200.

59. A. C. Kyser, Texas Highway Department, to Richard Holgin, May 29, 1970, ESRC.

60. The creation of such study teams was a common tactic for local, state, and federal road builders in the 1960s and 1970s wishing to demonstrate the government's commitment to citizens' engagement. See Mohl and Rose, *Interstate*, 155–156.

61. "La Porte Freeway Design Team Named," *Houston Chronicle*, July 19, 1970.

62. Bullard, in *Dumping in Dixie*, 26, discusses the importance of having representation on decision-making panels.

63. The members of the Harrisburg Freeway Study Team included Phil Wilson (Chairman, Engineer, Texas Highway Department [THD]); Dr. W. G. Adkins (Research Economist, Texas A&M); Forland Bundy (Bridge Field Engineer, THD); Dr. Don Davis (Sociology Professor, Texas A&M); Hilton Hagan (Public Information Specialist, THD); Robert Hays (Architect, THD); Dexter Jones (Supervising Design Engineer, THD); Irl Larrimore Jr. (Field Engineer, THD); William McClure (Engineer, THD); George Munson (Engineer, THD); Roy Rodman (Landscape Architect, THD); and Oliver Stork (Engineer, THD). Member roll, Harrisburg Freeway Study Team, Meeting Minutes, September 16, 1970, LPFE, CHPD, ESRC. The relationship between Texas A&M University and the Texas Highway Department is well known anecdotally and professionally. The Texas Transportation Institute, a think tank and policy center housed at A&M, was created with help from the Texas Highway Department.

64. Harrisburg Freeway Study Team, Meeting Minutes, September 16, 1970, LPFE, CHPD, ESRC.

65. "Progress Report, Harrisburg Freeway Study Team," January 8, 1971, LPFE, CHPD, ESRC.

66. Harrisburg Freeway Study Team, "Handout Pamphlet," December 1970, LPFE, CHPD, ESRC.

67. "Route Plans Aired at Public Meeting," *Houston Chronicle*, February 19, 1973.

68. Leora Cekosky, "Freeway Panel Meets with Progress Association," *Houston Chronicle*, February 10, 1971.

69. "Highway Department Standing Behind Plans for Harrisburg Freeway," *Houston Chronicle*, February 21, 1971.

70. Tom Steacy, "Highway Dept. Tells Tentative Route of Harrisburg Freeway," *Houston Chronicle*, January 11, 1973.

71. City of Houston Planning Department, "Houston's Neighborhood Improvement Planning Program: Magnolia Park Working Plan," 2.

72. USDOT et al., "Draft Environmental Impact Statement for State Highway 225," 11.

73. Ibid., 10.

74. Maggie Landron, "Harrisburg Freeway Will Destroy Barrio," *Papel Chicano*, February 20, 1970, HMRC, 3.

75. City of Houston Planning Department, "Houston's Neighborhood Improvement Planning Program: Magnolia Park Working Plan," 5.

76. USDOT et al., "Draft Environmental Impact Statement for State Highway 225," 8.

77. "HGAC Okays Building Harrisburg Freeway," *Houston Chronicle*, August 21, 1973; Frank Partida, interview by author, March 5, 2013.

78. "Route Plans Aired at Public Meeting," *Houston Chronicle*, February 19, 1973. Mohl, in "The Interstates and the Cities," 198, discusses the San Antonio North Expressway fight.

79. "Harrisburg Freeway Study Called Inadequate by EPA," *Houston Chronicle*, September 1, 1973.

80. Richard Holgin, testimony before the Houston City Council, City Council Minutes, October 9, 1973, HMRC, 37. See also USDOT et al., "Draft Environmental Impact Statement for State Highway 225," 10.

81. Richard Holgin, City Council testimony, October 9, 1973.

82. "Harrisburg Freeway Study Team Progress Report," March 1974, LPFE, CHPD, ESRC.

83. Dan Davis, City of Houston Planning Department, "A Few Comments on the Location of the Harrisburg Freeway," November 28, 1973, LPFE, CHPD, ESRC.

84. Houston City Council Minutes, May 21, 1974, Houston City Secretary's Office.

85. Roscoe Jones to Fred Hofheinz, Memo, May 22, 1974, LPFE, CHPD, ESRC.

86. Richard Holgin to Mayor Fred Hofheinz, July 5, 1974, LPFE, CHPD, ESRC. It is not clear how Holgin received a copy of this memo; it may have been sent to him by Jones or obtained by other means.

87. "Plan Asks Drastic Highway Cuts Here," *Houston Chronicle*, August 13, 1976.

88. John Castillo to C. J. Stewart, City of Houston Planning Commission, May 5, 1976, Ben T. Reyes Collection, Box 4, Folder 2, MSS 103, HMRC.

89. Ibid.

90. Richard Holgin, interview by author, February 22, 2012.

91. See the Houston Galveston Regional Transportation Study, "Status of Freeway and Expressway System Map, 1989," Map R-818, TXR MC B3, HMRC.

92. Richard Holgin, interview by author, February 22, 2012.

93. Altshuler and Luberhoff, *Mega-Projects*, 251–254.

CHAPTER 4

1. Fred Hofheinz, "Second Inaugural Address," January 2, 1976, Box 74, Folder 3, City of Houston Public Service Department (CHPSD) Collection, RG A 20, Houston Metropolitan Research Center (HMRC).

2. Ibid.

3. Teresa Tomkins-Walsh, "'A Concrete River Had to Be Wrong': Environmental Action on Houston's Bayous, 1935–1980" (PhD diss., University of Houston, 2009).

4. For work on black-brown coalitions and their impact on Texas politics, see Maximilian Krochmal, *Blue Texas: The Making of a Multiracial Democratic Coalition in the Civil Rights Era* (Chapel Hill: University of North Carolina Press, 2016).

5. Mary Ellen Curtin, "Reaching for Power: Barbara C. Jordan and Liberals in the Texas Legislature, 1966–1972," *Southwestern Historical Quarterly* 108, no. 2 (October 2004): 210–231.

6. Charles Rutheiser, *Imagineering Atlanta: The Politics of Place in the City of Dreams* (New York: Verso, 1996); Ethan N. Elkind, *Railtown: The Fight for the Los Angeles Metro Rail and the Future of the City* (Berkeley: University of California Press, 2014).

7. William Fulton, *The Reluctant Metropolis: The Politics of Urban Growth in Los Angeles* (Baltimore: Johns Hopkins University Press, 2001); Jonathan Richmond, *Transport of Delight: The Mythical Conception of Rail Transit in Los Angeles* (Akron, OH: Akron University Press, 2005); Elkind, *Railtown*.

8. See Miriam Konrad, *Transporting Atlanta: The Mode of Mobility Under Construction* (New York: State University of New York Press, 2009); Ronald H. Bayor, *Race and the Shaping of Twentieth-Century Atlanta* (Chapel Hill: University of North Carolina Press, 1996); Ruthieser, *Imagineering Atlanta*.

9. Tayna Snyder, "How Clayton County Turned It's Zero-Transit Nightmare Around," *Streetsblog*, November 7, 2014, accessed May 29, 2016.

10. For further discussion of the comparable transportation histories of these three cities, see Kyle Shelton, "What Old Transit Maps Can Teach Us About a City's Future," CityLab, October 10, 2014, www.citylab.com/commute/2014/10/what-old-transit-maps-can-teach-us-about-a-citys-future/381149, accessed March 11, 2017.

11. On 1970s social movements, ranging from taxation campaigns to environmental protection, see Fulton, *Reluctant Metropolis*; Adam Rome, *The Bulldozer in the Countryside: Suburban Sprawl and the Rise of American Environmentalism* (Cambridge: Cambridge University Press, 2001); Richard Walker, *The Country in the City: The Green-*

ing of the San Francisco Bay Area (Seattle: University of Washington Press, 2007); Robert Fisher, *Let the People Decide: Neighborhood Organizing in America* (New York: Twayne, 1994); Matthew D. Lassiter, *The Silent Majority: Suburban Politics in the Sunbelt South* (Princeton, NJ: Princeton University Press, 2006); Robert O. Self, *American Babylon: Race and the Struggle for Postwar Oakland* (Princeton, NJ: Princeton University Press, 2003); Colin Gordon, *Mapping Decline: St. Louis and the Fate of the American City* (Philadelphia: University of Pennsylvania Press, 2008); Lisa McGirr, *Suburban Warriors: The Origins of the New American Right* (Princeton, NJ: Princeton University Press, 2001).

12. Thomas J. Sugrue, *The Origins of the Urban Crisis: Race and Inequality in Postwar Detroit*, Princeton Studies in American Politics (Princeton, NJ: Princeton University Press, 1996).

13. Thomas Plaut, "Energy and the Texas Economy: Past Present and Future," University of Texas, Bureau of Business Research, 1982, 203; Joe Feagin, "The Global Context of Metropolitan Growth: Houston and the Oil Industry," *American Journal of Sociology* 9, no. 6 (May 1985): 1204–1230.

14. See Citizens' Environmental Coalition collections at the HMRC and the Special Collections Library, University of Houston (SCLUH); Bayou Preservation Association records at SCLUH; Tomkins-Walsh, "'A Concrete River Had to Be Wrong.'"

15. According to Walker, *The Country in the City*, not all environmental fights were the same, but nearly all were infrastructural.

16. Robert Bullard, "Dumping on Houston's Black Neighborhoods," in Martin Melosi and Joseph Pratt, eds., *Energy Metropolis: An Environmental History of Houston and the Gulf Coast* (Pittsburgh: University of Pittsburgh Press, 2007).

17. On California Proposition 13, see Self, *American Babylon*.

18. Gordon, *Mapping Decline*; Lassiter, *Silent Majority*; Self, *American Babylon*.

19. City of Houston Planning Department, "Houston Metropolitan Area Transportation Study Report No. 3: Public Transit," 1963, Box 5, Houston Metropolitan Area Transportation Study Reports, 1960–1963, City of Houston Planning Department Records (CHDP), RG A 004, HMRC, ix.

20. "CofC: Prime Mover for a Mobile City," *Houston*, July, 1963, HMRC, 47; "Building Freeways to the Future," *Houston*, December 1963, 1963 Annual Report, HMRC.

21. "Building Freeways to the Future."

22. These numbers are a combination of passenger cars, trucks, and other vehicles. See Houston Chamber of Commerce, "Motor Vehicle Registration in Harris County, 1950–1984," H-Chamber of Commerce-Statistics Vertical File (VF), HMRC.

23. See Houston Harris County Transportation Study Newsletter, January 1969, Box 40, Folder 3, CHPSD, RG A 20, HMRC; "Swinging, Surging, Soaring, the Shining Sixties," *Houston*, December 1969, HMRC, 20.

24. City of Houston Planning Department, "Metropolitan Area Transportation Study: Houston, Origin-Destination Survey, 1960," Box 1, Folder 12, CHDP, RG A 004, HMRC, 3.

25. UC Waigand to Thomas Tyson, March 12, 1970, Box 44, Folder 1, CHPSD, RG A 20, HMRC.

26. See, for example, Thomas Tyson to Louie Welch, December 19, 1969, where Tyson advocates for the construction of bus-only lanes on the Gulf Freeway, Box 43, Folder 1, CHPSD, RG A 20, HMRC.

27. City of Houston Public Service Department, "Road and Transit Study," July 1969, Box 38, Folder 9, CHPSD, RG A 20, HMRC, 56.

28. Eugene Maier, "Total Urban Mobility," speech delivered to the Houston Chamber of Commerce, September 1, 1971, Box 54, Folder 1, CHPSD, RG A 20, HMRC.

29. Alan A. Altshuler and David Luberhoff, *Mega-Projects: The Changing Politics of Urban Public Investment* (Washington, DC: Brookings Institution Press; Cambridge, MA: Lincoln Institute of Land Policy, 2003).

30. For discussion of the transit expansion in the postwar period, especially the role of federal involvement, see Sy Adler, "The Evolution of Federal Transit Policy," in Martin Melosi, ed., *Urban Public Policy: Historical Modes and Methods* (University Park: Pennsylvania State University Press, 1993). See also the Highway Action Committee (HAC) Papers in the Leonel Castillo Papers, Box 3, Folder 6, MSS 147, HMRC. For a general discussion of the creation and importance of the gas tax and the highway trust fund, see Theodore Sky, *The National Road and the Difficult Path to Sustainable National Investment* (Newark: University of Delaware Press, 2011), 154–181; Henry Petroski, *The Road Taken: The History and Future of America's Infrastructure* (New York: Bloomsbury USA, 2016).

31. Speech by Louie Welch, "Transit Financing: The Cities' Role," Box 53, Folder 7, CHPSD, RG A 20, HMRC, n.d., 1.

32. Gerald Hines to Frank Mancuso, January 6, 1972, Box 53, Folder 6, CHPSD, RG A 20, HMRC.

33. See Adler, "The Evolution of Federal Transit Policy." On the cost of the Voorhees study, see "Transit Advisers to Meet," *Houston Post*, September 14, 1971, Box 10, Folder 4, CHPSD, RG A 20, HMRC.

34. Tyson to Ford, May 8, 1973. The first Voorhees report was issued in June 1971 under the title "Transit Action Program: Concerns and Objectives," Box 2, CHDP, RG A 004, HMRC. The final report, titled "Transit Program for Houston: A Summary Report," came out in March 1973, Box 2, CHDP, RG A 004, HMRC.

35. All thirteen members of the TAP steering committee were wealthy men. The committee included the president of the University of Houston, the president of Humble Oil and Refining, and the president of American General Insurance. Eleven members were white, one was black, and one was Mexican American. Minutes of Steering Committee of the Transit Action Program, May 27, 1971, Box 58, Folder 5, CHPSD, RG A 20, HMRC.

36. "Transit Advisers to Meet," *Houston Post*. See also Louie Welch's letter to Houstonians, inviting them to become members of the CAC, February 11, 1972, Box 48, Folder 1, CHPSD, RG A 20, HMRC.

37. Wesley Phelps, *A People's War on Poverty: Urban Politics, Grassroots Activists, and the Struggle for Democracy in Houston, 1964–1976* (Athens: University of Georgia Press, 2014), 25–30.

38. Other prominent civic groups that called for mass transit included the Texas Society of Professional Engineers. See W. F. Herbert to Louie Welch, June 16, 1972, Folder 2, Box 56, CHPSD, RG A 20, HMRC.

39. Houston League of Women Voters, "Focus: Mass Transit," March 1971, Box 44, Folder 6, CHPSD, RG A 20, HMRC.

40. On environmentalism in Houston, see Tomkins-Walsh, "'A Concrete River Had to Be Wrong.'"

41. Testimony of Charles Trost, "Mass Transit: An Inquiry on the Recommendation of the Alan M. Voorhees Company," Citizens' Environmental Coalition Educational Fund, October 1972, Box 45, Folder 6, Citizens' Environmental Coalition Collection, 03/2007–001, SCLUH.

42. Testimony of Gene Robbins, in ibid.

43. Tyson to Ford, May 8, 1973.

44. "C of C Endorses Bill to Create Mass Transit Authority for City," *Houston Post*, n.d. 1973, Box 39, Folder "Mass Transit-Clippings," Kay Bailey Collection, MSS 17, HMRC.

45. Texas, Cities and Towns—Rapid Transit Authorities, 63rd Regular Session of the Texas Legislature, Chapter 141, General and Special Laws of Texas. Text of Senate Bill 642 available at the Legislative Reference Library of Texas, www.lrl.state.tx.us/legis/billsearch/BillDetails.cfm?legSession=63-0&billTypeDetail=SB&BillNumberDetail=642, accessed April 4, 2012.

46. For details of the plan, see Alan M. Voorhees & Associates, "Transit Program for Houston: A Summary Report, 1973," Box 2, Planning Reports 1968–1973, CHPD, RG A 04, HMRC; Transit Action Program, *Newsbriefs*, May 1972, vol. 2, no. 3, published by the City of Houston, CHPSD, RG A 20, HMRC.

47. Voorhees & Associates, "Transit Action Program, Section One," 4.

48. The nine board members were Willoughby Williams (president of American General Insurance, City Council appointee), Carole Pinkett (Humble Oil employee, community activist, City Council appointee), Mary Rollins (League of Women Voters official, City Council appointee), Mario Quinones (president of Houston Tile Company and chairman of Pan American National Bank, City Council appointee), Sam Bowman (president of Northwest National Bank, City Council appointee), Knox Askins (La Porte city attorney, municipalities appointee), Sebron Williams (Deer Park superintendent of schools, municipalities appointee), John Garret (president of Richmond Road and Engineering Company, county appointee), and Herman Lauhoff (president of the Greater Houston Civic Council, county appointee). Carole Pinkett is African American, Mario Quinones was Mexican American. They were the only two nonwhites on the board. See "City Council Names 5 to Mass Transit Board," *Houston Post*, August 15, 1973, Box 61, Folder 7, CHPSD, RG A 20, HMRC; "Mayors Name 2 to Board," *Houston Post*, August 17, 1973, Box 61, Folder 7, CHPSD, RG A 20, HMRC; "Transit Authority Positions Filled," *Houston Post*, August 24, 1973, Box 61, Folder 7, CHPSD, RG A 20, HMRC.

49. "Transit Appointees Agree: Educating Public Their Task," *Houston Post*, August 19, 1973, Box 61, Folder 7, CHPSD, RG A 20, HMRC.

50. Transit Action Program, *Newsbriefs*, May 1972, vol. 2, no. 3, published by the City of Houston, CHPSD, RG A 20, HMRC.

51. "Summary of SB 642," Box 44, Folder 4, CHPSD, RG A 20, HMRC; "A Good Mass Transit Bill," *Houston Post*, March 7, 1973, Kay Bailey Collection, MSS 17, Box 39, Folder 2.

52. Open letter from Louie Welch to Houstonians, September 1973, Box 5, Folder 19, Frank E. Mann Collection, MSS 049, HMRC.

53. Texas, Cities and Towns—Rapid Transit Authorities, 63rd R.S., Ch. 141, General and Special Laws of Texas, 12.

54. "Moving Mass Transit," *Houston Post*, May 17, 1973, Box 61, Folder 7, CHPSD, RG A 20, HMRC.

55. Quentin Mease, executive director of Houston YMCA, to Frank E. Mann, July 24, 1969, Box 4, Folder 7, Frank Mann Papers, MSS 49, HMRC.

56. Laura Keever to Ralph Conant, May 30, 1973, Box 44, Folder 6, CHPSD, RG A 20, HMRC.

57. Laura Keever to Louie Welch, May 30, 1973, Box 44, Folder 6, CHPSD, RG A 20, HMRC.

58. Keever to Conant, May 30, 1973.

59. "No Big Opposition Surfacing for Area Rapid Transit Plan," *Houston Post*, June 25, 1973, Box 61, Folder 7, CHPSD, RG A 20, HMRC.

60. Bernard Sakowitz, "Rapid Transit System Depends on You," *Houston*, June 1973, HMRC.

61. Statement of Laura Keever before the Houston City Council, June 27, 1973, Box 61, Folder 4, CHPSD, RG A 20, HMRC.

62. "Pasadena Council Opposes Mass Transit Proposal," *Houston Post*, June 27, 1973, Box 61, Folder 7, CHPSD, RG A 20, HMRC.

63. "Few Disagree on Rapid Transit Needs," *Houston Post*, June 27, 1973, Box 61, Folder 7, CHPSD, RG A 20, HMRC. Marshall's concern about the lack of information also echoes the opinion voiced by HARTA board member Carole Pinkett about a lack of information reaching the city's black community. Carole Pinkett, interview by author, April 13, 2012.

64. For more on Marshall's role, see Phelps, *A People's War on Poverty*, 99–101, 103–105, 132.

65. Carole Pinkett, interview by author, April 13, 2012.

66. Quote from "Transit Opposition Grows," *Houston Post*, July 18, 1973, Box 61, Folder 7, CHPSD, RG A 20, HMRC. For other suburban resistance, see "South Houston C of C Against Transit Authority," *Houston Post*, July 25, 1973, Box 61, Folder 7, CHPSD, RG A 20, HMRC; "Mass Transit Traveling Rough Road," *Houston Post*, July 12, 1973, Box 61, Folder 7, CHPSD, RG A 20, HMRC.

67. "Castillo Backs Own 16-Point Plan," *Houston Post*, August 30, 1973, Box 61, Folder 7, CHPSD, RG A 20, HMRC.

68. Press Release of Tom Bass, September 20, 1973, Box 61, Folder 4, CHPSD, RG A 20, HMRC.

69. "Drive Being Cranked for Transit Vote Ok," *Houston Post*, September 6, 1973, Box 61, Folder 7, CHPSD, RG A 20, HMRC.

70. "5 Legislators Taking Stands to Oppose Transit Authority," *Houston Post*, September 23, 1973, Box 61, Folder 7, CHPSD, RG A 20, HMRC.

71. For a discussion of issues between the city's communities of color and the Houston Police Department, see Dwight Watson, *Race and the Houston Police Department, 1930–1990: A Change Did Come* (College Station: Texas A&M University Press, 2005).

72. "Minority Lawmakers Criticize Area Transit Proposal," *Houston Informer*, September 29, 1973, HMRC, 1.

73. "Transit Fear Use Denied," *Houston Post*, September 28, 1973, Box 61, Folder 7, CHPSD, RG A 20, HMRC.

74. Carole Pinkett, interview by author, April 13, 2012; "Transit Plan Gains Support of Minorities," *Houston Post*, October 2, 1973, Box 61, Folder 7, CHPSD, RG A 20, HMRC. This thought echoes that of journalist Saul Friedman, who wrote about the transition away from the traditional black power broker of the city in his "Life in Black Houston," Manuscript, *Houston Chronicle* Series 1965, Saul Friedman Papers, Folder 9, SC123, Box 13, HMRC. See also "Transit System Needed by Inner-City Residents, Minority Spokesmen Insist," *Houston Informer*, October 6, 1973, 1.

75. Quoted in "Baptist Ministers, NAACP Strongly Oppose Transit Plan," *Houston Informer*, October 6, 1973, 1; "Architects Say Yes, Others No on Transit," *Houston Post*, September 30, 1973, Box 61, Folder 7, CHPSD, RG A 20, HMRC; "Both Sides Say Mass Transit Proposal in Trouble," *Houston Post*, September 30, 1973, Box 61, Folder 7, CHPSD, RG A 20, HMRC.

76. PASO press release, October 1, 1973, Box 61, Folder 7, CHPSD, RG A 20, HMRC.

77. KXYZ Editorial, "Opposition to Mass Transit Election Mounts," September 26, 1973, Box 61, Folder 7, CHPSD, RG A 20, HMRC.

78. "Confused over Transit?," *Houston Chronicle*, October 4, 1973, Box 48, Folder 5, CHPSD, RG A 20, HMRC.

79. "Transit Authority Crushed by Voters," *Houston Post*, October 7, 1973, Box 61, Folder 7, CHPSD, RG A 20, HMRC.

80. Ibid.

81. Thomas Tyson to Jerome Premo, October 16, 1973, Box 57, Folder 8, CHPSD, RG A 20, HMRC.

82. Carole Pinkett, interview by author, April 13, 2012.

83. "Welch Says Buying Buses Sole Option," *Houston Post*, October 8, 1973, Box 61, Folder 7, CHPSD, RG A 20, HMRC.

84. "Let's Get Rolling," *Houston Post*, October 12, 1973, Box 61, Folder 7, CHPSD, RG A 20, HMRC.

85. "Elliott Hopes to Develop Transit Plans," *Houston Post*, October 12, 1973, Box 61, Folder 7, CHPSD, RG A 20, HMRC.

86. Editorial, "Referendum Defeat Shows Houston Politics Has Changed," KXYZ, October 9, 1973, Box 61, Folder 7, CHPSD, RG A 20, HMRC. Carole Pinkett also reflected this sentiment, seeing the opposition in the communities of color as an outgrowth of the inability of transit supporters to effectively communicate with those groups. Pinkett believes that 1973 was a turning point in terms of a mainstream embracing of Houston's diversity. Carole Pinkett, interview by author, April 13, 2012.

87. Tax Research Association of Houston and Harris County (TRAHH), December 1977 newsletter, vol. 30, no. 12, H-Transportation-1976–1977 VF, HMRC.

88. Barry Goodman to Gerald Koszer, November 10, 1975, Box 72, Folder 1, CHPSD, HMRC.

89. "Hofheinz Faces Uphill Battle in Mayoral Runoff," *Forward Times*, November 17, 1973, 7A, Dolph Briscoe Center for American History (DBCAH).

90. City of Houston, "Race/Ethnicity: 1980–2000," www.houstontx.gov/planning/Demographics/docs_pdfs/Cy/coh_race_ethn_1980–2010.pdf, accessed January 28, 2014; Roberto Treviño Jr., *Church in the Barrio: Mexican-American Ethno-Catholicism in Houston* (Chapel Hill: University of North Carolina Press, 2006), Appendix A, 217; Harris County Census Records, 1970 and 1980, Social Explorer, www.socialexplorer.com, accessed January 28, 2014; "Table 21: Population of the 100 Largest Urban Places, 1980," US Census, www.census.gov/population/www/documentation/twps0027/tab21.txt, accessed January 28, 2014.

91. Harris, Brazoria, Montgomery, Fort Bend, and Galveston County Census Records, 1970 and 1980, Social Explorer, www.socialexplorer.com, accessed January 28, 2014; "Table 21: Population of the 100 Largest Urban Places, 1980," US Census.

92. The need to create a constituency among both white and nonwhite voters in order to create a transit authority can also be seen in Atlanta's attempt to create the Metropolitan Atlanta Regional Transportation Authority. See Konrad, *Transporting Atlanta*; Altshuler and Luberoff, *Mega-Projects*, 71; Clarence Stone, *Regime Politics: Governing Atlanta, 1946–1988* (Lawrence: University of Kansas Press, 1989).

93. Citizens' Environmental Coalition (CEC), "'A Fresh Look' at Mass Transit: An Inquiry Conducted Under the Sponsorship for the Citizens' Environmental Coalition Report," March 1974, Box 44, Folder 2, Citizens' Environmental Coalition Collection (CECC), 07/2007–001, SCLUH, 3–4.

94. Barry Goodman to Garvin Berry, August 21, 1975, Box 72, Folder 3, CHPSD, HMRC.

95. Tom Kiley, "The Transportation Issue in Harris County Today," Public Opinion Survey for the Office of Public Transportation, 1976, H-Transportation-1976–1977 VF, HMRC, 1–4.

96. Ibid., 6.

97. Office of Public Transportation (OPT) and Transportation Advisory Group (TAG), *TransPlan*, April 1977, vol. 1, no. 1, Box 64, Folder 5, CECC, SCLUH.

98. OPT and TAG, *TransPlan*, August 1977, vol. 2, no. 1, Box 64, Folder 5, CECC, SCLUH.

99. OPT and TAG, *TransPlan*, May 1977, vol. 1, no. 2, Box 64, Folder 5, CECC, SCLUH.

100. "Second Park and Ride Route to Open in May," *Houston*, May 1977, HMRC, 38–42.

101. "Creation of Mass Transit Panel Proposed by Hofheinz," *Houston Post*, August 9, 1977, H-Transportation-1976–1977 VF, HMRC. The METRO referendum was made possible by the passage of HB 657 by the 65th Legislature of the State of Texas in 1977. HB 657 renewed a city's ability, set out in 1972 legislation, to create an authority and gave authorities the ability to levy a sales tax. See Legislative Reference Library of Texas, www.lrl.state.tx.us/legis, for the text of the bills, accessed June 24, 2013.

102. OPT and TAG, *TransPlan*, May 1977, vol. 1, no. 2, Box 64, Folder 5, CECC, SCLUH.

103. City of Houston, "METRO Public Hearing," September 27, 1977, Box 72, CHPSD, HMRC, 3–5.

104. Ibid., 22.

105. OPT and TAG, *TransPlan*, October 1977, vol. 2, no. 3, Box 64, Folder 5, CECC, SCLUH.

106. For more information on Ninfa Laurenzo, see Chrystel Pit, "Deal with Us: The Business of Mexican Culture in Post–World War II Houston" (PhD diss., University of Arizona, 2011).

107. OPT and TAG, *TransPlan*, January 1978, vol. 3, no. 2, Box 64, Folder 5, CECC, SCLUH.

108. James Leach, "Regional Transit Planning Must Succeed," *Houston*, November 1977, HMRC, 70.

109. Terry Kliewer "'Agreed in Principle' MTA to Pay City $2.4 Million for HouTran," *Houston Post*, August 3, 1978, H-MTA-1978 VF, HMRC; "Transit Authority Setting Sights on HouTran," *Houston Post*, January 13, 1978, H-Transportation-Jan-Apr-1978 VF, HMRC.

110. "$3.1 Billion Regional Transit System Keys Metro Proposal," *Houston Post*, July 24, 1978, H-Transportation-1978-July-Aug VF, HMRC; Metropolitan Transit Authority of Houston and Harris County (METRO), "Regional Transit Plan," July 1978, MSS 074, Michael Berryhill Collection (MBC), Woodson Research Center (WRC), Rice University, 27.

111. METRO, "Regional Transit Plan."

112. OPT and TAG, *TransPlan*, June 1978, vol. 1, no. 2, Folder 5, Box 64, CECC, SCLUH; "Board Favors August 12 Election," H-Transportation-Apr-June-1978 VF, HMRC; "Aug. 12 Election on Transit Panel Gets McConn's Ok," *Houston Post*, June 20, 1978, H-Transportation-Apr-June-1978 VF, HMRC.

113. METRO, "Regional Transit Plan," 5.

114. Ibid., 7–8.

115. Ibid., 8–26.

116. On *El Sol* and other Mexican-American media outlets, see Pit, "Deal with Us."

117. "Houston's Blocking Transit Plan; Suburban Leaders Mixed on Future," *Houston Post*, June 18, 1978, H-Transportation-1978-Apr-June VF, HMRC.

118. Ibid.

119. "PASO Will Back Mass Transit Plan, But Says Promises Must Be Fulfilled," *Houston Chronicle*, July 31, 1978, H-Transportation-1978-July-Aug VF, HMRC; "MTA Takes Sidetrip for Chicano Support," *Houston Post*, July 30, 1978 H-Transportation-

1978-July-Aug VF, HMRC; "PASO Endorses Creation of Transit Plan," *El Sol*, August 3, 1978, HMRC; METRO, "Regional Transit Plan," 9.

120. "LULAC, 7 Black Leaders Support MTA," *Houston Chronicle*, July 27, 1978, H-Transportation-1978-July-Aug VF, HMRC.

121. METRO Advertisement, *Houston Informer*, August 5, 1978, HMRC; METRO Advertisement, *Houston Forward Times*, August 12, 1978, DBCAH.

122. "Black Leaders Temper MTA Endorsements," *Houston Post*, August 5, 1978, H-Transportation-1978-July-Aug VF, HMRC.

123. "Houston Needs MTA," *Houston Forward Times*, July 29, 1978, DBCAH.

124. "Mexican-American Forces Endorse MTA," *El Sol*, August 3, 1978, HMRC, 2.

125. Ninfa Laurenzo, "MTA and Its Importance to Houston Hispanics," *El Sol*, August 10, 1978, HMRC, 1.

126. Alfonso Vazquez, illustrator, "Vote for METRO" comic, *El Sol*, August 10, 1978, HMRC, 3A.

127. "Vote for MTA," *El Sol*, August 10, 1978, HMRC, 2.

128. Citizens for Better Transit, Speakers Guide for 1978 Election, H-Transportation-1970–1974 VF, HMRC.

129. "Metro Questions," Box 33, Folder 7, CHPSD, HMRC.

130. "Mass or Mess?," *Houston Post*, August 12, 1978, H-Transportation-1978-July-Aug VF, HMRC.

131. The 1978 referendum results are available at the Houston city secretary's office, Box Election Misc. 1922–1984.

132. John Kling, "The Question of Mass Transit," *Houston Chronicle*, July 30, 1978, H-Traffic-1950–1979 VF, HMRC.

133. "Transit Victory Shows Strength of This Area," *Houston Post*, August 15, 1978, H-Transportation-1978-July-Aug VF, HMRC.

134. Ibid.

135. "Supporters Toast Apparent Victory," *Houston Post*, August 13, 1978, H-Transportation-1978-July-Aug VF, HMRC.

136. "No Single Bloc of Voters Brought Metro Win Home," *Houston Post*, August 13, 1978, H-Transportation-Sep-Dec-1978 VF, HMRC; "Mexico-Americanos Dieron Su Apoyo" (Mexican-American Give Their Support), *El Sol*, August 17, 1978, HMRC, 1, translated by author; "Mexican-Americans, Affluent Whites Strongest for MTA," *El Sol*, August 17, 1978, HMRC, 1.

CHAPTER 5

1. Clipping, *Northeast News*, April 26, 1983, Central Chancery Files (CCF), Archives of the Archdiocese of Galveston-Houston (AAGH), Houston, Texas.

2. Neighborhood Transportation Forum, "Boondoogle" Door Hanger, Box 4, Michael Berryhill Collection (MBC), MSS 074, Woodson Research Center (WRC), Rice University.

3. The results of both elections can be found at the Harris County Clerk's Office in Houston, Texas.

4. For a discussion on devolution, see Mark Rose and Raymond A. Mohl, *Interstate: Highway Politics and Policy Since 1939*, 3rd ed. (Knoxville: University of Tennessee Press, 2012).

5. Robert Fisher, *Let the People Decide: Neighborhood Organizing in America*, 2nd ed. (New York: Twayne, 1994), 168–176.

6. William S. Clayson, *Freedom Is Not Enough: The War on Poverty and the Civil Rights Movement in Texas* (Austin: University of Texas Press, 2010), 150–156.

7. 2011 Annual Energy Review, United States Energy Information Administration, www.eia.gov/totalenergy/data/annual/showtext.cfm?t=ptb0518, accessed February 21, 2014. For a general discussion of changes in oil prices between 1979 and 1986, see Daniel Yergin, *The Prize: The Epic Quest for Oil, Money, and Power* (New York: Simon and Schuster, 1991), 699–764.

8. Joe R. Feagin, *Free Enterprise City: Houston in Political and Economic Perspective* (New Brunswick, NJ: Rutgers University Press, 1988), 85.

9. Beth Anne Shelton, Nestor Rodriguez, Joe R. Feagin, Robert D. Bullard, and Robert D. Thomas, eds., *Houston: Growth and Decline in a Sunbelt Boomtown* (Philadelphia: Temple University Press, 1989), 25; Nestor Rodriguez, "Latino Settlement Patterns in 'The Free Enterprise City,'" in Robert D. Bullard, J. Eugene Grigsby III, and Charles Lee, eds., *Residential Apartheid: The American Legacy* (Los Angeles: Center for Afro-American Studies Publication, University of California, Los Angeles, 1994), 203.

10. Stephen Klineberg, "Houston Area Survey (1982–2007): Findings from the 26th Annual Survey," Kinder Institute for Urban Research, Rice University, 2007, 2, http://has.rice.edu/downloads, accessed February 22, 2014.

11. Feagin, *Free Enterprise City*, 96–105.

12. Ibid., 254–255; Nestor Rodriguez, "Hispanic and Asian Immigration Waves in Houston," in Helen Rose Ebaugh and Janet Saltzman Chafetz, eds., *Religion and the New Immigrants: Continuities and Adaptations in Immigrant Congregations* (Walnut Creek, CA: Rowman and Littlefield, 2000), 24; Nestor Rodriguez, "Undocumented Central Americans in Houston: Diverse Populations," *International Migration Review* 21 (Spring 1987): 4–25; Arnoldo De León, *Ethnicity in the Sunbelt: Mexican-Americans in Houston* (College Station: Texas A&M University Press, 2001), 225; Fred von der Mehden, ed., *The Ethnic Groups of Houston* (Houston: Rice University, 1984), 63–112.

13. Rodriguez, "Hispanic and Asian Immigration Waves," 24; Shelton et al., *Houston*, 93–122; Rodriguez, "Latino Settlements," 204–216; Nestor Rodriguez and Ximena Urrutia-Rojas, "Impact of Recent Refugee Migration to Texas: A Comparison of Southeast Asian and Central American Newcomers," in Wayne Holtzman and Thomas Bornemann, eds., *Mental Health of Immigrants and Refugees* (Austin, TX: Hogg Foundation for Mental Health, 1990), 263–278.

14. For attitudes about immigration and the impact it had on the region, see the Kinder Houston Area Survey 2016, http://has.rice.edu/surveytopics, accessed February 22, 2014. From the 1980s onward, attitudes about immigrants have slowly become more positive, according to the survey and its reports. See Stephen Klineberg, "An Historical View of Immigration in Houston, Based on the Houston Area Survey," Center for Houston's

Future, 2008, http://has.rice.edu/downloads, accessed February 22, 2014. See also Rodriguez and Urrutia-Rojas, "Impact of Recent Migration to Texas," 273–277.

15. Statistics for the forty-one census tracts in the Hardy corridor, as defined above, from the 1980 US Census, surveying for race and income, from Social Explorer, www.socialexplorer.com, accessed February 23, 2014.

16. These conceptions of place-making owe a debt of scholarly gratitude to Matthew Klingle, whose conception of an ethic of place has helped influence my own thinking on how to view urban landscapes as simultaneously urban and natural spaces. For more on Klingle's thoughts on the ethic of place, see Matthew Klingle, *Emerald City: An Environmental History of Seattle* (New Haven, CT: Yale University Press, 2007).

17. John Mollenkopf, *The Contested City* (Princeton, NJ: Princeton University Press, 1983), 139–179. Mollenkopf discusses the fact that local decision-makers interpreted and implemented federal policies in different ways depending on a variety of local factors. Houston's rejection of a train system did make it an exception among major American cities in the early 1980s, many of which embraced such systems. See Alan Altshuler and David Luberoff, *Mega-Projects: The Changing Politics of Urban Public Investment* (Washington, DC: Brookings Institution Press; Cambridge, MA: Lincoln Institute of Land Policy, 2003), 208.

18. There was one suggestion of a shared right-of-way, but neither side could agree to the compromise, or decide which system should be built first. Texas Turnpike Authority, "Hardy Tollway–METRO Rail Compatibility Study: Preliminary Engineering and Financial Feasibility Report," May 1983, Planning Library, Texas Department of Transportation, Houston Branch.

19. Carl Abbott, *The New Urban America: Growth and Politics in Sunbelt Cities* (Chapel Hill: University of North Carolina Press, 1987), 185–262. Abbott argues that suburban political power and independence increased concomitantly with minority voices in urban areas. The contests between these two powerful political sectors represented a major factor in shaping Sunbelt metro areas in the 1980s.

20. "Mayor Reaches to Atlanta for Possible End to City's Police, Mass Transit Woes," *Houston Informer*, April 3, 1982; "Atlanta Transit Chief Resigns for Houston Job," *New York Times*, June 12, 1983, 26; Jan Rich, "Rail Likely to Stay Top Transit Issue in '83," *Houston Chronicle*, January 4, 1983.

21. Patrick Jankowski, "MTA's New Driver," *Houston*, August 1982, Houston Metropolitan Research Center (HMRC), 46–50, 71–72.

22. "Seize the Opportunity," *Houston Chronicle*, June 10, 1983, H-Elections-MTA Rail-1983 Vertical File (VF), HMRC. In agency publications, press releases, and newspaper articles, METRO officials pointed to systems in other cities as models. John Sedlak, who came to METRO from Atlanta with Alan Kiepper and originally began in the planning department, also recalled that METRO was aware of other ongoing transit projects. John Sedlak, interview by author, April 11, 2012, Houston, Texas, audio recording. Federal lobbying by local officials made it clear that they recognized they were competing against other locales for financial support. See Dan Arnold, interview by author, January 31, 2012. Finally, even critics were aware of mass transit projects across the nation. Texas highway commissioners grilled Dan Arnold about the efficacy of transit systems during the 1981 public hearing. State Highway and Public Transportation Commission (SHPTC), Public Hearing, June 23, 1981, Box 1990/11–1, Texas State Department of Highways and Public Transportation, Public Hearing Dockets, 1979–1988, Texas State Archives (TSA), 28–45.

23. Dan Arnold hinted at this desire at the 1981 Texas Highway Commission hearing, SHPTC, Public Hearing, June 23, 1981, 35. A number of scholars have discussed the drive to become an "elite" city by building a mass transit network. See Zachary Schrag, *Great Society Subway: A History of the Washington Metro* (Baltimore: Johns Hopkins University Press, 2006); Jonathan Richmond, *Transport of Delight: The Mythical Conception of Rail Transit in Los Angeles* (Akron, OH: Akron University Press, 2005).

24. John Sedlak was one such hire. The migration of transit experts from Atlanta to Houston highlights the exchange that existed between American cities. John Sedlak, interview by author, April 11, 2012.

25. METRO, "Draft Environmental Impact Statement: Southwest/Westpark Corridor Alternatives Analysis," September 1980, Box 2, MBC, WRC.

26. Mike Snyder, "TMO's Theory: Confrontation Gets Power," *Houston Chronicle*, April 4, 1980, H-TMO VF, HMRC. For more about COPS, the Industrial Areas Foundation, and its founder, the radical theorist and organizer Saul Alinsky, see Saul Alinsky, *Reveille for Radicals* (Chicago: University of Chicago Press, 1946); Saul Alinsky, *Rules for Radicals: A Practical Primer for Realistic Radicals* (New York: Vintage Books, 1971); Mark R. Warren, *Dry Bones Rattling: Community Building to Revitalize American Democracy* (Princeton, NJ: Princeton University Press, 2003); Susan Fainstein and Ann R. Markusen, *Urban Policy: Bridging the Social and Economic Development Gap* (Piscataway, NJ: Rutgers University Press, 1993); Ernesto Cortes, *Reweaving the Fabric: The Iron Rule and the IAF Strategy for Dealing with Poverty Through Power and Politics* (Piscataway, NJ: Rutgers University Press, 1993); Mary Beth Rogers, *Cold Anger: A Story of Faith and Power Politics* (Denton: North Texas University Press, 1990).

27. Alan Altshuler, *Community Control: The Black Demand for Participation in Large American Cities* (New York: Pegasus, 1970); Wesley Phelps, *A People's War on Poverty: Urban Politics, Grassroots Activists, and the Struggle for Democracy in Houston, 1964–1976* (Athens: University of Georgia Press, 2014); Clayson, *Freedom Is Not Enough*.

28. See Warren, *Dry Bones Rattling*, 15–72.

29. See ibid.; Fisher, *Let the People Decide*, 132–167.

30. See Ramona Toliver, interview by author, April 20, 2013.

31. See Clayson, *Freedom Is Not Enough*, 150–156.

32. Rev. Dan Scheel to Parish Council Presidents, November 25, 1980, Box 3, John McCarthy Files (JMF), Accession 98–18, AAGH. For a brief history of TMO's founding and its connection with Industrial Areas Foundation, see Warren, *Dry Bones Rattling*, 59–65; Rogers, *Cold Anger*, 143–154; Shelton et al., *Houston*, 60–63. On community organization in the 1970s and early 1980s, see Fisher, *Let the People Decide*, 132–167.

33. Roberto Treviño Jr., *Church in the Barrio: Mexican-American Ethno-Catholicism in Houston* (Chapel Hill: University of North Carolina Press, 2006), 167–171; Warren, *Dry Bones Rattling*, 190–198.

34. On black Catholic roots, see Bernadette Pruitt, *The Other Great Migration: The Movement of Rural African-Americans to Houston, 1900–1941* (College Station: Texas A&M University Press, 2013), 113–117; on Mexican Americans, see Treviño, *Church in the Barrio*; De Léon, *Ethnicity in the Sunbelt.*

35. Warren, *Dry Bones Rattling*, 193–195. On liberation theology, see Donal Dorr, *Option for the Poor: A Hundred Years of Vatican Social Teaching* (Dublin: Gill and Macmillan, 1983); Daniel H. Levine, *Popular Voices in Latin American Catholicism*, Studies in Church and State (Princeton, NJ: Princeton University Press, 1992). On Vatican II, see Jay P. Dolan, *The American Catholic Experience: A History from Colonial Times to the Present* (Notre Dame, IN: University of Notre Dame Press, 1992); Gene Burns, *The Frontiers of Catholicism: The Politics of Ideology in a Liberal World*, (Berkeley: University of California Press, 1992).

36. Treviño, *The Church in the Barrio*, 167–177; Rogers, *Cold Anger*, 107.

37. Rogers, *Cold Anger*, 145–146.

38. Warren, *Dry Bones Rattling*, 45, 49, 196.

39. Ibid., 196.

40. On the difficulty of bringing Protestant and Jewish members of congregations into TMO/COPs and the overlaps between the religions and the group, see Warren, *Dry Bones Rattling*, 198–205. For a broader discussion of engagement with social problems in Protestantism and Judaism, see David Chappell, *A Stone of Hope: Prophetic Religion and the Death of Jim Crow* (Chapel Hill: University of North Carolina Press, 2004); Ronald C. White, *The Social Gospel: Religion and Reform in Changing America* (Philadelphia: Temple University Press, 1976); Robert Wuthnow, *The Restructuring of American Religion: Society and Faith Since World War II*, Studies in Church and State (Princeton, NJ: Princeton University Press, 1988); Michael Lerner, *Jewish Renewal: A Path to Healing and Transformation* (New York: G. P. Putnam's Sons, 1994). On Jews and the civil rights movement in Houston, see Bryan Edward Stone, *The Chosen Folks: Jews on the Frontiers of Texas* (Austin: University of Texas Press, 2010), 193–214.

41. As an example of the public participation that went into the 1983 debates, more than eighty public meetings were held dedicated to the Westpark rail proposal alone. See Metropolitan Transit Authority (METRO), "Public Hearing: EIS on Southwest/Westpark Corridor," October 27, 1980, Box 2, Folder "Metro Hearing 1980," MBC, WRC, 9. Other debates produced a similar number of public meetings. This total does not include those hearings and meetings held at the state or county levels; nor does it include the individual meetings that the METRO board and the County Commissioners Court held during the debates. Dan Arnold, former METRO board chairman, estimated that he alone attended the meetings of at least twenty community groups during the buildup to the 1983 rail referendum. See Dan Arnold, interview by author, January 31, 2012.

42. On the power created by regional governance bodies, see Elihu Rubin, *Insuring the City: The Prudential Center and the Postwar Urban Landscape* (New Haven, CT:

Yale University Press, 2012); Louise Nelson Dyble, *Paying the Toll: Local Power, Regional Politics, and the Golden Gate Bridge* (Philadelphia: University of Pennsylvania Press, 2000).

43. SHPTC, Public Hearing, June 23, 1981, Box 1990/11–1, Texas State Department of Highways and Public Transportation, Public Hearing Dockets, 1979–1988, TSA, 25–35.

44. Several scholars have written about the process of fragmentation and incorporation. See Robert O. Self, *American Babylon: Race and the Struggle for Postwar Oakland* (Princeton, NJ: Princeton University Press, 2003); Colin Gordon, *Mapping Decline: St. Louis and the Fate of the American City* (Philadelphia: University of Pennsylvania Press, 2008); Matthew D. Lassiter, *The Silent Majority: Suburban Politics in the Sunbelt South* (Princeton, NJ: Princeton University Press, 2006).

45. When weighing in on the 1983 debates, the organization's publication, *Houston*, long a champion of Houston business development and booster of the central business district, began a steady shift toward the promotion of suburban growth. The most concrete signal of this shift would be the Chamber's name change in 1989 to the Greater Houston Partnership.

46. For more readings on NIMBYism's rise and its impact on American cities, see Michael Dear, "Understanding and Overcoming the NIMBY Syndrome," *Journal of the American Planning Association* 58 (Summer 1992): 288–300; Carissa Schively, "Understanding the NIMBY and LULU Phenomena: Reassessing Our Knowledge Base and Informing Future Research," *Journal of Planning Literature* 21, no. 3 (2007): 255–266. On NIMBYism as an environmental justice tactic, see Robert D. Bullard, *Dumping in Dixie: Race, Class, and Environmental Quality* (Boulder: Westview Press, 1990).

47. "Turnpike Authority to Ask OK for 3 Tollway Studies," *Houston Post*, January 24, 1979, H-Toll Roads-1979–1982 VF, HMRC.

48. "Council Authorizes Spending $10,000 on Toll Road Study," *Houston Chronicle*, December 19, 1979, H-Toll Roads-1979–1982 VF HMRC.

49. "Initial Feasibility Assessment: Houston Tollways," prepared by Wilbur Smith and Associates for the TTA, October 1979, Box 1, Folder 19, Hardy Street Toll Road Controversy Collection (HSTRCC), HMRC, 12.

50. METRO, "Draft Environmental Impact Statement: Southwest/Westpark Corridor Alternatives Analysis," September 1980, Box 2, MBC, WRC.

51. METRO, Public Hearing, October 27, 1980, 13–16, 29–30.

52. Ibid., 13.

53. "The Rail Alternative—Why We Oppose a Toll Road," February 1980, TMO File, CCF, AAGH.

54. "Planning Commission Dominated by Builders, Developers," *Houston Post*, March 2, 1980, H-City Planning-Clippings VF, HMRC.

55. Houston Interfaith Sponsoring Committee, Letter from TMO Leaders to Members, March 22, 1982, TMO Records, CCF, AAGH; Jan Rich, "New Group Forms on Toll Road," *Houston Chronicle*, November 19, 1982, H-Toll Roads-1979–1982 VF, HMRC; Charlie Evans, "Freeways Impact Growth, Land Costs," *Houston Chronicle*, June 16,

1980, H-Growth and Development-1980–1982 VF, HMRC; Alex Lieber-Alessie to Mayor Kathy Whitmire, February 8, 1983, Box 74, Folder 4, Eleanor Tinsley Collection (ETC), HMRC. For information about the Woodlands, see George T. Morgan Jr. and John O. King, *The Woodlands: New Community Development, 1964–1983* (College Station: Texas A&M University Press, 1987).

56. Brian McCann, "Chamber's Toll Road Approval Fuels City's Auto Dependence," *The Leader*, April 18, 1980, Box 1, Folder 20, HSTRCC, HMRC.

57. "Politicians Aim to Scotch Hardy Street Toll Study, Plan to Boost Rail System," *Houston Post*, February 19, 1980, H-MTA Rail-1980–1982 VF, HMRC.

58. "Gorczynski Favors Railway over Northside Toll Road Plan," *Houston Chronicle*, March 6, 1980, Box 1, Folder 20, HSTRCC, HMRC.

59. "Organization's No. 1 Concern Hardy Street," *Houston Chronicle*, July 19, 1980.

60. "Commissioners OK Resolution Against Toll Road," *Houston Chronicle*, August 8, 1980, H-Toll Roads-1979–1982 VF, HMRC.

61. Meeting attendance estimates are from "TMO Members Ask Council to Back Rail System in Hardy Street Corridor," *Houston Chronicle*, September 10, 1980, Box 1, Folder 7, HSTRCC; "350 Northside Residents Promote Rail over Hardy Toll Road at City Council," *Houston Leader*, September 10, 1980, Box 1, Folder 7, HSTRCC. The speaker list is from "350 Northside Residents."

62. "Consideration of Rail Transit for Hardy Road Corridor Urged," *Houston Post*, September 18, 1980, Box 1, Folder 7, HSTRCC, RG F 018, HMRC; Raul Reyes, "Council Recommends Rail System for Hardy Road Corridor," *Houston Chronicle*, September 18, 1980, Box 1, Folder 7, HSTRCC.

63. "Outdated Formula," *Houston Post*, October 21, 1980.

64. Dan Arnold, interview by author, January 31, 2012.

65. "Metro May Get Up to $750 Million for Rail Transit System, Senator Says," *Houston Chronicle*, January 15, 1983, H-MTA Rail-Jan-March-1983 VF, HMRC.

66. Dick Bryant, "North Houston Next in Mass Transit Plans," *Houston Chronicle*, December 18, 1980, H-Toll Roads-1979–1982 VF, HMRC.

67. Lynn Garner, "Highway Commissioner Critical of Opponents to Toll Road Plan," *Houston Chronicle*, October 1, 1980.

68. Joseph Fiorenza to diocesan priests, June 6, 1979, Correspondence Folder, CCF, AAGH.

69. McCarthy to TMO leaders, May 8, 1980, Box 3, John McCarthy Files (JMF), Accession 98–18.

70. Nene Foxhall, "Mayoral Candidates Face Tough Queries," *Houston Chronicle*, October 27, 1981, 12.

71. Feagin, *Free Enterprise City*, 164.

72. Houston Chamber of Commerce, Regional Mobility Plan, February 1982, HGAC Transportation Department Library, i.

73. Ibid., iii.

74. SHPTC, Public Hearing, March 16, 1982, Box 1990/11–1, Texas State Department of Highways and Public Transportation, Public Hearing Dockets, 1979–1988, TSA, 16.

All of the local political powers sent a representative to this public hearing to express support for the Regional Mobility Plan. See press release from Jan Wilbur, TMO co-chair, February 26, 1982, Box 1, Folder 18, HSTRCC, HMRC.

75. TMO Mass Transit Position Paper, February 25, 1982, Box 1, Folder 6, HSTRCC, 10; SHPTC, Public Hearing, March 16, 1982, 27.

76. Houston Chamber of Commerce, "Houston and Regional Mobility, Plans into Action: North Corridor and Hardy Road," July 1982, Box 1, Folder 8, HSTRCC.

77. Laurie Paternoster, "Citizen Groups Unite to Support Proposed Hardy Toll Road," *Houston Post*, April 28, 1982, H-Toll Roads-1979–1982 VF, HMRC.

78. "Rail System Has Been Planned Quietly for Months with Little Public Input," *Houston Chronicle*, September 30, 1982, Box 1, Folder 21, HSTRCC.

79. "Metro to Spend $190 Million for Land," *Houston Chronicle*, October 4, 1982, H-MTA Rail-1980–1982 VF, HMRC; Jan Rich, "Metro to Exercise Eminent Domain Right," *Houston Chronicle*, September 8, 1982, H-Transportation-1982 VF, HMRC.

80. Jan Rich, "New Group Forms on Toll Road," *Houston Chronicle*, November 19, 1982, H-Toll Roads-1979–1982 VF, HMRC.

81. "Kiepper Defends Metro 'El' as Resuscitation for Downtown," *Houston Chronicle*, November 3, 1982, Box 1, Folder 21, HSTRCC.

82. "Mayor Expects MTA to Call for Vote to Finance Rail Plan," *Houston Post*, November 4, 1982, H-MTA Rail-1980–1982 VF, HMRC; "Bond Election Predicted for Rail Plan," *Houston Chronicle*, November 4, 1982, Box 1, Folder 21, HSTRCC. Dan Arnold also discussed METRO's hesitancy to schedule a referendum on the rail proposal. Both Kiepper and the METRO board wanted to get construction underway as quickly as possible and did not think a vote was required. A March 1983 referendum was delayed at Mayor Whitmire's request. This delay frustrated Arnold and Kiepper. See Dan Arnold, interview by author, January 31, 2012; Laurie Paternoster, "Metro Officials Accuse Mayor of Blocking Vote," *Houston Post*, February 23, 1983, H-Transportation-MTA Rail VF, HMRC.

83. "Lindsay Leaning Toward County Responsibility for Toll Road," *Houston Post*, March 22, 1983, H-Toll Road-1983 VF, HMRC. For text of the bill, see SB 970, 68th Legislature, Regular Session, Texas Legislative Reference Library, www.lrl.state.tx.us, accessed November 9, 2012.

84. County Judge Jon Lindsay to Councilman Dale Gorczynski, March 23, 1983, Box 1, Folder 13, HSTRCC.

85. "City Council Hearing on Hardy Toll Project Draws 300," *North Freeway Leader*, April 28, 1983, Box 1, Folder 22, HSTRCC.

86. Urban Mass Transit Administration and METRO, "Supplemental Draft Environmental Impact Statement: Houston Rail Rapid Transit Project," March 1983, MBC, WRC, 5-2, 5-3.

87. "MTA Bond Plan Soundly Defeated: Just a Rail Bad Day for Metro," *Houston Chronicle*, June 12, 1983, H-MTA Rail-April-December-1983 VF, HMRC.

88. "Metro Combines Rail, Bus Expansion Projects into 1 Bond Election," *Houston Chronicle*, May 6, 1983, H-MTA Rail-April-December-1983 VF, HMRC.

89. "Groups Lining Up For, Against Metro Plan," *Houston Chronicle*, May 24, 1983, H-MTA Rail-April-December-1983 VF, HMRC; "County AFL-CIO Backs Metro Bond Referendum," *Houston Post*, June 2, 1983, H-MTA Rail-April-December-1983 VF, HMRC; West Houston Association Press Release, May 26, 1983, Box 1, Folder "Busway Editorials," MBC, WRC.

90. "Three Minority Councilmen Back June 11 Metro Bond Election," *Houston Chronicle*, June 2, 1983, H-MTA Rail-April-December-1983 VF, HMRC; Laurie Paternoster, "Reyes Supports MTA Bond Referendum," *Houston Post*, June 7, 1983, H-Elections-MTA Rail-1983 VF, HMRC; "Hispanos de Houston Apoyan Sistema De Tren-Autobus Del METRO" (Hispanics of Houston Support Train-Bus System of METRO), *El Sol*, June 8, 1983, Box 1982–1983, RG D 80, 45/143/B, HMRC, 1–2. A number of other prominent politicians and civic groups, both Latino and African American, supported the referendum. See "Election For," *El Sol*, June 6, 1983, Box 1982–1983, HMRC, 1–3.

91. "MTA," *El Sol*, May 11, 1983, Box 1982–1983, HMRC, 4; "Junio 11 Voto para Financiamiento del Metro" (June 11 Vote for the METRO Bonds), *El Sol*, May 18, 1983, Box 1982–1983, HMRC, 1.

92. "Get Out the Vote," *El Sol*, June 8, 1983, Box 1982–1983, HMRC, 3.

93. "Los Problemas de Transito Son Peores de lo que Nos Imaginamos" (The Problems of Transit are Worse Than We Can Imagine) Advertisement, *El Sol*, June 8, 1983, Box 1982–1983, HMRC, 16.

94. "To Get Houston Moving Is a Job for Us All," Advertisement, June 11, 1983, *Houston Informer*, HMRC; "We Care Enough About Your Vote on June 11 to Ask for It," Advertisement, *Houston Defender*, May 20, 1983, HMRC.

95. Cypress Creek United Civic Associations to Lindsay, June 3, 1983, Box 999, Folder 18, Judge John Lindsay Papers (JJLP), Harris County Arhcives (HCA); "M.C.I.A. Directors Oppose M.T.A Bond Proposal June 11," *The Meyerlander*, June 1983, vol. 14, no. 1, Folder "Editorials," Box 1, MBC, WRC.

96. David Legge, "Vote No on Heavy Rail," *Houston City Magazine*, June 1983, Box 2, Folder "MTA Postmortem," MBC, WRC, 120.

97. Jan Rich, "Metro Bond Election Gains More Support," *Houston Chronicle*, June 7, 1983, H-Elections-MTA Rail-1983 VF, HMRC.

98. Lynn Ashby, "We Can Gripe Until Eternity; Now's the Time for MTA Vote," *Houston Post*, June 11, 1983, H-MTA Rail-April-December-1983 VF, HMRC.

99. The voting numbers are from the official referendum election results for June 11, 1983, Metropolitan Transit Authority Bond Election, Harris County Clerk's Office, Houston, Texas. The number of registered voters is from Laurie Paternoster, "MTA Bond Plan Election Today," *Houston Post*, June 11, 1983, H-Elections-MTA Rail-1983 VF, HMRC. In other elections the turnout usually hovered around 4 or 5 percent.

100. Nene Foxhall, "Rejection of Bond Issue Crossed Geographic Lines," *Houston Chronicle*, June 12, 1983, H-Elections-MTA Rail-1983 VF, HMRC; "MTA Bond Plan Soundly Defeated," *Houston Chronicle*, June 12, 1983, H-Elections-MTA Rail-1983 VF, HMRC. Full, precinct-by-precinct results are available at the Harris County Clerk's Office, Houston, Texas.

101. Jim Craig, "Rep. Fields Calls on MTA to Drop Federal Funds Bid," *Houston Post*, June 13, 1983, H-Elections-MTA Rail-1983 VF, HMRC.

102. "Thinking Small Derails Big Bucks for Houston," *Washington Post*, June 16, 1983, H-MTA Rail-April-December-1983 VF, HMRC; "House Panel Approves Bill Reallocating Houston's 104.5 Million Share of Transit Funds," *Houston Post*, June 17, 1983, Box 1, Folder 22, HSTRCC.

103. "Soul-Searching Time for Metro Officials," *Houston Chronicle*, June 13, 1983, H-MTA Rail-April-December-1983 VF, HMRC.

104. "A $93 Million Question: To Rail or Not to Rail?," *Houston Post*, June 16, 1983, H-MTA Rail-April-December-1983 VF, HMRC; "Metro Planners Estimate They Invested $48 Million in Rail Plan," *Houston Chronicle*, June 22, 1983, H-MTA Rail-April-December-1983 VF, HMRC.

105. Laurie Paternoster, "MTA Begins 'Demobilizing' Rail Program," *Houston Post*, June 17, 1983, Box 1, Folder 22, HSTRCC.

106. "Work Started to Define New Plan for Metro," *Houston Chronicle*, July 27, 1983, H-MTA Rail-April-December-1983 VF, HMRC.

107. Jon Lindsay to Houstonians, June 13, 1983, Box 2, Folder "Toll Roads," MBC, WRC.

108. Nene Foxhall, "Lindsay Taking Bold Approach on Toll Roads," *Houston Chronicle*, July 31, 1983, H-Toll Road-1983 VF, HMRC.

109. Bill Coulter, "County Sets Toll Roads Referendum," *Houston Post*, June 24, 1983, Box 1, Folder 1, HSTRCC; Lindsay to Houstonians, June 13, 1983. Both Dan Arnold and John Sedlak referenced Lindsay's choice to place the Hardy Toll Road in a larger package of HCTRA projects as a key factor in the subsequent successful election. Dan Arnold, interview by author, January 31, 2012; John Sedlak, interview by author, April 11, 2012.

110. "City Council Prepares to Take Stand on Controversial Hardy Road Project," *Houston Post*, August 5, 1983, H-Toll Road-1983 VF, HMRC.

111. Laurie Paternoster, "Two MTA Rail Bonds Opponents Back Toll Road Plan," *Houston Post*, August 10, 1983, H-Toll Road-1983 VF, HMRC.

112. "New Group Formed to Oppose Proposal or Toll Road Bonds," *Houston Chronicle*, August 12, 1983, H-Toll Road-1983 VF, HMRC.

113. TMO, "A Critique of Judge Lindsay's Toll Road Program," Box 1, Folder 1, HSTRCC.

114. Jan Wilbur to George Pletcher, August 19, 1983, Box 20, Folder 25, Ben T. Reyes Collection (BTRC), MSS 103, HMRC.

115. George Pletcher to Jan Wilbur, September 8, 1983, Box 20, Folder 25, BTRC, HMRC.

116. Houston City Council members Johnny Goyen, Judson Robinson Jr., Frank Mancuso, and Ben Reyes to Bishop John Morkovsky, August 30, 1983, Box 20, Folder 25, BTRC, HMRC.

117. Bishop John L. Morkovsky to Judson Robinson Jr. et al., September 14, 1983, Box 20, Folder 25, BTRC, HMRC.

118. Pamphlet from Harris County Citizens for the Toll Road Alternative, Box 1, Folder 1, HSTRCC, HMRC.

119. "An Opportunity to Vote for Mobility," *Houston*, August 1983, HMRC, 73; Laurie Paternoster, "Return to 'Menu' Planned if Voters Reject Toll Road," *Houston Post*, September 13, 1983, H-Toll Roads VF, HMRC.

120. Lynn Ashby, "Houston's Tollway Plan Hardly a Road to Ruin," *Houston Post*, September 11, 1983, H-Toll Road-1983 VF, HMRC.

121. "County Voters OK Toll Road Referendum," *Houston Post*, September 14, 1983, Box 1, Folder 22, HSTRCC, HMRC. Election results are also available at the Harris County Clerk's Office.

122. The Papers of Houston City Council member Eleanor Tinsley contain numerous letters of support for the HCTRA. Almost all of the letters came from Harris County groups outside of the immediate city, such as the Humble Chamber of Commerce, the North Houston Association, and the Cypress Creek United Civic Associations. There is also a sheet listing the numerous supporting organizations. See ETC, Box 74, Folder 4, HMRC, for the letters and list.

123. "County Voters OK Toll Road Referendum."

124. "Toll Roads Will Help, but the Traffic Problem Still Must Be Faced," *Houston Chronicle*, September 18, 1983, Folder 19, Box 13, 2009–028, Sarah and Army Emmott Records, Special Collections Library, University of Houston (SCLUH).

125. Laurie Paternoster, "Toll Backers Spent $413,992 Records Show," *Houston Post*, October 13, 1983, H-Toll Road-1983 VF, HMRC; "444,992 Spent in Toll Road Campaign," *Houston Chronicle*, October 13, 1983, H-Toll Road-1983 VF, HMRC.

126. Bill Coulter, "Toll Road Authority Created," *Houston Post*, September 23, 1983, H-Toll Road-1983 VF, HMRC.

127. "County to Acquire Property to Build Hardy Toll Road," *Houston Chronicle*, February 16, 1984, H-Toll Road-1984 VF, HMRC.

128. Stephen Johnson, "Land Donated to Construct New Toll Road," *Houston Chronicle*, April 24, 1984, H-Toll Road-1984 VF, HMRC.

129. "Hardy Toll Road Opening Advanced," *Houston Post*, September 14, 1984, H-Toll Road-1984 VF, HMRC.

130. "Bicycle, Party Hardy on the Toll Road," *Houston Post*, September 18, 1987, H-Toll Road-1985–89 VF, HMRC.

131. Norma Martin, "Crowd Celebrates Toll Road Opening," *Houston Chronicle*, July 16, 1989, H-Toll Road-1985–89 VF, HMRC.

132. Fisher, *Let the People Decide*, 176–209.

133. Abbott, *The New Urban America*, 185–262. John Sedlak agrees that the result of the 1983 referendum pushed the agency toward greater suburban emphasis. John Sedlak, interview by author, April 11, 2012.

134. Jerry Laws, "Transit Plans Win Backing of Former Foe," *Houston Post*, October 11, 1984, H-Transportation VF, HMRC.

135. METRO, "Houston Has a Traffic Problem . . . and METRO Has Some Answers," 1984, H-MTA-1984 VF, HMRC.

136. Robert Bullard and Glenn S. Johnson, eds., *Just Transportation: Dismantling Race and Class Barriers to Mobility* (Gabriola Island, BC: New Society, 1997); Robert Bullard,

Glenn S. Johnson, and Angel O. Torres, eds., *Highway Robbery: Transportation Racism and New Routes to Equity* (Boston: South End Press, 2004); Karen Lucas, ed., *Running on Empty: Transport, Social Exclusion and Environmental Justice* (Bristol, UK: Policy, 2004); William Julius Williams, *More Than Just Race: Being Black and Poor in the Inner City* (New York: Norton, 2009), 25–62; William Julius Williams, *When Work Disappears: The World of the New Urban Poor* (New York: Knopf, 1996), 39–42, 223–224; Richard Hébert, *Highways to Nowhere: The Politics of City Transportation* (Indianapolis: Bobbs-Mill, 1972).

137. Christopher W. Wells, *Car Country: An Environmental History* (Seattle: Washington University Press, 2012). Wells discusses the creation of the nation's car-centric landscape. He argues that laws, development, and consumer action drove the nation to build a world that catered to, and even required, the use of cars.

138. For a discussion of post-referendum road construction, see Erik Slotboom, *Houston Freeways: A Historical and Visual Journey*, (Cincinnati: C. J. Krehbiel, 2003).

CHAPTER 6

1. There were nearly 120 public meetings between 2004 and 2008. Metropolitan Transit Authority of Harris County, "East End Corridor Environmental Impact Assessment," March 2009, 7-1.

2. Metro Transit Authority Bond Election Results, November 4, 2003, https://www.ridemetro.org/MetroPDFs/AboutMETRO/Board/Resolutions/2000s/2003/Resolutions-101-153_Sept-Dec-2003.pdf, accessed May 30, 2016.

3. Eric Jaffe, "Toward a Stronger Theory of NIMBYism," CityLab, February 9, 2016, www.citylab.com/housing/2016/02/nimbyism-define-club-chris-bradford/461946.

4. Alan A. Altshuler and David E. Luberoff, *Mega-Projects: The Changing Politics of Urban Public Investment* (Washington, DC: Brookings Institution Press; Cambridge, MA: Lincoln Institute of Land Policy, 2003). Henry Petroski, *The Road Taken: The History and Future of America's Infrastructure* (New York: Bloomsbury USA, 2016).

5. Two major community organizations, Houston Tomorrow and the Citizens' Transportation Coalition, were central to changing the conversation around transit in Houston proper. Houston Tomorrow was active in helping the light rail vote succeed. Both groups advocated for improving the system throughout planning and construction.

6. Jim Simmon, "Ex-Metro Chief Says Lanier Seeking Rail 'Death Warrant,'" *Houston Chronicle*, June 29, 1989.

7. Metropolitan Transit Authority of Houston and Harris County, "A History Lesson: Transportation and Transit in Houston, Texas," METRO public presentation, n.d.

8. Kyle Shelton, "What Old Transit Maps Can Tell Us About Cities," CityLab, October 10, 2014, www.citylab.com/commute/2014/10/what-old-transit-maps-can-teach-us-about-a-citys-future/381149.

9. For a list of Houston mayors, controllers, and City Council members, see the City of Houston's record, www.houstontx.gov/citysec/mayors.pdf, accessed March 16, 2014.

10. METRO, "Metro Solutions," 2003, H-MTA-Rail-2000s Vertical File (VF), Houston Metropolitan Research Center (HMRC).

11. Lucas Wall, "Rail Ridership Breezes Past Other Cities," *Houston Chronicle*, January 17, 2005, H-MTA-Rail-2000s VF, HMRC.

12. Rad Sallee and Don Mason, "Rail Opponents File Suit over Disputed Route," *Houston Chronicle*, April 13, 2007.

13. David Crossley, "If You Want More, Better Transit, Vote No on Metro," *Houston Chronicle*, October 29, 2012; Bill King, "King: Metro Vote Means End of Light Rail Project," *Houston Chronicle*, November 7, 2012.

14. Kevin Wilcox, "Houston Significantly Expands Light-Rail Line," *Civil Engineering*, February 2014.

15. See "Notice of Special Election," 2003 Metro Solutions Referendum; METRO, "METRO Solution, Harrisburg Corridor Study," February 2004, METRO Files.

16. For transit dependence, see Goodman Corporation, "Greater East End Livable Centers Plan," 2009, 2–7. On automobile ownership rates, see METRO, "Harrisburg Corridor Preliminary Study: Purpose and Need," February 2004, 11.

17. Kyle Shelton, "How Houston's East End Finally Got Transit," *Urban Edge*, May 26, 2015.

18. Rad Sallee, "Metro Will Use Light Rail for 5 Future Lines," *Houston Chronicle*, October 19, 2007.

19. S. R. Beard and Associates, HDR, "East End Conceptual Planning and Analysis Report," September 2006, 1, METRO Files.

20. For details about the business assistance fund, see METRO business assistance fund documents in possession of the author or available from the Public Relations Department of METRO upon request.

21. Rad Sallee, "Metro to Break Ground on Houston's 1st New Rail Line in Years," *Houston Chronicle*, June 25, 2008.

22. Charles Kuffner, "East End Community Meeting to Consider Harrisburg Grade Separation," *Off the Kuff*, June 15, 2011, accessed March 4, 2016.

23. Christof Spieler, "Temporarily Inconvenient on the East End," Citizens' Transportation Coalition, March 28, 2008, www.ctchouston.org/intermodality/2008/03/28/temporarily-inconvenient-on-the-east-end, accessed February 22, 2016.

24. Charles Kuffner, "Freight Rail vs. Light Rail," *Off the Kuff*, March 28, 2008, accessed February 22, 2016; Charles Kuffner, "Harrisburg Rail Resolution Progressing," *Off the Kuff*, April 25, 2008, accessed February 22, 2016.

25. Julio del Carpio to Bill White, January 26, 2009, Peter Brown Collection (PBC), in possession of the author.

26. Marilu de la Fuente to Bill White, January 27, 2009, PBC.

27. Rosanna Ruiz, "East End Residents Fight Plan for Metro Rail Overpass," *Houston Chronicle*, February 9, 2009.

28. Angie Martinez to Bill White, January 2009, PBC.

29. Charles Mayfield and Sylvia Medina interviews with author.

30. Houston Chronicle Editorial Committee, "Clearing the Tracks," *Houston Chronicle*, August 4, 2010.

31. City of Houston, "Houston Mayor and METRO Seek Common Ground on East End Line," press release, July 26, 2011.

32. Houston METRO Board Minutes, July 28, 2011.

33. Public Meeting notes, November 15, 2012, in possession of the author.

34. Garcia Special Election Campaign Mailer, in possession of the author.

35. The Alvarado campaign and City Council Member James Rodriguez also accused Garcia of supporting the overpass and actually being far removed from the community throughout the debate. See Rodriguez newsletter from January 8, 2013, in possession of the author.

36. Anita Hassan, "Garcia Wins Senate District 6 Seat," *Houston Chronicle*, March 2, 2013.

37. METRO Citizen Advisory Board Meeting Presentation, May 5, 2013.

38. METRO Citizen Advisory Board Meeting Presentation, June 4, 2013.

39. METRO, "Summary of Environmental Assessment & Response Actions for Hughes Underpass," August 6, 2013.

40. Charles Mayfield interview.

41. METRO Hughes Underpass Presentations, January 30, 2014, and February 27, 2014.

42. East End Community Leaders Gloria Moreno, Steve Parker, Elisa Gonzales, Charles Mayfield, Marilu de la Fuente, Wendy Thiessen, and Victor Villareal to Mayor Annise Parker, February 13, 2014, METRO Records of Letter Received, Public Meeting Documents, April 15, 2014.

43. Ibid.

44. Copies of the liability briefs prepared by law students at the University of Houston are in possession of the author. The briefs were prepared in April and May 2014 and focused on how METRO could avoid liability under the Comprehensive Environmental Response, Compensation and Liability Act (CERCLA) and the Municipal Setting Designation process. For mention of doubt about the pollution, see Allyn West, "What Kind of Overpass Will Metro Build for the East End?," OffCite, May 30, 2014.

45. Yolanda Navarro to Gilbert Garcia, March 6, 2014, METRO Records of Letter Received, Public Meeting Documents, April 15, 2014.

46. Julio del Carpio and Harrisburg Merchants Association to Mayor Annise Parker, March 12, 2014, METRO Records of Letter Received, Public Meeting Documents, April 15, 2014.

47. Alan Atkinson to Mayor Annise Parker, March 20, 2014, METRO Records of Letter Received, Public Meeting Documents, April 15, 2014.

48. West, "What Kind of Overpass."

49. METRO Press Release, May 22, 2014.

50. Steve Parker, Bolivar Fraga, and Victor Villareal, "East End Not Overjoyed About Metro's Overpass Proposal," *Houston Chronicle*, April 15, 2014.

51. Dug Begley, "Metro Rejects Pleas for Delay, Proceeds with East End Overpass Plan," *Houston Chronicle*, May 22, 2014.

52. Ibid.

53. Dug Begley, "Metro Proceeds with Rail-Only Overpass in East End," *Houston Chronicle*, June 30, 2014.

54. Kat Driessen and Mike Morris, "Council Set to Approve Rail Line Overpass Funds," *Houston Chronicle*, July 29, 2014.

55. Gail Delaughter, "City Council Agrees to Help Metro Build East End Overpass," KUHF-NPR, July 31, 2014.

56. See June 25, 2015, METRO board minutes.

57. The Garcia and Spieler quotations are from September 2, 2014, public meeting, METRO Records.

58. Rebecca Hennes, "Groundbreaking of Metro Overpass Unites Community," *Houston Chronicle*, March 14, 2015.

59. Houston Chronicle Editorial Board, "Not-So-Super TIRZ," *Houston Chronicle*, July 25, 2014.

60. Kyle Shelton, "Taking the Pulse of Houston's Newest Rail Line," *Urban Edge*, June 1, 2015.

61. Dug Begley, "Harrisburg Rail Overpass Delayed Again," *Houston Chronicle*, February 8, 2016.

CONCLUSION

1. Texas Highway Department, "State Highway 288 Final Environmental Impact Statement," August 1974, Texas Highway Department Files, Houston Branch Office, 11.

2. "Plans for US 59 Lamented, Lauded, Expansion to Aid Traffic, Dislodge Many in Fifth Ward," *Houston Chronicle*, January 1, 1991.

3. See "SPARC Growth Houston," an effort of the Greater East Management District, the Fifth Ward Community Redevelopment Corporation, the East Downtown Management District, and the Greater Northside Management District, www.greatereastend.com/sparc-growth-houston, accessed April 20, 2016.

4. Todd Litman, "Generated Traffic and Induced Travel Implications for Transport Planning," Report of the Victoria Transport Policy Institute, January 27, 2015.

5. Talking Points for Mayor Sylvester Turner, Texas Transportation Commission, Austin, January 28, 2016, www.houstontx.gov/citizensnet/TxTransComm20160128.pdf, accessed April 20, 2016.

6. Sylvester Turner, State of Mobility speech, May 17, 2016, www.houstontx.gov/mayor/stateofmobility2016.html.

7. A similar process is highlighted nationally by Owen Gutfreund, *Twentieth Century Sprawl: Highways and the Reshaping of the American Landscape* (New York: Oxford University Press, 2004), 106.

8. For information on the status of the parkway, see the updates posted by the Grand Parkway Transportation Corporation at www.grandpky.com, accessed April 20, 2016.

9. A number of cities have constructed or considered this type of project. Two of the most successful have been the Clyde Warren Park in Dallas, www.klydewarrenpark

.org, accessed April 20, 2016, and the Rose Kennedy Greenway in Boston, www.rose kennedygreenway.org, accessed April 20, 2016.

10. Carter and Burgess, Inc., "North Hardy Planning Studies: Alternatives Analysis Report (Highway Component)," November 2005. See also the timeline of the project on the TxDOT website for the effort, www.ih45northandmore.com/history.aspx, accessed April 20, 2016. This site is in and of itself an excellent example of the changing face of public documents in major projects.

11. The Pierce Elevated discussion fostered a wide discussion of the possibilities for the road. See Kyle Shelton, "Pierce Elevated May Go Back to the Future," *Urban Edge*, May 4, 2015; John Jacob, "Tear Down the Pierce Elevated, Make It the Pierce Promenade," *Houston Chronicle*, May 4, 2015; Lisa Gray, "Imagine the Pierce Elevated as a Park," *Houston Chronicle*, April 26, 2015.

12. The I-45 coalition was the most active citizen group in resisting the project. The group's website holds a great deal of information about their positions. See www.i-45 coalition.org, accessed April 20, 2016. See also Jennifer Friedberg, "Tunnels Under I-45 Proposed," *Houston Chronicle*, October 25, 2007; Tom Manning, "TxDOT's Plan for I-45 Has Another Delay," *Houston Chronicle*, November 10, 2005.

13. All told, for four major public meetings held between 2012 and 2015, more than 3,000 pages of documentation and public comment were collected. All the public meeting notes and comments are available on the project website, www.ih45northandmore .com.

14. Plan Houston, the general plan, was passed in September 2015. See www.plan houston.org, accessed April 20, 2016. The Houston Bike Plan was released in February 2016 and as of March 2017 was still pending City Council approval. See www.houston bikeplan.org, accessed April 20, 2016. The Bayou Greenways initiative will invest nearly $480 million to create linear parks along the region's waterways. See www.bayougreenways.org/bayou-greenway-initiative, accessed April 20, 2016. The bus system was reimagined in August 2015, prioritizing frequency of routes. See www.ridemetro.org/Pages /Reimagining.aspx, accessed April 20, 2016.

15. Kinder Baumgardner, "Beyond Google's Cute Car," *Cite: The Architecture + Design Review of Houston*, October 2015, 97; Tory Gattis, "How to Fix Houston's Traffic? Let's Talk MaX Lanes," *Houston Chronicle*, February 16, 2016.

16. John Rennite Short, "Why Is the US Unwilling to Pay for Good Public Transportation?," *The Conversation*, April 1, 2016; Phillip Kennicott, "We Caused the Metro Shutdown When We Decided to Let Our Cities Decay," *Washington Post*, March 16, 2016; Henry Petroski, *The Road Taken: The History and Future of America's Infrastructure* (New York: Bloomsbury USA, 2016).

17. Ellen Dunham-Jones and June Williamson, *Retrofitting Suburbia: Urban Design Solutions for Redesigning Suburbs* (Hoboken, NJ: Wiley, 2011).

18. Mike Lydon, Anthony Garcia, and Andres Duany, *Tactical Urbanism: Short-Term Action for Long-Term Change* (Washington, DC: Island Press, 2015); Janette Sadik-Khan and Seth Solomonow, *Streetfight: Handbook for an Urban Revolution* (New York: Viking, 2016); Gabe Klein and David Vega-Barachowitz, *Start-Up City: Inspiring Private and*

Public Entrepreneurship, Getting Projects Done, and Having Fun (Washington, DC: Island Press, 2015).

19. Joel Kotkin, "Houston Rising—Why the Next Great American Cities Aren't What You Think," *Daily Beast*, April 8, 2013; Steve Inskeep, "Fighting Gentrification with Money in Houston," National Public Radio, September 17, 2009, www.npr.org/templates/story/story.php?storyId=112888084NPR, accessed March 6, 2014; Lori Rodriguez, "Gentrification Revives City but Displaces Minorities," *Houston Chronicle*, May 6, 2001.

20. On recentralizing neighborhoods, see Steve Belmont, *Cities in Full: Recognizing and Realizing the Great Potential of Urban America* (Chicago: Planners Press of the American Planning Association, 2002); Alan Ehrenhalt, *The Great Inversion and the Future of the American City* (New York: Vintage, 2013).

21. Tim Beatley, "Sustainability in Planning: The Arc and Trajectory of a Movement, and New Directions for the 21st Century City," in Bishwapriya Sanyal, Lawrence Vale, and Christina D. Rosan, eds., *Planning Ideas That Matter: Livability, Territoriality, Governance, and Reflective Practice* (Cambridge, MA: MIT Press, 2012), 91–124.

22. Scott Campbell, "Green Cities, Growing Cities, Just Cities? Urban Planning and the Contradictions of Sustainable Development," *Journal of the American Planning Association* 62, no. 3 (Summer 1996): 269–313; Todd Litman and Marc Brenman, "A New Social Equity Agenda for Sustainable Transportation," paper presented at the 2012 Transportation Research Board Annual Meeting, published at Victoria Transport Policy Institute, March 8, 2012, www.vtpi.org/equityagenda.pdf, accessed March 6, 2014. One Houston-area professional whose work has consistently dealt with this issue is University of Houston architecture professor Susan Rogers, whose Community Design Resource Center brings architecture students and residents together to define the needs and desires for projects from a citizen-driven point of view. See Community Design Resource Center, http://cdrchouston.org, accessed April 20, 2016.

23. Litman and Brenman, "A New Social Equity Agenda"; Michael Greenberg and John Renne, "Where Does Walkability Matter the Most? An Environmental Justice Interpretation of New Jersey Data," *Journal of Urban Health: Bulletin of the New York Academy of Medicine* 82, no. 1 (2005): 90–100; Kevin M. Leyden, "Social Capital and the Built Environment: The Importance of Walkable Neighborhoods," *American Journal of Public Health* 93 (2003): 1546–1551; Lawrence D. Frank, James F. Sallis, Terry L. Conway, James E. Chapman, Brian E. Saelens, and William Bachman, "Many Pathways from Land Use to Health: Associations Between Neighborhood Walkability and Active Transportation, Body Mass Index, and Air Quality," *Journal of the American Planning Association* 72, no. 1 (Winter 2006): 75–87; Robert Bullard, "Can Houston Go Green Without Brown and Black?" *OffCite*, March 26, 2014; Jeff Speck, *Walkable City: How Downtown Can Save America, One Step at a Time* (New York: North Point Press, 2013).

24. Center for Transit-Oriented Development, "Why TOD? Why Now?" Reconnecting America, Federal Transportation Administration, 2007, http://ctod.org/ctod-research.php, accessed March 6, 2014; Center for Transit-Oriented Development, "Station Area Planning: How to Make Great Transit-Oriented Places," Reconnecting America, Federal Transportation Administration, 2008, http://ctod.org/ctod-research.php, accessed

March 6, 2014; Eric Dumbaugh and Wenhao Li, "Designing for the Safety of Pedestrians, Cyclists, and Motorists in Urban Environments," *Journal of the American Planning Association* 77, no. 1 (2006): 69–88.

25. Anna Clark, "Forefront Excerpt: The Lone Star Progressive," *Forefront*, March 10, 2014, http://nextcity.org/daily/entry/forefront-excerpt-the-lone-star-progressive.

26. Several nonprofits in Houston have done admirable work in creating more democratic decision-making models and building upon the existing assets of communities. See, for example, Neighborhood Centers, Inc., the ongoing work of the Metropolitan Organization, Avenue CDC, and Project Row Houses, among many others. See Bruce Katz and Jennifer Bradley, *The Metropolitan Revolution: How Cities and Metros Are Fixing Our Broken Politics and Fragile Economy* (Washington, DC: Brookings Institution Press, 2014); Michael Berryhill, "Houston's Quiet Revolution," *Places Journal*, March 2016; Molly Glentzer, "Project Row Houses Fights to Keep Third Ward Culture Alive," *Houston Chronicle*, January 22, 2014; Leah Binkovitz, "Third Ward Looks to Shift the Gentrification Conversation," *Urban Edge*, May 25, 2016.

27. A number of cities have used participatory budgeting to help disperse public funds. This has been particularly popular in the case of infrastructure funding. Several wards in Chicago have undertaken participatory budgeting approaches in partnership with the Great Cities Institute of the University of Illinois at Chicago. For more on that work, see PB Chicago, www.pbchicago.org, accessed December 26, 2016.

28. This is happening in Houston through the efforts of official and nonprofit agencies that are soliciting the opinions of Houstonians. See, for example, the Houston General Plan, www.houstontx.gov/planning/GeneralPlan, accessed April 20, 2016, and METRO's community engagement efforts, www.ridemetro.org/Pages/NewsPublicHearing.aspx, accessed April 20, 2016.

29. Susan S. Fainstein, *The Just City* (Ithaca, NY: Cornell University Press, 2010).

30. On the long legacies of infrastructure, see Alex Marshall, *How Cities Work: Suburbs, Sprawl, and the Roads Not Taken* (Austin: University of Texas Press, 2000); Petroski, *The Road Taken.*

31. TransitCenter, "A People's History of Recent Urban Transportation Innovation," http://transitcenter.org/peoples-history; Sadik-Khan and Solomonow, *Streetfight*; Klein and Vega-Barachowitz, *Start-Up City.*

32. On People's Park, see Don Mitchell, "The End of Public Space? People's Park, Definitions of the Public, and Democracy," *Annals of the Association of American Geographers* 85, no. 1 (1995): 108–133. On Brooklyn, see Suki Hawley and Michael Galinsk, "Battle for Brooklyn," Film, Rumur, Inc., 2011. The Brooklyn example echoes a new generation of downtown redevelopment methods in many ways as cities continue to work to remake themselves amid shifting demographic and residential patterns. As gentrification and densification occurs in many central cities, new amenities and infrastructures are generating great debate. For examples in Houston, see Gavin Benke, "Electronic Bits and Ten Gallon Hats: Enron, American Culture and the Postindustrial Political Economy" (PhD diss., University of Texas at Austin, 2012).

33. In 2011, Chicago mayor Rahm Emanuel pledged to make significant investments in bike lanes. See Rahm Emanuel, "Chicago 2011 Transition Plan," Document Cloud, May 10, 2011, https://www.documentcloud.org/documents/89709-chicago-2011-transition-plan.html, accessed on September 14, 2015. Numerous elements of that plan have begun to be implemented. See John Greenfield, "Chicago Gets First Curb-Protected Lanes; Many Other Bike Projects on Deck," Streetsblog Chicago, May 18, 2015, http://chi.streetsblog.org/2015/05/18/chicago-gets-first-curb-protected-lanes-many-other-bike-projects-on-deck, accessed September 14, 2015. On LA's long-running transit debates, see Ethan Elkind, *Railtown: The Fight for the Los Angeles Metro Rail and the Future of the City* (Berkeley: University of California Press, 2014).

34. Kyle Shelton, "Contested Spaces: Infrastructural Citizenship in the City," *Social Science Space*, November 4, 2015, www.socialsciencespace.com/2015/11/contested-spaces-infrastructural-citizenship-in-the-city. On road protests in Ferguson and Charlotte, see Taylor Wofford, "Police Arrest Dozens of Black Lives Matter Protesters, Body Slam Man in Ferguson," *Newsweek*, August 10, 2015; Paige Hansen "Protesters Stage 'Die-In' on Streets of Uptown Charlotte," WSOCTV, December 10, 2014.

35. DeWitt C. Greer, speech at the Dedication of IH-10, May 17, 1972, Box 2002/101–16, Folder "Speeches 1972," Texas Highway Department Historical Records, Texas State Archives.

36. Kyle Shelton, "Building a Better Houston: Highways, Neighborhoods, and Infrastructural Citizenship in the 1970s," *Journal of Urban History*, October 15, 2015.

INDEX